# Elvis: Still Taking Care of Business

Sonny West
with Marshall Terrill

## TRIUMPH
BOOKS

This book is available in quantity at special discounts for your group or organization. For further information, contact:

**Triumph Books**
814 North Franklin Street
Chicago, Illinois 60610
(800) 888-4741
Fax (312) 337-1807

Printed in U.S.A
ISBN: 978-1-60078-149-0
Design by Amy Carter
All photos courtesy of Sonny West and Russ Howe
unless indicated otherwise.

# The Ballad of the Memphis Mafia

Bright lights city moved their soul....

They strode into town

With a swagger and ready fist,

Protecting the people's King

Good ole boys, one and all,

Flashy badges and an orgy of excess,

Their life was for living

Hard, fast and fun,

Fighters and lovers

With a "downhome" cheeky grin,

If you were looking for TROUBLE

You'd come to the right place...

Be prepared...

As they'd "scatter" you all over the place

—*Anonymous, 2003*

# Contents

# Acknowledgments

I AM DEDICATING THIS BOOK TO SOME PEOPLE IN MY LIFE WHO DESERVE A LOT of credit. At the top of that list is my beloved wife, Judy, who shared a part of my life with Elvis Presley. Her incomparable patience, understanding, unselfishness, and love never wavered, and she gave me strength to get through some rough times during our life with Elvis, and also after. Judy has never tired—at least openly—of hearing the same stories I tell over and over everywhere we go. An occasional reward for her patience is when a fan asks something that sparks a story she has never heard. I love you so much, baby!

To my son, Bryan, who lived the first four years of his life in Elvis's house and whom Elvis dearly loved.

To my daughter, Alana, who, though born after the Elvis years, grew up very much with his presence through his music, movies, and, of course, stories she heard me tell of him. I know he would have loved you very much.

To my cousin Red West, who introduced me to Elvis in 1958, which is when it all began. Without the introduction I would never have had the opportunity to know my best friend and share most of my young-adult life with him.

To Colonel Tom Parker for the security measures he taught me when Elvis went back to performing concert tours around the country. But beyond that, I got to know the Colonel when he was around just the people he cared about. I feel fortunate to have been one of them. In private, he was relaxed and didn't have to be the "man in charge of everything." Much like Elvis, Colonel also had "the man and the image" thing to deal with. We had some great one-on-one conversations when I drove him to Palm Springs from L.A. over the years. To his widow, Loanne, a great lady who took care of the Colonel with such love and devotion and was always there for him. I want to thank her for her help and guidance in several stories about the Colonel that are in the book. Thank you, Loanne, for your treasured friendship.

To Barbara Leigh, a dear friend and a beautiful woman inside and out, who introduced me to Marshall Terrill, a man whose sensitivity and warmth enrich his talent as a writer. He is my cowriter and now dear friend. I have spent countless hours with Marshall in personal visits, on the phone, and through the Internet—writing, editing, and polishing this manuscript to our satisfaction.

To Marshall's wife, Zoe, whose friendship is highly valued.

To Marshall's parents, Carolyn and Mike Terrill, who lovingly opened their home to me and treated me like family. Their home was a refuge for me after spending long days with Marshall traveling back through the years bringing forth wonderful, exciting, but sometimes painful memories of my years with Elvis.

To our literary agent, Tony Seidl, who stuck with us to see that this project came to fruition.

To Pete Ehrmann and Cheryl Hosmer, who unselfishly spent many hours preparing this manuscript for publication.

To those now gone who remain a large part of my life—my mom and dad, my brother, Billy, and my mother-in-law, Opal, of whom Elvis thought the world. To my sisters, Liz, Barbara, Carolyn, Susan, and their loved ones they have lost—Bob, Russ, and Bill, all of whom I love dearly for always being there for me. To my nieces and nephews and their loved ones, too many to name, but you know who you are. I love you all.

To some of my fellow members of the Memphis Mafia, Marty Lacker, Lamar Fike, Billy Smith, and Dave Hebler, for their friendship and support through the years. You guys will always be dear to me. To the memory of Alan Fortas, Richard Davis, and Charlie Hodge for their friendship over the many years we shared with Elvis. As the rest of us have entered our twilight years and faced the health issues that come with them, it is important to me for you to know that I love you guys.

To my dear friend Russ Howe and his wife, Nereida, whom I have come to love since they entered my life so many years ago. A special

# ACKNOWLEDGMENTS

thanks to Russ for the photos that he has provided for me to use in this book and at other times over the years for my personal use.

To my dear friend Bud Glass, whom I love for his friendship and support since I met him so many years ago.

To my dear friends Butch and Kim Polston, whom I love and who have always been there for me and my family. Butch is one of the kindest and most honorable men I have ever known.

To my dear friend Sandi Pichon, for her unwavering support and for defending me with words of wisdom to those who know not of what they speak but who speak against some of us guys. To our mutual friends I met through her that do the same, I thank you.

To Jim Wilson, whom I love for his friendship that I value so highly and who has come to mean so much to me. For the opportunity he has afforded me, I am deeply grateful.

Thanks must also go to Bill E. Burk, who graciously answered several questions regarding various topics on Elvis Presley's life.

To the many people that I have met from around the world because of Elvis and have enjoyed a great friendship with over the years. Some I am closer to than others, and you know who you are.

To Elvis's adoring fans worldwide. You were special to him. And now your children and your children's children are keeping his memory alive.

And last, but certainly not least, to the man this book is all about. Thanks, Boss.

# Introduction: First Impressions of a Memphis Mafioso

First impressions are everything—and some even last fifty years. By the time this book comes out, it will mark the fifty-first anniversary of Elvis Presley's 1956 appearance on *The Ed Sullivan Show* in front of his largest American TV audience.

More than fifty million viewers watched the snarling, swivel-hipped singer do his thing. (In fact, he appeared again on the show in January 1957 and was filmed only from the waist up so that the audience couldn't see hips move!)

Actually, I saw Elvis two years before that iconic performance at my high school during a lunch break. At that point, he was just getting started in his career.

Elvis Presley's introduction to the music world in 1954 marked the beginning of his indelible imprint on modern culture as the man who introduced rock and roll into our lexicon.

But my personal first impression of Elvis didn't happen until four years later, when I met him in Memphis, Tennessee, at a private roller-skating party. My cousin Red West invited me and three of my sisters to meet Elvis before he joined the army. I was impressed with his warmth, charm, sincerity, and gentlemanly ways, not to mention his striking good looks. I had no idea then, of course, that he would have such a tremendous influence on my life in the years to come.

He became like an older, more worldly brother who took me along for a ride called *fame*. Let me tell you, it was one helluva ride. I eventually ended up going to work for Elvis and lived most of my young-adult life with him, including my early years as a husband and a father.

I became an integral member of a group known affectionately as the "Memphis Mafia" that accompanied Elvis everywhere he went. Like the not-so-affectionately regarded Mafia, we had our own code of silence and became a handpicked circle of insiders at Elvis's beck and call twenty-four hours a day. We played when he played and slept when he slept, putting up with his demands no matter how large or small. We served, as the occasion demanded, as his trusted friends, bodyguards, personal assistants, and, at the end, dwindling lifeline to reality. In the beginning, it was intoxicating.

The movie years (1960–69) were the most fun of my time with Elvis. We had more fun than probably anyone is entitled to, and Elvis enjoyed having us around and working with his costars and directors. We had a couple of blowups and confrontations over the years, usually caused by pride and stubbornness, but our love for one another overcame all that. We seemed to migrate back to each other and were always the better for it. Out of it came a deeper understanding and mutual respect.

I'm sure you will enjoy the many stories of our lives in Memphis, Los Angeles, Las Vegas, and Palm Springs, and there were no better times than at Graceland around the holidays. In July 1969, Elvis returned to the stage and took Las Vegas by storm at a monthlong engagement at the International Hotel. His triumphant return to live performing revived his career and deepened our relationship because I was called on by him to be his chief of security.

Security mattered greatly to him because even fans who meant him no harm sometimes ended up hurting him. He always had scratches and bruises from women who charged the stage to show Elvis how much they loved him. Once he even had a crown broken by one. While constantly wary, Elvis had great fun onstage, to the delight of the audience, with women who approached him slowly and respectfully and waited for him to do the kissing.

At the opposite end of the spectrum were the nutcases who threatened to harm and even kill Elvis. Even the FBI got involved in protecting him when a very disturbed man tried to extort $50,000 from Elvis. Another threat came in the form of Charles Manson, whose vicious and cold-blooded murders were a wake-up call to all celebrities. Elvis was extremely upset by the senseless killings and was determined that nothing like that would happen to him, his family, or his friends.

We obtained permits to carry concealed weapons and became very adept at using those weapons. I personally developed a fast draw that pleased Elvis so much that he enjoyed pitting me in mock duels against the policemen we worked with on tour. I didn't do it to show off, but because I realized there might be a time when someone could try drawing down on Elvis, and I wanted to be ready. I learned in my years with Elvis that there was more to being a good bodyguard than being a tough guy and packing heat. Most, if not all, of the security measures I learned were from one of the best in the business, Colonel Tom Parker, who at one time did security for President Lyndon B. Johnson when he was a senator in Texas.

That said, the tours were mostly good times and a lot of fun. After the hugely successful *Elvis: Aloha from Hawaii, Via Satellite* special beamed to more than one billion people all over the world in January 1973, Elvis was at the pinnacle of his fame. Simply put, he thought he had no more worlds to conquer. Or perhaps I should say no more *creative* worlds to conquer, because a world of prescription drug abuse was looming on the horizon. Conquering it was a whole different matter.

I believe everyone has his own demons to conquer, and it can be a lifelong war to wage. Some can be defeated, but some can't even be controlled. There are those who grow weary from the constant battle and surrender. I should know. I lost my brother to a demon called gambling, which had such a stranglehold on him that it ruined his life. He was in such denial.

Elvis was also in denial, but no one really likes to talk about that aspect of his life, and there are those who don't want to hear about it. Elvis actually believed that he needed the drugs so freely prescribed for him by doctors and that he was the one in control. It is true that he had his own *Physicians' Desk Reference*, and that he studied it religiously and often suggested to doctors what drugs he should have to treat maladies that often existed only in his mind.

There were several doctors around him who gave Elvis whatever he wanted, mostly in California and Las Vegas, and others who ignored the situation. It got to the point where my cousin Red, Elvis's bodyguard Dave Hebler, and I had to do something to get Elvis to understand how bad the situation was getting. We loved

Elvis and could clearly see the direction his addiction was taking him. We tried to intervene. We were fired in July of 1976.

Red once busted down a door of a bass player in the singing group Voice and broke the guy's toe. Then Red told him that if he continued giving drugs to Elvis, Red would come back and work his way up to the top of the guy's head, breaking everything along the way. We had some success in slowing down the supply line—just enough for Elvis to become aware of it and tell us to mind our own business because he was in control of things and knew what he was doing. "And if you don't stay out of it," he warned, "you will be looking for other jobs."

But, of course, we couldn't sit by and watch this man, as close to me as a brother, kill himself and not do a thing about it. Contrary to popular belief, Elvis's father, Vernon, didn't fire us; he just notified us of Elvis's wishes. Elvis also told Vernon to give us enough separation pay to live on for a couple of months. Instead of doing what his son requested, he gave us three days' notice and one week's pay.

We were told by Elvis's girlfriend at the time, Linda Thompson, someone for whom I have great respect and love, that it was his intention to hire us back in a few months. Linda took great care of Elvis and also tried to help him with his addiction, but she also ended up leaving the fold because she knew what was coming and did not want to watch Elvis die. After our dismissal, there was nothing else we could do about the drug abuse. We then came up with the idea of writing a book as a wake-up call to Elvis. It was our last resort.

Over the years, many have accused us of writing *Elvis: What Happened?* to get even with him for firing us. I was fired or quit several times during my sixteen years with him and never even considered writing a book. But this time his life was at stake, and it seemed the only way to reach him was the book. Some said we did it for the money. But if money had been our object, we could have just accepted Elvis's offer to buy us off for not writing the book. The more we told our story, the more we realized our love for him and great concern for his welfare. The bottom line is, if you really love someone and he or she is in a bad situation, you do what you think it takes to help.

The book was a startling revelation to the media and Elvis's fans. Elvis and Colonel Tom Parker had done a magnificent job over his career of carefully cultivating his All-American image, and the media and the public didn't want to believe that Elvis had a drug abuse problem. One media personality, Geraldo Rivera, went on national television and out-and-out called us liars. This is the same individual who, two years later as an investigative correspondent for ABC's *20/20*, exposed to the world in a groundbreaking report that Elvis was in fact addicted to prescription drugs. So much for his eye-opening revelation. Nobody ever accused Rivera of lacking nerve, and he actually invited Red to come on his show. Red agreed, with one stipulation: Rivera had to apologize to us on the air. Needless to say, we didn't go on the show. To my knowledge, Rivera has never publicly admitted that we told the truth about Elvis's problem, nor has he apologized for calling us liars.

The fans' passionate reaction to our book was not unexpected by us. We knew that because of their love for and devotion to Elvis, they would be angry about our revelations. To this day, there are some who don't accept the fact that Elvis had a problem. Elvis was a wonderful human being, but he had human frailties as we all do. Addiction is a human frailty, whether it be to medicine, alcohol, gambling, or overeating. You have to really want to beat your addiction and change your life to be successful. Elvis didn't even face the fact that he had an addiction.

Looking back almost thirty years later, I am forced to concede that even though our book sold three million copies, it was largely a failure. It didn't save Elvis, and neither did it convey to readers how much I loved the man. By focusing so much on Elvis's addiction and oddball behavior, I was remiss in not telling readers how much he meant to me.

In this book I want to give readers an insight into what Elvis was really like. Sure, everyone got glimpses of his private side, especially in the wonderful film *Elvis: That's the Way It Is*, which showed his crazy sense of humor. However, there was so much more to the man. Elvis had abundant charm, charisma, sensitivity, and class. He was well-read on a variety of subjects from religion to philosophy to world history. Elvis had a God-given talent in music and gave 100 percent all the time on stage and in the studio. But he likewise put all of himself into every emotion, and when he was mad, you always prayed it was at somebody else. If not, you felt you needed to get the hell out of Dodge.

Writing this book has truly been a labor of love and a catharsis. At times it's left me drained emotionally and physically. I have taken almost four years to put down my stories of my life with Elvis, and I truly hope you enjoy reading them. If you laugh a lot or are deeply touched and moved to tears and feel you know Elvis more personally by the time you are done reading this book, then I will have accomplished something very important to me.

Last, I've dedicated an appendix to dispelling rumors, untruths, half-truths, and exaggerations regarding the legend of Elvis Presley. Over the years there have been statements made by some concerning Elvis's views on race, religion, and politics. Elvis spent a lot of time discussing current affairs and articulating his positions. He purposely chose not to publicly convey his views so his fame would not influence anyone. Elvis served his country with distinction, and he believed that everybody is entitled to an opinion and freedom of choice.

He was once asked at a news conference about his view on a political issue, and he politely declined to answer. The reporter asked Elvis if he even had a position on the subject. Elvis stated he did but preferred to keep it to himself. That's quite a contrast to so many of our current celebrities who aren't at all shy about using their status to promote a political agenda.

In private, Elvis never shied away from telling anyone how great this country is. He was one of the most patriotic people I ever knew and was very proud of the men and women in our armed forces for doing their duty to protect our freedom. It's no mere coincidence that Elvis is the symbol of America to many people around the globe, and he would be very proud of that association.

I am happy to have been associated with Elvis Presley, a man who profoundly touched the lives of untold millions and enriched the lives of those who knew him.

—Sonny West

# Chapter 1

# Memphis, Tennessee

**W**HILE MOST PEOPLE ALREADY KNOW THE HISTORY OF ELVIS PRESLEY, VERY few people know the history of me, Sonny West.

Like Elvis, I was a product of the Deep South. We were born just a few years apart and were both children of the Great Depression. It's even quite possible there is some blood relation between the two of us. You see, my mother, Robbie Elaine Smith, was born on May 25, 1912, in the small town of Pontotoc, Mississippi—about twenty miles west of Tupelo, the birthplace of Elvis. My mother was from a family of loggers who carried the same last name as Elvis's mother, Gladys Smith.

My mom lost her father in a terrible logging accident when she was just a child. A batch of logs broke loose from their ties and rolled down the hillside, crushing him to death. Grandpa's last name was Smith. My grandmother later married the man I came to know as my grandpa, whose last name was Hopper.

Mom's features were very similar to the rest of the Smiths'— dark, exotic, and slender. At five feet eight inches, she had high, prominent cheekbones. She had chocolate brown eyes and dark brown hair. Her partial Cherokee Indian heritage was evident in her unique and striking beauty.

Like many poor folks in the South in those days, Mom went where the jobs were. Oh sure, there was plenty of work in the cotton fields working for pennies, but that was backbreaking work in the blistering humidity that sent a lot of people to early graves. My mother planned a better and longer life for herself. She passed away in June 2000, at the age of eighty-eight. But I'm getting ahead of myself.

Mom migrated north at age twenty-two, landing in Memphis in search of a better life. She hit the mother lode, so to speak, when she met Delbert Bryant West at a local dance hall. My dad, who was born April 13, 1905, on a farm in Corinth, Mississippi, was a strapping man, six feet tall and 190 pounds. His deep brown eyes, sharp features, and high cheekbones were catnip for my mother. Mom, who was seven years his junior, was swept off her feet.

Although my dad had a reputation as a hard worker, he was also known for playing just as hard. Over the years, I heard stories about him and his brother Tom. Tom, who was my cousin Red's dad, and Delbert West, were known as dudes you didn't mess with. To them, a good time was downing a few beers at the local bar, turning the mugs upside down, and then fighting back-to-back against the other patrons. And not just the rowdiest ones but everyone else in the joint. Then, after they had cleaned house, it wasn't unusual for the Wests to chug down a few more brews with the guys they'd just pummeled into the ground.

Dad's bad-boy reputation and handsome looks won the heart of Mom, who had a fun-loving side of her own. Their whirlwind romance led to the exchange of wedding vows on July 19, 1930; a family followed soon thereafter. Ann Elizabeth, the firstborn, arrived in 1931 and was followed by Barbara Ann in 1934 and Carolyn Mae in 1936.

My father drove a taxicab for a living and, after Carolyn Mae came along, took on additional side jobs to put food on the table. It wasn't unusual for him to have two or three jobs at a time, and he routinely got by on four or five hours of sleep a night. But financial and physical concerns were the least of his worries. Trumping them was the fear there'd never be a son to carry on the family name. That was put to rest when I was born on July 5, 1938, at the John Gaston Hospital in Memphis. It was a hospital for people who couldn't afford quality health care. That was us, and we took full advantage of the services there, such was they were, when I developed a case of double pneumonia as an infant.

One of Dad's side jobs was parking cars at the swanky Peabody Hotel in downtown Memphis. The Peabody was made famous by, of all things, a family of ducks that occupied an area of the boiler room at the hotel.

Legend has it that back in the 1930s, Peabody General Manager Frank Schutt and a friend, Chip Barwick, returned home from a weekend hunting trip in Arkansas full of Tennessee "sippin' whiskey" and thought it would be a hoot to place some of their live duck decoys (it was legal then for hunters to use live decoys) in the fountain of the Peabody.

The sight of three small English ducks splashing around in the centerpiece of the most posh hotel in town struck the guests as hilarious and precious, and so, rather than shoo the quackers away, the management made them a star attraction.

Every day at 11:00 AM these little guys would be led into the elevator to the ground floor. A red carpet would be rolled out for them, and when the elevator doors opened they would march to the fountain in the lobby of the hotel, where they would spend the day. Around 5:00 PM they would march back into the elevator to return to the boiler room. Hundreds of people would gather two times daily for this time-honored ritual.

But way back when, things weren't too ducky with me. Thanks to the double pneumonia, my temperature was close to 106 degrees for almost two days, and the doctors had no luck getting it down. If it reached much higher, there was a good chance I would start having convulsions. My parents were naturally upset and worried, and between cab fares Dad raced back and forth to the hospital to check on me. One day his boss at the Peabody noticed he was not himself and asked what was wrong. After Dad explained my condition and the inability of the doctors at John Gaston Hospital to bring down my temperature, his boss recommended bringing Dr. Harry Jacobson on the case. Dr. Jacobson was one of the city's most prominent pediatricians and was a patron at various dinners and functions at the hotel.

The reason I was at John Gaston to begin with was that we couldn't afford anything better. A topflight pediatrician like Dr. Jacobson was way out of our financial league, but Dad's boss insisted on calling Dr. Jacobson himself.

A few minutes later, he told Dad to check me out of John Gaston Hospital and rush me over to the Methodist Hospital, about five minutes away.

At John Gaston, a staffer saw Daddy preparing to cart me out of there and got the idea that he would stop him. He abandoned the idea, and spared himself a stint as a patient in his own hospital, after one of the toughest fighters in Memphis made it clear with just a look that there was no stopping him.

3

At Methodist Hospital I was gently deposited into the arms of Dr. Jacobson. He immediately placed me in a vat of ice and treated me with the latest antibiotics, and my temperature came right down.

My daddy often saw Dr. Jacobson at the hotel afterward, and when he did he would mention to the doctor he hadn't yet received his bill for saving my life. Dr. Jacobson always stated he would be sure to get one sent out. But not only did Daddy never get a bill from the doctor, he never received one from Methodist Hospital either.

I have no doubt that Dr. Jacobson footed both his own and the hospital's tab. My understanding is that he continued to practice medicine well into his eighties. His profession never had a finer, truer representative.

Once I was well again, my parents produced two more children: my brother, William Arnold, was born in 1940 and was followed by my sister Susan, the last child, born in 1945.

Growing up, I was pretty rambunctious and full of life. I was mischievous and got into plenty of trouble, but I was never mean-spirited or hateful. That didn't mean, however, there weren't lots of spankings to keep me in line. My mom's favorite thing to say was, "I'm going to tell your daddy when he gets home."

Actually, my mom was the disciplinarian when my brother and I were younger, and she was tight-lipped when it came to letting my daddy know that we were acting up. She'd often try to whip us by grabbing one of our arms with one hand and swinging a belt with her other hand. We'd start running around her in circles screaming, "You're killing me!" even when the belt missed its target, which it usually did, thanks to our gyrations.

By the time the mommy-go-round spun itself out, poor Mom was so dizzy that she usually didn't even know or care that the dreaded belt had hit mostly air.

When I was five years old, an attempt to find better work dropped us off in Tulare, California. All of Dad's jobs and prospects in Memphis suddenly went south. So we went west, and Dad went to work as a foreman on a turkey ranch.

We took the train out to the fabled coast, which in 1943 was more than ever considered the land of opportunity. Living on a ranch was a lot of fun for a kid with a strong imagination. It was a great place to play cowboys and Indians, but if you weren't careful, there was plenty of trouble around every corner. I remember following my dad as he was preparing a field for planting by pulling a rototiller behind him on the tractor. The tiller's big spikes broke up the earth, but this time they impaled my foot because of an equipment malfunction.

Unlike Mom's belt, one of those spikes scored a direct hit on me, going completely through my heel and pinning me to the ground. I screamed, and Dad had to pull the spike out himself. He always said that it was the hardest thing he'd ever had to do, because I was in such pain and he had to hold me down while he removed the spike. What really spooked him was that I never shed a tear during the whole ordeal, which I find hard to understand myself.

Anybody who's lived on a farm will tell you that disaster is never far away. That was further brought home to me when one of our neighbors suffered a gruesome death driving up an embankment on his tractor. When he pressed down on the accelerator, the tractor flipped over onto him, and the exhaust pipe pierced his heart, killing him instantly.

We never suffered anything that tragic, thank the Lord, but things started to go bad for us on the farm when my father warned the owner of the spread, Mr. Flint, that the incubator used for speeding up the process of hatching eggs was on the blink.

"I will take care of it," Mr. Flint assured my father, but either the matter slipped Mr. Flint's mind or he was Mr. Skinflint when it came to spending money on farm equipment. Sure enough, the incubator shorted out, causing a fire that destroyed the building and killed more than a thousand turkeys—practically the entire flock. The ranch was wiped out, and even though he had warned Mr. Flint well in advance of the potential tragedy, Daddy was fired. The West family headed back east.

My Uncle Tom—Dad's old bar-fighting partner—and his wife, Eloise, had three sons. Tom Jr. was the oldest, followed by Harold and then Red. They owned a two-bedroom home on Russell Circle in northern Memphis. They took us in and made us feel welcome. My cousins gave up their bedroom to my mom and dad and bunked with us in the living room, where we slept on pallets.

Uncle Tom had saved my father from a wretched existence on my grandfather's farm. Grandfather John William West sired six boys and one girl and greatly utilized them to help farm his land in Corinth, Mississippi. My grandfather wasn't a particularly warm man, and procreation was not done out of love for my grandmother but to make helping hands to work the land and tend the crops. Not only were the kids worked day and night, but the old man beat them severely and often. It amounted to downright physical abuse, and it was no wonder that as soon as they reached maturity, the kids bailed out in search of an easier life somewhere else. Tom was several years older than my father, who was the youngest boy. Tom came back to rescue his eighteen-year-old baby brother and brought him to Memphis in 1923.

I grew especially close to my cousin Red because he was only a couple of years older than me and I looked up to him. What Red lacked in size when he was a young boy, he made up for in heart. He was mentally and physically game for anything and was never one to back down from a challenge. To me, Red was always a big-brother figure. We spent many hours together during those months that we stayed with his family, playing football, baseball, and wrestling.

It wasn't long before my father got back on his feet and found work as a house painter. We were also accepted into Lamar Terrace, a government housing project for the underprivileged. In order to qualify for an apartment there, a family couldn't bring in more than $200 a month income. Most families got around this rule by taking second and third jobs but not reporting the extra income. My dad was no exception.

Lamar Terrace was located near the southeast edge of downtown Memphis and looked like your typical government housing project—downright dreary. The thirty or so red brick buildings each housed ten two-story apartments with about one thousand square feet of living space. The apartments were two and three bedrooms. Each apartment had a kitchen, dining area, and living room on the bottom floor; the bedrooms and bathroom were located on the second floor.

I considered Lamar Terrace my first real home because I lived there for more than five years. It was also the place where I began to come of age.

I was no different from most kids of the Eisenhower '50s. I loved sports and television and spent hours listening to the radio. *The Cisco Kid* was one of the most popular kids' Westerns of the day, and our whole family gathered around the radio every time it was on the air.

Hollywood held a certain fascination for me, and I frequented the Linden Circle movie theater around the corner from Lamar Terrace.

For 10¢, I could watch a Saturday matinée and a Hopalong Cassidy serial. It was no small wonder that I would become a part of movie-making magic in the years to come thanks to my association with Elvis. I had long pretended as a kid to be the cowboy, the soldier, the athlete, and the hero that I saw in the movies. I was never into comic books, but give me a movie to watch, and later a television show, and I was mesmerized for hours on end.

I usually wanted to be the good guy, but I also found a lot of satisfaction and freedom in being the bad guy or antihero—not evil, just a tough guy people admired and liked. When I entered the movie business many years later, I found I could do this. My hero as a teenager was James Dean, because of his look and attitude. I related to him so much that I used him as a role model in my acting class while interpreting the roles I played. I was in the air force when *Rebel without a Cause* came out, and I know I saw it at least a dozen times. Somehow, some way, I just knew I wanted a career in the film business.

When I wasn't in school or at the movies, I spent much of my time outdoors playing sports. At any given time, I could walk outside my door and play with literally hundreds of kids encamped on the lawns of Lamar Terrace. While I never wanted for playmates, sometimes the play got a little rough.

Lamar Terrace was home turf to perhaps the toughest gang in Memphis at that time, and no one in the project escaped its influence. The older kids took it upon themselves to make the younger kids tough, and often that meant making us fight each other. What it boiled down to was you were either going to survive by doing what it took, or you were going to get beat up.

Often the older kids stole money from the younger kids to buy cigarettes, so it was up to us to either fight back or run and hide from the older ones. If they caught you, they'd beat the tar out of you or at least subject you to their torture: they'd turn a bicycle upside down, manipulate the pedals so the back tire was spinning fast, and rub your arm on the rubber for a nice painful burn.

I'll never forget the advice my father gave me as I prepared to go outside and play one day: "There are good and bad kids in this place, so make sure you pick the right ones."

I realized I had picked wrong when our gang went looking for fresh victims outside of our neighborhood. We went up the street to

Bellevue and Lamar Avenue and spied a kid about our age walking and minding his own business. As punishment for breathing the same air as us, this poor guy ended up on the ground with a bloody nose. That act of sheer, senseless brutality caught me off guard, and I knew in an instant that I didn't like it. Seeing that innocent kid with his nose bleeding and a dazed look in his eyes didn't make me feel very proud of myself, and I knew right then that I wasn't going to be a very good gang member. I have always detested bullies, and the strength-in-numbers gang mentality wasn't for me. Shortly after that incident, we moved away from Lamar Terrace. All in all, I took away some wonderful memories from there and learned that I wasn't cut out to be a thug.

Luckily, I had sports to turn to.

Baseball was my game of choice, and there was always some sort of game going on. The Yankees, even though they were from another part of the country, were everybody's team, and Mickey Mantle was the person every kid in America tried to emulate. Not only did he have the catchy name and the All-American good looks, but there was also that magical aura of all home-run kings.

Mantle was the star of a training film the coaches often ran at church. I locked in on his wrists because they were so huge. They showed just pure brute strength.

While I dreamed of becoming Mickey Mantle at the plate, my real talent was in my arm—I had been told I was quite a pitcher. My specialty was a mean sidearm curveball that kept batters, umpires, and even me guessing. When I threw it, I never was sure where it was going to go. Sometimes it would go behind the batter, sometimes right at him, and sometimes even over the plate. Most of the time I had the batter "stepping in the bucket." When I got him to do that, I would come back with a sidearm fastball to the outside corner of the plate on the next pitch. The sidearm fastball kept them thinking a curve was on its way again.

We won the state championship when I was twelve and played for Bellevue Baptist Church on a team called the Supermites, coached by Billy Mashburn. I tallied a few no-hitters over the years and was elected to the All-Star team five out of six years.

Mantle and I had more in common than just our love for baseball—we also shared a love for the opposite sex. When I reached puberty, it didn't take me long to figure out that it might be more fun hanging out with females rather than those stinking, sweaty guys. The butterflies I got in my stomach when I went up to bat were nothing compared to the ones I got when I asked a girl out for a date.

I remember when I was just twelve, a girl named Patricia Parker, a blue-eyed blond from Texas, visited her cousin, Johnny Holly, in Memphis. Patricia's beauty took my breath away. It took some time, but I finally mustered up the courage to ask her out on a date. We went to a double feature and were well into the second film before I gingerly took hold of her hand. She didn't run screaming from the theater or go into convulsions or anything like that—and if there was a happier kid than me in all of Memphis right then, I'd like to have seen him.

Holding hands was as far as it went between the two of us, but it was enough for me. Other times we would ride our bicycles to the park and talk about Patricia's life in Texas and what we were going to do when we got older. Patricia came back the following summer, and we picked up right where we left off, hand in hand. I'll always treasure the memory of those two summers of innocent puppy love, when Patricia and I were so sweet to one another. I finally did work up the nerve to kiss her shortly before she left for Texas. It was one of those innocent-type kisses with closed mouths. It also turned out to be a permanent good-bye kiss because we moved away after that. I was lucky that my first experience with a female didn't end up in heartache but gave me some insight into the sensitivity of women and how we could both teach each other something when we let our guards down.

Thanks to Patricia, I learned I could let my guard down, but with members of my own sex, I was usually forced to be the tough guy.

# Chapter **2**

# Blackboard Jungle

IN SPITE OF MY FAILED GANG MEMBERSHIP, MY LAMAR TERRACE DAYS EARNED me a reputation as a tough guy and a badass. I'd say that over the course of my high school career I had close to twenty-five fights. They were usually over nothing in particular, other than standing up for myself when confronted by a bully or taking up for a friend getting picked on by one. That was one of my pet peeves—seeing a guy pick on someone who didn't want to fight or maybe didn't even know how to fight.

There was a kid named Randy, whose last name I don't recall, who had a stuttering problem. Randy was constantly being picked on by a hard case named Buddy Weller. To add insult to injury, Buddy lost his girlfriend to Randy. That was too much for big, bad Buddy. He wanted to humiliate Randy with his fists. After eating a steady diet of abuse, Randy finally agreed to meet Buddy in a field and have it out with him. I made sure I was there to see that it was a fair fight and that Buddy didn't kill him. I knew that Buddy knew that Randy couldn't fight, so I was already mad before it even started.

Sure enough, Buddy knocked him down with the first punch. As Randy got up, I could see he was groggy, so I stepped in and said that was enough.

Buddy didn't think so and wound up to hit Randy again. I shoved him back, and Buddy made the mistake of inviting me to take Randy's place in the fight. A couple of seconds later, he was on the ground taking a nap arranged by my right hand finding his jaw.

Buddy was not only a bully, but an unusually stubborn one. Not long after our first encounter, he came looking for me with a

11

pair of brass knuckles. When I saw them glinting on his hand, I picked up a piece of steel pipe about two feet long and got ready for round two.

But as is always the case when a bully no longer carries a guaranteed advantage, Buddy found something else to do and never bothered me or Randy again.

One confrontation I did lose was to another member of my own family—my father. Being a typical teenager, I was feeling my oats and decided to challenge my father's authority. During the summer, I had taken to hanging out almost every night with some friends at a local drugstore named Whiteway Pharmacy. After dinner one evening, I informed my mom that was where I was headed.

"No, you're not going out tonight," my mother told me. "It's late, and we're going to spend some time together as a family." Mom's tone told me it was not up for negotiation.

A quiet night with my parents was not my idea of how to spend an ideal summer evening, and I didn't hesitate to say so over the ominous rattle of my father's newspaper from the living room that signaled his imminent participation in the debate.

"I'll be back in a little bit," I said confidently as I walked toward the front door to leave. Without looking up from his paper, Dad said, "You heard your mother—you're not going."

Any parent will vouch for the fact that no teenager is really in his right mind, and that night I must've been especially out of mine, because instead of clamping my mouth shut and heading in the opposite direction, I put on my toughest sneer and said, "You're going to stop me?"

About a millisecond later, the undefeated bar-fighting champion of Memphis was out of his chair, looking as though somebody had swiped his beer. I managed to jump around him and grab him from behind in a bear hug. It was like wrapping my arms around a glowing volcano to keep it from exploding. I needed help fast—and got it when Mom called out from the kitchen.

"D.B., don't you hurt that boy!"

"Momma," I yelled, "open the back door for me!" God bless her heart, she did as asked, and with all of my might, I shoved my father away from me and ran toward the kitchen, pulling a chair down behind me in an attempt to slow his pursuit. I ran out the back door, through a screened porch area, and down the driveway at top speed, as though my life depended on it, which isn't much of an exaggeration. As I reached the front of the house, I thought the coast was clear when out of the corner of my eye I saw a dark shape come at me like a rocket. I yelled out as Daddy caught me with a flying tackle. The force made us both roll along the ground.

"What are you screamin' about?" he asked me when we finally stopped.

"Daddy, it's you!" I said, not believing my eyes. "How did you catch me?"

"As long as I'm your daddy, and when you get out of line, I will always be smarter, be stronger, run faster, jump higher, and be able to kick your butt up and down this street," he said. With that, we both laughed and pulled ourselves up off the ground. That was the first and last time I ever disrespected my father. Since then there have been more than a few times I have wished for just one more chance to spend a quiet night alone with him and Mom.

The main thing my father taught me was to be good to my family and to other people. "Be a big person, work hard, and always be honest, Son," was his simple advice to me.

Now that I think about it, it was ironic that Elvis once told me that my honesty would be my downfall. He said this after I got in the habit of correcting facts in the stories he told about various incidents that had happened to him. If I had been there with him when something happened, say, in Palm Springs, and later Elvis said it had happened in Las Vegas, I spoke up because I didn't want people to think he was making up the story. Elvis had a creative imagination, and from time to time he would embellish a story or change a detail or two to make it more interesting to his listeners. It wasn't malicious or anything like that, but it happened often enough for those of us around Elvis to find it amusing—unlike how he found my penchant for accuracy.

When I turned sixteen, I discovered many changes on the horizon. My first true love—baseball—was put to the ultimate test when I tried out for the team at Tech High. Over the years of church league and Little League ball, that sidearm curve pitch wore out my arm, and I was relegated to the outfield, where I was lucky if I got to field a pop fly or grounder every now and then. While I could still swing a pretty mean bat, I became bored in the outfield and quit playing ball after my first year.

After I lost interest in baseball, I acquired two hobbies to take its place: girls and cars—and not necessarily in that order. I was also working various odd jobs. I worked at A & P Groceries on Watkins Street and then at Whiteway Pharmacy, where I hung out at night. To work at Whiteway, I had to get a health card because I manned the soda fountain and handled food.

When I got to the health department and started filling out the forms for my card, a woman started screaming in the next room. After several minutes she came out with bandages on both arms as if she'd been warding off a machete attack. When it was my turn with the same technician, I asked what the problem had been with the screamer. He explained that he'd been trying to draw blood, but she had what was referred to as "rolling veins," meaning they rolled away from the needle upon contact and thus required numerous attempts to get a sufficient sample. I wasn't too crazy about needles at that time and shot straight with the technician, who was about to shoot straight into me.

I didn't know if my veins rolled, rock-and-rolled, or did the boogaloo, but I did know that no soda jerk's job was worth the pin-cushion treatment. I told the technician he had one shot to hit pay dirt. It worked.

On weekends and in summers I worked with my father, helping paint and putty nail holes on commissioned jobs. Daddy employed several people, including some black folks. Everyone who worked for my dad was a good painter, and he paid top wages. I remember hearing on several occasions after someone quit and went out on his own that his replacement said that he had waited a long time to get hired by my dad.

My dad had an excellent reputation as a fair-priced man who did top-quality work. He had a lot of repeat customers over the fifty years he worked as a painter. My brother, Billy, worked many years for my dad and learned the trade so well from him that when Daddy decided to retire, my brother took over the business. Billy would pay Dad a 10 percent commission for doing the estimates on the jobs for several years after his retirement. A lot of the painters who worked for Dad stayed on when my brother took over.

Unlike many Southerners at that time, I was color-blind—race simply wasn't an issue. My dad worked with black men who were as kind and trustworthy as anyone could ask for. Even though I brought my own lunch with me on the job, everyone was always

14

offering me some of theirs. I really liked all the men who worked for my dad.

When I was about twelve, after we had moved away from Lamar Terrace, a bunch of us kids used to meet on Saturdays to play football. There was a city water pumping station on this big piece of property that was just like a park. We referred to it as the "water-works."

The kids were white and black, and when the captains of each team started choosing up sides, they chose the best players available. It didn't make any difference what color they were. It was different off the gridiron, though. On the way home after one game, several of us stopped at a little neighborhood market for a cold soda. As we started inside, one of the black players fished out a nickel and asked me to buy him a Nehi grape soda.

In my naïveté, I wondered why he didn't just come in with me and get his own drink. His answer floored me. "Us colored folk can't go in there," he whispered, his eyes downcast, almost ashamed. Although I knew blacks went to their own churches and schools, I thought it was their own choice. Segregation and racism were concepts with which I was unfamiliar. But my blinders were coming off.

I was raised Southern Baptist and went to Bellevue Baptist Church, where I was baptized when I was about ten. When I was a teenager, a bunch of us used to attend the East Trigg Baptist Church, with a mostly black congregation, for the late-night services that were still going on after our own evening services had ended. We had to sit in the balcony because by the time we got there the down-stairs was filled. I didn't like anybody telling me who I could associ-ate with, and the idea that somebody was inferior to me because his skin was a different color smacked of the kind of bullying I always despised. I have always instinctively abhorred racism. It angers me.

The same was true of Elvis Presley, who drew heavily upon the influence of black performers. The first time I ever saw Elvis was when I was a sophomore at Tech High in 1954. That was the same year he released "That's All Right" on the Sun Records label, which he cut on July 5, 1954—my sixteenth birthday. Elvis came to our campus to sing a few other songs while promoting his new single.

I remember it was during lunch period, and I was walking out-side after eating, when I saw this group sitting on the grass and heard the sounds of a guitar strumming and a distinctive voice.

"Man, that sounds familiar," I said to a friend alongside me. "Is that the guy who they've been playing on the radio?"

"Yeah," my friend replied.

"Man, he's pretty good," I said, quite impressed with his soulful voice. As I approached the group, I heard the murmurs of the girls, who of course thought Elvis was good-looking and sexy. "Oh, would you just look at him," said one of them. The crowd was polite, not the frenzied mob that later was the norm at his shows. He moved around then just as he did when he performed later on television and in concert.

At the time, Elvis's first record was being featured on *Red, Hot & Blue*, a top-rated show hosted by a disk jockey named Dewey Phillips on WHBQ radio. Dewey was not related to Sam Phillips of Sun Records, who first recorded Elvis. Dewey's was the hottest radio show going at the time and was one of the first programs to play R & B and rock and roll during the early '50s in the Memphis area. All the kids listened to it because *Red, Hot & Blue* played their music, not their parents'. For a local boy like Elvis to be on the show was considered big time.

Who would have thought this young man singing and playing the guitar on our school campus would become the most famous entertainer the world has ever known? I certainly never would have guessed that just six years later this guy would radically and irrevocably alter my own life.

The balance of my high school career was basically a battle to keep from being bored. I made good grades naturally, but I never pushed myself to be an excellent student. Like many teenagers, I did just enough to get by and never gave much thought to how education would relate to my future. So when my friend Bobby Moore asked me to join the military with him, I couldn't think of any reason not to.

At first, Bobby wanted to enlist in the navy, but I vetoed that on account of my fear of water and sharks. My Uncle Terry, my mother's baby brother, was in the navy, and I remember him telling my dad and some of my other uncles a haunting story about a ship called the USS *Indianapolis* that went down. Hundreds of crewmen survived the sinking ship only to be eaten by sharks. I was about seven years old at the time, which is such an impressionable age. That story stuck in my head, and the fear of sharks was forever etched in my psyche.

"No, I'd rather join the air force and fly," I told Bobby, who readily agreed. On July 8, 1955, Bobby and I officially joined the air force, and five days later we were on a train to San Antonio, Texas, to take basic training at Lackland Air Force Base.

Although I already had a relative with the same name as the one I had just inherited, the new one was going to be an overbearing boss for the next few years.

His name was Uncle Sam.

# Chapter 3

# Lucky Thirteen

ALTHOUGH THE NUMBER THIRTEEN IS CONSIDERED BY MANY PEOPLE TO BE A bad omen, it's always been a lucky number for me. On April 13, my father was born. When I played roulette, thirteen always seemed to pay off for me. On July 13, Bobby Moore and I took a train from Memphis to San Antonio, Texas, for basic training.

Now, you can argue there's nothing lucky about basic training or even joining the armed forces, but my hitch in the air force was nothing but a pure joy—at first.

However, I suffered a minor setback right out of the gate when Bobby was sent home for a disability he had kept from recruiters when he signed up. Turned out Bobby had a badly broken arm when he was younger, and the doctors inserted several plates that hindered his arm movement at certain angles. He said good-bye, and all of a sudden I was on my own for the first time in my life. I must say it was a lonely and scary feeling with no friends or family around me.

But it didn't take me long to make new friends in Flight 60. In basic training, the units were called flights. Each flight had consisted of four squads. I quickly earned the respect of my fellow airmen, especially that of my training instructor, Airman First Class James Bolton.

Upon arriving at the train station in San Antonio, we boarded an air force bus. On the way through town we passed several bars, and I made a mental note to come back to town that night and check a couple of them out. Little did I know it would be eight weeks before anyone in our flight was allowed to leave the base.

The first thing we did after stopping at the barracks and picking out our bunks was march over to pick up our uniforms. From that point on for the next eight weeks, we marched everywhere we went.

In fact, just about all we did was march and have classes on becoming responsible airmen and what Uncle Sam expected out of us. In between, we had breakfast, lunch, and dinner. We couldn't even smoke until given permission to do so, and believe me, that wasn't often. And on top of that, when we did smoke, we had to share a cigarette. All of us took turns puffing on the same butt. We were lucky to get two drags off of it apiece. Then we had to "field strip" the butt when we were done, meaning we had to shred it into such minute fragments that it would blow away like dandelion fuzz. That included the filter.

Going to the firing range for target practice was another thing we did in basic training. We fired .30-caliber rifles at the range, and I qualified as a marksman. It sounds impressive, but in fact, not only was "marksman" *not* one of the top qualifying titles, it was the lowest. That didn't mean someone with that qualification was Mr. Magoo, but he wasn't rated expert. Most of us were marksmen, but there were a few deadeyes who earned higher qualifying titles such as sharpshooter or expert. I suspect a lot of the better shooters did a lot of hunting growing up. The first time I ever fired a rifle was in ROTC in high school, and I did it only once.

Basic training was an eleven-week program at that time. The classes ended after the eight-week drill competition was completed, and then it was time to learn how to do the things that went on in all the war movies—learning how to survive in the field and fight.

Airman Bolton was the man who was going to teach us.

He was tough but fair. Bolton was clean, immaculate, and the epitome of what an airman should look like. He could size up a person quickly, and he liked what he saw in me. He had special communication skills and earned the respect of everyone in Flight 60.

His assistant, Airman Third Class Ewing, was not a very good man. I got the feeling Bolton didn't respect Ewing very much, and I sure as hell didn't. Once while marching, we were ordered to halt, and my left foot didn't land in the right position, so I slid it a couple of inches forward. Ewing came over yelling at me and kneed me in the left thigh. I buckled and willed myself not to punch him in the face, knowing that if I did I would have had a very short career in the air force.

Bolton saw what happened and quickly made his way over to us. Seeing that I was in pain from Ewing's assault, he asked me if I wanted to fall out. I told him I was okay. Bolton was clearly unhappy with Ewing's tactics but chose not to confront the situation at the time in front of his men. Ewing hadn't been assigned to us when we first got there. He came along after the first week. Before that, I had been called out by another airman and took care of him in short order. There wasn't much to it. He threw the first punch, I blocked it, and then I flattened him with my counterpunch. The guys in the flight were happy to see him get what he deserved, as he had bullied a couple of them. I earned a lot respect for standing up to him.

After the Ewing incident, those near the front of the barracks could hear Bolton in his quarters chewing out Ewing for his actions against me and threatening disciplinary action against him if he did anything like that again.

He also told Ewing that he'd better hope I didn't catch up to him after basic training was over, when I would hold the same rank as Ewing did and wouldn't have to worry about going after a ranking airman.

I had a couple more fights before training was over, and the word that I was somebody who didn't take crap from anybody must've gotten back to Ewing, because one day he came up and apologized for what he'd done. Good thing, too, because I had compiled a shit list to take care of after basic, and Ewing's name was the first one on it.

Our flight won the six-week drill competition, and our reward was a trip to the snack stand. We had our first cheeseburgers and fries in a month and a half while listening to the jukebox. The good life, however, was short-lived, because the next day we began training for the eight-week drill competition. We took third place in that one, but only two demerits separated first place from third. Far from being angry that we lost, Bolton told us, "You guys were the best out there, bar none. You have nothing to be ashamed of." With that, he gave us our first weekend pass, and we were off to check out some of those bars we had passed weeks earlier on our way to camp. If I was ever going into battle, I would want Airman Bolton to lead the charge.

We capped off our field training with a week of bivouac, which replicates situations you might face in combat. We crawled under barbed wire, ran an obstacle course, dug up foxholes, and, worst of all, entered a building filled with tear gas.

The assignment was to go in with our gas masks on and then remove them to find out what it was like to breathe tear gas. What it's like, I found out, was getting hot pokers shoved into your eyes. We had to stay inside the building for a certain amount of time before exiting into the sweet, fresh air. Then the trick was not to rub your eyes, because this would only make it worse, but to stand there and let the air and your own tears cleanse your eyes of the stinging chemicals. I'll take a bad case of rolling veins over getting teargassed any time.

During bivouac, we lived in tents and prayed it didn't rain because it was already miserable enough in the fields. Luckily for us, it rained just once while we were training. I heard horror stories from the other guys about enduring an entire week of rain and mud and wearing the same smelly, wet clothes.

Overall, basic training was a great experience and helped me to become a more mature and responsible young man. That said, I wouldn't want to do it again.

In the first few days of basic, we had all taken vocational tests to see where we could do the air force the most good after all that marching was done. My lowest test score was in mechanics. My highest was in radio and radar, so naturally I assumed I'd be slotted as a technician in this field. In fact, I was even counting on it because the training would take place at Keesler Air Force Base in Biloxi, Mississippi, where I had relatives I could stay with on weekends and enjoy plenty of home-cooked meals. But my Uncle Sam had different plans for me. The military wants you to learn to do things their way.

According to the results of my basic training aptitude test, I was least suited for any kind of duty involving mechanics. So naturally my assignment was to Sheppard Air Force Base in Wichita Falls, Texas, to become a jet engine specialist. But first they kept me at Lackland for two more months and made me a "KP Pusher," with my stripe, airman third class, then put me in charge of running the mess hall. The only kitchen I'd ever known was my momma's kitchen, and she was always the one in charge there. What the hell did I know about running a kitchen?

I quickly figured out that I could get along quite well by delegating responsibility and telling people what to do. In fact, I got so good at the latter that I kind of morphed into the kind of arrogant bastard I'd always despised, who took himself too seriously and abused his authority. It's amazing how one little stripe on my sleeve went right to my head. I'm surprised I didn't see Airman Ewing when I looked in the mirror.

One day when my fuse was particularly short, an airman in my detail seemed to be not working as hard as the others. He deserved to be chewed out, but I went further than I should have and decided to make an example of him by getting in his face, yelling, and calling him some choice names.

As I ranted on, tears began to well up in this young man's eyes, and his lips began to quiver, and all of a sudden I realized that I was as bad as any bully I'd ever taken on. I told the kid to take a break, and from that point on, unless I had a real smart-ass in my group, I did my best to be a decent boss and fair to everyone. Much like my future boss, Elvis, I learned that to be successful you found out who was made of what, surrounded yourself with good people, and rewarded them when they performed. I had my favorite guys that I gave extra smoke breaks to, because they earned them.

When my orders finally came through for Sheppard AFB, Airman Bolton, with whom I had developed a friendship, took me aside to give me some ominous pointers about Wichita Falls, Texas.

"Watch yourself when you get there, Sonny," he told me. "Even though the town economically benefits from the base, the townspeople and the merchants don't want us there. Just know that." He warned me that the local rednecks liked to fight in numbers and considered targeting airmen a form of entertainment. "They'll waste you if they get the chance," he said.

After ten days at home in Memphis with family and friends, I boarded a Continental Trailways Bus for Wichita Falls to spend the next few months training to be a jet engine specialist. En route there the bus had an hour layover in Fort Worth, and, with Bolton's warning in mind, I took a stroll to some nearby pawnshops and bought myself some brass knuckles. If the Wichita Falls Welcome Wagon tried to run me over, it would get a few dents in the process.

When I stepped off the bus in the Falls, wearing my dress blues, there were five guys lounging against the wall of the bus station. They weren't there to carry my duffel bag to the base for me.

"Hey, Blue Boy!" one of them called out in a thick Texas drawl.

"Yeah?" I said, turning toward them with all the confidence in the world, thanks to the weight of the shiny new brass knuckles in my right pocket.

"You better shine those shoes up, or they'll toss you in the brig," the bigmouth said, drawing appreciative laughter from his peanut gallery. If that's the best one-liner the punk-ass could come up with, then he wasn't worth my trouble. I turned and walked away, heading for a cab.

"Hey, Blue Boy, we're not done talking to you," yelled the guy. That did it. I stopped, turned around, dropped my duffel bag, and answered, "You don't have anything to say that I want to hear, badass."

"Oh my, boys, we got us a big bad one here," he drawled to his yokel posse.

"That's right, you do. And I ain't going anywhere, so if you want some, come and get it." I reached in my pocket and produced the brass knuckles, slipping them on my hand. It didn't go unnoticed. We stared back at each other for a minute or two, and when it was clear I wasn't going to break down they decided, as all bullies do in the face of resistance, to slink away.

Sheppard was a huge base with several thousand airmen stationed there. Because it was a training base, there was a large turnover as airmen came and went.

Although I'd already waited a couple of months to start my training, on arrival at Sheppard, I learned that there would be a further delay—for a slot to open up in my specialty. But once again, I lucked out and was chosen by my commanding officer, Lieutenant Kenneth Herndon, to be a temporary charge of quarters (CQ). Three of us were chosen for that job, and we each had an assistant CQ assigned to us. As a team, we worked every third night at the command quarters from the time it closed in the afternoon until it reopened in the morning. It was a twelve- to fourteen-hour shift, but, as I said, it happened only every three days. In between, we were free to do whatever we wanted.

Our duty consisted of securing the building and taking any emergency calls that came in, directing them to the proper person. It was really a piece of cake, unless you made the mistake of falling asleep on duty—and getting caught.

One night on my shift we learned that one of the guys in our flight had been savagely beaten with a pipe by a group of thugs at a local dance hall. His jaw was broken in the attack. When we got the news, Herndon called about twenty-five of us together for a war council.

"God forbid if this was the navy or the marines, because this town would be in trouble," Herndon said. "Dammit boys, the air force has to have some pride, too!" If his call to arms was a little roundabout, it was because Herndon could've been charged with conduct unbecoming an officer had he come right out and told us it was ass-kicking time. But we got the message loud and clear: if you pick on one of us, you pick on all of us.

The next weekend, a bunch of us dressed in civilian clothes, squeezed into five cars, and headed for the dance hall where our comrade had been beaten. We intended to two-step on a few redneck heads. Some of the guys were even packing lead pipes, intending to dish out some of their own medicine.

I'll give 'em this: the yokels were game as hell.

They charged right at us as soon as we entered the door. It was a typical Western-style brawl, and I waded right in like John Wayne himself, swinging at everything in front of me. I was having fun in spite of a split lip I got from someone's wild punch, and I was so wrapped up in my work that I didn't see that the cops were coming. By the time I did, I ran for the door (after flattening another guy) and ended up right in the arms of one of Wichita Falls' finest. And he didn't want the next dance.

Only two of us were arrested, and I didn't even know the other guy. It turned out that he was assigned to another squadron on base and had just happened to be at the dance hall that night. He felt it was his patriotic duty to help his fellow soldiers. God bless him.

When they found out we were servicemen, they called the provost marshal's office at the base. Two air policemen were dispatched to pick us up and take us back to the base to face military justice. When they arrived, they were very businesslike with the police, but once we were all in the car, the air force cops softened their spit-and-polish attitudes and even commented admiringly on our handiwork back at the dance hall.

The brass back at the base was a whole other story, though. That we were defending a fellow airman's honor cut no ice with them, and the provost's office recommended a court-martial for tarnishing the image and reputation of the U.S. Air Force.

That was averted when Herndon suggested an Article 15 instead. An Article 15 is a lesser disciplinary action that can range from taking a stripe to restriction on the base to KP duty. It also goes on your permanent record.

In my case, they took my stripe, put me back to the rank of airman basic, and restricted me to the base for two months. I would get the stripe back before I left the base, thanks to Herndon. He had felt bad that his obtuse "Win one for the Gipper" speech was the cause of the whole mess, and he had pushed for the Article 15 to keep me from being booted out of the air force altogether.

Unfortunately, Herndon couldn't change the fact that the incident would permanently stay on my service record and, more important, permanently change my feelings about working for Uncle Sam.

From that point on, I was counting the days when I would get out of a uniform and back into civilian clothes.

# Chapter 4

# Casualty of War

**M**Y FINAL AIR FORCE STOP WAS DAVIS-MONTHAN AIR FORCE BASE IN Tucson, Arizona, where I was a jet engine specialist in the 43rd Bomb Wing.

I arrived in Tucson in late May 1956, and, of course, the first thing that hit me like a ton of bricks was the heat. Texas was humid and hot, but Tucson was stifling. It's a dry heat, sure, but so's the heat in your oven, and who wants to live there? For fun, some of the airmen would take out a piece of sheet metal in the middle of the day, lay it on the concrete, and literally cook eggs on the burning surface.

I had some good times in Tucson and got along fine with my fellow airmen. The accommodations weren't bad, either—three men to a room with a toilet and a sink for shaving. We still had to go down the hall to take a community shower, but for a young man all of seventeen, it wasn't a bad life. All that and $90 a month!

After breakfast each morning, I walked over to the hangar and spent most of the day working on jet plane engines, some in the hangar itself and some outside on the flight line. You really had to be careful working on a plane out in the sun, because the metal parts turned excruciatingly hot and you could get seriously burned.

Nobody was more surprised than I was when I turned out to be a halfway decent jet mechanic. It wasn't nearly as bad as I thought, either. Unlike car engines, which are usually covered with oil and grime, jet engines are relatively clean, and almost everything is on the outside of the engine and therefore pretty accessible. Go figure.

There were times when we wouldn't have any work for hours on end. But there were many base alerts, readiness drills, and scramble drills, all designed to prepare us and keep us fit for the air force mission of defending freedom. I was very proud to be a member of the Strategic Air Command, called SAC by those of us in the service.

My off-duty hours were filled with fun activities with the guys I hung out with. Mostly we'd ride dirt bikes around nearby Mount Lemmon and Sabino Canyon. At first, I rode on the back of a friend's bike, but then I went out and bought a used 1956 BSA Golden Flash bike.

There was also the time Elvis Presley came to the Tucson Rodeo Grounds for a concert on Sunday, June 10, 1956. At the time, I was courting a prim and proper young lady whom I admired and whose beyond-her-years maturity and obvious good breeding made me wonder what the heck she saw in a guy like me.

On a previous date, the subject of Elvis Presley had come up. I happened to mention that my cousin, Red West, hung out with the young King of Rock and Roll. Because Elvis was coming to Tucson and my young lady expressed a detached interest in seeing what all the screaming was about, I got us tickets.

In the years since I first saw Elvis during lunch break at my high school, he had broken out of his Deep South base to become an international phenomenon. By 1956, he was the hottest rock-and-roll star on the planet and an icon to kids all over the world.

On the night of the concert, my date came to the door looking good, tastefully dressed to the nines. When we reached the wooden gates of the old rickety rodeo grounds, thousands of teenage girls were already screaming their heads off in anticipation of seeing their idol. But not my girl. In a dignified and ladylike fashion, she accompanied me in that sea of pandemonium as if we were entering a country club cotillion.

All of a sudden, at the other end of the rodeo grounds, the gates opened up. In came this long, black limousine with a police escort on either side. There were two cops each side of the front fender and two at the back. A couple of policemen ran alongside the car, which was leaving a huge cloud of dust in its wake.

When the limo stopped, a policeman opened the right rear door and Elvis got out. Even from a distance, I could see that cocky swagger he had. He took two steps and then suddenly fell down to his knees in the dirt. Man, those girls went absolutely nuts and started jumping out of their seats to get to him.

The strains of the first song rang out, and every female on the premises lost control of her heart, senses, tear ducts, and, in some cases, bladder. That was the power Elvis Presley had over women—and the one I was with was not immune. My cool, calm debutante was suddenly screaming as loud as anybody and trying her damnedest to get down to the fence separating Elvis from the crowd, while I did my best to hold her back. Believe me, no rodeo cowboy ever had a harder time tussling with a bull than I did keeping my desert rose–turned-wildflower from throwing herself at the heartthrob with the ball-bearing hip joints. She was the first girl I lost to the King, but she wouldn't be the last, although, of course, I didn't know that at the time.

As my hitch in the service inched closer to the end, the air force tried to lure me into reenlisting by offering me a tempting cash bonus. But I really never gave it much thought. For some reason, it felt like something else was calling me back to Memphis. While the air force was overall a great experience for me, I was eager to get back home and get on with my life as a civilian. So in the summer of 1958, upon receiving my discharge, I headed back to Memphis.

It was good to be in the South again where I felt at home. But I didn't stay in my comfort zone for long.

Tragedy struck the family soon after my arrival on August 14. My Uncle Tom died from a heart attack. He was just sixty. We were all devastated. He had meant so much to all of us. When we came back from the turkey farm disaster in California, Uncle Tom took us into his home and took care of us for several months until Daddy got his house-painting business established.

He was a good and kind man, and I never heard him raise his voice in anger. Family meant everything to Uncle Tom, and losing him was as bad as it got.

We weren't the only family mourning for a loved one on that day. Several hours before Uncle Tom died, Gladys Presley—Elvis's beloved mother—went to her reward. Mrs. Presley passed away at approximately 5:00 AM on August 14, and Uncle Tom passed away later that same day around 10:00 or 11:00 PM.

The funeral services were held one day apart at the Memphis Funeral Home in the same stateroom.

The stateroom was packed with family, friends, and well-wishers from the community paying their last respects to Uncle Tom. I was sitting with my father in the family section when I heard a noise behind me. It was Elvis, stumbling through a side entrance. His appearance startled me because his eyes were bloodshot from crying over his own loss. His mom had been laid out in that same room just twenty-four hours earlier. Elvis walked right up to my cousin Red. They embraced. Then they walked arm in arm to stand beside Red's father's casket.

"Red, I know how you feel, man," Elvis said tearfully aloud. "My momma was right there just yesterday. Oh God, I miss her so much. And I know how much you loved your daddy, and you miss him as much as I miss Momma." Then Elvis hugged Red again as his emotions overwhelmed him.

"I gotta go, Red," Elvis said in between sniffles. "It hurts too much to be here. If you need anything or if there's anything I can do, please let me know. Whenever you're ready, come on out to the house, okay?"

With that, Elvis rejoined his cousin Gene Smith and friends Lamar Fike and Alan Fortas, who were waiting in the wings, and departed.

In the sixteen years I would spend with Elvis, that was the most emotional I ever saw him. His mother was so special to him. Many times over the ensuing years, I joined Elvis at her grave, watching this man who brought joy to so many become aggrieved at a loss still raw. His taking time out of the day after his mom's funeral to comfort my cousin over his loss is one of my most special memories of Elvis.

I finally met him a few weeks later. We were at the Rainbow Skating Rink at an after-hours private skating party. Red made the introductions.

Red West and Elvis had a special relationship that went back to their high school days.

One day in 1952, at Humes High School, Red was heading for football practice after class. He spotted Elvis leaning up against a wall. As he approached, Red noticed that Elvis looked all shook up— but not the way he sang about.

Red greeted him and asked if there was something the matter. Elvis told him that at that moment there were three guys waiting for him to leave the building so that they could beat him up. Even before he was famous, because he wore his hair differently and dressed to suit himself, Elvis was an attention getter. Some of that attention was hostile.

My cousin and I were a lot alike. We were mostly shy and pretty laid back most of the time, but we absolutely hated bullies. While it took a lot to provoke me, Red had a reputation as a fearless fighter. I can't recall a time when he lost a fight. In high school, Red stood five feet eleven inches and weighed about 160 pounds. When crossed, Red came down like a landslide on his transgressor. He had a hair-trigger temper, and woe to the person who became the target of it. Or, in this case, persons. Numbers didn't matter to Red.

"Let's go and see what this is all about," he told Elvis, leading him out onto Manassas Street. There slouched three hulking fellows whose combined IQs wouldn't have reached double figures if you spotted them a couple points. What they indeed had in mind was teaching the long-haired, duck-tailed, flamboyant greaser a lesson in pain and humility.

"I understand you three badasses are gonna whip this little guy's ass," said my cousin, opening the proceedings on a diplomatic note.

The biggest one answered that it was none of Red's business, that all they wanted to do was talk to Elvis.

Red had a better idea. Because conversation was all the Three Stooges wanted, he would be happy to stay and chat with them, while Elvis, who was more into singing than talking, went on home.

Elvis left, and the trio proved they were smarter than they looked by not trying to stop him.

Another time, Red walked into a school bathroom and discovered Elvis in the clutches of three different dudes who had in mind cutting off some of that soon-to-be-famous slick brown coiffure. Without hesitating, Red strode right into their midst and asked what was going on. One of them said they were going to give the boy a haircut. Red responded with, "He doesn't look like he wants one to me. Elvis, you want a haircut?" Elvis shook his head and softly said no. The guy spoke up and said it didn't matter what he wanted, they were going to cut it anyway. Red said, "Naw, that's not going to happen guys." Noting his steely gaze and unflinching manner, the would-be barbers let go of Elvis and left in search of flies whose wings they would tear off.

Elvis never forgot what my cousin had done for him, and in the fall of 1954 when Presley-mania was first taking off, Elvis invited Red out on the road with him as there were bullies out there just like there had been in school.

It was Red's senior year of high school, and his football team was about to board a bus to play cross-town rival Central High. Red noticed Elvis in the parking lot. Elvis had graduated the year before and was back visiting the school with some friends. It wasn't hard to miss him, as Elvis was decked out in a black-and-white cowboy jacket and black pants. He was already riding high from the success of "That's All Right" for Sun Records. The record had sold thousands of copies and was constantly getting radio airplay. Being on the radio back in the 1950s was like being a movie star. When Red and Elvis renewed their acquaintance that afternoon, Elvis invited him to one of his concerts. From that point on, Red became one of his best friends and picked up where he'd left off as Elvis's protector.

They shared a lot of crazy times. In my opinion, Elvis was the first authentic rock star of the post–World War II generation. The raw sexuality he oozed made him a target for females who couldn't resist him, as well as for their boyfriends, who resented their girls' lack of resistance and especially the man who caused it. In the Deep South, back in those days, if a woman was with a date and she went onstage to kiss Elvis, that was like asking the guy she was with to go outside for a fight. Red often saw the boyfriends smolder while their bobby-soxer girlfriends openly lusted over Elvis. And when Elvis saw the women reacting to his suggestive wiggling and jumping around, he laid it on twice as thick, resulting in the girls getting wilder and the boyfriends getting angrier. When things got out of hand, Red waded in like the U.S. Marines.

Once at a club outside of Lubbock, Texas, Elvis caused a ruckus that engulfed the entire place. According to Red, Elvis was onstage doing his thing when a guy in the audience yelled out an insult at Elvis. Then one drunk in the crowd told another one to shut up, and all hell broke loose. Suddenly, it looked like a scene from one of Elvis's movies, with beer bottles flying, tables overturning, and more than one hundred people beating the hell out of each other. Things started to get really ugly when a brawler put his foot through one of Elvis's guitars, and then blood started flowing as thick as the whiskey.

Normally, Elvis would have been frightened, but this time he actually seemed to be enjoying what his gyrations had ignited. In fact, with chairs, bottles, and buddies crashing all around him, Elvis actually began to sign autographs. Red finally grabbed Elvis and half dragged him outside.

As they sped away from the scene, Elvis began laughing like a madman. He had never turned a crowd on like that before, and he loved the pandemonium. A moment later, Red was roaring, too.

They had a bond that bordered on brotherhood. But when you consider that each had lost a parent on the same day, that bond seems almost predestined.

The Memphis Draft Board notified Elvis in December 1957 that he would soon receive his draft notice. Elvis's manager, Colonel Tom Parker, quietly arranged with the army to postpone his induction for several months so that Elvis could fulfill his contractual obligations. Elvis's meteoric rise in 1956 had netted him several hit records, millions in record sales, lucrative performing dates, and successful money-making films in Hollywood.

Finally, on March 24, 1958, Elvis Presley reported to his local draft board in Memphis and became a sworn member of the U.S. Army.

About six months later, Private Presley prepared to ship off for Germany for the next eighteen months. Along with his grief over his mother's passing, Elvis was worried about his career, which he was afraid would be dead in the water by the time he was stateside again. Luckily, that proved not to be the case.

Although he was grown up, Elvis was a kid at heart who liked to do fun things that he had missed out on as a teenager, such as rollerskating. Many times, Elvis rented out the entire Rainbow Skating Rink after its regular business hours. The owners were happy to accommodate Elvis and let him use the facility from midnight to whenever he felt like leaving. Usually, that was well into the wee hours of the morning. It was a time for Elvis to gather his close friends around him and just be himself instead of the public image he was to the world. On this night, Red extended an invitation to me, my sisters, Barbara, Carolyn, and Elizabeth, and Barbara's husband, Bill Thorpe, for a late evening of fun, Elvis-style.

I was standing at rinkside with my brother-in-law Bill, an all-around athlete and a local Amateur Athletic Union welterweight boxing champion, when Red and Elvis skated up to us.

"Elvis, I want you to meet the new meat," Red said, rubbing his hands together expectantly as Elvis extended warm greetings to us.

"What do you mean, 'new meat'?" I asked him. Elvis put up a reassuring hand and said, "Oh, that doesn't mean anything." He was boyish, charming, and just as nice as he could be. The fame and fortune hadn't gone to his head, and he took everything in stride. He was just a good guy, and I took an instant liking to him. "Well, look, there's this game we're going to play called 'War,'" Elvis said. "Why don't you guys just watch and see how it's played. When we have our first break, you can join in." I said that would be fine.

The object of the game, as far as I could tell, was for the teams that formed on opposite sides of the floor to, at the signal of the referee, Junior Smith, Elvis's cousin, skate as fast as they could into one another and knock everybody down. I'd never seen anything like it in my life. The "game" combined the worst elements of skating, hockey, football, and demolition derby. A barroom fight looked like a walk through the park compared to this. A person who didn't know how to roller-skate very well would be in serious trouble.

A person, for instance, like me.

Before the game started, I noticed that everyone on the floor went over to a big cardboard box in the corner and took out elbow and knee pads to wear. I went over and got some for myself. Then, after I saw what went on, I went back to the box and padded each arm from wrist to shoulder and each leg from ankle to knee. If there'd been a full suit of armor, I'd have put that on, too.

When it was my turn to go in, I was paired opposite a girl named Melinda Mullinex. She was the only girl Elvis let participate in War, and her qualifications were obvious. Not only was she built like a brick shithouse, but she could skate like Gordie Howe on ice. But even so, I was reluctant to square off against a member of the opposite sex. There was no way I was going to knock down a girl. When Junior blew his whistle to start the game, Melinda came shooting at me as if fired from a cannon. Gallantly, I tried to ward her off with a gentlemanly wave of my hand. The next thing I knew, I was on the floor looking up.

When I regained my feet and started looking around for the number of that truck, Melinda grabbed me by the collar of my shirt and jerked me off my feet once more. I don't know what hurt more, crashing onto the hardwood floor or my pride.

I got up the second time, and I kept one eye out for Melinda, while the other one sought out somebody my own speed that I might have a reasonable chance of knocking down. As I scanned the crowd for octogenarians and wheelchairs, a pile driver to the back of my knee sent me reeling to the floor once again. The three-knockdown rule was not in effect, so when I got up and inched my way over to the rail, Melinda sent me down a fourth time. I crawled on my hands and knees the rest of the way to the rail. The timeout whistle blew. As I sat there licking my wounds, Elvis and Red skated over.

34

"Sonny, what are you doing?" Red asked, not holding back his laughter.

"Man, I'm just resting," I gasped, the sweat pouring down my face. "All I've done is hit the floor, get up, and hit it again. Every time I get up, that girl over there just knocks me on my ass. I can't seem to escape her." By this time, Elvis doubled over with laughter. Then he called Melinda over, and when she arrived, Elvis put an arm around her and said good-naturedly, "Now, Melinda, why are you picking on Red's cousin here?"

"I don't care who he is; he tried to knock me down!" Melinda said to Elvis, glaring at me like bad-boy boxer Sonny Liston.

I gently pointed out that I had actually tried to *avoid* hitting her. I then offered to skate as fast as I could in the opposite direction from her when the game resumed if she would please refrain from trying to kill me.

"Melinda, how about that? Is that a deal?" Elvis asked. He later told me that he had watched the whole thing unfold from a distance to gauge my reaction. He said he saw my true personality that night and liked what he saw. I guess that was an audition to be a charter member of the group that would later be known as the Memphis Mafia, although it would be a year and a half before we were officially given that title. I asked him later if he had in fact set the whole thing up, and Elvis denied it. To this day, I am not sure whether he had told me the truth or not.

Although Melinda had grudgingly agreed to a truce, I didn't fare much better the rest of the night and ended up with cuts on my head and cheek as well as a badly bruised shoulder. Elvis always had a first-aid technician present on skating nights, and he earned his money that night just keeping me together.

Before I left, I went over to tell Elvis that I enjoyed meeting him and had had a good time. He said, "I'll see you tomorrow night. You're coming out here again, right?"

"I won't even be able to walk tomorrow night," I answered, which made him smile.

"You may not be able to walk, but you'll be here skating, right?"

I smiled back and agreed. Battered and bruised as I was, right then the pain of letting Elvis Presley down would have been more than I could bear.

# Chapter 5

# The King's Court

O N SEPTEMBER 22, 1958, TOTING A DUFFEL BAG AND WEARING HIS ARMY uniform, Elvis walked up the gangplank of the USS *Randall* to set sail for Germany, where he would serve for the next eighteen months.

Elvis didn't know if he would have a career in show business when he got back, just as I didn't know what the future held in store for me.

When I got back from the air force, I paid my parents room and board and lived with them and my little sister, Susan.

After I settled in, I went to work for Ralston Purina as a feed mixer. My primary duty was to lift hundred-pound bags of barley, calcium, salt, and other ingredients onto a two-wheeled dolly; slice them open; and dump the contents into different bins to be mixed with food for animals. I mixed dog food, cow food, cat food, and just about every kind of animal chow you can think of. It was back-breaking work that took an immediate toll on my back and hands. Invariably, I came home dirty, sweaty, and in pain from wrestling those huge bags.

That being the case, I was hardly in the mood to go out at night and sow some wild oats (which sounded too much like something animals eat, anyway).

After a couple months of this, my dad recommended that I look for new work. "Son, you don't need to be doing a job that is caus-ing you this much pain," he said.

When I pointed out that I was making pretty good pay, he trumped me by asking, "How much are you enjoying that good pay?"

I looked in the paper and saw an ad for an assistant parts manager at Ace Appliance on Summer Avenue. I applied for the job and was hired on the spot. It took me about three months to figure out that repairmen technicians made better money, so I asked the owner, Mr. Gatlin, if I could train to become a technician. Admiring my get-up-and-go, he agreed to send me to a technician school for washer and dryer repair. After maintaining jet engines in the air force, repairing washers and dryers was a breeze, and soon I was going on house calls as an assistant. Within two months, I was making my own house calls with my own assistant in tow.

With the money I made, I traded in my 1951 two-tone green Pontiac for a brand-new white 1959 Ford Galaxie 500 convertible. Life was good, but I had no direction beyond cruising around town in my convertible, hanging out with my friends, and chasing the girls. That was until March 1960, when honorably discharged Army Sergeant Elvis A. Presley returned home to Memphis.

In early 1959 Red came back from visiting Elvis in Germany. He had been something of a fish out of water in Europe, and his undefined role in Elvis's life and unsettled lifestyle there had worn on him. Red spent many hours in the local watering hole until Elvis came home from duty. As a result, he got a little testy with the locals and had his fair share of scrapes. Elvis hadn't started a payroll system yet, so Red didn't have any money and was too proud to ask for any. All he got was a little here and there from Vernon Presley, Elvis's father, for cigarettes or the occasional beer. Red had gone over with Lamar Fike to lend Elvis moral support and to dispel the doldrums of army life. Elvis didn't give much thought to his friends' needs because his own were always provided for, and I'm sure he thought his dad was giving them money to spend on other things. Elvis didn't even carry money on him. He probably figured that supplying Red and Lamar with food and shelter was enough.

Before Red left Germany, Elvis told him, "Tell Sonny to come see me when I get home." A couple of weeks after Elvis returned, I got in my convertible and drove down Democrat Road to visit him at his home, known to the world as Graceland.

During the five-mile trip from my house, I was a little apprehensive wondering if Elvis would actually remember me, Red's assurances notwithstanding. After all, it had been a year and a half since we first met at the roller rink. Maybe I'd have to fall down to refresh his memory.

I turned onto Highway 51 South—later to be renamed Elvis Presley Boulevard—and headed to the outskirts of Memphis. Elvis's home, Graceland, was still in the county, as the city of Memphis had not annexed into the community of Whitehaven yet. When I drove up to the famous wrought-iron gates, I got excited. Stepping out of my convertible, I met Elvis's uncle, Travis Smith, the security guard. Travis would later become my favorite of Elvis's relatives.

"Can I help you?" he asked.

I replied, "I met Elvis before he left for Germany, and he said for me to look him up when he got back."

Travis asked my name, and when I identified myself, he asked if I was kin to Red. I confirmed I was indeed. He then called the house, and Junior Smith, Elvis's cousin, answered the phone. He gave Travis the go-ahead. As I passed through the gates, I knew I had been granted access to a very special world that only a privileged few ever got to see.

Today Graceland is the second-most-visited home in the United States, after the White House, and millions know it by both name and sight. Graceland started out in 1861 as a Hereford cattle farm owned by S.E. Toof. Toof, publisher of the *Memphis Commercial Appeal*, named the estate after his daughter, Grace Toof. Grace's niece, Ruth Moore, actually built the house in 1939.

When Elvis offered $100,000 for the home and its thirteen and one-half surrounding acres, Moore, then separated from her husband, sold it to him on March 19, 1957. A month later, the Presleys moved into the beautiful, enchanting mansion.

I rang the doorbell. Junior answered and invited me inside. There were Elvis and his army buddy Rex Mansfield working out in their karate gis. Elvis stopped, wiped the sweat off his brow, and introduced me to Rex and Elisabeth Stefaniak, Elvis's German secretary. I already had met everyone else there—Lamar Fike, Junior, Gene Smith, and Billy Smith (Travis's son), all of whom are Elvis's cousins, except Lamar.

After a few minutes of small talk, Elvis asked me if I'd ever heard of karate. I told him I hadn't. He and Rex began a demonstration. Watching them instantly brought back the memory of an incident while I was in the air force.

I may not have heard of karate, but in the service I'd seen first-hand a demonstration of what someone trained in this devastating martial art could do. It was in the parking lot of a Tucson bar in which I was having a drink with a former serviceman who'd just returned from a long stint in South Korea. A hulking cowboy looking for a fight set his sights on my companion, on whom he had about one hundred pounds. But the weight advantage counted for nothing as the guy used his flying feet to reduce the cowboy in less than a minute to a blubbering pile of broken bones.

When I told Elvis the story, he started laughing. I think he always identified with the "little guy," the reluctant underdog with the capability to kick ass when sufficiently provoked. That's why karate fascinated him so much. He was eager to show me the finer points he'd learned studying under his own personal instructor in Germany.

As Rex, in the role of the aggressor, tossed punches at him, Elvis expertly blocked them and countered with blows with the back of his hand, his elbow, his forearm, the side of his hand, and his fingers. It was an impressive show, and Elvis clearly enjoyed putting it on for us. The thought came to mind: what would happen now to anybody who tried to give him a haircut against his will?

I spent the rest of the day with Elvis and the gang, just hanging out, swapping stories, and keeping the conversation light.

As I was about to call it a night, Elvis invited me back to Graceland the next day. Then he said, "We're going to go to 'Holiday on Ice' tomorrow at Ellis Auditorium. Wanna go with us?" I gladly accepted. When the King of Rock and Roll invites you as his personal guest for a night on the town, anything else is like a visit to the dentist's office.

The next evening I drove to Graceland after work. There I joined a group that included Gene and Lamar, Joe Esposito, Charlie Hodge, and Cliff Gleaves, the latter three whom I met for the first time. We were a lively bunch, to say the least, and a privileged one, hanging out with Elvis.

The evening after that, we all watched movies at the Memphian Theatre, rented out for the occasion to the city's own movie star. I thought it was so cool that a guy could rent an entire movie theater and watch movies all night long. It was good to be the King, yes indeed; and it was also good to be with the King.

Saturday, March 19, was the day I think I really earned Elvis's trust. We were back at the Rainbow Skating Rink for an evening of roller-skating wars with the guys.

This time, however, I wasn't the freshest meat on wheels. In fact, since Melinda the Merciless had blitzed my ass that first night, I'd made it a point to do some practicing when Elvis was in Germany, and now I was, if not hell on wheels, at least no longer helpless on them.

On this night, my new skating skills came in handy. An outsider who'd been invited through a friend of a friend thought he'd get cute and show off for his girlfriend by gunning for our host. The first time out he blindsided Elvis with a forearm check that sent him to the floor. These things happen in a rough-and-tumble game like War, but when it happened a second time and then the guy went smirking over to his girlfriend, I figured he was playing a private game of "Let's Humiliate the Superstar" and decided that I would ruin his fun.

Sure enough, when the action resumed, I noticed Elvis's stalker positioning himself for another sneak attack. This time he came up behind Elvis. I came from the side, and, just as he was about to strike, I exploded into him from out of a crouch. A split second before I nailed him, he spotted me coming. The fear on his face was almost cartoonish. It was replaced by pain as he hit the floor after flying about ten feet and then skidding into the wall.

The first-aid tech attended to him, and we heard that the guy suffered some cartilage separation in his rib cage. Sorry about that, guy. We never saw him at the rink again.

"Good hit, Sonny," was all Elvis said to me about the incident, but the look in his eyes relayed that he knew I was protecting him. Red was out in Hollywood working in TV and the movies, but for now, there was another West taking care of business back home.

Not long after that, Elvis invited me to a recording session in Nashville at RCA's Studio B. It was the first time I got to watch the King in his element.

Elvis chartered a bus. Skating from the previous night had left me with a black eye, prime fodder for everyone to give me a hard time about having been popped by somebody's angry boyfriend.

We arrived in Nashville around noon and were joined in the studio by Scotty Moore, D.J. Fontana, and the members of the Jordanaires who sang backup on Elvis's records—Gordon Stoker, Neal Matthews, Hoyt Hawkins, and Ray Walker. I liked the Jordanaires right off because they were fun and loose, which made them a good fit for Elvis. Rounding out the roster were musicians Hank Garland, Buddy Harman, Floyd Cramer, and Bob Moore. I later heard they were told they would be working on a Jim Reeves session so word wouldn't leak out about Elvis being there, which would've caused problems with marauding fans.

It was Elvis's first recording session since June 1958, and I could tell he was a little nervous. The session started at 8:00 PM and lasted until 7:00 AM.

Elvis was methodical but loose in his approach to recording. The first thing he would do was get everyone to relax by greeting everyone and catching up on what they had done since the last time they saw each other. Once everyone felt comfortable, Elvis took control.

"Hey look, guys, let's cut some songs!" he said, and everyone took their places. He had already picked out the demo songs he wanted to record, and the producer played them over the speakers for the musicians and singers to hear. Elvis discussed with the musicians the sound, rhythm, and style he was looking for, and everybody would chime in with their own thoughts during repeated playbacks.

Then slowly they started playing along with the tape as Elvis picked out the melody. The session men added their own signature to the music, and everyone worked until they achieved a unique sound to put down.

It was a great sound, thanks mostly to the fact that Elvis was a tireless perfectionist who worked on something until he got it right. He and the band would rehearse until the sound in his head was matched by what the musicians were playing, and then he would be ready to record it. Elvis would have made a helluva producer himself and was the perfect example of a singer taking command of a song. It was a phenomenal process to witness.

Elvis recorded six songs during that all-night session, including "Stuck on You," "Fame and Fortune," "Make Me Know It," "Soldier Boy," "A Mess of Blues," and "It Feels So Right."

It was apparent to everyone in the studio that "Stuck on You" would be an instant hit. But it was "Fame and Fortune" that really knocked me out. Written by Fred Wise and Ben Weisman, the message of the song was universal: what good is fame and fortune if you don't share it with anyone? That basically summed up Elvis's personal philosophy and the way he lived his life.

Once the recording was done, RCA wasted no time doing its part. The company's pressing plant in Indianapolis worked overtime pressing and shipping a million copies of "Stuck on You" and "Fame and Fortune" in just two days to record stores. The former became his first Number 1 hit since his two-year army hiatus. "Fame and Fortune" didn't fare badly either, entering the Top 20 and making the disc a double-sided hit.

When we got home, there were more skating parties and all-night movies at the Memphian. And now that Rex had returned to his home in Dresden, Tennessee, I was Elvis's partner in his karate workouts. After one of our sessions, we headed to the kitchen, where Elvis really stunned me—but not with a kick or punch.

"Sonny, man, would you like to come to work for me?" he asked as we settled in at the kitchen counter.

"Doing what?" I asked, hardly believing my ears. "Everything. Whatever I need you to do—performing errands, looking after my cars, keeping jealous boyfriends off my back," he said, smiling.

In addition to all that, he said he needed friends around to keep him company. That part would be easy, I thought, never guessing that keeping Elvis Presley company would be the hardest part of the job.

I was making pretty good money at the appliance store, about $75 a week, and I was working for a boss who was a good man. But how many chances would I get to work for and play with the world's greatest superstar? Working for Elvis would be a wilder ride than I could ever get in my Ford Galaxie 500. And if that didn't work out, there were always washers and dryers that needed fixing.

"Yeah, sure, I think that would be great," I finally said. I didn't even think to ask how much he was going to pay me, but the delighted expression on Elvis's face blanked out a lot of questions.

I told Elvis that I would have to give two weeks' notice to my boss, and he said that was fine. In fact, he respected me for that. He said he had to go to Miami to film a television special with Frank Sinatra and he would see me when he got back. I subsequently found out when I received my first paycheck from Elvis that I would be making $35 a week before taxes were taken out compared to the $75 a week I was making as a repairman.

But the way I looked at it was that I might be taking a cut in pay, but I would start living like a king.

# Chapter **6**

# The Hollywood Waltz

**E**LVIS'S WORLD WAS INTOXICATING TO ANYONE ENTERING IT, AND THAT WENT in spades for an impressionable twenty-one-year-old who came from such humble beginnings. To have the world on a string, beautiful girls at your beck and call, and enough money to buy whatever you wanted was not only intoxicating but addicting. I took just one whiff of his lifestyle and was instantly hooked.

While I finished out my last two weeks at Ace Appliance, Elvis and a few of the guys rode a private railroad car to Miami for "Frank Sinatra's Welcome Home Party for Elvis Presley" on NBC-TV in late March. They stayed in the penthouse of the world-famous Fontainebleau Hotel, partied it up, and were treated like royalty. Meanwhile, I was busily prying apart washing machines and trying to figure out how to make them run again. It didn't take a genius to figure out which was the better job.

The $35 a week I made when I signed on with Elvis was all free and clear because everything I needed was taken care of. My laundry, dry cleaning, food, and transportation were all courtesy of my generous boss. The only thing I really needed money for was cigarettes. They were quite cheap back in those politically incorrect days when smoking was considered manly and sexy. I even turned over my 1959 Ford Galaxie 500 white convertible to my brother Billy, who was just getting out of the army. When he asked me what I would be driving instead, I told him, "Cadillacs, Lincolns, and just about any car or motorcycle Elvis owns." And it was true—anything Elvis owned, I was free to drive.

Entering the King's court was like entering a special brotherhood. We all became loyal friends at first, but over the years certain ones in

45

the group seemed to become more focused on their own self-interests and came to believe they were more important than the rest of us. Joe Esposito even concluded that he was Elvis's closest friend. Those of us who didn't suffer from such delusions of grandeur were more than content with the reality of the situation, which was that we were all close to Elvis and didn't need to make more out of our friendship than what it was. Some others, however, whether from low self-esteem or too much ego—I suspect mostly the latter—embellished their place in the scheme of things and even made a cottage industry of doing so.

As for me, I'm content to make the statement that Elvis was my employer for sixteen years and also happened to be my best friend. I feel it should be up to him to say who was his best friend and not up to someone else to make that claim on his own. I know I never heard him say that about anyone. I loved him and know in my heart he loved me, and that's good enough for me.

The group that surrounded Elvis eventually became known as the "Memphis Mafia" because we had taken up the peculiar habit of dressing in black mohair suits and wearing dark sunglasses and snazzy hats; it was the Blues Brothers look twenty years before they made it famous. One time, around 1962, we pulled up at a casino in Las Vegas, and as we exited the limo someone asked if we were the Mafia. "Yeah," answered an onlooker, "the Memphis Mafia." I believe that onlooker happened to be James Bacon, a well-known entertainment columnist with the *Los Angeles Herald Examiner*. He was also the source for the coining of the "Rat Pack" phrase about Sinatra and his group of guys.

Just as in the real Mafia, the Memphis Mafia had its own code of silence within the group. We became Elvis's official entourage, a group of gatekeepers and confidants who protected the Presley name and image for years.

Elvis handpicked his friends with great care. The two things he looked for were personality and loyalty, especially the latter. Personality granted you entrance into Elvis's world, but loyalty kept you there. Disloyalty, or even the hint of it, was cause for immediate banishment. But Elvis was a person of great charity, and if the circumstances warranted it, he believed in second chances. Those of us around him tried to follow his lead.

However, Joe blew it when Elvis found out that he was reporting to the Colonel about Elvis's activities. Elvis cut him loose, and

Joe returned to his wife and children in Los Angeles. He discovered that he had burned a lot of bridges by abusing his authority and carrying on as if he was the power behind the throne. "Diamond Joe" found out real quick that on his own he was not even worth fool's gold. In fact, without the Presley cachet, he had trouble finding work as an extra in Hollywood, where he'd previously tossed his weight around and treated people as though they were serfs.

I felt sorry for Joe and his wife, Joan, and their two daughters, Debbie and Cindy, even though Joe had asked for it. When MGM decided to make a television pilot called *Kissing Cousins*, I approached Jim Dobson, the studio's casting director for extras. I kindly asked Jim to put Joe to work on the production so he could put food on the table for his family.

If Joe reads this, or someone else does and tells him about this, he will realize for the first time that I got him the job, because I never mentioned it before. Over the years, Joe has said some hurtful things about me, which is baffling, because when he first went to work for Elvis in 1960 we shared the left front bedroom upstairs at Graceland, which later became Elvis's wardrobe room. I felt that Joe and I were pretty good friends.

Before Elvis entered the army, he was largely viewed by the mainstream world as a rock-and-roll outlaw who threatened the moral fiber of society. But he emerged from the military with a much higher approval rating. He had served his country, and now even adult America was taking a second look at this polite young man who seemed to have the swiveling hips under control.

Having gone from antihero to All-American hero, Elvis was primed to become bigger than ever, not just as a recording artist, but also as a well-rounded entertainer. That meant movies as well, and Hollywood wasted no time setting its cap for the dashing heartthrob. The result was a multipicture deal worth many millions of dollars to Elvis. With his financial security assured, Elvis could now afford to put his family and friends on his payroll. Now Elvis had his own production company, Elvis Presley Enterprises, Inc., and he needed people working for him full time.

Initially on the payroll were Elvis's father, Vernon; his cousin, Gene Smith; Joe Esposito; Lamar Fike; Charlie Hodge; and myself. Red was already out in California working in the movies and was added to the payroll later. Not long afterward, Elvis added Alan Fortas,

Marty Lacker, and Elvis's cousin, Billy Smith. Eventually Richard Davis and Jerry Schilling completed the roster of Memphis Mafia for the rest of the decade. A few others worked for Elvis for a short time, but the nucleus remained pretty much the aforementioned names. Another Elvis cousin, Junior Smith, was also salaried, but he reported to Vernon and didn't travel with us when we went to Hollywood.

In addition to being his friends and employees, we were Elvis's lifeline to the outside world. Many books have portrayed Elvis as a "prisoner of fame," but that wasn't altogether true. Elvis went riding around, shopped, visited nightclubs, and did many of the everyday things most people did, especially during the movie years from 1960 through 1969. Granted, some outings had to be meticulously planned. Obviously, Elvis couldn't just stop in any restaurant and order a meal without being overwhelmed by people who wanted autographs and pictures. When we did go out to eat, it was mostly in restaurants that had private dining areas available to us. But eating out wasn't that high on Elvis's list of things he liked to do a lot, anyway. He could afford to rent an amusement park or movie theater for our enjoyment, and he did so often. Elvis was always the first person to admit that he did whatever he pleased. In fact, Elvis reveled in his fame and fortune and loved to share it with his family, friends, associates, fans, and even, at times, total strangers. Make no mistake, he loved being Elvis Presley.

His first cousin, Gene Smith, grew up with Elvis in Tupelo, Mississippi, and was perhaps the closest person to him then. They shared the bond of family, and because Elvis didn't have any other siblings, he loved Gene like a brother. They were only about six months apart in age, and they shared that same weird, off-the-wall sense of humor along with their memories of constant struggle growing up in the post-Depression years.

I got along particularly well with Gene, and we became good buddies. When someone else would say something wacky or funny, I could look at Gene's face and in an instant know what he was thinking. We shared a lot of laughs. I was especially close to Gene during Elvis's early movie years.

Gene ran interference for Elvis during that time, but when Presley-mania went international, Gene was relegated to duty as Elvis's companion on the road, and Joe Esposito became Elvis's chief foreman. Once when the question was put to Gene as to what he did for Elvis, he looked at the guy with a steady gaze and said, "I'm his cousin; I don't do a damn thing." When Elvis heard about that, it broke him up. In fact, Gene did do something for Elvis, and he did it very well. He made Elvis laugh a lot. When he wasn't doing it, Elvis would say to Gene, "I pay you a lot of money to make me laugh, and today I haven't even cracked a smile." Gene would get a shocked look on his face and mutter something like, "Is that right?" or "It ain't that damn much," and that alone would break Elvis up.

Joe Esposito was a smooth talker, but that wasn't his only appeal to Elvis. For some reason, Elvis thought that Joe had some extended family connection to the Mafia, through his older brother Frank who lived in Chicago, which made him that much more intriguing. To be honest, I don't think Joe went out of his way to set the record straight in that regard, figuring that if Elvis got a kick out of thinking that he was "connected," why rock the boat? Although he took over Gene's role, Joe was still jealous of Gene's closeness to Elvis. Sometimes when Elvis would go for a ride or to visit a young starlet, he wanted just one guy with him, and it was always Gene unless he was upset at Gene for something. The rest of us accepted that because Gene was kin, but Joe didn't like it one bit. It was important to Joe that he be the number one guy. It's almost pathetic to hear him still referring to himself today as Elvis's best friend.

But at the start, Joe was alright, just one of the guys. He was the outsider, being the only "Yankee" working for Elvis at the time. He seemed to have the kind of playful sense of humor we all had, but over the years, his need to view himself as the most important person in Elvis's entourage caused him to distance himself from the rest of us over time.

Joe's favorite words were *I* and *me*, and his inflated self-importance intruded in most situations. He may have been "foreman" and "road manager," but when we toured, the most I can remember him doing was distributing itineraries, which were made up by the Colonel's staff. These itineraries included departure times, instructions for taking wardrobe to the facility where Elvis was going to perform, and travel arrangements for vacations. Fact is, Colonel Parker made all the important arrangements, such as hotels, security, and schedules. Even when we were making movies, the Colonel's staff handled almost everything. Billy Smith once told me that Elvis was getting ready to can Joe near the end of his life and asked Billy if he could do what Joe did. Billy answered, "What does he do?" I wasn't there for that moment, but knowing Elvis, I know that brought a big grin to his face.

Other than that, Joe did a beautiful job.

Lamar Fike was Elvis's personal court jester and king of the one-liners. A natural-born raconteur, Lamar served as the butt of Elvis's personal jokes (although we all took turns in that position) and as his personal assistant. But Lamar had a pretty wicked tongue himself, and he could get under Elvis's skin like nobody else in the group. They often traded barbs like a couple of lounge comedians, and the repartee could really sizzle. But Elvis's affection for Lamar was obvious to all.

Lamar also had the gift of insight into Elvis's psyche. He could read Elvis's mind quite well, and though he pushed the envelope pretty hard sometimes, he usually knew when to back off. When Lamar didn't back off, he suffered the consequences.

When Elvis began performing again in 1969, Lamar became lighting director for all of his shows. I grew more fond of Lamar over time and came to see the sensitive side he usually hid well. The big man was, at root, a pussycat. A bunch of us have stayed in regular contact over the years, and it's always a treat to talk to "Lamoyne," an affectionate nickname I nearly always greet him with. He had another nickname bestowed on him. Elvis called him "Lamasides" because he resembled *Ironside* actor Raymond Burr. Elvis had a unique way of connecting things so that you could easily see what he meant, and his sense of humor was quite keen.

Cousin Red was the enforcer of the group and instilled the fear of God in everyone, including Elvis. He didn't hesitate to physically confront anyone hassling Elvis, and he wasn't afraid, either, to tell Elvis when he was out of line. That was necessary from time to time, especially when we were in Hollywood. Red also had a sensitive streak in him and was quite a gifted singer/songwriter. His song "If Every Day Was Like Christmas" is one of my favorite Elvis tunes and is always played in my home during the holidays. He also became a highly skilled actor, landing many roles in films, television, and commercials.

As for me, my role was pretty well diversified. I supplied Elvis with companionship, ran errands, protected him when needed, and shared his zest for sports, especially football. Elvis loved to play football, and if we weren't playing it we were watching it on TV, especially the NFL broadcasts on Sunday.

Elvis was a die-hard Cleveland Browns and Baltimore Colts fan, and he loved to watch Jim Brown and Johnny Unitas play. He was thrilled when he had the opportunity to meet both in the '60s when they visited him on movie sets.

Elvis's entourage also included a plethora of friends, fringe characters, and hangers-on who straggled in and out of the picture over a period of years.

George Klein and Elvis went back to their days at Humes High School, where George was class president. Their friendship blossomed anew after George became one of Memphis's top disc jockeys. George was a good friend who never turned down any request from Elvis, no matter how outlandish. And some were mighty outlandish.

In the mid-1950s, for instance, Elvis was considering having surgery on his nose. It was just a trim job, but plastic surgery wasn't the cottage industry it is today, and Elvis was skittish about going under the knife.

So he asked his pal George to have the operation first to see if it was safe. When George agreed, Elvis contacted Dr. Maury Parks, one of Hollywood's leading authorities on early plastic surgery, and arranged (and paid for) everything. After George came out of it, healthy and looking spiffy, Elvis took the plunge himself. Dr. Parks was also the doctor who pinned Priscilla's ears closer to her head after Elvis requested she have the surgery.

George went the extra mile for his famous pal another time, in 1967. We were headed back to Graceland after filming a movie and were somewhere around Little Rock, Arkansas, with Elvis himself at the wheel of the bus that automobile guru George Barris had customized for him. As we came within range of Memphis's WHBQ, where George deejayed, a new single by Tom Jones called "Green, Green Grass of Home" was playing. That's the one about the prisoner who dreams about home and Mom and Dad just before he wakes up for his own execution. It's a tearjerker, and hearing it so affected Elvis that he actually pulled over to the side of the road to listen. I never saw Elvis so emotionally into a song before, and when it ended he wiped his eyes and shouted, "God almighty! Call George and tell him to play it again!"

Keep in mind, this was long before cell phones came into the picture, so we had to drive down the highway until we spotted a phone booth from which Alan Fortas would call George at the station on his private line. When he was told Elvis really liked the new Tom Jones single and wanted him to play it again, George happily complied, telling listeners that a "good friend" of his driving in from the West Coast had made the special request. It didn't take a whole lot of imagination to figure out it was Elvis.

The song came on again, and for the second time Elvis got emotional. He instructed Alan to call George back and tell him to play it a third time.

While George worshiped Elvis, this time he got a little out of joint and pointed out to Alan that there were Federal Communications Commission rules against playing a record over and over on the air.

"Tell Elvis I could get fired if my station manager finds out about this," George told Alan. But Elvis wasn't to be denied, and in a heartbeat he came up with the perfect solution to George's problem.

Elvis said, "Tell George to play it again, and if he gets fired, I'll buy the damned radio station and he can run it." George played it again and a few others in between to save his butt.

By the time we pulled up to the gates of Graceland, Elvis had it memorized.

All of this might have been avoided had Elvis simply listened to Red a year earlier. Red had heard "Green, Green Grass of Home" on a Jerry Lee Lewis album and told Elvis he should record the song. Red even played it for him, but for some reason, Elvis didn't hear the song's potential after hearing Jerry Lee's rendition. He told Red it was a pretty good song, and that was the end of it. Elvis couldn't believe it when Red told him it was the same song he had heard a year earlier. "Man, I really missed that one," Elvis said. Believe me, it was one of the rare occasions he did.

Back to George for a moment—to this day he is very much in denial about Elvis's addiction to prescription drugs. But he was not alone. Joe Esposito and even Priscilla initially denied the allegations when they were first brought to light. I am well aware that George was not around as much as the rest of us guys who worked for Elvis in the end. But it is hard to believe, which I don't for one second, that George doesn't think Elvis had a problem. If he didn't want to talk about it, which I believe is the case, that's fine. But he hasn't even admitted that much as far as I know. Being a good and loyal friend, which George was, doesn't mean you have to be in denial about a friend being in trouble. I know there are some of you who will say you would rather have a friend like George than me, and that is your prerogative. Good luck. I am a firm believer in that old saying, "A good friend won't always tell you what you want to hear, but what you need to hear."

I would like to say for the record, there are two kinds of friends in this world. One is a friend who will risk whatever it takes to be honest with you and accept all that brings with it, good or bad. The second kind of friend will tickle your ears and tell you what you want to hear. For those who think I should have been the second kind of friend, I accept their anger, disdain, criticisms, and even hatred of me for doing what I tried to do for a dear friend in trouble. But then they must accept my feelings of anger, disdain, and criticism because they did not go to the limit to do what was necessary to help or protect a friend.

I will end this by saying that I like George even though I am aware of some disparaging remarks he has made about me over the years, even fairly recently. Yet, a few years ago, at the funeral service of Richard Davis, he leaned over and quietly said, "I love you, Sonny West." I was taken aback somewhat. I answered him with "I love you, too, George," and I meant it. I don't know how George will take the things I have written here, but I write as I speak—always from the heart, right or wrong.

It was through George Klein that Elvis met and befriended Alan Fortas, whom Elvis dubbed "Hog Ears." Alan was a stockily built, talented All-Memphis tackle at Central High who later played at Vanderbilt University and Southwestern before dropping out of school. But Alan was no dummy, and he came from good stock. His uncle was Abe Fortas, the U.S. Supreme Court justice, and his father was a successful businessman. In addition to smarts, Alan possessed a congenial personality and wit, and he was an all-around good guy who was just plain fun to have around. We were roommates on and off when he was working for Elvis.

Someone else who drifted in and out of Elvis's life was Cliff Gleaves, a college kid from Mississippi who met Elvis backstage at a show. Cliff had show business aspirations of his own, and he had the tenacity and drive to become successful. The problem with Cliff was that he just didn't know whether to be a singer, songwriter, actor, or comedian. Full of energy and as flaky as they come, Cliff was definitely a breed apart. Very smart and intelligent, he lacked good old-fashioned horse sense and was often his own worst enemy.

"Wait a minute, mister. Let's get this straight," was Cliff's signature tagline when he wanted to produce a laugh. Though Cliff was funny and entertaining, Elvis could handle Cliff only in small doses. Cliff had this constant need to be "on," and Elvis would finally say, "I need a break, man. The guy just wears me out." But I loved Cliff. He was truly a colorful character and one of a kind.

Diminutive Charlie Hodge, only five feet three inches, was another close friend who became tight with Elvis when they served together in the army. Charlie and Elvis actually first met backstage in Memphis at a gospel concert before they were drafted. A native of Decatur, Alabama, Charlie sang in a gospel quartet called the Foggy River Boys, which appeared weekly on ABC television. When they met again on the army ship bound for Germany, Elvis was grieving the loss of his mother. Charlie kept him in stitches for hours with jokes and stories, easing Elvis's emotional burden.

Charlie wasn't just loyal to Elvis; he existed for Elvis.

In the early '60s, Charlie left Elvis for personal reasons and then hooked up with country star Jimmy Wakely and toured with him on his shows for a few years before coming back to the group in the mid-1960s. He never left again. He performed with Elvis for the first time onstage in 1968 on the *Singer Presents Elvis* special. When Elvis opened in Vegas in July 1969, Charlie was with him and would be as long as Elvis performed.

Family meant everything to Elvis, and his father, Vernon, oversaw Elvis's finances with a bookkeeping firm called Spain and Fisher, and he signed all the payroll checks. Vernon had only a grammar school education, but he kept control of the purse strings like a veteran bean counter.

As a person, Vernon Presley was capable of great coldness. Unlike his son, generosity and charm didn't come easily to him. He disapproved of Elvis's spending habits, and he made no bones about disapproving of the friends Elvis put on the payroll. It must've killed him to sign our checks, and I have no doubt Vernon would have canned every one of us without blinking an eye. He was obviously jealous of our relationship with his son, and he never did see that Elvis needed us around to keep him sane.

While Vernon was a good one to avoid, Vernon's mom, Minnie Mae Presley, was a peach. She helped fill the void and ease the pain Elvis felt when his mother died.

"Dodger," as Elvis affectionately called her, was a tall, slender, feisty gal who wasn't much on words and didn't much care that Elvis was a celebrity. Minnie Mae always had a room in Elvis's homes and a special place in his heart. He visited with her quite often and always before leaving to go on the road.

I loved her, too. I spent a lot of time talking with her, because, in a way, Minnie Mae filled a void in my life as well. My paternal grandmother died when I was young, and my other grandmother lived in California, and we didn't get to see her often. Elvis's grandma became sort of a grandma-by-proxy to me. Minnie Mae was not some old fuddy-duddy who spoke just to hear herself talk. She was an interesting lady with plenty on her mind. She got especially animated on the subject of her ex-husband, a dapper gentleman who made his home in Kentucky. He was quite the Lothario, I guess. I met him a couple of times, and he did seem to have a real zest for life. Too much, apparently, for Minnie Mae, who wasted no time throwing the old chap out on his butt when she caught him with another woman. I told her about meeting him and how he seemed like a nice man. She patiently sat and listened to what I had to say. When I was finished, she leaned forward in her chair and said, "Sonny, now that you have said your piece, let me say mine—don't ever talk about him again, ya hear?" Minnie Mae didn't say it with anger or disdain; she simply wanted to get her point across. I never mentioned him again.

I know that Minnie Mae's feelings toward me were warm, as she once told Elvis that she really enjoyed visiting with me and that I was her favorite. It was understandable, as I spent much more time with her than any of the other guys did. I truly loved her; she was an interesting and grand lady.

Family and music were the two big loves in Elvis's life. A lot had changed on the music scene while he was away for two years serving his country. Elvis's biggest musical contemporary, Buddy Holly, had died in a tragic plane crash, while crosstown rival Jerry Lee Lewis's career came crashing down after it was discovered that he married his thirteen-year-old cousin. Little Richard had found religion and didn't know if he wanted to sing or preach to the masses. Bill Haley and his Comets flamed out after a few hits, and Fats Domino's career went on a crash diet when the 1950s ended. The raw energy that fueled rock and roll and made it dangerous gave way to safer, homogenized artists such as Fabian, Paul Anka, Pat Boone, Frankie Avalon, Ricky Nelson, Bobby Darin, and the Four Seasons. For Elvis, whose trademark sound and look in the 1950s was raw and animalistic, it was time for a career makeover. Musically, the emphasis of his music went from raw rock and roll to polished pop.

In Germany, Elvis spent a lot of his free time singing and playing the piano at his home. His voice became stronger, and he developed a fuller, richer sound, clearly different from the twangy quality of his first recordings. The songs "It's Now or Never" and "Surrender" would not have even been recorded by the pre-army Elvis. If they had, they would not have sounded anything like they did in 1960.

Another reason for the change in musical direction was that song publishing had become big business. This prompted Elvis's manager, Colonel Tom Parker, to sign a publishing deal with Hill and Range, a firm based out of New York City and owned by Jean and Julian Aberbach.

The arrangement with Elvis's old publishing company, Gladys Music and Elvis Presley Publishing, was that he could record any artist he wanted, but Hill and Range set up a specific song list and put together a team of writers to bring songs directly to Elvis.

Under the new deal, RCA would also book the top studio musicians to accompany Elvis's majestic voice, making available the latest in recording technology and giving him every possible edge over his competition.

In early April 1960, Elvis loaded up all the guys on a chartered bus for another trip to RCA Studio B in Nashville. The marathon session reaped quite a harvest of hits for the album *Elvis Is Back*.

In twelve hours, Elvis recorded a dozen songs. The two standout tracks in my mind were clearly "It's Now or Never" and the hauntingly beautiful "Are You Lonesome Tonight?"

"It's Now or Never," written by Aaron Schroeder and Wally Gold, was an instant smash and ultimately became Elvis's biggest hit, with total international sales, according to *The Guinness Book of World Records*, of twenty million records. The song shot straight to Number 1 in America and the United Kingdom, opening new doors for Elvis with adult listeners. Many easy-listening stations with more mature audiences found the song disarming and gave it regular play.

Artistically, Elvis broke new ground with "Are You Lonesome Tonight?" a song he grew to love so much. The track just knocked everyone out, and Elvis listened to the playback over and over. Each time he focused on something different—instruments, the harmony, whether everyone was on key and hitting the beat at the right time. That was actually standard operating procedure for Elvis. He would play a record over and over again in the studio, listening for any real or imagined flaws until he was satisfied there wasn't much else to do. He might say, "You need to bring up the guitar a bit higher," or note something else that only his ear had picked up. He helped create the total sound that made up the finished product. What was amazing about Elvis was that, for all his perfectionism, he worked rather quickly. That's if he was really into the project. If not, he dragged his heels or let his attention wander.

His musical instincts were usually right on, but in the case of "Are You Lonesome Tonight?" Elvis was afraid to release it as a single. He thought fans might not like it because of the narrative in the middle of the song, paraphrasing William Shakespeare's sentiments that "all the world was a stage."

"Anytime you love something so much, it usually means that other people aren't going to like it as much as you," Elvis told me. "If you like something so much and nobody else does, the fall is so big."

It took a lot of lobbying to change his mind. "Elvis, you've got to release that record," Cliff Gleaves told him. "It's so good." We all seconded the motion, but Elvis thought we were just stroking his ego. Even when other performers came by the house, heard the song, and raved about it, Elvis wasn't convinced.

It took more than seven months for him to relent and release "Are You Lonesome Tonight?" Its takeoff was nothing short of astronomical. The single shot straight to Number 1 and stayed there for six weeks, boosted by airplay on easy-listening stations across the country. In Britain, it topped the charts for four weeks and was his sixth Number 1 single in the United Kingdom.

One day around that time, I was feeling my oats; I playfully claimed credit for his fourteenth chart-topping record.

"See boss, I told ya it was a hit," I said with a slight grin.

"You were right, Sonny," Elvis said with a twinkle in his eye as he handed me a Hav-a-Tampa cigar. I didn't normally smoke cigars, but I did that one. Then he lit one for himself, and as we sat back to enjoy them, he quietly said it again: "You were right."

It was one of those moments that friends share that is no big deal, just nice. And it's the only time I ever recall Elvis lighting a cigar for me.

# Chapter 7

# The Colonel and the Chairman

G.I. BLUES WAS ELVIS'S FIFTH MOVIE, AND IT WAS THE FIRST TO USE A formula aimed at garnering huge profits for the studio at the expense of plot, dialogue, and most other things that went into making a decent film.

This formula usually featured Elvis in a fish-out-of-water experience where he sings, gets the girl, and punches out a few guys to show his masculinity. For years, producers had labored to find a surefire method of making films that scored huge profits, and the Elvis formula was the safest bet.

"The only sure way to making money in the movie business is to have Elvis Presley in a film," producer Hal Wallis once said. "His movies might make a whole lot of money, or very little, but they always make money."

In the beginning, Tinseltown was an experience in itself. Elvis hated to fly in airplanes ever since a hair-raising, near-death experience in a small chartered plane when it nearly crash-landed in Arkansas. Elvis swore he'd never set foot in one of those death traps again. But later on he overcame his fear of flying and spent several million dollars on private jets to carry him back and forth to concerts and anyplace else he felt like going.

In mid-April 1960, Colonel Tom Parker rented two private railroad cars on the Southern Pacific Sunset Limited for a three-day whistle-stop journey to Los Angeles. It was the first time I got a chance to meet Colonel Parker and see him work his magic.

It was no coincidence that hundreds of people came to the Memphis train station to wish Elvis a safe trip to Hollywood. Colonel Parker had seen to it that the multitudes knew exactly where Elvis would be, and he circulated throughout the crowd passing out signed 8-x-10s of Elvis.

Over the years, many people have criticized the "evil Svengali" influence Parker exerted over Elvis, but I've always had a different take on the subject. They represented a perfect merging of manager and talent and made up the greatest team in the history of entertainment.

In the unconventional world of show business filled with all manner of colorful characters, few out-rainbowed Colonel Tom Parker.

Much has already been speculated and written about Parker and his past, and I'd prefer to leave that subject to the historians. I simply knew him as the only man who could manage Elvis Presley.

Colonel Parker broke into the music business in the late 1930s by managing Gene Austin ("My Blue Heaven") and later a young singing talent named Eddy Arnold. Parker brought Arnold to the top of the charts as a country-and-western singer. He worked very hard for his client (it was Parker's choice to represent only one client at a time, though he was approached by many others), and it paid off for Arnold with success in records, radio, television, and movies.

By 1953, Eddy Arnold and Colonel Parker parted ways. Looking for someone to represent, Parker heard through one of his associates about a young boy who had recently graduated from Humes High School in Memphis.

The very next year Elvis had flourished into a regional star, having performed at state fairs and school functions and recorded for Sam Phillips at Sun Records. It was a gentleman named Oscar Davis who brought Elvis to the attention of Colonel Parker. Parker's innate instinct for nosing out talent told him right off the bat that this Presley kid had the potential to be a big star. Although Elvis already had a manager, Bob Neal, Parker began to talk to the young singer, filling his head with visions of superstardom the likes of which he could never achieve under Neal.

Colonel talked RCA Records into buying out Elvis's contract with Sam Phillips's Sun Records, a pivotal move in the singer's career. Parker used his contacts from the Eddy Arnold days to get Elvis the exposure he needed. Presley appeared on *Stage Show* (hosted by Tommy and Jimmy Dorsey, aka the Dorsey Brothers) for six consecutive telecasts; starred in a major motion picture, *Love Me Tender*, and was on his way to superstardom with the velocity of a Mercury rocket.

Over the years, Parker has been criticized by many in the Elvis world for the decisions he made on behalf of his client. But Parker's decision to have Elvis record a series of songs before going into the military, and his insistence that RCA stagger the release of these songs, kept Presley fresh in the hearts and minds of his legions of fans until Elvis came out of the service in 1960.

It was a decision that very possibly saved Elvis's career.

There was also the decision to keep Elvis from performing overseas. Up to his untimely death in 1977, Elvis Presley, with the possible exception of his army stint in Germany and a brief engagement in Canada in the late 1950s, never sang a song outside the borders of the United States. The millions of overseas fans who make up a large part of the fan base that has kept Elvis's memory alive for the past few decades unfortunately never got to see him perform in person.

For the most part, Colonel Parker's association with Elvis Presley has been well documented, so there's no need to go into more detail here. Suffice it to say that Elvis was a young boy who needed better management than he had in Memphis, and Parker provided that. Elvis became the first rock-and-roll megastar, and Parker became a megamanager.

When I first laid eyes on him that day at the Memphis train station, I said to myself, Man, this guy here is the boss! I was totally impressed. The Colonel was clearly in control of the Elvis juggernaut, and he wasn't afraid to let anyone know it.

For his part, Elvis showed 100 percent loyalty and did whatever the Colonel told him to do. Parker told Elvis what was going to happen, when it was going to happen, and how Elvis should react.

"Yes sir," Elvis would say, nodding his head up and down as he listened. "Yes sir."

Many of Elvis's family and friends came to see us off for Hollywood that day, including Vernon Presley and Charlie Hodge. As we got ready to take off, Elvis turned to Charlie and made him the offer of a lifetime.

"Charlie, you want to come with us?" he asked. Charlie's plan was to go back to Graceland and then head back to Decatur, Alabama. Elvis's unexpected overture really took him aback.

"Elvis, I don't have anything with me," Charlie said.

"Daddy can send all of that stuff to you in California. Get your mom and dad to send stuff out from home."

He didn't have to ask twice. Charlie leaped aboard the train, and Elvis turned to Vernon and said, "Daddy, put him on salary."

The day before we shoved off on the trip, Elvis took me upstairs to his closet bedroom at Graceland and then to a closet in the attic with more clothes.

"Sonny, ya gotta look sharp if you're going to Hollywood," he said with a gracious smile. He went through all of his clothes racks and started handing me suits, shirts, ties, and slacks. Back then, Elvis and I had the same waist size (I had only about five pounds on him at the time). It was an act of incredible selflessness—and one typical of Elvis at his best.

The Colonel always made sure Elvis was comfortable, and for this trip he pulled out all the stops. When the King rode in style, so did his court, which now consisted of Lamar, Gene, Joe, Charlie, and myself.

Our accommodations on the train were nothing short of first class, including a private stateroom and sleeping car for each of us. A lounge car with all the creature comforts of home included a fully stocked bar, overstuffed couches and chairs, game tables, and a state-of-the-art hi-fi system that played so loud I'm sure passengers at the front of the train must've felt their teeth vibrating. It was a three-day party on wheels.

During one of the more sober moments, we were sitting in the club car and I was wearing one of the suits Elvis had given me. He gave me the once-over and said, "Sonny, that hairdo is not going to cut it in Hollywood," referring to my flattop haircut, which I had had for years. "You have to let that moss grow. Get that Tony Curtis look, you know?" He pretended he was combing his hair back and then doing a little forward flip as if to bring a lock of hair down on his forehead. I took his advice and began letting it grow. My coif turned out great, but it looked more like James Dean's hair than Tony Curtis's. It got me by.

On the way to Los Angeles the train stopped in all the major cities to pick up new passengers. The Colonel used these occasions as another opportunity to promote Elvis.

"We're approaching our next big city in fifteen minutes, and we'll be greeting the fans," Parker would announce.

The Colonel worked tirelessly to keep the PR fires stoked. Even before the train pulled out of Memphis, he was on the phone to all the big-city media in the cities we'd be stopping at along the way, informing them that Elvis would be passing through their towns. Parker provided all the necessary background information regarding this being Elvis's first movie since his discharge from the army and so forth. He practically wrote the copy for the reporters, and whenever possible, he made Elvis available for exclusive interviews. As far as I was concerned, the Colonel was a genius who could've given lessons to P.T. Barnum.

We whistle-stopped like politicians on the stump for votes. From his perch on the caboose, Elvis would sign autographs, shake hands, and answer questions from the media, while the Colonel handed out signed 8-x-10s. In El Paso, Texas, the train was practically mobbed, which was exactly what Parker wanted. As long as the masses clamored for Elvis, we were all still in business.

In between stops, we spent a lot of time playing poker. With the Colonel were three assistants, plus Freddy Bienstock, who ran Elvis's two publishing companies, and Jean and Julian Aberbach, co-owners of Hill and Range Publishing.

Freddy was an impeccable dresser who wore a scarf draped around his neck and had a tan that would make George Hamilton jealous. And he had class to match his personal wealth.

I started the trip with about $60 to my name and promptly dropped two-thirds of it in a game won by Freddy. He came up to me later and asked how much I lost. When I told him it was about $40, Freddy stuffed two twenties in my shirt pocket.

"No, Mr. Bienstock, I lost that money fair and square," I protested.

"I'll take the money from the Colonel because he can afford it," he said in his thick German accent. "But not from you."

The farther west we traveled, the more excited I became. We weren't going out to be turkey farmers. For most of my young life, I had dreamed of going to California, perhaps even breaking into show business myself. All those hours sitting in the movie theater as a kid only whetted my appetite to see and be a part of the Hollywood scene.

Elvis's presence assured all of us not only the keys to the kingdom but that everything was going to be first class. Elvis himself insisted on it.

As we got to the Los Angeles county line, I remember seeing rows and rows of homes and not believing how vast the city was. A few minutes before our scheduled arrival at Union Station, the train stopped on a siding. Elvis and the Colonel disembarked and got into an awaiting cab, leaving to avoid the mob scene at the terminal. The whistle-stop media circuses, encouraged and orchestrated by Parker along our route, were one thing, but now it was time to get down to business.

The rest of us continued to Union Station. Nobody made a big deal about welcoming us to town, which was just as well because we had to round up all the luggage—no small job—and get it loaded onto a truck.

The Colonel had arranged for a white limousine to transport us along the 405 freeway north to Sunset Boulevard, then east to our destination—the world-famous Beverly Wilshire Hotel.

Built in 1928, the hotel is nestled at the famous intersection of Wilshire Boulevard and Rodeo Drive. The building's ornate European facade included distinctly rounded awnings fronted by rows of sculpted trees.

It was our home for the next few months.

Elvis took a two-bedroom suite on the sixth floor and shared it with Gene and Joe. Lamar, Charlie, and I shared the penthouse, which sounds a lot more impressive than it was. What we had was a huge room with a bath and studio beds. Lamar and I took the pull-out beds, and a rollaway was brought up for Charlie because he was the smallest. There was an exit from the penthouse to the roof, and Elvis often came up to lay out in the sun. The hotel was the tallest building in the area at the time, so we'd do our sunbathing there instead of by the pool so as not to be bothered by anyone.

Our primary duties were to keep both suites stocked with food and to drive Elvis wherever he wanted to go. Lamar and Junior had driven out the white Cadillac and black Lincoln limo and had both of them at our disposal. Later, when Elvis wanted to do some driving himself, he leased a candy-apple red Cadillac convertible. That car was a real honey, and we would always fight over who would drive it. Occasionally I won, and I always made sure to treat that car as I would a beautiful lady. I'd drive with my arm up on that windowpane and one hand on the steering wheel, like Joe Cool. Cruising around Beverly Hills, I imagined people thinking, *There goes another snobby Beverly Hills brat*, and I wondered what they'd say if they knew I was making a whole $35 a week.

In L.A. we reunited with Red and Cliff Gleaves, who had come out earlier hoping to break into show business. Red found employment as an extra on the popular television series *The Rebel*, starring Nick Adams. He and Adams had first met in 1957 on the *King Creole* set in New Orleans when both were visiting with Elvis. They hit it off. Adams told Red that if he ever was in California to look him up. Red did, and, true to his word, Nick put him to work on his series.

Aaron Spelling, another actor on the set of *King Creole*, wasn't in the film but was visiting with his wife and Elvis's costar, Carolyn Jones. Spelling made a similar offer to Red, but he lacked Nick Adams's character. Years later, after Spelling became one of the biggest television producers Tinseltown has ever known, Red came calling. But Spelling never even bothered to return his phone calls. Spelling obviously forgot where he came from—that once, he too had struggled for a foothold in the business. He made it, but then he pulled the ladder up after him. That hurt Red because the Wests weren't that way. Our word was our bond. When we said something, it was a done deal. That kind of integrity, plus Red's drive and talent, helped him to succeed in spite of Aaron Spelling.

Cliff didn't have as much luck as Red. Cliff was genuinely talented but had a weird knack for talking himself out of work after he had already nailed the part. He'd do an audition or reading, they'd tell him, "You're perfect for the part," and then Cliff would have to explain at great length to the casting director why he and the part were made for one another. After a torrent of his gibberish, the casting director would say to himself, "I can't hire this lunatic!"

Cliff infuriated Vernon Presley to the point that Vernon telegrammed Colonel Parker from Memphis stating that Cliff wasn't connected with the group in any way, shape, or form. I don't know what Cliff did, but he sure had a talent for pissing people off.

Elvis didn't have much time to relax on the West Coast. The day after we arrived in Los Angeles, Hal Wallis started preproduction on *G.I. Blues*. Preproduction consisted of meeting the director and costars, attending music and script rehearsals, and having wardrobe tests. The whole point of the movie was to cash in on all the publicity given to Elvis's service in the army. The story, in case you missed it, concerns three army buddies who assemble a rock-and-roll band called the Three Blazes to pass the time during their tour of duty in West Germany.

About the best thing that came out of the whole experience for Elvis was his association with director Norman Taurog, who ended up being his favorite director.

Taurog had a lot more in common with Elvis than met the eye. A onetime child actor, in his twenties Taurog won an Academy Award for *Skippy*, in 1931. Like Elvis, he had an entourage and people fawning all over him wherever he went. Taurog was flamboyant, wearing capes and berets on the set. He had a long and well-respected career directing such well-regarded films as *Mad about Music*, *The Adventures of Tom Sawyer*, *Young Tom Edison*, *Palms Springs Weekend*, and *Boys Town* (for which he was nominated for another Academy Award).

By the time *G.I. Blues* was offered to him, Taurog had seen and done it all. Because he had consistently delivered good, moneymaking films to Paramount Studios, Hal Wallis needed a steady hand and experienced filmmaker to bring the movie in on time and within budget. He knew Taurog would deliver. While Elvis and Taurog established instant rapport, it was a different story with his costar, Juliet Prowse. The native South African actress-dancer played a sexy nightclub dancer and Elvis's love interest in the film, but there were no sparks between them right off the bat.

"Man, I'll tell you, that is one cold chick," Elvis told me one day on the set.

Miss Prowse's icy veneer could have had something to do with the fact that at the time she was engaged to be married to a pretty well-known operator by the name of Frank Sinatra.

Although the two superstars had recently filmed a successful television special together, the Chairman of the Board was on record as disapproving of the music that made Elvis Sinatra's successor at the top of the charts.

"His music is deplorable, a rancid-smelling aphrodisiac," Sinatra told reporters when Elvis first hit it big. "It's the most brutal, ugly, degenerate, vicious form of expression it has been my displeasure to hear." Even though Sinatra's vitriol was said in the 1950s, Elvis never forgot the remark.

Sinatra was nothing but cordial to Elvis in person, and I truly feel he liked Elvis, but I've always felt Ol' Blue Eyes was just a little jealous of Elvis because he dared to steal the mantle of teen idol and usurp Sinatra's popularity. While Sinatra was the idol of millions of bobby-soxers in the 1940s, Elvis became the gold standard by which every entertainer was measured.

Whatever her initial reservations about Elvis, the Presley charm, charisma, and wit worked their magic on Juliet Prowse, and she loosened up after a while. We even discovered she had a great guffaw-like laugh. In no time she warmed up to everyone, and we ended up having a lot of fun.

Exactly how much fun Juliet and Elvis were having together off the set has long been a matter of speculation. I know they were greatly attracted to one another and they spent an inordinate amount of time in Elvis's trailer on the set. I don't know if they were just going over their lines or if they were acting out their love scenes in private, but I did notice that Elvis got quite antsy the first time he heard Sinatra was on the set looking for his girl. He and Juliet were ensconced in Elvis's trailer, and with Red in the lead, we decided to have a little fun.

"Elvis! Elvis!" Red rasped outside the trailer door. "Don't try anything, Elvis! Frank's coming around the corner!"

There was the sound of frantic scrambling from inside the trailer, and then Elvis appeared at the door, looking very concerned.

When he asked where Frank was, we laughed and said we were just kidding. "You sons of bitches," Elvis said. At least he was smiling.

Juliet laughed, too. Everybody enjoyed our little prank so much that we repeated it several times. Predictably, as in the case of the boy who cried wolf, nobody took us seriously anymore.

Then one day during a lunch break, this little dapper figure appeared on the horizon strolling through the big soundstage doors with that porkpie hat and silhouette. It wasn't Mickey Rooney. I remember thinking, *Man, I hope there isn't anything going on behind closed doors.*

"Elvis, man, it's Frank! Frank's coming!" I hissed at the trailer door.

"Get away from that damned door," ordered that familiar drawl from the other side.

"No shit, Elvis, we're serious!"

"Go to hell!"

By that time, our visitor was at the threshold.

"Hi fellas."

"Yes, Mr. Sinatra. How are you, sir?" I said, trying to stall.

"I'm fine, thank you. Do you happen to know where I can find Juliet Prowse?"

"Yes sir, she and Elvis are going over their lines right now," I answered, trying to knock on the door. I'd have tried to stall Sinatra a little longer, but he just didn't look as though he was in the mood to shoot the shit right then.

Luckily, Elvis and Juliet heard Frank's voice from inside the trailer. Whatever was going on in there stopped, and when Elvis opened the door, Juliet was sitting on the couch with the script on her lap.

We never repeated that prank again, but it didn't put an end to our worries about keeping Elvis in one piece if Frank ever found him and his fiancée in a tryst.

It almost happened again, according to Lamar, when Elvis decided to have a "reading" with Juliet in his bedroom at the Beverly Wilshire Hotel. Lamar was there, and Elvis asked him to go gas up Juliet's car.

Did I say "car"? Automotive wet dream is more like it.

Frank had given Juliet a Dual-Ghia, a rare, fabulously expensive American-Italian hybrid car. Sinatra and Dean Martin each had one of their own, and I'm sure you could count on one hand all the Ghias in Los Angeles (only 125 were made over an eight-year period).

As Lamar was filling up the tank with gas, damned if a limousine didn't pull up right next to him. And double damned if Frank Sinatra didn't pop out of the rear door.

"Lamar, can I ask you a question?" Frank asked politely.

"Sure, Frank," Lamar gulped.

"What are you doing with my car?"

"Puttin' gas in it," Lamar said. It wasn't a brilliant answer, but it was a truthful one.

"Where's Juliet?" Frank inquired a little less politely.

"She's back at the hotel with Elvis rehearsing their lines," Lamar said.

Frank's limo almost did a wheelie peeling out of there, and as soon as the smoke cleared, Lamar took off in the Ghia in the same direction. Their destinations were the same: the Beverly Wilshire.

Sinatra got there first, and as Frank strode toward the elevator, Lamar ran for the house phone.

"Frank's coming up!" Lamar yelled when Elvis answered.

"Oh, not this again!" Elvis groaned.

"No, Elvis, it's the truth!" Lamar screamed. "He's on his way up! The man is getting on the elevator and he's coming up."

Elvis and Juliet were fully dressed when they greeted Sinatra at the door a minute later. The first time they weren't caught was pure luck. The second time, I'm fully convinced, was divine intervention.

# Chapter 8

# Lights, Camera, and a Helluva Lot of Action

WHILE JULIET PROWSE WAS STRICTLY AN ON-THE-SET ROMANCE, IN HIS spare time, Elvis always managed to do plenty of freelancing.

In addition to Juliet, he began seeing Judy Rawlins, who had a smaller part in *G.I. Blues*. Judy was a beautiful starlet who later married singer Vic Damone. Where women were concerned, Elvis was a man of discretion. Even though Juliet and Judy worked long hours together, as far as I know, neither ever found out about the other's relationship with the star or anything else!

Off the set, Elvis also managed to find time to date Sandy Ferra, whose father, Tony Ferra, owned the Crossbow, a country-and-western nightclub in Van Nuys.

Red actually discovered the bar and became friendly with Tony, who paid him to be the bouncer when Red wasn't getting acting parts. Lance LeGault, a rhythm-and-blues singer from Louisiana, was the house entertainer. But for Elvis, I think Sandy was the real drawing card.

Although just a teenager, Sandy was mature and beautiful beyond her years; her shapely figure was eye candy at its sweetest. Alan Fortas later nicknamed her "Sandy Ferrari," because "She's got the shape of a Ferrari!"

I grew to love Sandy as a friend and became her protector. Often, when she and Elvis went out on dates in Beverly Hills, I ended up taking her home in the wee hours of the morning. The drive to the Valley was about thirty minutes, and she'd curl up in the front seat and sleep. Years later, she married Wink Martindale, the Memphis deejay who also was the host of a popular TV show called *Dance Party*, which had the same format as *American Bandstand*. Wink later earned nationwide fame as a game show host.

It's a good thing Elvis's love life glowed so intensely, because musically his career took a turn for the worse with the recording of the *G.I. Blues* soundtrack.

Before any actual filming took place, Elvis had to record the songs for the movie that would later be used on the set for playbacks. The process started when they sent the script to Hill and Range, who picked the songwriters to write songs tailored to the appropriate scenes.

Several songs composed by prolific songwriters Jerry Leiber and Mike Stoller had been arranged for *G.I. Blues*, but they were set aside because of the composers' business differences with Hill and Range. The songwriting duo, responsible for some of the biggest songs of their generation ("Love Potion No. 9," "Poison Ivy," and "Yakety Yak"), balked at the stipulation that they had to share publishing rights with Elvis's company, an understandable position. When word of their difficulties with Hill and Range got out, the other top songwriters in town sided with them, resulting in decidedly inferior songs, unworthy of the man known as the King of Rock and Roll. Elvis knew it—his ear for good music was impeccable—and he was unhappy about the situation.

Adding to his distress was the fact that the recording studio at RCA on Sunset was set up differently from what Elvis was used to in Memphis and Nashville, and it immediately made him uncomfortable. Recording soundtrack music with three-track machines made it easier to match the sound of the film more accurately, but Elvis was a creature of habit. If he wasn't comfortable with a situation, he became disinclined not to give it his all, and in this case it showed.

Also infuriating was a new union contract stipulating the length of the recording sessions, impeding the flow of Elvis's creativity in the studio. Once Elvis got into a groove, he wanted to keep the momentum going no matter what. I remember one time a union representative insisted on a seventy-five-minute break after a six-hour session. Another time, the rep interrupted a session with a mandatory lunch break. Then, at 10:00 PM, he pulled the plug for the night.

Elvis's bitching about "these damn unions" didn't exactly endear him to the guys in the control room, either. All the fun was being taken out of making records for Elvis, and the spark would be a long time returning.

Meanwhile, Elvis was a magnet for other celebrities who made the pilgrimage to the set in a steady parade. Some were royalty in their own right. I recall meeting three Scandinavian princesses: Margaretha of Sweden, Astrid of Norway, and Margretha of Denmark. A few days later, King Bhumiphol and Queen Sirikit of Thailand came to visit, as did the king and queen of Nepal.

Hollywood's own royalty also came to pay their respects to the King. I remember meeting many of my childhood idols, most notably John Wayne, Robert Mitchum, Rock Hudson, Dean Martin (whom Elvis admired tremendously), Jerry Lewis, Warren Beatty, and Shirley MacLaine.

While Elvis was always polite to the celebrities who courted him, he mostly preferred the company of regular folk, like Ed Parker, a Kenpo karate instructor with whom he sought a strong friendship.

Elvis had first studied karate with Jurgen Seydel, who was known as "the Father of German Karate." Seydel admired Elvis's perceptiveness and often called Elvis one of his most talented pupils. Seydel stressed self-defense, preaching doing everything possible to avoid a fight; but he said that if a fight was unavoidable, it was best to know how to defend yourself. Elvis adopted this as his own personal credo.

I think because he was a great showman, Elvis also loved karate because of the elaborate choreography involved. Karate utilizes virtually every part of the body as a weapon rather than just a kick or punch. The repertoire of moves is exciting to watch, and Elvis never tired of demonstrating moves he learned from Seydel and, later, Parker.

Parker was born in Hawaii and was raised in the Mormon faith. After a stint in the U.S. Coast Guard, he learned about karate while attending Brigham Young University. Parker quickly sailed through the ranks, achieving black belt status. Even more impressive was his development of a new, more flexible style of karate, incorporating street-fighting techniques he'd picked up as a brawler in Honolulu.

The first time we saw Parker, we were all sunbathing on top of the roof at the Beverly Wilshire Hotel. We heard a commotion coming from a patio area close to the pool. It was Parker putting on a karate demonstration. Elvis was spellbound. Afterward, he pushed to meet the karate master.

"I don't know if you have heard of me, but my name is Elvis Presley," he said, holding out his hand. Elvis's humility instantly touched Parker, and their friendship blossomed from there. They were both trailblazers in their respective fields. Parker explained to Elvis that his new style of martial arts was being met with a lot of resistance by purists in the field who condemned his ideas and labeled him a radical. Elvis knew the feeling well, having gone through the same wringer when he burst onto the national scene in the mid-1950s. A strong and lasting friendship began between the two of them and lasted until Elvis's death. Ed gave me some private lessons when he would come to Las Vegas or on the road when touring. He was a dear friend to me also.

Being on a movie set for the first time was almost a religious experience for me. I ate up the entire landscape, watching from behind the scenes to see what everybody's job duties were and how they were executed. Making a movie is, to me, the ultimate American art form. So many people and elements have to come together for the picture to get off the ground. And it all starts with a good script. Once that is presented, casting the right actors is essential. A star of Elvis's magnitude can green-light a project, but that doesn't mean it will be any good if he's not right for the part. The same goes for the people who work behind the cameras, chiefly the director. Once all the preproduction is finished, other considerations must fall into place for principal photography to go well. Is the location right for the story? Is the cinematographer on the same page with the director and getting all the right angles? Is the lighting adequate? What about makeup and costumes? How about the sound? Are the props used in the film authentic? Are all the stunts believable?

Once the picture is in the can, the film is by no means finished. Postproduction includes editing, film score, credits, and—perhaps most important of all—promotion, today called marketing. If any one of those elements is lacking, in all likelihood it means the film will die in the stretch. It's almost an act of God when a movie earns big money. That's why it's truly amazing that almost all of Elvis's films were profitable.

While the experience of moviemaking fascinated me, I don't think the same could be said for Elvis. After *King Creole*, which was his favorite and finest role, I think his acting endeavors ceased to be challenging for him. For the star of the picture, especially, tedium can quickly set in. To capture just two or three minutes of usable film, it takes about a whole day of actual shooting and preparation. What it amounts to is that movie stars spend an awful lot of their time on the set just sitting around waiting to act.

One way Elvis relieved the boredom was by giving karate demonstrations for the cast and crew. Everybody seemed to enjoy watching Elvis exhibit his skills as a martial artist. It also fulfilled his craving to be the center of attention.

One day on the set of *G.I. Blues*, he was giving a board-breaking demonstration. It started off as a joke with cigar boxes, which were little more than cardboard and therefore no big deal. But as the crowd got a little larger, up to about fifty people, Elvis decided it was time to get serious. He had us fetch a few real boards, which he easily broke with the side of his hand to generous applause. Then Elvis got even more daring and decided to break a board with a clenched fist.

The board held on his first try. Now it was a matter of pride for Elvis to break that sucker. He stepped back, measured his distance, assumed the correct karate stance, and attacked the board once again.

"Hiyaaaahhh!" Elvis screamed, mustering up all the drama he could as his fist punched the board. It broke into two pieces, and the audience applauded and cheered as Elvis bowed and casually took his leave behind a wall on the set. Once out of sight, he bent over with his left hand holding his right in great pain.

"Sonofabitch!" he panted, "I almost broke my hand!" His right hand was in fact swelling up, and if you look carefully, there is a scene in *G.I. Blues* where Elvis is strumming a guitar with a swollen right hand. But that was Elvis: he'd take a bruised hand any day over a bruised ego.

Off the set, we blew off steam roaming the streets of Hollywood, checking out the local nightlife. When we weren't at the Crossbow, we'd get dressed up to the hilt and go see Dean Martin, Bobby Darin, and Sammy Davis Jr. at the Moulin Rouge, Coconut Grove, Cyro's, Roosevelt Hotel, or the Cloister in Hollywood. The best tables in the house belonged to us. On weekends, we'd drive to Las Vegas and see shows by Billy Ward, Red Skelton, Don Rickles, and Della Reese; the latter two Elvis greatly admired.

The first such excursion to Las Vegas got under way, and everyone was in great spirits. Charlie, Joe, and I had never been to Vegas, and we were pumped as we left L.A.

We took two cars—Lamar and Charlie drove a white Cadillac, and Elvis, Gene, Joe, and I went in a black Lincoln.

Near Barstow, California, we stopped at a restaurant to eat and gas up. As we exited the cars, Elvis asked Gene for his kit bag, telling him he wanted to brush his teeth. One of Gene's responsibilities was to bring the kit bag everyplace Elvis went. It did in fact contain a toothbrush, some jewelry, and other items—and Elvis's "medications." These were the uppers Elvis had started taking over in Germany. He was increasingly relying on them and didn't think the rest of us knew—but it wasn't hard to figure out.

On this occasion, Gene had forgotten to bring the kit bag. When Elvis found out, he went ballistic. "Everyone back in the car, dammit!" he exploded. Lamar and Charlie again took the Caddy, and Elvis got behind the wheel of the Lincoln. When he pulled out of the parking lot, he turned back in the direction of Los Angeles. At first he drove like a madman, ranting and carrying on as if we'd deliberately sabotaged his plans for a great weekend. Finally, he sank into a sullen funk, and in the gathering quiet, Gene, Joe, and I began to doze off.

"There'll be no damned sleep!" barked Elvis, punctuating his outburst with a sharp slap at Gene, who was sitting next to him in the front seat. The slap hit Gene in the chest hard enough to make him groan.

"No cuz, no sleeping," Gene replied as he came out of his stupor.

For the next hour or so, we struggled to keep our eyes open as ordered, with various degrees of success.

Joe was next to me in the backseat, surreptitiously catching a few z's while simultaneously managing to continue smacking his chewing gum. Elvis wasn't having any of it.

"Joe, dammit, I said no sleeping!" Elvis yelled.

"I wasn't sleeping; I was just looking out the window," Joe explained.

When we finally pulled up to the Beverly Wilshire Hotel, disappointed and dead-ass tired, we dragged our luggage upstairs and literally fell into bed and right to sleep.

Less than an hour later, it started all over again. Joe called our room and told us to haul ass downstairs. "Elvis has decided he wants to go to Vegas again."

We got up, dressed, and headed downstairs. There was Elvis, ready to get moving again and in a hell of a better mood than before. Once again, Elvis took the wheel of the Lincoln, and we barreled down the highway in the dark. He couldn't wait for us to see Las Vegas in all its lit-up glory, and he regaled us with tales of his past exploits there. Elvis's excitement was contagious, and before long we were all feeling an adrenaline rush.

Just before we reached the Vegas city limits, as we were still jetting along at about eighty miles per hour, the left front tire blew out on the Lincoln.

"Whoa, you sonofabitch, whoa!" Elvis yelled as he fought to keep the car under control. The front end of the car began shaking violently, which caused a hubcap to go flying off and the horn assembly on the steering wheel to fall into Elvis's lap.

Elvis wrestled the car to a stop on the side of the road, and we all sat there for a moment too stunned to speak. Then Elvis looked around at each of us and said, "One helluva ride, wasn't it, boys?"

His statement took away our anxieties, and we all broke into laughter.

We got out and inspected the damage. The left tire was in shreds, and that's when we noticed the hubcap was gone.

"I can't believe it! A brand-new car and the damn tire blows out on it! I'm going to trade this damn thing in when we get to Vegas!"

The absurdity of the situation deepened after we took the luggage out of the trunk to get to the spare tire.

"And why they hell would they put a blue tire instead of a whitewall tire for a spare?" Elvis asked. He didn't realize the blue strip was there to protect the whitewall, but we did our best to explain it to him.

When we got the spare on and were ready to roll, Elvis decreed that he was not about to appear in Las Vegas in a car without a hubcap. I spotted the wayward hubcap in some shallow water beneath a flash flood bridge. Before I waded in to retrieve it, I took off my shoes and socks and rolled up my pants, all the time thinking of how many snakes might be between me and that damn hubcap. I guarantee you, I was never quicker than that morning. With the hubcap safely back on the tire and the blue covering over the whitewall removed, the car was made presentable again, and we proceeded into town.

After checking into the Sahara Hotel—which became our Vegas headquarters—Elvis wasted no time heading for the craps tables and dropping a quick ten grand. At that point, the casino manager stepped in and told Elvis that he was free to play with house money for the rest of his stay and that he didn't need to worry about losing any of it.

That was the signal for Elvis to embark on one of the most incredible winning streaks I ever saw. As a huge crowed gathered around him, he could do no wrong with those bones. As they kept falling his way, people began to piggyback on Elvis's bets, winning big, too.

This went on for about an hour, until Elvis decided to call it quits.

As he turned to exit the casino, a high roller who had been betting on Elvis the entire time and made a small fortune offered to give Elvis a big cut of his action in gratitude. Elvis thanked him, graciously turning down the money.

Elvis handed each one of us a little white pill out of his kit when we got to the suite. It was Dexedrine, he explained, a common prescription drug relied on by over-the-road truckers to keep them awake on their cross-country hauls.

"We don't have much time guys, and we don't want to sleep our weekend away over here," Elvis said. "This here will keep you awake."

It was my first introduction to amphetamines, and all of a sudden, I could understand Elvis's attachment to that kit bag. That little pill provided me with an abundance of endurance unlike anything I'd ever felt.

The pills were fun as long as the high lasted, but sometimes it got to the point where I almost got sick. They would dry out your mouth like cotton, and I was constantly gulping liquids to counterbalance the pills. And when you came down, it happened as fast and totally as if somebody had pulled a switch. That's why they call it "crashing," I guess.

But we took the pills because Elvis insisted that our schedules and body clocks be totally in sync with his. If we could have managed that without taking the pills, we would have. But Elvis never kept bankers' hours.

"You sleep when I sleep, you eat when I eat," was Elvis's mandate to the guys. If he stayed up around the clock, then, by God, so did his entourage.

Many times during the week, I'd try to find a well-hidden place to sleep on the soundstage. A gaffer on the catwalk above the set pointed me out to Elvis once as I was napping on the set of *G.I. Blues.* Elvis was working on the club scene set next to the one where I was taking a nap. I woke up startled when a table next to me was upended.

"Dammit, Sonny," Elvis yelled. "Wake up!"

As I scrambled to get away from him, Elvis laughed up a storm. It was a big joke to him.

It was all fun and games in the beginning, nothing but young men trying to squeeze as much as they could out of life. Of course, later on, Elvis's drug use was no laughing matter.

In fact, it became a matter of life and death.

# Chapter 9

# The Beverly Hillbillies

ELVIS SPENT MOST OF THE '60s IN HOLLYWOOD, BUT HE ALWAYS CAME BACK to Memphis between films. Graceland was not only his home but his safe haven away from the prying eyes of the public.

When *G.I. Blues* wrapped in the latter part of June 1960, Elvis sought refuge behind the gates of Graceland. Elvis still had a phobia about airplanes, so we traveled back and forth between Memphis and Hollywood in cars. A decked-out motor home was customized by George Barris for Elvis in 1963, and then he got a bus a couple of years later.

It was on these road trips that Elvis really let his hair down and the superstar transformed back into a regular guy. He would talk about anything that came to mind—the movie he had just finished, the song he was about to record, men, women, religious philosophies, life on other planets—anything was fair game. We were just a bunch of friends talking and hanging out. The only time the superstar attitude came out was when Elvis was in Los Angeles, where everyone made a big fuss over him.

Elvis didn't have a care in the world when he was driving that motor home, singing his head off, and sporting special driving gloves and a hat.

The trips home usually took anywhere from four to five days, depending on how fast Elvis wanted to get back to Memphis. Sometimes we'd drive straight through in thirty hours, with some of us taking a driving shift, including Elvis.

Sometimes we'd start in the morning and drive until dusk, stopping every few hours to take a break, gas up, or eat. Other times we'd drive all night and check into a motel at dawn, sleep until dusk, get up, eat, and be on our way. It really depended on what Elvis felt like doing. Sometimes if we spotted an open field, we'd hop out and throw the football around to stretch our legs, or Elvis would give a karate demonstration.

Elvis was like a little kid on our road trips, and his carefree enthusiasm was infectious. I can't remember one that wasn't pleasant and fun.

However, this time, Elvis's mood changed when we arrived in Memphis and learned that Vernon Presley and Davada "Dee" Elliot Stanley were about to tie the knot almost two years after Elvis's mother passed away.

My reading of the situation was that Elvis was a little suspicious of Dee, and with good reason. Dee had made a play for Elvis when she invited him over for a home-cooked meal while he was stationed in Bad Nauheim, Germany.

Elvis declined, suggesting they meet for coffee at a later date, which he never intended to do. Then he sent Vernon in his place thinking it would be okay because of her marital status. Turned out it wasn't okay.

Dee was in her early thirties, and Vernon was instantly smitten. The fact that Dee was married to a soldier and had three kids didn't stop Vernon from asking her out. In fact, her husband, Bill Stanley, who'd once been a bodyguard for General George Patton, often joined Vernon and Dee, the three of them drinking until closing time at a lot of the American military clubs.

Not surprisingly, Dee and Bill's marriage eventually came apart, and Vernon stepped up his courtship. Afterward he moved Dee into Elvis's home in Bad Nauheim while she shipped her three sons, Ricky, David, and Billy, to live with her sister in Norfolk, Virginia, until she returned to the States. Both actions deeply offended and worried Elvis.

To his credit, Elvis never openly criticized Vernon in front of anyone, and he was always kind and gracious toward Dee and her three children.

"She seems pretty nice," Elvis told a reporter for the *Memphis Press-Scimitar*. "I only had one mother and that's it. There'll never be another. As long as she understands that, we won't have any problems."

But those of us close to him knew Elvis was deeply hurt by his father's actions, and the final straw was when Vernon wanted to live with Dee in Gladys's room at Graceland. There was no way Elvis was going to ever let that happen. Not in a million years.

"It really hurt me when Daddy started seeing someone so shortly after Momma passed away," Elvis confided to a group of us at McKellar Lake at Riverside Park in Memphis. "I didn't think Daddy was like that."

In fact, the very day we went to the lake, July 3, 1960, was Vernon and Dee's wedding day in Huntsville, Alabama. Elvis opted to be with his friends instead of attending the ceremony. He also had Vernon sign over a quitclaim deed assigning Elvis sole ownership of Graceland. In exchange, Elvis agreed to buy the newlyweds a place of their own a few blocks from Graceland. Later, when a house at 1266 Dolan Drive became available, Elvis bought it, and they sold the other house. The backyard of the Dolan Drive house was adjacent to Graceland's pasture by the barn. That way, Vernon and Dee could have their privacy without rubbing Elvis's nose in their relationship. It was the best solution to a potentially volatile situation.

"She needs to understand who she is," Elvis said to me. "She's not my mother but my daddy's wife." I don't think it took too long for Dee to get the message.

I believe that it was because of Dee that Elvis never dated married women. Elvis was upset that Dee's marriage to Bill Stanley broke up because of Vernon. When I went to work for Elvis, he forbade all of us guys to date married women.

Unmarried was a whole different story, however, especially where Elvis himself was concerned. Plain and simple, Elvis loved women, and women loved Elvis.

Friend George Klein introduced Anita Wood to Elvis in July 1957. A gorgeous, petite, pert blond, Anita was a nineteen-year-old beauty contest winner, singer, aspiring actress, and co-host of Wink Martindale's *Top Ten Dance Party*, a popular local television show for teens.

Anita had style, class, and morals, everything in a woman that I admired. Elvis admired her, too; she was smart and a lot of fun to be around. More important, she enjoyed being around the guys and didn't mind sharing Elvis—in fact, the more the merrier. I just liked her from the get-go.

Anita was Elvis's number one girl at the time, but certainly not his only one. There was Bonnie Bunkley, also nineteen and, like Anita, a beauty queen. Bonnie met Elvis when she appeared on the steps of

Graceland with her voice teacher to collect money for a benefit for Whitehaven High School.

Bonnie was very sweet and surprisingly shy. Elvis tried to bring her out of her shell, and she did open up around him. The two dated a few times, and Bonnie later married Tony Barrasso, the younger brother of a friend of mine, Ernie Barrasso, the car salesman who sold me my 1959 Ford convertible.

What neither Anita nor Bonnie knew was that half a world away in Germany, Elvis had safely stashed away a spirited teenage girl (she was fourteen when they met) named Priscilla who would, in the not-so-distant future, knock everything (and everybody) into a cocked hat. But while she was in Germany, Elvis, a superstar in his mid-twenties, was like a kid in a candy store—and was determined to sample all the different flavors.

Back in Memphis, the emphasis shifted from hard work to hard play, and we engaged in all sorts of fun activity. We often rented the Memphian Theatre for all-night movies, and we had many nights of fun at the Fairgrounds, later renamed Libertyland, Elvis's favorite amusement park, where the fast, up-and-down, exciting rides were indicative of the way he lived his life.

When we were really feeling our oats, we'd partake of a night of War at the Rainbow Skating Rink.

Because I had become more or less proficient on skates, I continued in my role of Elvis's protector. There never seemed to be any shortage of new guys who thought the surest way to impress their dates was knocking Elvis Presley on his ass. The fact is that for all his fame and stardom, Elvis retained that aura of vulnerability that had caused him to be a target for bullies in high school. The people who loved him felt protective of Elvis, and I was no exception. He was like a big brother to me. Even today, whenever anybody knocks Elvis, it brings out the Terminator in me.

It sure did one night at the Rainbow when a newcomer tried to make Elvis look silly. I singled out the predator after he'd made a couple vicious passes at Elvis, and I sent him flying fifteen feet in the air through an opening in the rail surrounding the rink. He slammed into the wall and slid onto the floor, just like in one of Elvis's movies. Then I skated over to the perpetrator and fixed him with my steeliest gaze as his senses slowly returned. When I knew he could comprehend the English language again, I told him, "And that's just the start of it, guy. That's just the first shot." For the rest of the night, the dude watched the action from a safe table off the rink.

Before we knew it, our monthlong layoff was over. On August 1, 1960, Elvis was to start preproduction on *Flaming Star* for 20<sup>th</sup> Century Fox. On our way to Los Angeles, we made the usual pit stop in Las Vegas.

There we took in Bobby Darin's opening act for George Burns. Bobby was one of Elvis's favorites. His recording of "Mack the Knife" had scorched the charts and was in heavy rotation on radio stations all over the country.

I'll never forget a show we attended a few years later where Darin was the headliner and Elvis gave Darin something to think about. Bobby's shows always had a lot of energy, but when entertainers know there's another entertainer in the audience, they kick it up another notch. Elvis was quite vociferous in his appreciation of the show, and the audience loved it. They and Darin got a little more than they bargained for, though, when Bobby switched gears at one point. He mentioned his earlier hits were somewhat of an albatross around his neck and said he liked to think he had moved on to a deeper level of artistry and better songs. It seemed almost as if he was apologizing for recording them and didn't want to sing them anymore.

All of a sudden, Elvis's voice rang out throughout the room: "Don't knock what made ya, Bobby!"

When the words reached him onstage, Bobby hunched his shoulders and let out a long, "Ooohhh!" to signify that Elvis had scored a direct hit. The audience's loud, spontaneous applause seconded the motion.

But to Bobby's credit, he instantly saw the light. "That hurt, but you know what? He's right," Bobby said. Then he launched right into "Splish Splash" and the rest of his back catalog of hits, and an already great show got even better.

After the show, Elvis told Darin that maybe he shouldn't have spoken out as he did, but Bobby wouldn't hear of it.

"No, Elvis, you're right," he said. "I will never do that again. I never realized those songs really mean something to people."

"Bobby," Elvis said, "Never apologize for your work. Ever."

We continued on to Hollywood and settled into the Beverly Wilshire Hotel so that Elvis could start work on *Flaming Lance*, which became *Black Star*, and ultimately *Flaming Star*. Written with Marlon Brando in mind for the leading role, *Flaming Star* was a drama. Elvis sincerely thought the starring role would be his dramatic break-through. He related to the character of Pacer Burton, a half-breed Kiowa Indian. Maybe it was because Elvis had a little Cherokee Indian in him from the Smith side of the family or just because, like the character in the movie, he always felt like an outsider growing up. In any case, the role strongly appealed to him.

"I know I have a long way to go, but a man has to have a goal, and acting's mine," Elvis told a reporter at the time. "The part I have in *Flaming Star* is the least like myself, but I would love to move on to new dramatic frontiers. I'm hoping in time to handle only straight roles."

The film takes place in the years after the Civil War, when western Texas was an uneasy meeting ground between the white and Native American cultures. Pacer Burton is a half-breed Indian, the son of a white rancher played by John McIntire. Dolores Del Rio played McIntire's beautiful Kiowa wife and Elvis's mother. Steve Forrest was Pacer's white stepbrother. When fighting breaks out between the settlers and the natives, Pacer is pulled into the deadly violence despite his peace-making efforts.

Elvis was going to wear brown contact lenses to really look the part, but the dust kicked up during filming got into the contacts and irritated him too much. It looked weird, too. When we saw him with those brown eyes, we said, "Man, you walk, talk, and sing like Elvis, but you sure don't look like Elvis."

Elvis took the role seriously. The film required not only a certain dramatic flair but also that Elvis perform most of his own stunts and ride a horse.

On the second day of preproduction, Elvis went to 20$^{th}$ Century Fox Studios in West Los Angeles. The property back then was nothing but wide-open land with ranch houses, mock Western towns, barns, and corrals.

The head horse wrangler, whose name was Jimmy, brought out several horses for Elvis to try out to see which one he wanted to use throughout the movie. Elvis chose one named Big Red, mounted up, and rode off with Jimmy.

They were gone about ten minutes when I heard a loud commotion, looked over my shoulder, and spotted Elvis and Big Red by the corral gate. Elvis was hanging on the saddle horn with both hands to keep from falling off, as the horse was taking him on the ride of his life. The ground right in front of the gate was paved asphalt where the trailers unloaded the horses into the corral. Big Red was running so fast that as he came through the gate, his hooves slid on the slick surface, causing his rear legs to spread-eagle. Elvis hung on some-how, and the horse regained its balance. Big Red made it through the gate with Elvis still in the saddle. He charged up to a barn that had a low roof overhang in front of the stalls. Elvis had to duck his head as they came under the roof, or he would have been badly hurt.

When Elvis jumped off the horse, he decided to show the animal who was boss.

"You dumb sonofabitch!" he yelled as he hauled off and whacked Big Red in the jaw. I swear, that horse's eyes rolled up in his head, and his front legs slightly buckled from Elvis's heavyweight punch. About this time, Jimmy rode up, his face pale and huge drops of sweat run-ning down his face. He quickly dismounted and went over to see if Elvis was okay. Seeing that the studio's big investment was unhurt, Jimmy took Big Red's reins from Elvis, led the horse out from the under the overhang, and mounted him. Jimmy then took a tight grip on the reins as he spurred Big Red hard in the flanks. The horse lunged forward. Jimmy jerked back on the reins, causing the animal to pull up imme-diately. This was repeated several times, until the white froth coming from the horse's mouth became speckled with little spots of blood.

Jimmy finally dismounted Big Red, apologized once more to Elvis, and asked him to pick out another horse to ride.

"No sir, I'm riding Big Red," Elvis said determinedly. "After the lesson you just gave him, that horse would be a crazy sonofabitch to try something like that again." The statement brought a grin to every-one's face, especially Jimmy's, and we all breathed a sigh of relief.

Big Red behaved himself during the entire filming of the movie. We learned later that the horse hadn't been ridden for some time and had developed "tough mouth," meaning it wasn't tender enough where the bit fit in his mouth. But Jimmy had taken care of that.

As for me, whenever I see the movie *Blazing Saddles*, in which Alex Karras punches his horse in the jaw and knocks him down, I always think of Elvis and Big Red and get a big chuckle.

Elvis had an easier time with director Don Siegel, one of the darlings of France's cineastes of the '60s. Siegel had style, flair, and several hits under his belt including *Invasion of the Body Snatchers* and, later on, *Dirty Harry* and *Escape from Alcatraz*. He also had a good sense of humor. Elvis respected him tremendously.

When we weren't filming, we spent a lot of time playing football and practicing karate in the hundred-degree heat. As was the case during the filming of *G.I. Blues*, Elvis enjoyed breaking boards for audiences of admirers on the set. He also enjoyed tossing me around to demonstrate his prowess at hand-to-hand combat. I was a willing fall guy, and whenever the mood struck Elvis, we gave a demonstration for all who cared to witness.

Siegel forever endeared himself to Elvis one day on the set when he challenged Elvis to take his art form to a higher level.

"Why don't you break some of those big pieces of wood that are used for leveling the arc lights?" challenged the director. These pieces were about three by eighteen inches and sturdy as hell. When Elvis demurred on the grounds that the huge boards could probably withstand a blow from a sledgehammer, Siegel told him, "Hell, I can break one of those boards right now."

"I don't think so, Mr. Siegel," Elvis answered politely. With that, Siegel yelled at one of the prop men to bring him one of the boards. Then the director, who smoked a pipe and wore a bandanna around his neck, made a big inspection of the wood, psyching himself up for what he was about to attempt.

"You may want to think twice about this, Mr. Siegel," Elvis warned. "You might break your hand."

"Hurt my hand?" Siegel scoffed. "Son, I'm tough as nails." Siegel then wondered if Elvis wanted him to break the board with his fingers or the side of his hand.

"Anyway you want to break it is fine by me, Mr. Siegel," Elvis said, smirking at the director's showmanship. "If you want to go over there and drive a truck over it, that's fine with me, too."

Siegel went into an unorthodox karate stance and let out a scream as his arm came down on the beam. It split wide open as Elvis and the crew stood there in openmouthed shock.

Then all of a sudden Elvis said, "Wait a minute. Let me look at that board." Sure enough, it was aged balsa wood, a stunt prop that a five-year-old girl could've broken.

Many biographers have stated that Siegel didn't take Elvis seriously as an actor, but that certainly wasn't my take on their relationship. Siegel appreciated that Elvis took the role seriously. The problem wasn't Elvis's acting (even though he was not his usual loose self), nor Siegel's direction, but rather the jumbled and cliché-laden script.

In the film's climactic death scene, Elvis was called on to utter such lifeless lines as, "I have to return to my heritage and die!" and, "Maybe someday, somewhere, people'll understand folks like us." I think that even Brando would have had problems reciting such hokum.

It also might have contributed to the fact that *Flaming Star* flamed out at the box office, ending up as one of the least profitable movies of Elvis's career. Despite the critical reviews and box-office failure of the picture, Siegel publicly lauded Elvis's acting ability, and years later he approached Elvis about starring in *Dirty Harry*. By then, Elvis was on to the next phase of his career in Las Vegas and touring. Siegel then offered the part to Clint Eastwood, and the rest is cinematic history.

Barbara Eden, the female lead in *Flaming Star*, was not the first actress to get the part. An actress from England named Barbara Steele landed the role first, but after just a few days, she was replaced by Eden.

Barbara Eden was a beautiful and talented actress. Elvis really liked her, but she was married to an actor by the name of Michael Ansara, who starred in a series on ABC-TV called *Broken Arrow*. He seemed to be a nice enough guy but, like most actors, was pretty insecure. Michael was especially wary of the relationship between Elvis and Barbara and spent a lot of time on the set to keep an eye on his better half. Elvis liked to flirt with attractive women, and Barbara certainly fit that criteria. She had an hourglass figure and a warm personality to go along with it, and Elvis enjoyed her company. I'm sure Michael saw some of the flirting between the two of them, which only served to fuel his suspicion. However, Michael could have saved himself a lot of grief if he had known Elvis's thoughts regarding dating married women.

Determined to invest his part with as much authenticity as possible, Elvis did most of his own stunts in *Flaming Star*. He came out unscathed, but Red, who played a Kiowa Indian brave on the picture, wasn't so lucky. Though it has been widely reported that Red broke his arm in a fight scene, it didn't happen. Red had a bad elbow from football, and whenever he bumped the arm against anything, it would swell up with fluid. It happened in the movie during a knife fight with Elvis. Red got knocked back by Elvis and smacked his arm against a rock. It swelled up badly. But it wasn't broken. Rudolph

Acosta, the actor portraying the Indian chief Buffalo Horn in the movie, fell off his horse and broke his arm.

But all the excitement on the set couldn't match the around-the-clock rodeo at Beverly Wilshire Hotel, where the management and other guests were growing tired of our upside-down hours, screaming, roughhousing, and rambunctious bad-boy behavior. Our escapades included the impromptu karate demonstrations, music blaring at all hours of the night, numerous pratfalls, food fights, football games in the hallway, water and shaving cream fights, and a constant parade of visitors in and out of our suites. The wealthy patrons of the hotel who lived there year-round weren't exactly in tune with our manic energy or our sophomoric brand of humor. They started turning the screws on the management to crack down on the Beverly Hillbillies.

The final straw was an indoor water fight involving Elvis, Joe, Red, and me that escalated into an all-out war using high-powered squirt guns and buckets of water. The three of us tackled Elvis. I held down his legs while Joe held him around the torso and Red pinned his arms. Red took the palm of his hand and rubbed it back and forth over Elvis's nose. The tickling drove him bonkers, and by the time we let go of him, Elvis was totally enraged. Red and I took one look at him and knew it was time to depart. Joe's escape was foiled when he tripped and fell down. In an instant, Elvis was all over him, kicking and punching him. When Joe rolled away, Elvis grabbed the nearest thing he could find, which was a guitar, and began swinging at him. He connected once on Joe's arm, and it swelled up just like Red's did on *Flaming Star*. Seeing Red and me out of the corner of his eye, Elvis turned and ran toward us. When it was clear he wasn't going to catch us, he angrily heaved the guitar in our direction. As the guitar flew down the hallway, one of the permanent residents opened his door to check out the commotion. The instrument whizzed within an inch or two of his nose, and he immediately retreated into his room and called the hotel management.

Our eviction notice, couched in Beverly Hills niceties, arrived soon after that. We were never kicked out of a nicer joint, that's for sure.

# Chapter 10

# Till Death Do Us Part

JOE ESPOSITO ARRANGED TO RENT A NICE ASIAN-STYLE HOME DESIGNED BY Frank Lloyd Wright Jr. in swanky Bel-Air. It was a place to call our own, but we sure missed the room service, having our beds turned down each day, and mints on our pillows.

The residence, located on Perugia Way, was the former home of Ali Khan, who was the sister of the shah of Iran. Elvis signed a six-month lease on the property overlooking the Bel-Air Hotel golf course, and he paid the handsome sum of $1,400 a month for rent. We would live there on and off for the next five years. It wasn't the Beverly Wilshire; still, it had its perks.

Perugia Way was a cul-de-sac that had trees and underbrush in the middle of the road, sort of like an island, surrounded by pavement. Unlike at Graceland, the wooden double gates in front were usually left open. There wasn't much of a front lawn because the home was situated on a winding hillside road with a massive asphalt driveway and a three-car garage.

The house had a circular design, and there was with a fifty-foot round patio in the middle with shrubbery and plants along the outer perimeter. Inside, the house's modern decor included thick, plush, white shag carpeting. Because he grew up with antiques in his home, Elvis wanted to go the total opposite way with California-style furnishings.

Alan Fortas decided to join us around this time, and it didn't take much persuasion on Elvis's part. Elvis had earlier tried to convince Alan to join him in Germany, but Alan turned him down flat. Alan was Jewish, but Elvis didn't make the connection. Alan didn't want to go to where six million of his people had been killed not that long before. California seemed a much better proposition.

Elvis also hired Jimmy and Lillian Jackson to take care of us in the new house. Jimmy was a jack-of-all-trades, and Lillian did the cooking. Both did the housecleaning.

Jimmy was a personable enough fellow, but Lillian could get a little bossy at times. She pretty much had her own way of doing things, unless, of course, Elvis wanted them done differently. Both were good at performing their duties and running the household. Everyone liked them, and later, when Elvis leased other homes in Los Angeles, Jimmy and Lillian came along with the deals.

The Perugia Way home was the place where Albert Goldman said, in his 1981 book, *Elvis*, wild sex orgies took place. Nothing could be farther from the truth. If anything, it was more like the movie *Porky's*, with a bunch of us guys hanging out in the game room just shooting the bull and passing the time. On the other hand, we weren't choirboys. Let's just say for the record that we were hot-blooded young men in the prime of our lives in search of a good time—and we usually found it. I can remember just one occasion when a couple had sex and was viewed by Elvis and Tuesday Weld through a special two-way mirror that had been installed at the house. The lovebirds didn't take long, and moments later Tuesday and Elvis exited the room, giggling like two naughty schoolchildren. There was no panting or hard breathing by either of them.

Sure, we had our fair share of parties, but a better term might be "hanging out." Mostly, we watched television, conversed, or listened to the jukebox.

People dropped by almost every night, but usually it was less than a handful. Elvis was pretty low-key on weeknights because he went to bed early. He had to wake up at 4:30 in the morning to report to the studios by 6:00 AM and wanted to be fresh.

It was on the weekends when we had the larger parties, which usually ran in the neighborhood of thirty to fifty people. Because Elvis couldn't go out into the world, he brought it to him.

The word got out in Hollywood that if you were a fine young filly and wanted to meet Elvis, there was no better place than his own pad on a party weekend.

The home had a wet bar, and in addition to assorted refreshments and chips, we served liquor to our guests. Elvis rarely drank, but when he did, the results usually weren't good. We generally followed his lead. Being drunk and not doing your job was a sure way to incur the Presley wrath. I found out firsthand when I made the mistake of drinking too many mai tais on location one time in Hawaii. More about that later.

Most of our hanging out was done in the main den, watching television on a big console. Elvis had his favorite spot right in the middle of the couch, with the rest of us surrounding him.

He decided what played on the TV, though most of the time the sound wasn't even on. There was usually music playing in the background, always other artists. Elvis never played his own records. Elvis liked listening to every kind of music, especially rock and roll, gospel, and R & B. He listened and constantly played songs by Tom Jones, Jackie Wilson, Roy Orbison, Billy Eckstine, Roy Hamilton, Brook Benton, and Tony Orlando. Elvis especially liked Tony's 1961 "Halfway to Paradise" single, always keeping it on the jukebox and playing it often. It was also a favorite of mine.

One artist on Elvis's jukebox was in a category all his own. Cliff Gleaves, in one of his many different career phases, recorded a song. Cliff asked Elvis if he could put his record on the jukebox in the den, and with much skepticism, Elvis gave him permission. The name of the song was "The Long Black Hearse," and much to everyone's chagrin, it died a very slow death in the household.

The story line of the song was about a guy not being able to face the day since his love died, or something like that. Cliff's voice left a lot to be desired, but even more unnerving was the amount of times he played the song and sang along in person. He drove us all nuts, Elvis especially. Of course, he didn't play it that often when Elvis was in the room because he knew Elvis would have the record taken off the jukebox.

Cliff would be drinking and singing along with the song, while at the same time in between the lyrics, he'd be saying, "Sonny! Do you see what I mean? The guy can't face the day without his love! He can't make it without her!" What Cliff failed to realize was that if he played that song one more time, we couldn't face the day because it was so damn bad. One of the lines in the tearjerker contained the hokey sentiment, "Hold back the dawn."

When Cliff did play the song in front of Elvis, the boss would shoot him a look that threw daggers. Sometimes Alan would talk

Cliff into playing it just to irritate the rest of us, which usually did the trick.

On weekends, Elvis was devoted to organized games of football at Beverly Glen Park, nestled in a discreet location off Sunset Boulevard and Beverly Glen. Elvis invited his Hollywood pals to play. It wasn't unusual for Robert Conrad, Lee Majors, Ricky Nelson, Pat Boone, Max Baer Jr., Ty Hardin, Gary Crosby, Michael Parks, and Kent McCord to join us on the gridiron.

Parks later starred in *Then Came Bronson*, a television series about a sensitive guy who gave up his menial nine-to-five life to travel around the country on a motorcycle. He was quiet and a little intense, but a nice enough guy.

McCord was more amiable. He portrayed a college buddy of Ricky Nelson's in the family series *The Adventures of Ozzie & Harriet*. Kent's birth name was Kent McWhirter; he changed it when he got into acting. But most people will remember him as the young police officer in *Adam-12*, costarring Martin Milner.

In the series, he was a handsome and trim 180 pounds. But when he played football with us in the early '60s, he was a 240-pound behemoth.

I remember Ricky smiling widely one Saturday morning when he brought this one-man wrecking crew for "a little workout."

We matched Alan Fortas up against McCord. Alan had been an All-Memphis football player at Central High School in Memphis and even played some college ball later on. McCord easily blew by him with his speed and was in the backfield on almost every play. After a few downs, Alan asked me to switch with him.

I weighed about 190 pounds at the time, but I was much faster than Alan. I was able to hinder McCord just enough to keep him from making the big play every down, but I paid the price dearly. McCord had me by about fifty pounds, and he put such a licking on me that the entire right side of my body was bruised from trying to block him. For the next few days, I couldn't even lift my right arm up high enough to comb my hair. Out of necessity, my left hand learned a whole new set of skills by the end of the week.

When McCord didn't show up the next Saturday, I didn't send out a search party. But Kent and I did remain friends over the years. We even studied acting together with Peyton Price, a drama coach in the San Fernando Valley.

By this time, Elvis was welcoming more and more people into his inner circle, including seventeen-year-old Patty Parry.

Elvis was driving down Santa Monica Boulevard in the fall of 1960 in his Rolls-Royce when Pat, who was with a friend in an old black Buick, pulled up next to him and airily said, "You look familiar. Do I know you?" Her brash sense of humor broke Elvis up, and he asked her to pull over to the curb. They did, and the friendship that began that day blossomed into a close and warm relationship that would last until Elvis's death.

Pat stopped by the house to visit with Elvis and us guys almost on a daily basis. After she became a hairstylist, she cut Elvis's hair for a while; I was a customer for even longer. I love Pat dearly, even though we lost touch for a number of years. She was upset with me for cowriting *Elvis: What Happened?* but still cared for me. We now communicate by phone or email several times a week. I am happy to say she has maintained her sharp wit and sparkling personality, and she still looks great.

She refers to herself as the only female member of the Memphis Mafia, but in reality, there was no female member. If there had been, it would have been Pat, as she was the closest to Elvis and us during all those years. We all adopted her as our little sister and looked out for her.

Principal photography for *Flaming Star* wrapped in early October 1960, and Elvis was eager to get back to Graceland. After the usual pit stop in Vegas, we returned home, but rest was the last thing on Elvis's mind.

Elvis was able to combine relaxation and play through touch football, and sometimes his enthusiasm for the game surprised even me.

He broke his finger playing football at an elementary school near Graceland while running for a downfield pass on a long bomb. He hauled it in. As he neared the goal line for a touchdown, Elvis got tackled from behind, the momentum carrying him into the end zone. He stretched his hands out in front of him, holding tight to the ball. As we all ran over to him to congratulate him on a great catch, he held up his right hand to show us his little finger bent backward so far that the tip of it touched behind the knuckle of his ring finger.

"I think I broke my finger," said Elvis as calmly as if he was announcing that his shoe had come untied. We headed right for the emergency room, where a plaster cast was placed on his hand. Then, instead of heading to Graceland for rest and recuperation, Elvis insisted that we go right back to the field to resume our game. We did, and, playing with his usual reckless abandon, Elvis broke the cast, leaving us with no choice but to go back to the emergency room so a second cast could be applied. Before they let him go this time, the doctor made Elvis sign a release form stating that he would not hold him or the hospital responsible if he suffered further injury to his finger. Reluctantly, Elvis called the game off.

We adjourned to Graceland for less risky undertakings, chief among them getting Elvis inducted into the Tau Kappa Epsilon fraternity at Arkansas State University. That was the brainchild of Rick Husky, TKE president with a flair for public relations.

Looking for some notoriety for his fraternity, northerner Husky hit on the idea of taking a poll to see who the most famous man in the South was. At the time, *G.I. Blues* was dominating the box office, its soundtrack topping the album charts. "It's Now or Never" had spent five weeks at the number one spot on the *Billboard* singles charts, followed by "Are You Lonesome Tonight?"

Who do you think finished first in Husky's poll?

Husky sent a letter to Elvis naming him Tau Kappa Epsilon's "Man of the Year." I would've loved to have been a fly on the wall when Husky opened up a telegram from Elvis not only stating that he would be honored to become a fraternity brother but also inviting TKE members to hold the induction ceremony at Graceland at 7:30 PM on October 16. That's one of the things I loved most about Elvis: he loved to blow people's minds.

At the appointed time, Husky and a handful of his fraternity brothers appeared at Graceland handsomely dressed in suits and ties. They followed Elvis, sporting his newest cast, into the music room for the proceedings to take place.

Acting as Elvis's big brother, Husky conducted the ritual whereby Elvis recited the fraternity pledge with his right hand raised. Rather than play it for laughs, Elvis showed the utmost respect for the young men and their mysterious traditions.

To seal the deal, Husky whispered in Elvis's ear the secret password and enjoined him to never forget it. Husky removed the fraternity pin on the lapel of his suit and placed it on Elvis's shirt. He presented the new pledge with a plaque that read: "Distinguished Member of the Year: In recognition of the remarkable achievements in the world of entertainment and as a prominent American, to Elvis Presley, Distinguished TKE Member of the Year." Elvis was rendered almost speechless, and I think he was deeply touched.

"This is one of the nicest awards I've ever received," he humbly said. "It will occupy a place of honor in my home." He wasn't stroking his guests, either: the plaque hung in the same room as his many gold records for years.

Not long after that, it was back to Nashville's Studio B to record an album that was a radical departure for the reigning icon of rock and roll.

It was a long-standing ambition of Elvis's to produce a full gospel album, the music that first motivated him to start singing. The result was *His Hand in Mine*.

Though I had heard him sing gospel songs in private, that was the first time I ever heard Elvis sing that style in the studio. His majestic voice and unique interpretation of classics such as "Mansion over the Hilltop," "Swing Down Sweet Chariot," and "If We Never Meet Again" just blew me away.

There was a transformation that took over Elvis when he sang gospel, and I'd never seen anything like it before. It was apparent that the music had a hold on him. It was as if the Lord was using Elvis as a conduit, bringing everything out of him. He was trying not only to sound technically perfect but to get the feel as well. I guess you could say it was a different approach. I had a feeling when he sang those songs that his mother, Gladys, was tucked away in the back of his mind as the inspiration for the heartfelt sound that came out of his mouth. He might have even been singing just for her.

I recall Elvis telling me that when he first started out he wanted to sing gospel, and he even auditioned for a chance to be the lead singer with a local gospel group but was turned down. Some of his favorite gospel groups were the Blackwood Brothers, the Golden Gate Quartet, and the Statesmen. As Elvis told me about his rejection, I thought, *How could they miss a talent as great as his?* Maybe he was too raw and not polished enough, or perhaps they saw the magnitude of his charisma while he sang and it scared them. In any case, there's not a doubt in my mind he would have become the number one gospel singer in the world.

Then again, being the King of Rock and Roll was nothing to sneeze at.

While gospel fed Elvis's soul, it was making movies that put food on the table. By November, he was back to work at 20th Century Fox.

Elvis followed *Flaming Star* with yet another drama called *Wild in the Country*. Although the original concept called for no Elvis music to be involved, producer Jerry Wald didn't want to repeat the same mistake as was made with *Flaming Star* and insisted that four songs be inserted into the script.

Adapted by famed writer Clifford Odets from a J.R. Salamanca novel, *Wild in the Country* stars Elvis as Glenn Tyler, a rebellious back-woods delinquent gifted with a rare literary talent. Hope Lange is the sympathetic psychiatrist who tries to help him, and Tuesday Weld and Millie Perkins round out an all-star cast as his seductive cousin and childhood sweetheart, respectively.

Millie was not Elvis's type, being thin and frail looking, but she was perfect for the part of a small-town innocent. Her husband or boyfriend, I can't recall which at the time, was actor Dean Stockwell. He visited with her on the movie set in Napa and back at the Fox lot. I remember him taking a lot of pictures of her during the shoot. Many years later, Millie ended up playing Elvis's mother in the TV series about a young Elvis, produced by Elvis Presley Enterprises, of which, coincidentally, Elvis's fraternity brother Rick Husky was the producer/writer.

Tuesday played the part of the wild, independent girl intent on doing pretty much anything she wanted. Though total opposites, Tuesday and Millie's characters both were in love with Elvis's character. However, in the movie he ended up falling for the Hope Lange character, a self-assured woman totally unlike the other two.

Tuesday Weld was one of the sexiest women I had ever been around. She was also sweet, wild, and totally unpredictable— and she definitely did not fawn over Elvis. One time in the Beverly Wilshire Hotel, Elvis said something she didn't like, and she grabbed a whole carton of milk and threw it out of the window into the street several floors below. She didn't even look to see if there were people down below. We all rushed over to the window to see where it landed, and there was just this big white mark down on the street where it hit and exploded. She was just that way, very impulsive.

Tuesday was also spoiled, because she grew up from a very young age in the business and had been catered to for most of her life. Like Elvis, she was quite capable of yelling at one person while simultaneously conducting a polite conversation with someone else.

Elvis and Tuesday occasionally dated, but unlike so many women, she was never bowled over by him. To her, Elvis was too domineering when it came to women, and she was too much of a free spirit to be led around or dictated to by a man. I think that trait is also what attracted Elvis to her in the first place.

Elvis was also romancing the classy Nancy Sharpe from St. Louis, who was the head of wardrobe on the set. She was also a stark contrast to the type of women Elvis usually dated. He preferred young, kittenish types in or barely out of their teens. Nancy was a tall, slender blond, fresh looking like Doris Day, with a college education. She was sweet, and all the guys really liked her and thought she had a lot on the ball. Elvis enjoyed talking and spending time with her. Nancy was also talented in her own right, with perfect pitch and tone. You could hit any note on the piano, and Nancy could tell you what it was. All I know is that she hit all the right notes with Elvis.

As if he didn't already have enough on his plate, Elvis also cast an eye in Hope Lange's direction. But Hope had too much common sense and dignity to get caught up in a fleeting on-location romance with a fellow actor. I believe they had a lot of respect for each other, so they decided to become friends instead of lovers. However, Hope tested the bounds of their friendship when she literally caught Elvis with his pants down.

During the filming of *Flaming Star*, Elvis developed a nasty boil on his tush from spending a lot of time on horseback. By the time he started filming *Wild in the Country*, the boil was a problem that interfered with even normal activity. Finally, Elvis decided to have it lanced by a studio doctor. First he spent a weekend locked in his Napa Valley motel room, soaking the boil with very hot cloths that we brought to him. We were trying to bring the boil to a head, per doctor's instructions.

It would have been a lot worse, but thanks to a complimentary case of wine sent over by the Napa Valley Wine Growing Association, not even Elvis was feeling any pain. In fact, he, Joe, Gene, Alan, and I all had a decent buzz going when Hope Lange showed up at the door. She said that she'd heard that Elvis had some kind of physical problem, but no one would tell her the nature of the trouble so she came over to check on him personally. She was escorted into Elvis's bedroom, where he was lying on his back with a pillow under his hips in order to apply the hot compresses onto the boil. He was unclothed but covered by a sheet.

When Hope asked what was wrong with him, Elvis straightforwardly told her, "I've got a boil on my ass." The wine had loosened his inhibitions, but he still wasn't prepared for what happened next.

"Well, where is it?" Hope asked, pulling the sheet away quickly for an up-close-and-personal eyeful of a naked Elvis. Elvis instantly flushed as red as his boil and said, "Whoa now, Miss Lange, wait a minute," as he frantically re-covered himself with the sheet. Unfazed, Miss Lange said, "Well, I just wanted to see how you're doing."

"I'm okay!" Elvis replied almost pleadingly. After she left the room, Elvis turned to us and asked incredulously, "Can you believe her? Jerking up that sheet like she did?"

"There's nothing like looking a situation straight on to know where one stands," Alan said, cracking everybody up as we broke out another bottle of wine.

Elvis was going stir-crazy in the motel after the boil was lanced, so we made a jaunt to San Francisco for a weekend excursion at the famous Mark Hopkins Hotel. I was behind the wheel of Elvis's white Cadillac limo; Alan was sitting up front with me. Elvis was in the rear sitting in his usual spot on the right side. Next to him was Nancy Sharpe, Joe, and Gene. We were cruising along at around seventy miles per hour when a car passed us suddenly on the right.

"Sonny, pull up beside that car," Elvis ordered. I pressed the accelerator to the floor, and within moments we were adjacent to the other vehicle. As I edged ahead, Elvis put down his window and pointed a derringer gun at the driver. When he saw it, the guy swerved and literally drove his car off the freeway and down an embankment. Elvis put his window back up and calmly said, "That just goes to show you, you never know who you are messing with." Only then did I learn that someone in the other car had given the finger to us as it passed our limo. It wasn't the first time Elvis had pulled a gun on someone, nor would it be the last.

We arrived late on a Saturday evening, and after an elegant dinner in Elvis's suite, Elvis and Nancy called it an evening. Gene also decided to stay at the hotel. Alan, Joe, and I, however, were in the mood for fun. We had heard the Golden Gate City had an incredible nightlife, and we wanted an unforgettable experience. This brings to mind the old saying, "Be careful what you wish for."

We told the bellhop we wanted to go to one of those "after-hour" clubs we had heard so much about. Seeing three single guys in San Francisco, he thought he knew just the place where we could find some excitement. He called a cab for us, and we were taken to a place called the Broken Drum. It was so smoky when we walked in that we could hardly see in front of our face. We sat down and ordered drinks.

As our eyes acclimated to the haze, we noticed something awfully peculiar about the place—it was filled with guys sitting with guys and girls sitting with girls. Maybe this wasn't our kind of club after all. We decided to finish our drinks and find ourselves another club. But just then, out of nowhere, a young lady appeared and plopped herself down in Alan's lap, put her arms around his neck, and hugged him.

"You're just like this big ol' teddy bear I have at home," this little sexpot proclaimed. "You're so cute." Alan grinned from ear to ear, put his arms around her, and said, "Well hi, honey."

Maybe we would stick around for a while after all.

Then out of the corner of my eye, I saw a hulking figure heading in our direction from another table and instinctively knew it wasn't to sell us any Girl Scout cookies.

Sure enough, when the bruiser reached our table, with a voice that would've scared Charles Bronson, this person growled, "That's my woman you're holding." The face was pretty scary, too, and it certainly didn't help when we realized this Dick Butkus look-alike standing so menacingly over us was a female, at least by medical standards. Coming from Tennessee, this was just something totally new to us, and we sat there openmouthed as Lady Godzilla attempted to pull her girlfriend off Alan's lap. "Get over there and sit down and behave yourself!" the manly woman said. When the girl balked, the giantess yanked her by the arms and repeated her command.

"Hey, don't do that," said Alan, his gentlemanly breeding finally kicking in. Only five foot ten, Alan weighed about 220 pounds, which still put him at a distinct disadvantage against the Great Dame. Alan continued, "Look, I just don't want you jerking her around. If she's your girlfriend, that's fine, but she came over here. She was just cutting up and having a little fun. Nothing serious."

Meanwhile, off to the side I noticed three more "ladies" taking an interest in matters, and in my head I envisioned the headline in the next day's newspapers: "Memphis Mafia in Lesbian Dustup." Wouldn't Elvis be tickled pink about that! Fortunately, the bartender saw what was happening and jumped all over the woman, "Get on over to your table and take your friends with you, and stop this right now. Go on." She must have been a regular, and she did as she was told.

The bartender turned to us, apologized, and offered us a drink on the house. We politely declined, and I said, "We are obviously in the wrong place, so we are going to go now. But thanks anyway." Then we got the hell out of there. The situation rather dampened our enthusiasm for club hopping, so we headed back to the hotel. Elvis roared with laughter when we told him the story, and he ribbed Alan about going toe-to-toe against a woman.

"Look, Elvis," Alan insisted, "she might have technically been a woman, but otherwise she was all man."

The rest of our trip went without a hitch, which was just fine with me. We had had enough action for the two days we were in San Francisco.

A few days went by, and filming resumed at the 20th Century Fox ranch about fifteen miles north of Santa Monica. But then there was other erratic behavior by Elvis that caused worry.

I don't know if it was an accumulation of the amphetamines or the tremendous pressure Elvis was under because the film's shooting schedule was cut from fifty to thirty-seven days, but he began showing a side I'd never seen before.

At the time, Joe was dating Christina Crawford, who had a minor role in the film and later was the author of the best-selling tell-all book about her mother, Joan Crawford, called *Mommie Dearest*. Christina was about as feisty as Tuesday Weld, and one evening at Elvis's house she tested the bounds of Elvis's temper.

Elvis was used to having his cigars lit for him by whichever one of us happened to be nearby. None of us ever gave it a second thought. At one point, Joe leaned over to light one for him, and Christina was incensed, considering it an act of abject servility. She objected by knocking the cigar out of Elvis's mouth and yelling at him, "He shouldn't have to light your cigar!"

In a flash, the enraged Elvis grabbed Christina by the hair, dragged her across the coffee table, and ordered her out of the house. It was a stunning scene that was wholly out of character for Elvis. I know the two patched things up later on, because they were laughing and joking with each other on the set about a week after the incident. Christina sent him a peace offering of sorts in the form of several cases of Pepsi-Cola, which just so happened to be Elvis's favorite soda.

Despite the fact that he kissed and made up with Christina, it was becoming uncomfortably clear that Elvis was changing—or something was changing him.

In December, *Wild in the Country* wrapped for the holidays, and we were free to go home to Memphis. Colonel Parker always made sure that Elvis had Christmas off. It was always such a special time for him, and for all of us. At the time, everyone working for Elvis lived in Memphis except Joe, who, if I remember correctly, headed for his home in Chicago to be with his family.

Elvis rented out a club that New Year's Eve, and we had a great time. The party was just for his close friends, including Marty Lacker and Richard Davis, who would soon join us working for Elvis. Right before we went to the club that night, we had a big fireworks battle at Graceland shooting off Roman candles and bottle rockets. One of the bottle rockets went into the side of the house and started a small fire. The people inside yelled that smoke was filling the house. I ran over and got the water hose. After pulling the rocket out of the hole it made in the house, I stuffed the running hose in the hole and went back to join the battle. Soon those inside were yelling at us again, this time because the room was flooding. Elvis told us his daddy was going to be mad at us for setting the house on fire and then flooding it, as if it hadn't been him who shot the rocket off in the first place. Sometimes Elvis reminded me of a child who was too big for his britches, but he was a lot of fun to be around. Memories of those times are very special to me.

After the New Year, Joe, Alan, Gene, and I returned to Los Angeles with Elvis. By the third week in January, the film was in the can and Elvis was free to go home. On the way, we stopped off in Las Vegas and took in some shows: Don Rickles, the Clara Ward Singers, and a few other acts Elvis really enjoyed.

Elvis's cousin Junior Smith died of alcohol poisoning in early February 1961 while staying at his Uncle Travis's home. Junior, a Korean War veteran, had suffered post-traumatic stress disorder and was never the same after he returned home. Elvis was brokenhearted over Junior's death as Junior had always been good to him when he was a young boy. On more than one occasion, Elvis had talked about what Junior had gone through in Korea. Even more heartbreaking to Elvis was that he couldn't attend Junior's funeral because he had been called back by 20th Century Fox to shoot an alternate ending to *Wild in the Country*. In the original ending, Hope Lange's character died of carbon monoxide poisoning. Test audiences or studio brass apparently turned thumbs-down on that, and the studio decided to go with something less grim.

Regardless of the new fan-friendly ending, the film didn't do well at the box office, even though Elvis gave a wonderful performance.

It seemed to be a sign that his fans wanted him to sing in his movies and leave the dramatic stuff to Olivier.

# Chapter 11

# Hawaiian Wedding Song

IN THE LATE 1950s, ELVIS BEGAN ONE OF HIS GREATEST LOVE AFFAIRS. He fell head over heels for a beautiful mistress he courted with tremendous admiration and respect for the rest of his life—the great state of Hawaii.

Elvis first stepped on the shores of Hawaii in November 1957, greeted by four thousand shrieking fans.

Once in Hawaii, Elvis became a different person. He said the state gave him peace and tranquility like no other place on earth. He also loved the native people because they were friendly and seemed real and down-to-earth to him.

Hawaii unofficially became Elvis's second home over the years. He performed several concerts and made three movies and an iconic TV special there, as well as taking countless Hawaiian vacations. Elvis was even arguably the state's greatest booster at one time, with several of his movies promoting Hawaii in a way that a brochure from the office of tourism couldn't match. It was definitely a two-way love affair.

We first found out we were going to Hawaii in January 1961, when Colonel Parker held a press conference at the Hawaiian Village Hotel in Honolulu to announce that Elvis was going to hold a charity concert there for the navy.

A month before, the Colonel had read in the *Los Angeles Herald Examiner* about the nineteenth anniversary of the Japanese bombing of Pearl Harbor. The piece recounted how approximately a thousand U.S. sailors were entombed in the battleship of the USS *Arizona* after a bomb ripped apart the bow, splitting the hull. The ship sank in a matter of minutes, and the bodies on the *Arizona* were never recovered.

Over the years, dozens of plans to memorialize the crew of the *Arizona* had come and gone. For almost two decades, efforts to raise funds by the Pacific War Memorial Commission had run into choppy waters.

An estimated $500,000 was needed to complete a memorial, and only about half was in the commission's coffers. Organizers wanted to start construction by the twentieth anniversary of Pearl Harbor but needed about $50,000 to begin. They needed someone to kick-start the struggling building fund.

"I know a young man whose services can be a big help," Colonel Parker said.

Around that time, the Colonel had also arranged a benefit show for Elvis in Memphis. The show garnered more than $50,000 for several charities. Elvis was always generous to those less fortunate and gave a large amount of money to charities in Memphis every year. Despite what you may have heard, Colonel Parker was also a charitable man who gave each year to his own favorite causes. His requirement was that the majority of the money go to the purpose for which it was intended. He not only believed in giving back but put his money where his mouth was, and that says a lot about a man.

Elvis himself was not only charitable but also had a patriotic streak in him a mile wide. Elvis believed strongly in his country and was proud to be an American.

Although Elvis didn't speak out publicly regarding his views on politics and policies, he voiced them around us, often with great passion.

The USS *Arizona* memorial benefit concert was an opportunity for Elvis to ease back into performing for a live audience after serving in the military and also to do something for his country. Not only did Elvis not receive any money for doing the concert, but he and Colonel Parker bought the first two tickets as a gesture of goodwill.

The show was held at the four thousand–seat Bloch Arena. Opening for Elvis were Grand Ole Opry star Minnie Pearl and comic Sterling Mossman. They gave it their all, but nobody complained when it was time for the main event.

This was the second time Elvis had performed in concert since I started working for him, and I was surprised at how nervous he was. He had concentrated on making movies for the year I had been with him, and, of course, that was a whole different and slower-paced forum. I eventually learned that Elvis was always jittery before going onstage to perform.

He used to do stretching exercises just before he walked out on the stage to relieve some of his anxiety—but once he was out there, magic happened. Elvis seemed to channel his nerves into a positive force that exploded on stage.

Outfitted in a ten-thousand-dollar gold lamé jacket with silver-sequined lapels and cuffs, black slacks, a guitar with inlaid mother-of-pearl slung around his shoulder, and a lei of fragrant orchids around his neck, Elvis was ready to rock the house.

The hysteria that greeted his entrance was unbelievable. More than five minutes passed before the crowd settled down enough for him to launch into a nineteen-song set that included "Heartbreak Hotel," "Don't Be Cruel," and "All Shook Up."

Backed by the Jordanaires and several Nashville musicians he had recorded with just a month before, Elvis gave an inspired and playfully uninhibited performance that wasn't anything like his '50s concerts but wasn't as polished as his later Vegas shows, either.

The concert was a resounding success on all fronts. The fans got their money's worth, and Elvis regained his confidence in front of a live audience. The show raised more than $62,000 for the memorial fund.

The spotlight that the concert shone on the memorial effort helped revive public interest in the project. That September, Congress donated $150,000, and the Hawaiian legislature added another $50,000 contribution to the pot. With the $250,000 already collected from federal and state sources combined with the $275,000 in public donations, construction on the memorial began in March 1962. It was ready for dedication by the following year—all thanks to a swivel-hipped singer and a former carnival barker.

Elvis dovetailed the triumph of the concert with the filming of *Blue Hawaii*, the biggest box-office success of his film career, raking in more than $14 million, with a soundtrack that sold five million copies. To put this into perspective, $14 million then would be in the $250 million to $300 million range in profit margin today, with *Blue Hawaii* costing less than $1 million to make. Unfortunately for Elvis, the huge success of this movie was the catalyst for the films that followed, which were usually similar in content.

The film was a return to the formulaic, lighthearted musical comedies the public had come to know and expect from Elvis. After two movies with more drama—*Flaming Star* and *Wild in the Country*—which had little or no music in them, both Colonel Parker and Hal Wallis needed to strike gold this time out for their respective clients.

Two days after the concert at Bloch Arena, Elvis reported to the shoot tan, relaxed, in good spirits, and happy to be in the capable hands of Norman Taurog, his favorite director.

Hal Kantor, who had directed *Loving You*, wrote the *Blue Hawaii* screenplay and tailored the script to Elvis's personality, charisma, and comedic timing. Elvis's double takes and timing in the film reminded me of Cary Grant, the master of comedy takes.

In the movie, Elvis plays Chad Gates, who has just returned to his home in Oahu after serving a two-year stint in the army. Of course, the script included two crucial elements to any Elvis movie: beautiful women and songs.

Elvis's life off the set somewhat mirrored his on-screen life when he began dating actress Joan Blackman.

Joan had a few movies under her belt, was a good actress, and was very sexy. She was a little standoffish at first with us, as had been Juliet Prowse and all of Elvis's leading ladies where the Memphis Mafia was concerned. It took a while to warm up to us. I mean, how many leading men had a constant entourage of guys around them like Elvis did? But as soon as they discovered we were just a regular bunch of guys with a little "crazy" streak, they would relax and have a lot of fun on the set. And I always made sure to treat Elvis's costars and the women in his private life with the utmost respect in every manner. Joan had the most beautiful blue eyes I had ever seen, which were accentuated by the dark makeup they used to make her a Hawaiian beauty.

Naturally, Elvis didn't limit his dating to just one girl. During the filming he saw several women, including ingénue Pam Austin and a few others on the set. Many of the actresses in the movie would hang out with us at the end of the day, which made for some late nights. Whether it was because of their bloodshot eyes or lethargic manner in the morning, Hal Wallis found out about our after-hours goings-on and hastily moved the female cast to another wing of the hotel, imposing a strict 10:00 PM curfew. Sly dog that he was, Elvis switched to dating local women who didn't work on the movie.

Colonel Tom Parker was also in high spirits throughout the filming of the picture. A fan of practical jokes, the Colonel—sporting a straw hat, a Hawaiian shirt, shorts, and sandals—interviewed tourists with the aluminum casing of his cigar as his microphone and announced he was a representative of "Radio Pineapple." Parker would ask if they were having a good time and if they planned to see the movie when it came out. He would also offer them free slices of pineapple, courtesy of Hal Wallis.

One day while we were shooting at the Honolulu Airport, the Colonel set up a gag to play on Wallis himself. Parker was big on hypnotism and enlisted me to play one of his subjects.

We had already been on the set for about three hours when Wallis, with a newspaper under his arm, came to claim his chair. This wasn't just any chair, of course, but rather a large director's chair with high legs for better supervision of the movie set. To remove any doubt whose chair it was, on the back was stenciled in large black letters the name "Hal Wallis."

I was sitting in it, staring straight ahead, unblinking. Hal approached and saw me in his exalted throne and noisily cleared his throat to signal his arrival so I could vamoose. The crew and actors were in on the gag, and their snickering made it difficult for me to keep a straight face.

As he reached his chair, Hal cleared his throat again, this time louder and more imperiously. I remained staring straight ahead. Finally, the exasperated producer spoke.

"Excuse me, you're in my chair," Hal said. He might as well have been talking to a statue. Then the Colonel spoke right up on cue. "I'm sorry about this, Mr. Wallis," he said. "Sonny had a very long night, and I've got him hypnotized, and he's getting a little sleep right now."

"He is?" Hal asked, as startled as if he'd been told I had died in his precious chair.

"Well, I hypnotized him," said the Colonel with a totally straight face. "Give him just a few more minutes, and I'll get him out of it. Is that okay with you?"

"Sure," Wallis said, standing there with his hands on his hips, almost hypnotized himself by the unfolding scenario. "This is really something," he added.

Then the Colonel, who knew Hal suffered from a chronically stiff neck, said to him, "You know, Sonny gives very good neck rubs.

Would you like to have one?"

"Yes, sure," Wallis said, perking up. "That might be nice."

"Well, I have to wake up Sonny now," the Colonel said. Then he turned to me and intoned, "Sonny, when I wake you up, I want you to get out of the chair and rub Mr. Wallis's neck for a little while. On the count of three, I would like you to awake. One, two, three...WAKE UP!" At the snap of his fingers, I sat up straight, looked at Hal, and said, "Hello, Mr. Wallis, how are you today?" as if laying eyes on him for the first time that day.

"Well, I'm fine, Sonny," Hal responded. "Did you get enough sleep?"

"Yes, sir! I feel very rested now," I said, leaping out of the chair. Then I asked, "Would you like your neck rubbed, sir?"

Wallis plunked down in his chair. As I massaged his neck, he smiled brightly and said to the Colonel, "Boy, he's good. This feels great, Colonel." Keep in mind this was Hal Wallis—one of Hollywood's all-time leading producers and hard-nosed businessmen. He couldn't see the Colonel's face because Parker was standing to the side of him, but I could, and the twinkle in Parker's eye and smile on his face made it clear that there was nobody in Hawaii having as much fun right then.

Hal Wallis never did know that the Colonel was putting him on.

After two weeks in Honolulu, the shoot moved to the remote island of Kauai. All of the footage there (about the last twenty minutes of the movie) was shot on the grounds of the Coco Palms Resort Hotel, ushering the property into immortality.

The grounds included a two thousand–tree coconut grove and was the closest thing to the Garden of Eden I could imagine on earth.

I wasn't going to have an acting part in *Blue Hawaii*, but one day in Kauai, Hal Wallis said he was going to walk in a scene as an extra. He asked if I'd like to join him, and I readily agreed.

Ours was the scene in which Elvis was driving a carload of women in a tour company station wagon. As Hal and I started walking out the driveway of the Coco Palms, Norman Taurog yelled for action.

Elvis had no clue I was going to be in the scene, and Hal wondered how I thought he would react when he saw me. "He's probably going to try and run me over," I said with a straight face, knowing how crazy Elvis could be.

"Well then, maybe you should walk on the outside of me," Mr. Wallis said without missing a beat. Elvis did look shocked when he saw me, but he curbed his urge to run me down because of Hal Wallis's presence. I was also an extra in the wedding scene where Elvis and Joan Blackman were floating down the lagoon on the raft.

Other than filming my two scenes in the movie, there wasn't much to do in Kauai because it was so remote. Everything on the island was connected to the hotel, and all the meals were served at set times. If a guest showed up late for a meal, well, that was too bad. There wasn't a convenience store or a fast-food joint around those parts. The hotel food was the only choice, and I happened to miss out on dinner one evening.

The meals were served in a big open-air dining room that had a lagoon running alongside it. The hotel had nightly entertainment on a small stage in the dining room, which I had watched many times with Elvis and the guys after our meals.

Across from the entrance to the dining room was a bar. I spotted two young ladies there on vacation and decided to greet them and see if I could join them for a drink. They were sipping on an interesting-looking concoction, and I decided to have the same thing myself. They were mai tais, a special drink from the island made with a mixture of rums. I had never had one before, and it went down pretty smoothly. So I drank a few of them fairly quickly, and before I knew it I was feeling no pain. Of course, drinking on an empty stomach only accelerated the alcohol's numbing impact on me. To put it simply, I was quite drunk.

When it came time to bid the ladies adieu, I kindly escorted them to their rooms. They were staying in the back area, so we walked across this little bridge over the lagoon. Failing to convince them to have a nightcap in their room, I headed back to the dining room.

As I approached the bridge, I saw an attractive couple singing the "Hawaiian Wedding Song." In the islands, it was not unusual to see people playing ukuleles and singing, so I walked up to the singers, put my arms around their shoulders, and began to sing along with them. I should add that I'm no Elvis Presley. My crooning has been likened to the keening of a walrus with a toothache—and that's when I'm on key.

In my inebriated condition, I was totally oblivious to the fact that I was crashing the floor show of which the singers on the bridge were an integral part. All the other shows that I had seen in the dining room had been performed inside on the little stage, but never outside. The screams of laughter from the diners made no impression on me at all as I kept belting out that lovely tune with my new friends.

I was also unaware that Elvis and the rest of the guys were in the audience contributing to the laughter as they watched my drunken musical debut.

Upon finishing our song, I gave my partners a hug, told them they sounded great, and walked toward the dining room entrance. Although Elvis laughed as heartily as anyone while I made a complete fool of myself, he sent Joe to intercept me and tell me not to come to his table. He didn't want any of the other patrons to know I was with his group.

People began to exit because the "Hawaiian Wedding Song" was the final number in the show. As dozens of guests filed past me, there was much laughter, and many nodded to me. But one lady stopped and fixed me with a glare that would've scared me if I had been in my right mind.

"Young man, you have ruined my fifteenth wedding anniversary!" she sobbed. The man behind her, apparently her spouse, was grinning and giving me a look that said, "Don't worry about it." I wasn't, because that would've required at least a couple of functioning brain cells.

The wife wasn't the only one irate with me. The next morning, as I was trying to get it together with a terrible headache and hangover, Red informed me that Elvis didn't want me to come around him on the set that day. Red then described what I had done the night before, which made me want to just climb back in bed and pull the covers over my head. Not to mention that I would rather have done that anyway, because my head felt as big as a basketball and was throbbing something fierce. Not having that luxury, I went to the set with everyone else, but this time I rode in a different vehicle from Elvis. On the set he shared what I had done with all the members of the crew and cast who hadn't witnessed it themselves. In telling it, he'd laugh and seem to enjoy it, but anytime he'd spot me he would glower and give me the cold shoulder. I thought he was being a little two-faced by laughing about it with everybody else while giving me the fish-eye. I finally went up to him and asked him if I could talk to him for a minute. Without even looking at me he said, "Yeah. Go ahead." His manner was cold and detached. I explained to him that when I went to work for him a year earlier he told me that whatever I did, good or bad, it would reflect on him. I admitted I acted stupid by getting drunk and making a fool of myself. I apologized and told him that he never had to worry about that happening again. In that moment, his whole demeanor changed, and he looked at me for the first time during the conversation. With warmth and compassion, Elvis said, "I know it won't, Sonny. Everything's okay." Then he grinned and added, "It *was* funny as hell, though."

I thought everything was fine, but I was still concerned about changes that had taken place in Elvis. My concerns were realized when we reached the mainland again.

One night Elvis had a few people over to the house. Alan Fortas and Gene Smith were there when Tuesday Weld brought over an attractive friend named Kay.

Elvis didn't really drink, but around Tuesday, he imbibed to deal with her. She got silly and was prone to fits and fits of giggles when she drank, which was more often than not. All of us guys were enamored with Tuesday, especially Alan. He had a huge crush on her and was like putty around her.

Elvis was drinking pretty good that night, and knowing that he was hooked up with Tuesday, I turned my attention to her friend Kay, a slender, pretty brunette who was a nurse.

She and I were sitting at the bar having a conversation when Elvis suddenly inserted himself between us. He looked at Kay and said, "Damn, you're pretty," and gave her a little kiss on the cheek. As suddenly as he had appeared, Elvis disappeared into his bedroom, located just off the den we were all sitting in. "What was that all about?" asked Kay. I grinned and said, "All he did was state a fact. But he left out the word *very*." She smiled and thanked me. Not a bad recovery on my part, I thought.

I didn't realize it at the time, but the game was pretty much over for me at that point. Kay and I were finished before we even got started. Whenever Elvis Presley wanted something, whether a car, a gun, a badge, a house, or a woman, he got it. Tuesday Weld, one of the most beautiful and sexy stars of the day, was his date for the evening, but Elvis had decided that he wanted Kay, too.

A few minutes later, Elvis came back and interrupted our conversation once more to plant a big kiss on Kay. This time he kissed her passionately on her mouth, and she responded in kind. Game over.

I slid off my bar stool and walked over to where Alan and Tuesday were sitting at a table. Tuesday was giggling as she watched Elvis and Kay, who was now eagerly responding to his kiss. Alan had that big grin on his face that was so funny to me, and he said in an admiring tone, "Smooth as silk, isn't he?" I smiled ruefully and said, "Yeah, he shot me right outta the saddle."

Then I went over to the couch where Gene was and sat down next to him. Gene said, "Burnt." That was shorthand we used for "shot down in flames." I chuckled in agreement, and then I leaned over so no one else would hear me and said, "Gene, if you had your choice between Tuesday and that girl, which one would you choose?" His immediate answer was no surprise: "Tuesday, man."

"Me, too," I replied.

Don't get me wrong. Kay was a very pretty girl, but Tuesday's beauty was so overpowering she could make your knees knock.

Elvis saw Gene and me with our heads together and had a fit of paranoia.

"What did you say about me, Sonny?" he said loudly from across the room. It signaled to me that he was looking for some sort of reaction from me regarding Kay. At first, I thought he might be joking, but then I realized he was dead serious.

"Nothing really, Elvis," I said. "I just asked Gene a question, but it wasn't about you."

This didn't satisfy him at all, and, his voice rising, Elvis said, "Dammit, Sonny, you said something about me and I want to know what it was!"

I was stupefied and didn't know what to say or how to react. I certainly didn't want to confess that I was talking about which girl we'd rather be with, so I just repeated that it wasn't about him. Then something surreal happened. Elvis grabbed a soda bottle and came toward me with bad intentions. Now you have to remember that Elvis was drinking and that he didn't hold his liquor well.

"Tell me or I'll break your damn head open with this bottle," he said from between clenched teeth. I'd seen Elvis angry before, very angry, but nothing like this. I stood up quickly, my anger rising as well.

"You're not going to hit me with no bottle," I said evenly. Then the anger boiled out of me, and I let him have it. "Man, you have changed! You are like a gestapo officer! I don't want to be around you anymore! I quit!"

We had both crossed the line—Elvis by threatening bodily harm to me, and me by standing up to him and embarrassing him in front of the ladies. Elvis stepped right in front of me to block my path and said, "You can't quit. You're fired!"

There was no going back.

"Call it anything you want, Elvis," I replied, "but I'm outta here."

No one ever dared talk that way to Elvis before, especially with an audience. Without warning, Elvis unleashed a sucker punch that caught me squarely on the jaw. The blow turned my head, but I turned back and looked at Elvis right in the eyes. The punch didn't hurt me all that much, but the emotional pain I felt was overwhelming.

Tears welled up in my eyes. Elvis Presley was like an older brother who looked out for me, gave me a better life, and even literally gave me the clothes off his back. But he was also capable of flashes of rage and prone to heaping abuse and humiliation on anyone who crossed him.

"I never thought you could do that to me," I said quietly to Elvis, tears welling up in my eyes. It was the only time in my life I never returned a punch. It never even crossed my mind to defend myself against Elvis.

I turned away and immediately went to my room to pack, with Tuesday and Alan at my heels.

"I'm so sorry, Sonny," Tuesday said. She was crying while Alan stood by silently as I hastily placed clothes in my suitcase. "If I hadn't brought Kay over," Tuesday said, "this would've never happened."

"Tuesday, this has nothing to do with you or Kay," I said firmly. "Elvis hasn't been himself for a while now, and I just called him out on his behavior. I'm just tired of it all." Elvis reminded me of the character he played in *Jailhouse Rock* when he became full of himself.

About this time, Elvis appeared in the doorway and asked the others to leave. I found out later that he had asked Gene what I said after I had left the room. When Gene told him, Elvis realized he had messed up. He was too proud to apologize. Not once did I ever hear him apologize for bad behavior or ill temper. His apologies usually came in the form of gifts or grand gestures instead of a simple, "I'm sorry." Elvis asked what was going on, and I told him again that he was different from when I first started working for him. I also told him he couldn't hold his liquor very well. The remark got his hackles up again, but he held himself in check. He confessed that he had a lot of pressure on him regarding his career and a few other things going on in his life. I responded that I could accept that, but I didn't think he would ever hit me for any reason and that he was wrong for even contemplating it. However, there was no apology forthcoming. Instead, he asked me where I was going and what I was going to do. While I continued to throw items in my suitcase, I told him I was going to stay at a friend's place while I figured out what I was going to do.

Elvis then asked if I had any money.

"I'm okay," I said. I might have had a few bucks in my pocket, but nothing to tide me over for the long term. Elvis instinctively knew that and had one of the guys draw a check for $200. I took the check, folded it, and put it in my pocket. "Thanks, Elvis," I said, not making eye contact.

"Can one of the guys take you someplace?" he asked, showing in his indirect way that he was concerned for my welfare.

"No, I already called a cab," I said. I asked Elvis if I could pick up the rest of my clothes another time, and he said that would be fine.

No more words passed between us, but when my cab pulled away from the driveway I could see Elvis's silhouette in the doorway. Even though I was the one wronged that night, I couldn't help but feel sorry for Elvis. Despite all of his fame and wealth, there was something deeply sad and lonely about him. For him to be so insecure about my love for him and commitment to him that he would behave the way he did—that's what really packed a wallop.

The next day, I called a couple I had met in Hawaii who owned a bar in Phoenix called The Carnival Room. They had told me if I ever needed work to look them up. I took them up on the offer much sooner than I had ever anticipated, and they were gracious enough to keep their word.

I flew to Arizona and started bouncing at the club with the idea from them that I might manage it one day. But after a couple of days I began to miss the excitement of Hollywood and was itching to get back. I thanked my benefactors for their hospitality and flew back to Los Angeles.

About a week later, I met up with Elvis and the guys at Paramount Studios, where they were finishing up interiors for *Blue Hawaii*. My presence immediately put everyone on the set ill at ease. When Elvis was mad at someone, he made it intimidating for the other guys if they were friendly with the person out in the cold.

Then again, I had been guilty of this same type of behavior in the past. Whenever Elvis had a flare-up with one of the guys, I automatically took Elvis's side against the other guy. Now I was the one on the outs, and it didn't feel so hot. Go figure.

When Elvis came off the set and saw me, he stopped right away. Much to my delight, he greeted me warmly with a big hello.

"Hi boss, how ya doing?" I asked politely. We exchanged some small talk, and then Elvis motioned for me to join him inside his portable dressing room. Joe was sitting there reading one of the trade papers. When I entered, he looked shocked and bewildered. Elvis asked him to leave so we could have some privacy.

Elvis sat down in front of the dressing room mirror and looked at me in the reflection. He grinned, and then that contagious laugh burst forth.

"Sonny, you crazy sonofabitch," he said. I couldn't help it—I started laughing, too.

"Me crazy?" I asked. "It wouldn't have happened if you could hold your liquor." That broke us up all over again. When the laughter subsided, Elvis told me Gene informed him what was said that night. "It was just a misunderstanding was all," he said. He then gave me an opening to get my job back if I wanted it, but I didn't take the bait. When I didn't bite, Elvis asked me what it was I wanted to do.

"Well, I was thinking of hanging around and trying to get some work in the movies, but I know it's pretty hard," I said. "I'd like to join the Screen Extras Guild, and I need someone of influence to get me in. I thought you might be able to do that for me." I told him that a letter needed to be written by him on my behalf.

"All right, if that's what you want," Elvis said without hesitation. In no time he had the letter drawn up, and the next thing I knew, I was a card-carrying member of the guild. The other guys wanted to join the union, too, so Elvis got them in at the same time. There was a long list of people dying to get into the union, but Elvis had the clout to get me and the guys in right away, and I appreciated it. I respected him for the fact that even though we had our flare-up, he didn't hold a grudge or resent that I wanted to do something else with my life.

At that time, I thought that this was the end of the road for Elvis and me as employer and employee. We had a good run and ended our relationship on nice terms with a handshake.

It seemed like a Hollywood ending.

# Chapter 12

# Independence Day

**M**Y INDEPENDENCE FROM ELVIS DIDN'T COME AT A TERRIBLE PERSONAL PRICE because our friendship remained intact. But I did suffer a mild case of sticker shock once I got back out in the real world. When I lived under Elvis's roof I never had to pick up a check or pay for any living expenses. Elvis paid the rent and bought the food, gas, and other necessities. Now that I was on my own, I realized I needed work, and fast.

Getting a job in the entertainment business was a whole lot easier as a card-carrying member of the Memphis Mafia than not. The smartest move I made was not to burn any bridges in dealing with people in the industry. Fortunately, many of them came through for me when I was striking out on my own.

Norman Taurog heard about my falling out with Elvis and pulled me aside at the tail end of *Blue Hawaii*. If there was anything he could do for me, he said, I should give him a call. Norman never forgot how nicely I treated his children and that I always behaved professionally on his sets.

I told Mr. Taurog that Elvis got me a union card but that I needed work.

"Certainly, I can do that for you," he said. He promptly instructed his secretary to get Sheldon Shraeder on the line. Shraeder was Taurog's son-in-law as well as the first assistant director on the Western television series *The Outlaws*.

They spoke for a minute or two. Then Taurog hung up the phone, turned to me, and said, "Report to wardrobe at 7:00 AM tomorrow on the Paramount Sunset lot." Just like that, I had a steady paying gig.

*The Outlaws* starred Barton MacLane, Don Collier, Bruce Yarnell, and Slim Pickens, and was about halfway through its first season when I reported to what amounted to about three months of steady employment.

I worked five days a week and was guaranteed at least $22 a day as a utility stand-in. That went up to a whopping $24 a day if I actually worked in a scene. It doesn't sound like much, but the money helped me pay the dues on my union card, get a few acting lessons, put gas in my car, and cover the rent on my tiny efficiency in Hollywood. The days were long and the work sometimes grueling, but I was happy to be gainfully employed in a profession I truly loved.

I was so busy, in fact, that I didn't have the opportunity to witness my cousin Red's marriage to nineteen-year-old Pat Boyd in July 1961.

Pat possessed both beauty and brains, and she worked in the office at Graceland as a secretary for Vernon. Red was smitten the instant he set eyes on her, and the two have been inseparable for more than four decades.

I finally got a chance to visit with them in mid-August when Elvis shot interiors for *Follow That Dream* at Samuel Goldwyn studios. Elvis and I visited as well, and we chatted amicably. He knew I could use more work and arranged for me to be an extra in a courtroom scene. But that lasted only a few days, and like all working actors, I began to worry about when and where I would get my next job. *The Outlaws* was about to go on summer hiatus, and I was getting down to my last couple of dollars when I bumped into director Don Siegel on the Paramount lot. Siegel remembered me from *Flaming Star*, and while we made small talk I worked up the nerve to make a pitch for employment. My timing couldn't have been better. Siegel was about to shoot interiors for *Hell Is for Heroes*, a World War II ensemble piece starring Steve McQueen, Bobby Darin, Fess Parker, James Coburn, and Bob Newhart.

McQueen wasn't yet the big international superstar he was destined to become, but he was already definitive in his approach and movements, and it was interesting to watch him work. He was intense, a loner, and gave off a vibe that made it obvious that unless he expressly invited you to speak to him, you shouldn't. When he wasn't shooting a scene, he pumped weights, often joined by costar James Coburn, with the grim intensity of a guy trying to work off a lot of pent-up tension.

A few years later, I was in a limousine with Elvis on Beverly Glen as we made our way to MGM Studios when McQueen rolled up alongside us at a stoplight in an expensive sports car.

"Elvis, is that you?" McQueen said, squinting into the back of the limo. Elvis rolled down the window and said, "Hey, Steve. Whatcha doin'?" McQueen said he was working at 20th Century Fox on *The Sand Pebbles*, a movie in which his acting skills earned him a nomination for an Academy Award.

Elvis respected McQueen's work on his TV series *Wanted: Dead or Alive* and especially in the hit movie *The Great Escape*, which he screened many times at the Memphian Theatre. But I always thought Elvis was a little professionally jealous of McQueen. Steve got a lot of plum dramatic roles in the 1960s that appealed to Elvis, including *Baby, the Rain Must Fall*, which Elvis very badly wanted to do. A few years down the road, Elvis and McQueen would compete head-on for the affections of a beautiful starlet named Barbara Leigh, but I'm getting a little ahead of myself.

I had worked as an extra on *Hell Is for Heroes* for about a week when I got a phone call from Sheldon Shraeder. Coming through for me in the clutch again, Sheldon got me a long-running stint on the television series *Dr. Kildare*, starring Richard Chamberlain. Sheldon must have liked my work ethic because he also got me work in a 1965 feature film called *Joy in the Morning* starring Chamberlain and Yvette Mimieux. I was a stand-in for Richard Chamberlain for the entire shoot.

All the while I also continued my acting lessons with Cory Allen. Then, Elvis himself provided my next big break when he called me in late October to work with him on *Kid Galahad* for United Artists.

The movie, Elvis's tenth, was shot mostly on location in Idyllwild, California, about one hundred miles east of Los Angeles in the San Jacinto Mountains. The studio put Elvis up in a spacious two-story log home for the location shoot. On weekends he headed down the mountain for a little rest and recuperation in Palm Springs, where he rented a home. I stayed up on the mountain in a cabin that the studio provided for all the extras, at a local mainstay called the Hidden Lodge.

The film was actually a remake of an old Warner Brothers drama starring Edward G. Robinson, Bette Davis, and Humphrey Bogart. The story was based on a *Saturday Evening Post* serial written by Francis Wallace in 1936.

In our version, Elvis portrays Walter Gulick, who returns to his hometown in upstate New York from a stretch in the army and looks for work as an auto mechanic. But Gulick is roped into serving as a sparring partner for a local pro boxer and, of course, turns out to be the better fighter, whereupon it's good-bye auto mechanics, hello big-time boxing for our hero, dubbed "Kid Galahad." The writers tailored the role for Elvis by incorporating songs, throwing in a few fight scenes, and making sure a love story somehow found its way into the plot, making *Kid Galahad* another typical Elvis flick.

What was not typical, however, was Elvis's appearance when shooting was about to start. He shocked everyone, including me, by tipping the scales at a hefty two hundred pounds. Because it was a boxing picture, after all, he would be required to appear without a shirt in a lot of scenes. To his credit, Elvis went right into heavy training, just like a real boxer. He started running every day, hitting the punching bag, shadowboxing, and even sparring with some hired pro boxers. And he went on a high-protein diet.

I got into tip-top shape myself, because I was going to play a boxer who dukes it out with Elvis in a fight montage. But I got TKO'd by an old football injury.

Mushy Callahan, a former World Junior Welterweight Champion, served as the technical adviser on the film. I had worked out a fight scenario that he wanted to show a friend who was visiting the set.

"Sonny, let's show my buddy what you and Elvis are going to do in the ring," Mushy said, motioning me up to where the two men were standing on the stage door ramp. Mushy and I took our boxing positions, and when I threw a right punch, my left foot slid off the edge of the ramp and my knee twisted badly. I went down and my knee was locked in a position that I couldn't straighten out. Alan Fortas took me to a nearby medical clinic and, later, an orthopedic doctor. The cartilage had torn in my knee, and he couldn't get it out of the locked position. He admitted me to the hospital and the next morning performed surgery on me. Red took my place in the fight scene.

While I didn't get a chance to show my stuff in the ring, with Elvis's help and that of Colonel Parker, I still put on an Oscar-worthy performance on the set, although not in front of the cameras.

Directing *Kid Galahad* was Phil Karlson, who had worked in the business since the 1940s, directing several crime B features. He was not the director Elvis originally wanted for this film. Michael Curtiz, who directed the original *Kid Galahad* in 1937 and who had so expertly directed him in *King Creole*, was Elvis's first choice.

Undoubtedly, Karlson felt more than just a twinge of insecurity knowing this, and I didn't help matters when Colonel Parker "hypnotized" me and ordered me to dress down Karlson in front of the troops. This happened early in the shoot before Karlson knew that I was with Elvis. He thought I was just an extra, hired to work on the film.

During a break in the shooting, I walked up to Karlson in front of the entire crew and told him that his movie, if you could even call it that, stank to high heaven and was a waste of the actors' time and the studio's money.

Karlson was stunned, of course, and sat there in shock as I coolly and loudly berated him as an incompetent director and disgrace to the movie industry. Finally, he snapped out of it, glared at the lunatic in front of him, and screamed for Dave Salven or *somebody* to remove me from the set. When Dave, who was in on the joke, didn't respond, Karlson was about to go ballistic. Colonel Parker, who had this great way of laughing that caused his whole body to shake, stepped in to save the day. He told me to wake up on the count of three and snapped his fingers near my face, causing me to come out of my "trance."

"I'm sorry about that, Phil, but I had Sonny under hypnosis," the Colonel announced sheepishly. "He couldn't have said those things any other way."

The Colonel wasn't a bad little actor himself, and Karlson went for it.

"Is this true?" the director asked me. "Yes, sir, it is," I said politely. Karlson looked properly impressed. Later the Colonel let Karlson in on the joke, and instead of being upset, Karlson bought me a drink, and we had a good laugh about the incident. We got along famously for the rest of the shoot. A few years later, he even cast me in *The Wrecking Crew*, a Matt Helm movie starring Dean Martin. That part came with a big stipulation, though.

"I'll put you to work, Sonny, but promise me you won't pull any more crap," Karlson said with a grin. I dutifully agreed.

During the *Kid Galahad* shoot, Elvis got his nose a little bent out of shape by actor Charles Bronson, who portrayed Elvis's boxing coach in the movie. As he did on all of his pictures, between takes

Elvis often demonstrated his karate moves for the cast and crew. While the others at least acted impressed, Bronson never joined in the applause. That rankled Elvis big-time.

"That muscle-bound sonofabitch wouldn't know something good if it hit him right in the face," Elvis said of his craggy-faced costar. Bronson, though, was a true professional. I never heard him bad-mouth Elvis once. Both of them were able to give the impression that the two had a tremendous chemistry on screen.

Elvis got along better with actress Joan Blackman, who played his love interest in the film. Even though their off-screen romance was over after *Blue Hawaii*, the two still worked well together.

Elvis's off-camera love interest during the picture was actress Connie Stevens.

At the time, Connie's career was red hot; she was named *Photoplay*'s most popular female star for 1961. Connie's résumé included a major role in the ABC–TV detective drama *Hawaiian Eye*; she also had a Top 5 record hit with actor Edd Byrnes called "Kookie, Kookie (Lend Me Your Comb)," and a successful nightclub act.

At five feet three and 118 pounds, the pixie actress from Brooklyn was a stunner. Her trademark short blond hair, long black eyelashes, and frosted lips exuded a bubbly sexuality.

With Connie, what you saw was what you got. She was smart, sassy, not afraid to speak her mind, and genuine and warm. She was also in her early twenties and still lived with her parents.

Elvis arrived for their first date at the Stevens home on Deervale Drive in Sherman Oaks wearing a sailor's cap and lots of Old Spice. Connie's father was watering the lawn when Elvis arrived in his new Rolls-Royce Silver Cloud sedan. But it wasn't Elvis's fancy car or celebrity that won Connie's father over; rather it was the down-home Southern charm that Elvis turned loose on him. Connie eventually came out of the house to see who was making her father laugh so loudly.

While Connie was a star in her own right, it took a while for her to get used to Elvis's level of celebrity. For starters, she wasn't used to having ten other guys tag along on a date. Not exactly shy, Connie voiced her disapproval and said that from then on it had better be just the two of them.

Trouble was, Elvis was so used to having somebody else take care of details such as paying for movie tickets and buying popcorn and soda, that he didn't even know the normal dating protocol anymore. When he and Connie went to the movies on their second date, Joe had to make sure Elvis had enough cash on hand before he picked up Connie.

Then, they got to the theater a few minutes after the movie started, which was standard operating procedure so Elvis wouldn't be mobbed by other moviegoers. That's why he also always left theaters before the movie ended.

"This is a helluva way to date," Connie said to herself out loud.

Their relationship ended abruptly when Elvis sent Joe to pick up Connie one night for what she thought was going to be a quiet evening alone with Elvis. Then she discovered that several of the guys and their dates were also at the house, at which point Connie decided things weren't going to work out. But she and Elvis always remained on friendly terms. I think Connie's father took the breakup harder than his daughter, who later married and divorced actor James Stacy and singer Eddie Fisher.

Connie told Larry King in 2003 that her father always said about Elvis, "That's the boy you should have married!"

It didn't take long for Elvis to get over Connie. It happened as soon as he laid eyes on the gorgeous Elizabeth Montgomery, who happened to be *Kid Galahad* costar Gig Young's wife.

Elvis was quite taken with the future *Bewitched* star's breathtaking beauty, and he could barely contain himself. (However, nothing happened between the two of them. She was married, after all.) One night after shooting, Elvis spotted her slow dancing in the lobby of the Hidden Lodge with Bronson, who was also quite enamored of her.

Going up to Young, seated at a nearby table, Elvis told him, "Man, I have a new Rolls-Royce; I'll trade you for her."

Gig enjoyed his cocktails after the cameras stopped rolling. He looked up from his drink and quipped, "Not bad. The Rolls-Royce is a newer model."

While Gig possessed a droll and self-effacing sense of humor, he was, like most actors, basically insecure and found it hard to mask his jealously when Elvis showered his wife with undivided attention.

One afternoon while Elvis was in the boxing ring filming a scene, Elizabeth dropped by the set. Elvis perked right up, which didn't go unnoticed by Gig.

Young's verbal abuse of his wife was an almost daily occurrence, and once Elvis had to intervene when it appeared that Gig was going to strike her. Elvis privately told us that he didn't have much respect for Gig because he was a hopeless alcoholic, and he wished that one day Elizabeth would come to her senses and ditch him.

Elizabeth, who was Gig's third wife, eventually did. After six tumultuous years together, she went to Mexico for a quickie divorce. It was a good thing, too. In October 1978, Gig married his fifth wife, actress Kim Schmidt, who was thirty-three years his junior. Three weeks later, Gig shot Schmidt with a .38 revolver in a jealous rage. He then turned the gun on himself, completing the murder-suicide.

Elvis liked having his guys around to help relieve any tension, and just before we were to begin shooting the movie *Kid Galahad*, he welcomed someone else into the fold—Marty Lacker.

Marty, who is Jewish, moved to Memphis in 1952 from New York and attended Humes High School with Elvis. Although the two never really hung out with each other until a few years later, they did eventually discover they both had a passion for music.

Marty was pursuing a career in radio in the hopes of becoming a disc jockey, and he soon crossed paths with George Klein. Marty accompanied George one night during a visit to Graceland, where he and Elvis got reacquainted. Marty noted that the shy kid he knew in high school sure had come a long way.

"Yeah, God has been good to me," Elvis said humbly.

Their friendship endured through Elvis's army tenure (1958–60), and Elvis affectionately named him "Moon," after the popular Andy Williams song "Moon River"—or at least Joe's version of it, which went, "Moon Lacker, wider than the sea...." Elvis added his own lyrics: "Moon Lacker, you poor old bald-headed sonofabitch...." And that's how Marty became forevermore known as "Moon."

When Elvis discovered Marty had left his job in radio in 1961, he offered Marty the opportunity of a lifetime: to join the Memphis Mafia. Marty didn't bite at first because he was married and had a kid. Like most smart men, he realized any life-altering decisions ought to be discussed with his wife, Patsy.

Offended that Marty didn't jump on the opportunity right away, Elvis picked up a newspaper, ruffled it open, and said in a biting tone, "Well, don't think about it too damn long!"

Marty literally had one night to decide, as Elvis was leaving the next day for California to film *Kid Galahad*. Luckily for all of us who came to know him, Marty came on board.

Elvis nicknamed everybody, including Ray Sitton, who was called "Chief." Ray hung out at the gates of Graceland, and he stood out on account of his six-foot, four-inch, 380-pound frame. Whenever Elvis spotted him, he would casually say, "Hey, Chief, how's it going today?" Of course, Elvis used that nickname interchangeably with such other generic ones as "Ace" and "Hoss."

One night, everyone was in the den when one of the guys told Elvis that "Chief" had asked if he could come inside.

"Well, who the hell is that?" Elvis asked.

"Guy said you knew him, boss," came the reply.

"Hell, I call everybody 'Chief,'" Elvis said, cracking up. But he let Sitton come up to the house.

Chief was a little off, to say the least. Looking back, it's easy to see that he was socially immature and slow to pick up on a lot of subtleties within the group. Because of his size, he got picked on a lot. That probably drove him to drink too much, and he got a reputation for cornering women at parties and making them feel uncomfortable.

He also got a deserved reputation as an awful driver, because he liked to get behind the wheel of Elvis's expensive vehicles with a snoot full. It came as no surprise to anyone when Chief dinged up a few of Elvis's cars. After that, he was banned from using any of Elvis's wheels. Elvis was concerned that the Chief's drunken driving would result in an accident, a lawsuit, and a ton of bad publicity. So what did Chief do when Elvis issued that edict? He went out the very next night, got drunk, took out one of Elvis's cars, and got into an accident.

Chief also got on my bad side one night at the pool table. While Cliff and I were playing pool, Chief was drinking and began to play grab-ass with Cliff. "Keep your hands off me, Chief, or I'm going to bust you open with this pool cue," Cliff warned him. Before the situation got out of hand, I stepped in and told Chief to knock it off.

"I'm not talking to you, Sonny. This is none of your business," he said, giving me a shove. My reflexes went on automatic pilot, and I hauled off with a right-hand punch to Chief's face. The shot was so hard it launched him over the nearby sofa. When Chief got up, he was holding his head in his hands. It was a sight that I'll never forget: his nose was literally pushed to the other side of his face. One of the other guys drove Chief to the emergency room at the UCLA Medical Center, where the doctors had to set what was left of his nose twice to get it to stay in place.

You'd think that would have caused Chief to change his ways, but it didn't. He sealed his fate one night in Memphis when he got loaded in one of Elvis's cars, was pulled over by a policeman, got belligerent, and ended up in a nasty scrape with the cop. When Elvis found out about it, Chief was history.

My own friendship with Elvis was pushed to the brink during *Kid Galahad*. It started before the cameras rolled, when I arranged for a woman named Linda Rogers and her friend Nancy Czar to visit me on the set on location in Idyllwild.

Linda, whom I had dated a few times, was a struggling actress I met at the Pancake House on Sunset Boulevard, where a lot of young actors hung out. Nancy was an Olympic figure skating hopeful who later also became an actress and even dated Elvis for a little while during the filming of *Girl Happy*.

The girls and I were supposed to meet on the set on Friday afternoon, but I never connected with them. That's because when they showed up, Elvis zeroed right in on them and invited them to spend the weekend at his place in Palm Springs. I found out later that Elvis and Linda had a brief tryst, and I'm sure he pulled out all the stops to impress her.

While it bothered me that Linda had gone with him, I was more upset with Elvis for his betrayal. He could have had any woman in the world, but he honed in on my action. It wasn't the first time, either. He had stolen one of Lamar's girls once before, and he justified it by saying, "Hell, she wasn't going to do anything with Lamar anyway."

Elvis eventually noticed that I wasn't hanging around anymore on the set with them, and he asked the guys what my problem was. When nobody spoke up, Elvis sent Marty to see me. Marty approached me the next day on the set and asked why I was making myself scarce around Elvis. He assured me that it was just the guys wanting to know and that he wouldn't tell Elvis. Marty felt bad about deceiving me and later apologized, telling me that Elvis had told him to do so. I told him I understood and that it was okay.

The next day, Elvis made it a point to see me. While he didn't apologize for his behavior, he said he didn't know I was seeing Linda and that he would break it off for good.

"No, Elvis, that's fine," I said. "She obviously likes you and wants to see you, so it's okay. Really."

I couldn't stay mad at him, and in no time I was a regular visitor to Elvis's new home at 10539 Bellagio Road, just around the corner in Bel-Air. He decided to stay put for Christmas that holiday season, and he invited me along on an all-expense-paid trip to Las Vegas to ring in the New Year.

Although I wasn't officially back on the payroll, I was at least back with my friend once again. And life was beautiful.

# Chapter 13

# Possessions

**E**LVIS WAS BY NATURE A CREATURE OF HABIT, WHO LIKED AND DEPENDED ON routine—he ate the same foods, tended to have the same taste in women, pretty much drove the same cars, and hung with the same small group of friends. For all of the excitement surrounding Elvis Presley's life, there was also plenty of monotony, even boredom.

Not surprisingly, once Elvis discovered something he really liked, it was as if nothing else existed. He played his favorite records until he wore out the grooves, he dated women until they no longer held his interest, and he ate the same meals for several days in a row. Now, with *Kid Galahad* wrapping up, big changes were ahead for him.

Elvis moved from his Perugia Way place to a new rental home just around the corner at Bellagio Road before filming ended. The Mediterranean-style home was Old World opulent, with lots of marble and columns and high vaulted ceilings.

The front entrance wasn't used, but the driveway curved around to the back of the house where there was a four-car garage and a large parking area. A large entry opened to a stairway leading up to the second floor and its four bedrooms.

Off the main-level entrance, there was a large living room to the right. To the left was a dining room and kitchen with a breakfast nook, and there was another room that served as an office. Stairs led down to the huge recreation room housing a bar, pool table, and big movie screen. That's where we had most of our parties.

Elvis made the move to accommodate the ever-growing number of guys in the group. In addition to Joe, Marty, Charlie, Lamar, Alan, cousins Gene and Billy, and Chief, Elvis welcomed into the fold

Richard Davis and Jimmy Kingsley. I introduced both of them to Elvis in the early '60s when we played football on weekends.

Both guys were from Tennessee, but that's about all they had in common. Richard was easygoing and had a great sense of humor. He was one of the best dancers in Memphis, and at local sock hops the girls lined up to dance with him to the point that some of us had to tell Richard to take a cigarette break so we could get a crack at them. Elvis called him "Broom" because of his slight stature and eventually used him quite a bit as his stand-in on movie sets. Richard was a dear and very loyal friend to Elvis and me. He would go to various men's stores, pick out clothes to take to Elvis, and then return the ones Elvis didn't like. Richard instinctively knew Elvis's taste in clothes.

Jimmy was more into himself than Richard was. He was also pretty sarcastic and mouthy at times. I once saved him from a serious ass-whipping at a drive-in restaurant called Monte's on Summer Avenue in Memphis. Jimmy was running his mouth at the wrong guy, and, luckily for him, I stepped in before things got out of hand.

Jimmy was also a taker. Once he mentioned how much he liked Elvis's watches, and Elvis promptly slipped the one he was wearing off his wrist and gave it to Jimmy. Anybody else would've done a handspring in gratitude, but Jimmy made it plain that he wasn't impressed. Jimmy leaned on Elvis to get him into the Screen Extras Guild so he could work in films. That was fine, but he groused about everything and even began bad-mouthing Elvis behind his back—the kiss of death to those of us who genuinely loved our boss.

Marty didn't much like Jimmy to begin with, and one day after overhearing some of his smart-ass comments about Elvis, he suggested that Jimmy pack his bags and leave. To just about everyone's relief, Jimmy did as advised.

Another new member of the entourage was a party animal we called "Scatter," a three-foot, forty-pound chimpanzee obtained by Elvis from Memphis TV personality Captain Bill Killebrew. Scatter and his brother, "Chatter," were regulars on Captain Bill's kids show.

Elvis had Lamar, Marty, and Alan transport Scatter from Memphis to Los Angeles in a cage in back of a Chrysler station wagon. Everything was fine until they checked into a motel room in Flagstaff, Arizona, off Interstate 40.

Scatter started swinging on the window drapes and then pulled the drapes down and took a large-sized monkey dump on them.

Then Scatter scattered his own mess by flinging it all over the room. The boys locked him in and retreated to the restaurant to eat and come up with a way to explain the situation to motel management.

They hadn't gotten very far at either when Lamar looked out the window and saw the maid knocking on their room door. The guys rushed out to stop her from letting herself in, but they were too late. As they arrived at the room, the screaming maid was exiting with Scatter riding her piggyback, his legs wrapped around her waist and his hands covering her face.

The fellows managed to separate them, but then Scatter promptly clambered up a drainpipe to the roof of the motel, where he did an impression of a pint-sized King Kong, thumping his little chest and obviously enjoying the predicament.

Luckily, the guys had paid for their room in advance when they checked in. So while Alan jumped in the car and got it turned around and Lamar rolled down the back window of the station wagon, Marty ran into the office and threw the keys on the front desk. Then they slowly headed toward the exit, and Scatter, thinking he was being left behind, quickly scuttled down and dove into the back of the car for a seamless escape.

Alan pretty much ended up taking care of Scatter, and he enjoyed dressing the monkey in suits, Hawaiian shirts, and caps. Alan often tooled around the Hollywood hills with Scatter in the Rolls-Royce limousine. When other cars pulled alongside them at traffic lights, Alan would duck down out of sight, and the other drivers would glance over and freak out seeing Scatter, sporting a chauffeur's cap, apparently out for a solo drive.

Elvis liked to bring Scatter to his movie sets, but that ended the day the monkey escaped from Elvis's locked dressing room at Samuel Goldwyn Studios while we were off watching the daily rushes. A security guard found us and asked if anyone owned a chimpanzee. When Alan fessed up and assured him that Scatter was locked up, the guard begged to differ. "He's sitting at Mr. Goldwyn's desk right now," the guard said.

Sure enough, Scatter had escaped and found his way to the studio mogul's second-floor office, which he promptly trashed. When we got there, papers, mementos, and pictures were strewn everywhere, and Scatter was in Mr. Goldwyn's chair looking as though he'd just kicked Mighty Joe Young's ass.

Goldwyn had the monkey banned from the studio, perhaps making Scatter the first animal to be blacklisted in Hollywood.

Things weren't much better on the home front. Scatter tore out the phone lines at the house on Bellagio Road, and it took repairmen days to restore service. Scatter also ripped a hole in the recreation room movie screen by swinging on the drapes in front of it. But Elvis didn't go ape shit until Scatter bit his butler, Jimmy. Jimmy and his wife, Lillian, were liked by everyone, and when Jimmy threatened to walk unless Scatter was reined in, Elvis and Scatter had a man-to-monkey talk.

"You coconut-headed little bastard, you'd better get downstairs to your cage," said Elvis. "And you'd better not ever bite anybody anymore, or I'm going to ship your ass back to the jungle, and the only thing you'll ever bite is a ripe banana." Scatter got the message. He slunk away to his cage beneath the stairs, and he even closed the door behind him, whereupon Elvis fell on the floor laughing.

Usually, though, Scatter was the life of the party. Elvis liked to have people over and let them get nice and comfortable in the den before giving the signal to let Scatter out of his cage. Then, all of a sudden, would come the "Whoo-whoo-whoo" noise announcing Scatter's grand entrance. It sounded like an oncoming freight train. Like the good alpha male he was, Scatter would make a beeline for the nearest female, whose reaction was to start screaming like Fay Wray.

One time, a young aspiring songwriter and his date stayed overnight, and they were in one of the bedrooms, doing what came naturally, when Elvis decided to turn Scatter loose. He leaped onto the bed, and the poor woman started screaming. Her partner grabbed Scatter and heaved him out the door, but the lovemaking was over for the night.

One of Scatter's favorite tricks was to hide in the bathroom when one of Elvis's female guests entered to use the facilities. That was always good for an ear-splitting scream. Scatter also enjoyed lifting up skirts to peek under the hood. He did it once to Pat Parry, who was sitting at the bar. Pat took no bullshit from any man, much less a three-foot chimp. "Do that again and I'll knock the hell out of you," she warned him. When Scatter went for two, Pat jumped up and belted him with an uppercut to the chin. Scatter literally turned a back flip, landing on the couch.

Scatter loved beer, and he could throw down a glass of whiskey when he felt like switching to the hard stuff. And just like a lot of men, drinking made him horny. When soused, Scatter would lie on his back on the edge of the sofa and raise the hem of any passing girl's skirt and try to stick his head up there. With a buzz on he was also wont to play with himself in front of the ladies.

The neighbors were not fond of Elvis's pet monkey. Once Scatter got loose and chased a Japanese gardener, who jumped into the swimming pool to get away. The gardener told the owners of the house about it, and they turned in a report to the Bel-Air Home-owners Association. After they dashed off a letter to Elvis, that was the end of Scatter's run in California.

Scatter was shipped back to Graceland and spent the rest of his days in a climate-controlled building constructed especially for him. Minus the stimulating company and free rein he enjoyed in Bel-Air, Scatter turned into one mean monkey. He regularly bit the maid Daisy when she brought his food, and once he ripped the wig off her head. His untimely death, presumably by natural causes, was not cause for great mourning at Graceland.

Scatter wasn't the only one to depart from our tightly knit little group. Marty decided that all the traveling wasn't conducive to mar-riage and parenthood. He didn't like all the time spent away from his wife, Patsy, who was pregnant at the time with their son, Marc. Marty moved back to Memphis and got a job in radio doing pro-duction work for WHBQ. A few months later, he got a job in New Orleans, where he stayed for almost a year.

Lamar also temporarily left the fold. He got a great opportunity to become singer Brenda Lee's road manager, which also included doing the lights for her show. The latter experience would come in handy years later when Elvis started doing live performances. The job with Brenda went smoothly for about a year until she got married and pregnant and stopped traveling. Lamar stayed in Nashville and went to work for Hill and Range Publishing, running the Nashville office. His job was trying to find songs for Elvis to record until 1970, when he went back to work for Elvis.

Charlie Hodge also became one of the dearly departed when he accepted an offer to tour and record with veteran country singer Jimmy Wakely. Charlie returned to the fold in the mid-1960s and stayed with Elvis to the end.

Perhaps the saddest departure that year was that of Gene Smith, Elvis's cousin and closest confidant. Gene went back to Memphis to spend more time with his family.

The rest of the guys who had been around a while were starting to show signs of domesticity. Red had his own life with Pat, while Joe was married to Joan Roberts, a Las Vegas dancer he met in a revue at the Sands Hotel. Even Billy Smith was itching to get married to his childhood sweetheart, Jo.

It was around this time that Elvis discovered the *Physicians' Desk Reference*, and over time it became his personal bible, as he slowly changed from being a dabbler to being dependent on drugs.

His drugs of choice were mostly uppers—Dexedrine, Dexamyl, Escatrol, and Desbutal. But Elvis also took downers, including Valium, Percodan, Tuinal, and Seconal. Elvis's consumption and constitution were almost superhuman in those days, and the amount of pharmaceuticals he took would likely have done in any other man. In fact, it almost killed his cousin Gene.

In March 1962, Elvis bought a Dodge motor home for $10,000, and decided to drive it cross-country from Memphis to Los Angeles to start work on the movie *Girls! Girls! Girls!* for Paramount Studios.

Both Elvis and Gene had been wired for three days straight on what Elvis called "go-go pills." They were Dexedrine, a potent form of speed. Gene couldn't sit still and was driving everyone nuts. When he announced that he was going to "fix things" in the motor home, everybody was so happy to get him out of their hair, they neglected to remind him that it was brand new and didn't need any fixing.

Armed with a screwdriver, Gene went around tightening up anything he thought needed it. Elvis was driving the motor home at the time, and as they were traveling down the highway at top speed, he looked down to find his cousin fiddling with the accelerator. Elvis ordered Gene to get away and then gave him five hundred milligrams of Demerol to calm him down. When the synthetic opiate apparently had no effect on Gene, Elvis prescribed another five hundred milligrams of the stuff. Gene took the pill and went back to the bedroom.

After a while, Elvis asked Billy to go back and check on his cousin. Billy was familiar with Gene's sleeping pattern and thought Gene was breathing oddly. When he touched Gene's skin, it felt unusually cold. Frightened, Billy began to shake him. It had been only a year or so since Billy had found Junior dead, and it looked as though the same scenario was unfolding now. When Gene didn't respond to his shaking, Billy ran out of the bedroom and screamed for Elvis to pull over.

Elvis slammed on the brakes and stopped the motor home on the side of the highway. Then he, Billy, and Joe ran to the bedroom and tried to pummel Gene awake. Nothing worked, and then somebody got the idea to carry Gene outside into the freezing cold. He finally stirred, and for the next three hours they took turns walking Gene back and forth along the highway until he was out of danger. Maybe it was good that Gene left the fold.

Elvis accumulated quite a pill collection from several doctors, and the drugs made him impulsive, mercurial, and wildly unpredictable.

I'll never forget the time I asked two actresses to the Bellagio Road house for an impromptu party. The one I had my eye on was named Judy Alden. The other was Annie Marshall, the daughter of the great English actor Herbert Marshall. They were naturally thrilled by the prospect of meeting Elvis, but this time, thanks to the drugs he'd taken, he was far from his usual hospitable self.

When we got there, Elvis was shooting pool with a couple of other guys. I introduced them to Elvis and several others present, but Elvis was not his usual warm self. He paid no attention to my female guests, and he asked me to join him in a game of eight ball against the other guys. When Elvis Presley asked you to do something, it was hard to say no. So I picked up a cue. As the game progressed, Elvis grew increasingly frustrated as he missed a lot of easy shots he normally would have made.

He wasn't the only one growing frustrated. One of the girls I'd brought over, Judy, was bored. This wasn't what she had expected at all. Finally she got up and walked over to me at the table and said that she wanted to leave. She asked me politely if I would move my car, which was blocking hers in the driveway.

Her request came just as Elvis was lining up a shot, and he barked, "Sonny, what the hell does she want?"

"Nothing, boss," I replied quietly, hoping to downplay the situation. "She's leaving, and she just wants me to move my car so she can get out."

Elvis blew. "Hell, man, you're playing pool! Let her get someone else to move the car."

Judy replied, "I don't know anyone else here," and then she turned to me more determined than ever to leave. Once again, she politely asked me if I would move my car.

"Dammit!" screamed Elvis. "Didn't you hear what I said? Get someone else to move the car!"

Then it was Judy's turn to get mad. "Go to hell, you sonofabitch!" she screamed at Elvis. At that point, he threw his pool cue at Judy, striking her in the chest. She fell to the floor, and when I ran over to her, she was crying. "Why did he do that?" she whimpered. "I never did anything to him." I didn't have a ready answer. Elvis did have a bad temper, but he would never do something like that to a woman if he wasn't under the influence of something. On this night he had taken some uppers.

Although clearly stunned and disgusted by his own behavior, Elvis could not bring himself to come over and apologize. I calmed Judy down, walked her outside, and told her how very sorry I was. She asked once again why Elvis would do that to her, and I replied that he was under a lot of stress. Judy stated he was in the wrong, and then she and Annie got in her car and drove off. We never dated again, but I did see her around over the years, and we never discussed what happened.

Amazingly, Judy never sued Elvis. I hate to admit this, but none of us would have backed her up. To this day, I don't feel good about that statement.

Elvis's movie obligations usually kept him on the straight and narrow. They required him to keep fairly normal hours and stay focused on the task at hand. He took his movie roles and preparation seriously.

While I wasn't around for Elvis's next two movies, *Girls! Girls! Girls!* and *It Happened at the World's Fair*, I knew the work was a welcome distraction from his everyday life. Not that his life was a shambles then, but it was easy for Elvis to get overstimulated. Everything he ever wanted was his for the taking—houses, cars, women, friends, luxury items. It was all too easy. Self-indulgence became his outlet and, over time, his greatest enemy.

I think that's exactly why he allowed a young lady named Priscilla Ann Beaulieu to reenter his life, and he started entertaining the idea of "settling down." On its face, that was as about as absurd as trying to become celibate in a brothel. At the start, at least, Priscilla represented a new conquest for Elvis, and it was a relationship he pursued with vigor.

The pair had traded transatlantic phone calls, letters, and pictures for two years. Elvis had proudly shown us pictures of Priscilla every now and then. Her natural beauty was undeniable. Her age, however, was a whole different matter—especially in the eyes of the law.

When they had met two years earlier, Priscilla was fourteen and Elvis twenty-four. Like the song Elvis would sing a few years later, that spelled "T-R-O-U-B-L-E."

An even more bizarre situation involving a young girl had famously derailed fellow Memphian Jerry Lee Lewis's red-hot career a few years before. Lewis had married his thirteen-year-old cousin Myra Gale Brown and the revelation of their marriage was a public relations disaster. Tours were canceled, Jerry Lee's records were blacklisted from radio playlists, and his fee for personal appearances dropped from $10,000 a night to $250. He was reduced to playing one-night stands in seedy bars and juke joints to pay the bills.

Colonel Parker had spent lots of energy convincing Elvis not to get married to Anita Wood, who was still in the picture and hoping that Elvis would come around. But that changed when Anita herself found letters to Elvis from Priscilla stuck in the pages of a book lying around his house.

It's a pretty good bet that the Colonel almost swallowed his cigar when he found out that Elvis was determined to bring Priscilla, then sixteen, to the States from her home in Germany. That required some intense negotiations with her father, Captain Paul Beaulieu. He was naturally a little leery of Elvis's intentions with his teenage stepdaughter, but the King's natural charisma and unfailing politeness broke down the captain's defenses. Beaulieu even took a leave of absence from his military duties to accompany Priscilla when Elvis sent two first-class plane tickets for L.A.

The Beaulieus stayed at the Bel-Air Sands Hotel. At the house on Bellagio Road, Elvis issued a stunning edict: no more parties. He did, however, encourage the guys who were married to bring their spouses around to his suddenly family-friendly abode. Elvis poured on the hospitality, making sure Priscilla and Captain Beaulieu were taken in his Rolls-Royce to all the famous sightseeing spots in Los Angeles and on scenic ocean-side drives in Malibu. He fervently promised Captain Beaulieu that he would see that Priscilla received the best education available, and he openly expressed his desire to marry her—but only when she was old enough.

Within a few months, Priscilla was a permanent fixture in his life. But permanent doesn't mean without change.

# Chapter 14

# Live-In Lolita

I'VE NEVER HAD A SINGLE DOUBT THAT ELVIS PRESLEY LOVED PRISCILLA Beaulieu. But to this day I still have my doubts that he wanted to marry her after they were together for several years. When the time finally came, the ol' U.S. Male got a touch of what is commonly referred to as "cold feet."

That's no knock against Priscilla but merely a factual statement about where Elvis was at that time in his life. He was the lion of the jungle, and he wanted to roar in that vast Hollywood forest of beautiful women. Young, handsome, and sexy, Elvis was on top of the world. He was the King of Rock and Roll and the world's most famous celebrity, and with that came a go-go lifestyle that he really dug.

To say that Elvis loved women is like saying the president of the United States has a powerful job. The world was one big tasty smorgasbord of opportunities for Elvis, and he wanted to sample it all. He never wanted to settle down in the prime of his career, if ever.

So why, then, did Elvis eventually marry Priscilla? It was a combination of things. If she had been a local girl, he wouldn't have had to make special arrangements for her to live in Memphis as his live-in Lolita. But because she lived out of the country and was underage to boot Elvis had to fight tooth and nail to get his way.

Elvis was also fascinated with the idea of molding a young lady into the woman of his dreams. I believe in his head he had a specific fantasy female in mind, and he proceeded to cast Priscilla in that mold. When you compare Priscilla, Ann-Margret, Debra Paget, Anita Wood, and many of the other women he was attracted to, there are quite a few similarities. Their physical shapes and sizes were strikingly similar. In addition to having great figures and beautiful faces, they were mostly petite and had soft features. Elvis dictated the style of clothes, hair, and makeup Priscilla wore. He was sculpting her into his vision of the ideal woman.

Over the years, Priscilla has stated that she and Elvis rarely had any privacy due to the omnipresence of the Memphis Mafia. I recollect it in a different way. Anytime Elvis wanted private time with a woman, all he had to say was, "Well, guys, it's about that time." That was our signal to disappear. What Priscilla never came to terms with was that Elvis chose to have us around. There were times when he wanted some private time with her and they had it, but it was only when he wanted. That obviously wasn't enough for Priscilla. It was that way before she came into the picture and while she was there, and it was that way after she left.

The fact is, he didn't even want Priscilla living with him in Los Angeles and cramping his freewheeling bachelor lifestyle. He wanted his princess tucked safely away in the castle at Graceland. Elvis always liked to have us guys around him. It sounds like I'm tooting my own horn, but we meant too much to him. We were a lifeline in his insane world of megastardom, and Elvis needed us.

I think Priscilla obviously thought that Elvis would change after they married and had Lisa Marie, but he didn't. Not for Priscilla or any of the women who followed in her footsteps. He was who he was.

Priscilla herself changed quite a bit over the years. In the beginning she was shy, sweet, demure, and extremely sensitive around the guys. She was understandably nervous about her new life and what to expect from Elvis. What sixteen-year-old wouldn't have been? At the same time, she was very sophisticated for her years without being uppity. She had a nice, easy charm about her, and she fit right in.

When Priscilla arrived on the scene, she had a delicate China doll quality to her. The first time I saw her, she was wearing a white sailor's outfit with her hair pulled back in a ponytail. Her appearance would dramatically change after Elvis got a hold of her. He took a fresh-scrubbed teenage schoolgirl and transformed her into a vixen. Elvis insisted that she dye her hair jet black to make her blue eyes stand out more and have it teased high into a beehive do. He also had her painted with enough heavy makeup, eyeliner, and mascara to rival Elizabeth Taylor in *Cleopatra*.

Elvis also took great pains to shield Priscilla from the public and, sometimes, even his friends. One night in Memphis, after we all took in a movie at the Memphian Theatre, it was back to Graceland for the night. Jerry Schilling went to the kitchen to fix himself a snack, and he bumped into Priscilla. They struck up a friendly conversation that was abruptly terminated after a few minutes when Elvis stormed in.

"What the hell are you two doing down here?" he shouted. "Cilla, you don't need to be roaming around here late at night!"

As Elvis prepared to march her back to their room, he turned to Jerry and said, "If you want to keep your job, son, mind your own damn business."

He made it clear that Priscilla was not to enter any room in which other males were present unless Elvis was already there. Any violation of that mandate let her in for the third degree. What was she doing there? Who engaged whom in conversation first? What did they talk about, and why did it go on for so long? Elvis was so possessive, anyone would've thought it was Priscilla, instead of him, who was the serial dater.

Elvis enrolled her in Immaculate Conception High School, an all-girls Catholic school on Central Avenue at Belvedere Boulevard in Memphis. She was forbidden to have classmates over to the house lest her cohabitation with Elvis become public knowledge. Nevertheless, some of Priscilla's friends did discover what was going on, but somehow this never made it into the newspapers.

Once they were nearly busted when a local reporter spotted Elvis and Priscilla on a motorcycle in the parking lot of Chenault's restaurant. Elvis had his own separate back entrance to a private room he often reserved there. Elvis turned on his megawatt charm and told the reporter that Priscilla was the daughter of an army officer who had befriended Vernon and his wife, Dee, and had sent her Stateside so she could graduate from high school on schedule. At the time, she was living with Vernon and Dee. Elvis told the newshound that he was just taking her out for a milkshake. The reporter flipped his notebook shut.

Hollywood gossip columnist Rona Barrett and *Memphis Press-Scimitar* reporter Bill Burk knew the real story, but they were acquainted with Elvis and never made a peep about Priscilla.

It was an era when even the White House press corps turned a blind eye to President John F. Kennedy's many Oval Office dalliances.

I doubt that Elvis's secret relationship would remain a secret very long in today's era of "gotcha" journalism and paparazzi ambushes. But it was vastly different in those days.

Priscilla's after-school activities were strictly limited and monitored. One day she was chastised for playing with her toy poodle, Honey, on the front lawn.

Vernon forbade Priscilla from entering his office in the back, and she usually visited with Minnie Mae or the wives of the men who worked for Elvis. She also spent time bowling, seeing movies, or grabbing a hamburger and milkshake at Leonard's Drive-In, a famous Memphis hangout at the corner of Bellevue and McLemore.

She also spent hours with Elvis's double first cousin, Patsy Presley, on shopping sprees. Priscilla developed a great love for spending Elvis's money, in spite of Vernon's grumping about the bills.

With Priscilla ensconced at Graceland, Elvis went back to work on *Fun in Acapulco*. You'd think from the sound of it that the movie was shot on an exotic beach location south of the border, with lots of sun and gals in bikinis. The bikini beauties were there, all right, but we never set foot in Mexico. There was a great urban myth that grew up in the late 1950s about Elvis disparaging Mexicans as a nationality and talking about their "black, greasy hair." Because Elvis's own locks were black and greasy, it's preposterous to think he would ever say such a thing. But somebody who obviously hated Elvis spread that slander, and his name became mud in Mexico. Radio stations there boycotted his records, and one even organized a rally to which people brought albums and pictures of Elvis to toss into a bonfire. Somebody even took out a full-page newspaper ad urging "Death to Elvis Presley!" The FBI had a copy in its file on Elvis.

Everything came to a head in October 1962, when a riot broke out at a screening of *G.I. Blues*, resulting in a total ban on Elvis movies in Mexico. It also moved Colonel Parker to arrange with Paramount Studios to have *Fun in Acapulco* made in Hollywood. Some second-unit background shots were filmed in Acapulco, with a brave actor doubling for Elvis.

The script itself was totally safe and predictable. Elvis played Mike Windgren, a former trapeze artist who developed a fear of heights after the fatal fall of his brother and partner. Windgren trades in his life in the circus for a little fun and sun as a lifeguard at an Acapulco resort.

Elvis's love interest in the film was Ursula Andress, one of the silver screen's most seductive ingénues of that time. Fresh from her turn as Honey Rider in *Dr. No*, in which she tantalized audiences by strolling on the beach in a sexy white bathing suit, the Swiss-born siren was instructed by Paramount Studios pooh-bahs to tone down her sensuality this time. She was forbidden to use lipstick or mascara; was told to wear a wholesome, Sandra Dee–type ribbon in her hair; and was not paraded around in a bikini.

Ursula went along with the program in front of the cameras, but off-screen she let it all hang out in hopes of snaring private time with her costar. Elvis didn't tumble to her overtures for several reasons, including the fact that Ursula was married to actor-turned-director-turned-photographer John Derek, who had shot pictures of his wife in a layout for *Playboy*. John still had his matinée idol looks, but that didn't stop his wife from setting her cap for Elvis. But Elvis didn't much care for messing with married women. Besides, Ursula wasn't Elvis's type. He liked demure, petite women. Ursula had sharp features, broad shoulders, and wide hips. Demure she was not.

Alan, on the other hand, was as nuts for Ursula as he had been for Tuesday Weld. He was the proud owner of the *Playboy* featuring Ursula bared, and he spent hours on end ogling her assets. Alan even offered to hold the lights if she ever decided to pose for her husband again.

Ursula actually took him up on his offer, calling him early one morning with the news that a sexy shoot was getting under way and that her husband needed Alan's beefy muscles to hold the lights and reflectors. Alan raced to their house in record time, managing not to trip over his own tongue, or anything else. When he got there, John Derek took him aside to explain what he was to do, and then out walked Ursula wearing a football jersey and blue jeans and licking an ice cream cone.

"Ursula, don't ever call me again to take pictures," said the deflated Alan, drawing loud guffaws from her and John.

Obviously Derek didn't mind a good joke, but when it came to Ursula, his possessiveness was scary. Elvis couldn't help but notice Derek constantly glaring at him on the set, and what really threw Elvis for a loop was the car Derek gave his wife. On the steering wheel was engraved: "Baby, you're indispensable."

Unfortunately for Derek, the feeling wasn't mutual. She'd reportedly had affairs with several actors, including James Dean, and made no secret of her hots for Elvis.

"Guys, don't leave me alone with her in the dressing room," Elvis said early in the shoot. "I always want one of you in here with me." I was with him there once when Ursula walked in, and I decided to have a little fun.

"Well, boss," I said, "I've got to go get something to eat at the commissary."

"Oh, hell, you can eat later, Sonny," he said to me with more than a trace of alarm. "But I'm hungry, boss," I said. "Elvis, let Sonny go eat," chimed in Ursula. Elvis shot me a look indicating if I left I should not come back. After watching Elvis squirm for a few more moments, I decided to let him off the hook and stay.

Ursula wasn't the only one wanting a piece of Elvis during the shoot. In a scene in which Elvis makes a high dive into the ocean, the script called for him to emerge triumphantly from the water and be hoisted into the air by six men and carried to the dining veranda. The scene should have been done in one take, but Elvis was blowing the shot by twisting and turning around as the guys carried him off. He came over to us and said in exasperation, "One of those guys keeps putting his hand on me down there. I thought the first time it was an accident, but the next take, damned if it didn't happen again. That hand is moving, and he doesn't let go!"

Somebody spilled the beans to assistant director Mickey Moore, who knew most of the extras in the scene. He immediately suspected who had the roving hand. He went up to the guy and said there were too many people in the shot and told him to sit it out. The next take went just fine.

The crotch-grabbing extra wasn't the only problem on the set. Actors Elsa Cárdenas and Alejandro Rey were in the doghouse with director Richard Thorpe for screwing up their lines. Both Latino actors spoke broken English and had trouble getting their dialogue straight. Thorpe had directed more than one hundred films (including *Jailhouse Rock*), and one day his patience ran out. "Jesus Christ!" he shouted at Cárdenas and Rey. "Can't you get the lines right?"

When word of Thorpe's outburst got back to Elvis, he took the sixty-seven-year-old director aside and said, "Mr. Thorpe, those people were hired to do the part and were hired specifically to speak the way they do. They are working very hard to get it right. I don't think they should be yelled at because of their difficulty with the English language, which the producers knew about when they were hired.

144

We'll work with them if we have to, but don't make them feel bad."

To his credit, Thorpe apologized to the two actors, and the movie commenced without any further problems. To me, that epitomized the Elvis who never failed to show proper respect for older people and could always be counted on to root for, and protect, the underdog.

When principal photography for *Fun in Acapulco* finished in March 1963, Elvis rushed back to Memphis and into Priscilla's awaiting arms. They resumed their Pygmalion type of relationship, with Elvis as teacher and Priscilla as his ever-willing pupil. He taught her his likes and dislikes, how to walk with proper posture, and how he wanted his lady to dress.

The last item was particularly important. One time, Priscilla came down in a patterned dress and was lectured for looking "too distracting." Solid colors were preferable, she was told, except for brown, dark green, and anything khaki.

Elvis watched her every move like a hawk and reviewed every word out of her mouth. It was exhausting, especially when her presence was required at all of Elvis's parties, jaunts to the skating rink, amusement park visits, and all-night film festivals. With school during the day, Priscilla probably would never have managed it all without help from Elvis's bottomless supply of Dexedrine, which fueled a lot of our boundless energy in those days. Elvis also turned her on to Placidyl to help her sleep.

While I'm not one to discuss what goes on behind another couple's closed doors, I don't consider myself bound by that convention given Priscilla's claim that Elvis wanted her to save herself for marriage. In her autobiography, *Elvis and Me*, she claims that they were never intimate until their May 1967 wedding. Yet she also says that before she and Elvis were married they did sexual role-playing using pictures, videotape, and even other teenage girls. Under the circumstances, it's hard for me to believe she was still a virgin in their wedding bed. But maybe she used the same definition of sex as former president Bill Clinton did during his impeachment mess.

Let me state for the record that Elvis never shared with me any details about what went on in the bedroom between him and Priscilla. Having said that, I do know that Elvis practiced the early withdrawal method to prevent impregnating his sex partners. I don't think it was mere coincidence that Priscilla gave birth nine months to the day of their wedding. It leads me to believe one of two things: their wedding night was the first time he never withdrew prematurely, or they never had that kind of sex until that night. Another thought to keep in mind is that Priscilla was under legal age for the first few years at Graceland, and he definitely did not want to get her pregnant. Priscilla has always maintained they never consummated their relationship until their wedding night. Because Elvis never said anything about their sex life, I'll accept what she says. But knowing him as I did, something else was going on besides some private and personal Polaroid picture taking.

While Priscilla had almost slave-like devotion to Elvis, his commitment to her was not the same. He still got phone calls and letters from Anita Wood, which drove Priscilla insanely jealous. He also got pestered by the indomitable Ursula Andress, who always asked for Alan as a way around Priscilla's radar. Whenever Elvis was in Hollywood, he felt free to cast a wide net. It was a double standard he freely embraced, and if the shoe had been on the other foot, Priscilla would have been out of the picture with the snap of his finger. That would change later.

But Priscilla's competition for Elvis wasn't just other Southern belles and sexy Hollywood starlets. She constantly had to vie for his attention when he was around the guys with whom he spent so much of his time. Elvis was as much a man's man as he was a sex symbol to women. Men who got to know him admired him very much. I remember one night in Las Vegas when football star Joe Namath showed up at one of Elvis's shows. Elvis turned to Priscilla and said, "Honey, you go along now and I'll catch up with you later. Tonight's gonna be a men's night."

Elvis consciously created an ultracompetitive atmosphere around himself in which everyone jockeyed for his time and approval. Some in our group tried hard to curry favor with the boss, constantly plotting to ride in the car with him to the movie lot, to the recording studio, or even on a simple pleasure ride to the Sunset Strip.

Priscilla learned early that it was not a good idea to offer an opinion unless it was expressly asked for. After Elvis played her a few of his latest records, she asked him, "Why don't you ever play rock and roll anymore, like you did in *Jailhouse Rock*?"

"Goddammit!" Elvis erupted. "I didn't ask for your opinion on what style I should sing. I asked if you liked the song, that's all. I get enough amateur opinions as it is." Then he stomped off to his bedroom, slammed the door, and sulked for a few hours.

Slowly but surely, Priscilla found her place in the household. She made sure the temperature was always to Elvis's liking, that his meals were properly prepared by the cooks, and that she was always back from school by 3:00 PM. When Elvis got out of bed, Priscilla made sure that his Spanish omelet, pound of bacon, orange juice, and coffee were ready when he emerged from his bedroom.

At night, they created their own private universe. They took their meals in Elvis's room, watched television, read, listened to music, had pillow fights, played hide-and-seek, talked baby talk to one another, and, with visual aids, explored their sexual fantasies through role-playing.

So used to being catered to by his mother, Elvis, at last, had a suitable replacement in Priscilla, and their relationship blossomed. To use an old military term, Priscilla had adapted and overcome. She learned to laugh when Elvis laughed, kept out of his way when he was in a foul mood, and, like the rest of us, was on call twenty-four hours a day.

Given the load she had to bear, it was quite a feat when Priscilla graduated from high school. Elvis rewarded her on graduation day with a brand-new red Corvair. As proud of her as he was, Elvis was also proud to have kept his word to Captain Beaulieu that his daughter would graduate.

Elvis then allowed Priscilla to enroll in the Patricia Stevens Finishing School, figuring it would be a pleasant diversion that would only enhance his wife-to-be. Priscilla got runway experience modeling the latest fashions for a swanky Memphis boutique. Modeling held only a passing interest for Priscilla, who decided that dancing was the true outlet for her self-expression and creativity. She took lessons at a local studio and learned interpretational and modern jazz dance as well as ballroom dancing. A quick study, Priscilla soon mastered the cha-cha, tango, waltz, fox-trot, and jitterbug.

She also started going with Patsy Lacker to gospel music concerts at the Memphis Auditorium. Priscilla became rather infatuated with Mylon LeFevre, a seventeen-year-old singer in the Southern Gospel Quartet, and she often visited with the good-looking blond singer backstage. That was risky, given that Elvis always made sure that family and friends reported to him about where she went and whom she saw. Priscilla somehow failed to mention to LeFevre that she was Elvis's girlfriend. He found out on his own and made himself scarce.

While Priscilla never acted on her feelings for LeFevre, Elvis had no hesitation pursuing anyone to whom he was attracted. He proved that anew when he met his distaff equivalent, the one everyone called "the female Elvis."

# Chapter 15

# The Female Elvis

IN EARLY 1963, COLONEL PARKER INKED A LANDMARK DEAL WITH METRO-Goldwyn-Mayer Studios that made Elvis Presley the highest-paid actor on the planet.

While Elizabeth Taylor reportedly received $1 million to star in the epic stink bomb *Cleopatra*, the Colonel quietly got Elvis $1 million per film *plus* 50 percent of the profits. The terms of the contract demanded one film a year for four years, which guaranteed Elvis's long-term financial stability.

One of the big perks of Elvis's contract was the opportunity to work with the lovely and talented Ann-Margret in his first MGM film under the new agreement, *Viva Las Vegas*.

Fresh from her breakout role in the film version of *Bye Bye Birdie* (loosely based on Elvis's induction into the army), the sultry Swede was the biggest female star in Hollywood. Dubbed "the female Elvis" by the media because of her high energy, vivacious personality, and mesmerizing effect on members of the opposite sex, Ann-Margret was considered the perfect woman by every man with eyes in his head.

Discovered by comedian George Burns a few years earlier, her ascension to the top was fast and meteoric. With only a few films to her credit—*A Pocketful of Miracles* (which is where I first spotted her as I was an extra on the film) and *State Fair*—it was *Bye Bye Birdie* that truly showcased her talents as an actress, singer, and dancer and introduced her to American audiences as a sizzling new sensation.

When the male and female Elvises were introduced at the studio for publicity shots, both were formally dressed. Elvis sported a suit and tie, while Ann wore a double-buttoned white turtleneck with her hair up. When they met face-to-face for the first time, they each said the exact same thing: "I've heard a lot about you."

A few days later, Elvis and Ann serenaded each other in the studio when they sang two duets in the movie and its soundtrack—"The Lady Loves Me" and "You're the Boss."

Despite their six-year age difference and the fact they were born in different countries, the two had similar personalities and qualities.

Both hailed from simple backgrounds and were shy around people they didn't know. But singing and performing transformed them into almost wild, sensual beasts.

"We both shared a devil within," Ann wrote of Elvis in her 1994 memoir. "At heart Elvis was no saint or king but rather a kid. We were soul mates, shy on the outside, but unbridled within."

The electricity between them was instant and could have easily lit up the unplugged Vegas Strip on a Saturday night for several hours. It was a high-voltage love affair almost from the start, despite the fact that Elvis had Priscilla stashed away at Graceland, while Ann was dating someone else I knew, Burt Sugarman, back in Los Angeles. Burt lived in the same apartment building I did on Fountain Avenue. He wasn't in the entertainment business at the time but ran a high-priced exotic car business on Wilshire Boulevard in Beverly Hills. Later, he became the producer of the successful late-night TV concert series called *The Midnight Special*.

Ironically, he also later became the personal manager of Priscilla Presley, but he could never make a real go of her career. Today he is married to the beautiful Mary Hart, longtime host of *Entertainment Tonight*.

This was clear: once Elvis and Ann met, Priscilla and Burt were, at least for the moment, out of the picture.

In my opinion, *Viva Las Vegas* was the best and most fun film experience of Elvis's movie career. He was in tremendous spirits because he was in love with someone who appeared to be his physical and spiritual equal. Not only was Ann beautiful and extremely talented, but she was also a wonderful lady. We were all just crazy about her.

Playful, funny, and intelligent, Ann was a good sport and fit right in with us guys. When Ann was at the house, everybody had a great time as a group. Whenever Elvis wanted to be alone with her, he'd give us the "It's about that time, guys," line, and we'd say goodnight and leave. They had all the privacy they wanted, when they wanted it.

I'll never forget when Alan asked Ann in front of Elvis if she would run around the block four times and lend him her pants. After a moment of silence, Ann and Elvis simultaneously threw back their heads and boomed with laughter. Alan had a wacky, inoffensive humor that put everybody at ease. Anybody else who had said what Alan did to Ann—and also Tuesday Weld and Hope Lange, by the way—would have probably been put through a window by Elvis. But Alan was like a big teddy bear, and everybody loved him.

We called Ann "Rusty," which was her character's name in the film, and also a reference to her beautiful and wild red mane of hair. Elvis called Ann "Scoobie" and "Bunny," although I'm at a loss to tell you why.

Ann was secure enough about herself that she didn't seem to mind vying for Elvis's attention, and I think she actually enjoyed being surrounded by a lot of men. Not that Elvis wanted us around that much, all of a sudden.

In Vegas we occupied the entire twenty-eighth floor of the Sahara Hotel, with Elvis encamped in the Presidential Suite (compliments of owner Milton Prell). Ann's room was a few floors below. But it didn't take long for her to trek upstairs on weekends when she and Elvis holed up in his suite. Usually they opened the door only for room service. Big surprise.

One time Red and Lamar tried to smoke them out by lighting a newspaper on fire and shoving it under the door. When they finally did come up for air, Elvis and Ann would take off on motorcycles (Ann was an accomplished rider). One of the rare times they ventured out together in public was at the New Frontier Hotel to catch Clara Ward's act. The owner of the place hailed from Memphis and had been bugging Elvis to come over. He and Ann were seated right before Clara's show, but their waitress was one of the few people in town who didn't recognize Ann, and she made the mistake of demanding to see identification before serving Ann a drink.

Elvis was so bothered that he abruptly rose and made for the door. When the owner approached to find out what the problem was, Elvis exploded.

"Let me tell you something," he said. "If I ever come back to this goddamn hotel again, you tell the waitress never to ask anybody I'm with for any f——ing identification!"

The Elvis-Ann romance hit its first rough patch when the filming of *Viva Las Vegas* switched to a Los Angeles soundstage. Elvis noticed that director George Sidney was spending more time on Ann's production numbers during rehearsals. He suspected that Sidney was infatuated with his costar, which was a major understatement. When Elvis saw in the dailies that Ann was getting plenty of flattering close-ups while he was relegated to window dressing, he was certain that something was up. Also, a lot of time and effort was put into her song-and-dance numbers per Sidney's direction. Elvis's scenes were simpler with hardly any production.

Of course, Ann had nothing to do with what was going on. It was Sidney who had decided on his own to make her the star of the movie—both the public one and his own private reel. I never saw proof, but the big rumor was that Sidney once had a cameraman shoot a four-minute close-up of Ann's bottom.

Sidney and Ann had a history. He had directed her in *Bye Bye Birdie*, and the way the story went was that when Ann signed on, her role in the movie was actually quite small. Janet Leigh was the big female lead. But by the end of the picture Ann's had grown into a full-blown feature role with many close-ups, thanks to director Sidney's machinations.

At the conclusion of a studio screening of the film, while the other stars of the movie—Dick Van Dyke, Bobby Rydell, Maureen Stapleton, Ed Sullivan, and Paul Lynde—dutifully clapped, Janet Leigh walked up to Sidney, slapped his face, and called him a "son-ofabitch."

Now history seemed to be repeating itself on the set of *Viva Las Vegas*. Elvis really didn't mind that Ann was getting more face time on camera, but he did object to the underhanded diminution of his role. So he put in a call to Colonel Parker to do some serious damage control.

The Colonel came down like a ton of bricks on producer Jack Cummings, the son-in-law of legendary Louis B. Mayer, the studio's former iron-fisted boss.

"Ann-Margret may be a big star right now," the Colonel told Cummings, "but Elvis pays the freight!"

When the smoke cleared, the close-ups were divided equally between the two stars, and Sidney was ordered to delete a duet on "You're the Boss" in which Ann really vamped it up for the cameras.

None of this, by the way, had the slightest effect on the personal relationship of the two megastars. In fact, Elvis's next move was to press Colonel Parker to take over management of Ann's career.

Ann was unhappy with her incumbent manager and was looking for new representation. When Elvis found out, he went right over to the Colonel's place at the Wilshire-Comstock Apartments. Parker's wife, Marie, answered his knock and told Elvis the Colonel was at his office on the Paramount Studios lot. Rather than going over there, Elvis asked Marie to summon the Colonel to their apartment.

When he arrived, Elvis told him Ann-Margret was outside in the car and was quite upset, and then he added, "I'm very unhappy about this, Colonel, and if I don't feel better, I'm going to go back to Memphis."

The Colonel knew that pulling up stakes in the middle of a picture could get you blackballed in Hollywood for good.

"You're on a picture, Elvis," Parker said. "You gave your word."

"I don't care," Elvis replied. "Ann's out there crying, and she needs you to manage her."

The Colonel's mind went into overdrive. He knew not to embarrass Elvis or try any kind of power play at the moment. The best way to deflect Elvis's request was to appeal to his ego. The master bit down on his cigar and went to work.

"Elvis, I have been asked by other stars to manage them, and I have always turned them down," Parker said. "But since you asked me to do this for Ann, I will do it—just as long as you know that from now on I'll have to devote 50 percent of my time to Ann. That would only be fair to her, right?"

The old sharpshooter scored a bull's-eye. Elvis thought for a moment and then, narrowing his eyes, said: "Okay, Colonel, let's just forget the whole deal. I will tell her that you just have so much to do managing me that you don't think it would be fair to her."

The Colonel was one shrewd customer.

But the good times rolled on for Elvis and Ann. Once he picked her up at MGM and they went riding on Elvis's Harley. Only he didn't check the gas, and they ran out at the corner of Venice Boulevard and Overland. Luckily enough, there was a gas station right there. Unluckily enough, Elvis didn't have a cent on him, and neither did Ann. So they did what any stars would do in that situation: they bartered their autographs in exchange for a tank of gas. The next day, Elvis dispatched Joe to the station to pay the owner in full.

It didn't take long for the scandal sheets to get wind of the torrid affair, and pretty soon the gossip columns were rife with predictions that a marriage was imminent. That idea was fueled by a studio publicity photo that showed Elvis and Ann getting hitched at the Little Church of the West in Vegas. It was a still from the final scene in *Viva Las Vegas*, but to the press it was a harbinger of things to come.

Naturally this was very upsetting to Priscilla, who devoured every article she could get her hands on, including a Hedda Hopper column in the *Memphis Press-Scimitar* that went on at length about the hot and heavy romance between the male and female Elvises.

She promptly called Elvis to get it straight from the horse's mouth. "Hell, no!" he replied when Priscilla asked if there was anything going on with him and Ann. "I have told you how it works—the studios like to generate publicity for the movies so they invent these stories. Ann comes around to ride motorcycles and hang out with the guys every once in a while, but that's all."

When the movie wrapped in early September, Elvis returned to Memphis. Ann called him regularly, but at Vernon's place on Dolan Street, about a block from Graceland. When he signed to make *Kissing Cousins* in Los Angeles, Priscilla pleaded with Elvis to let her tag along. Surprisingly, Elvis relented.

Then it really hit the fan when a UPI news story from London, where Ann was attending the royal premiere of *Bye Bye Birdie*, quoted her as admitting she was in love with Elvis and claiming that they were engaged to get married.

I have my doubts about the authenticity of the story. I've seen Ann interviewed by Johnny Carson, Jay Leno, and David Letterman and on many other talk shows, and she never talks about Elvis because their relationship was very personal to her and she has too much class. I'd be surprised if it was different when she was in London.

But the story still went out and caused a tidal wave of publicity that Elvis couldn't fend off, and it caused him to break his own golden rule. "Even if you're caught in the act, never admit to it," he always advised.

Now he conceded to Priscilla that he and Ann had engaged in a brief affair. Then, on the advice of Colonel Parker, he sent Priscilla back to Graceland, out of reach of the press.

Elvis never told us why or how it happened, but his romance with Ann ended abruptly. My understanding is that Elvis invoked the promise he had made to Captain Beaulieu to marry his daughter. He may not have been monogamous, but Elvis Presley was a man of his word.

I have no doubt that Elvis loved Ann. But deep down he knew she wouldn't ever take a backseat to his career, and rightfully so. Ann was going to be a major superstar in her own right, and nobody knew it more than Elvis.

As a son of the Deep South, Elvis had definite ideas about what his wife's role should be. And it wasn't a starring role. That was for him alone. I remember when director Hal Wallis, who produced many of Elvis's films, met Priscilla. Taken with her beauty, he asked if she was interested in a movie career. Elvis answered with a resounding "No!" and from then on, for the most part, kept Priscilla off his movie sets.

Going back to when I first met him in 1958, Elvis was always possessive of his women. I was the same way. So were all the guys who tried to take a poke at Elvis over the years because they were jealous of his effect on their wives and girlfriends.

A week after Elvis married Priscilla, Ann married actor Roger Smith of 77 *Sunset Strip* fame. Roger took over her career and pretty much gave up his own. She went on to become an international star and earned an Oscar nomination for best supporting actress in the 1971 film *Carnal Knowledge*. Ann also appeared in several high-profile TV specials and became a hugely successful act in Vegas.

Before every opening engagement, she received flowers from Elvis. They remained close friends until the day he died.

*Viva Las Vegas* preserved their passionate affair on celluloid and gilded their status as box-office dynamos. The picture was one of Elvis's biggest movies ever. The impact of the movie in Sin City more than forty years after its initial release is remarkable. Still shots of Elvis and Ann singing and dancing adorn the walls of many Las Vegas casinos today.

*Kissin' Cousins* was at the opposite end of the spectrum. With all the distractions in his life then, I'm not even sure Elvis read the script before agreeing to make the film. Of course, he would have had to make the movie anyway as he didn't have script approval in his contract. Still, it was easily his worst film to date.

Elvis reported for work in Big Bear, California, in mid-October. Nestled in the San Bernardino National Forest and close to seven thousand feet in elevation, the location offered breathtaking views of the mountains and Big Bear Lake. Not so majestic, though, was the movie script, which called for Elvis to play the dual role of Jodie Tatum/Josh Morgan, a pair of look-alike cousins who were polar opposites.

The plot called for a sophisticated soldier (Josh) to convince his hillbilly cousin (Jodie) to allow a missile site to be built on his land. Of course, it featured lots of fistfights and song-and-dance numbers.

Elvis's female costar was Yvonne Craig, who had previously starred with him on *It Happened at the World's Fair*. Yvonne was later known for her role as Batgirl on the hit TV series *Batman*. A former ballet dancer, she had a sexy and voluptuous body to match her beauty. Naturally, this didn't go overlooked by Elvis, and they got romantically involved. He also resumed his affair with Anne Helm, his brunette costar in *Follow That Dream*.

The worst part about the shoot for Elvis was having to wear a blond wig. He felt silly in it and thought that with the wig and his lumberjack shirt, jeans, and mountain boots he looked like the cartoon character, Li'l Abner. More than once he had to be coaxed out of his trailer in the getup.

It didn't help matters when Colonel Parker strolled around the set wearing a similar hairpiece he got from the wardrobe department. Everyone laughed but Elvis.

Compounding Elvis's frustration was the fact that producer Sam Katzman, known in the industry as "King of the Quickies," had budgeted the film for a mere $800,000 and slated just fifteen days to shoot. Quality was obviously not a consideration, and when the Colonel tried to placate Elvis by telling him it would be just like shooting a TV show, Elvis wasn't having any of it. He felt the whole deal was shortchanging the fans.

When production wrapped, Elvis couldn't get away fast enough. He rounded up the troops and headed down the mountain in the motor home. The road was narrow and treacherous, with a dramatic drop-off on one side. Elvis was behind the wheel when the brakes gave out. He frantically honked the horn to warn the car ahead, which carried members of the film crew, and shifted gears to slow the big motor home down. After several hair-raising minutes, he managed to bring the vehicle to a halt.

Later, Elvis joked about the narrow escape, but I believe it motivated him to take a good look at his life.

# Chapter 16

# Wandering Spirit

M UCH HAS BEEN WRITTEN ABOUT ELVIS PRESLEY'S SPIRITUAL QUEST FOR inner peace. It's been well documented that Elvis's mother, Gladys, introduced him to the Pentecostal church at an early age, and they spent many hours at the Assembly of God church. The gospel music and the fire-and-brimstone messages he heard there were ingrained into his soul.

While he often strayed from the lessons of the Bible (as a lot of us have a tendency to do), Elvis had a deeply rooted belief that God was the creator of all that is and watched over the universe. He believed in Jesus Christ as the Lord and Savior and Son of God.

Elvis developed a passion for gospel music. Often he would slip into an all-black Baptist church to hear some of the finest music in the Deep South. His very first musical ambition was to become a member of a gospel quartet.

With Elvis's fame came the introduction of a fast-lane lifestyle, but as long as his mother was around to offer him love, support, and spiritual guidance, he was safe from a world that offered him temptations on a daily basis.

After Gladys died, the love, compassion, generosity, and warmth she instilled in him as a child stayed with him the rest of his life. The same was true of his spiritual love for the Lord and faith in him.

Elvis's devotion to his Creator extended far beyond his love of gospel music; he had a real knowledge of the Bible, which he kept at his bedside.

By 1964, Elvis's spiritual direction shifted. He questioned why he was the recipient of such tremendous success at such a young age.

As Elvis approached thirty, a pervasive refrain began running through his head: *what is my purpose in life?*

At that time in American history, we were still mourning the death of President John F. Kennedy. We also saw the civil rights movement move to the forefront of our country's consciousness, while the realities of the cold war made everyone realize that civilization could go up in a mushroom cloud at any time.

The musical landscape changed as well. The Beatles invaded our shores on a tidal wave of popularity not seen since the likes of— Elvis Presley.

Although Elvis's public attitude was "There's room on top of the mountain for everybody," I don't think Elvis was happy about relinquishing his rock-and-roll crown to a bunch of long-haired boys from England.

Their arrival heralded the "British Invasion," changing the face of music forever. Young people were caught up in a counterculture movement fueled by folk and rock music, clothes, and antigovernment attitudes. Almost overnight, Elvis became part of the status quo that the youth culture railed against.

It had been almost two years since Elvis topped the charts with "Good Luck Charm." He still had registered a few Top Ten hits every now and then, but his records were mostly a by-product of his movies.

In January 1964, Elvis returned to musical form when he recorded Chuck Berry's "Memphis." He stamped his signature sound to the song, which anyone with ears could tell would be an instant chart-topper. Public release was set for May.

Elvis loved his interpretation of the song so much that he played it for anyone who would listen, including a new friend named Johnny Rivers. Johnny was just starting to make a name for himself in the music industry and was a regular at the Whiskey a Go Go on the Sunset Strip. At Elvis's invitation, Rivers started dropping by the Perugia Way home, and on one of his visits Elvis got out the acetate of "Memphis" and played it for him.

"Damn, Elvis, that is hot!" Rivers said. "Play it again, man!"

Rivers asked to hear the record several more times, and Elvis happily and innocently complied. He was really pleased that Johnny liked it so much. It was a few months later, as we were driving back from the studio in Elvis's Rolls, when we turned on the radio and heard "Memphis." Not by Elvis, but by Johnny Rivers.

Elvis turned up the volume and listened in stunned silence. When the song was over, Marty piped up.

"Elvis, you can put your record out real quick and kill his," Marty said.

"Naw, if it means that much to him, let the little sonofabitch have his hit record," Elvis said. "He needs it more than I do. I wish him luck, but I don't want him coming around anymore."

A few weeks later, Johnny came up to the house. Marty and Alan were in the courtyard and called him a thief and every other name in the book and ordered him to get the hell out of there. He didn't show up again for many years.

Johnny's version of "Memphis" hit Number 2 on *Billboard*'s Top 100. Elvis's record would undoubtedly have topped the charts, but now it would be another five years before he had another Number 1 single.

Things didn't go any better on the movie front, either. Elvis's next picture, *Roustabout*, was another lightweight effort in which Elvis portrayed Charlie Rogers, a drifter with a chip on his shoulder who ends up working in a carnival.

*Roustabout* was jinxed from the start for everybody involved, including me.

Paul Nathan, Hal Wallis's associate producer at Paramount Studios, asked if I wanted a bit part as a guy who gets into a fight with Elvis. Nathan set up an interview for me with director John Rich, whose credits included TV shows such as *Bonanza*, *Gunsmoke*, and *The Dick Van Dyke Show*. But Rich somehow thought I looked too much like Elvis because we had the same kind of hairdo. I really didn't think anybody would have trouble telling me from the King of Rock and Roll, but Rich was adamant even after I offered to shave my head for the part. Instead, he gave it to Glenn Wilder, a former football player at USC who was in training to become a stuntman. He later became a very good one, but back then he made a mistake that could have been costly to the studio.

Four days into filming, Wilder accidentally kicked Elvis in the head when he improvised in a fight scene with Elvis. He was supposed to bend over when kicked in the stomach by Elvis and then fall to the ground when Elvis came back with a chop to the back of the neck. Instead, Glenn did a forward flip when kicked, and his heel caught Elvis just over the eye as he attempted the chop to the neck.

You could actually hear the impact of the kick on the soundtrack. Real blood began flowing from a cut above Elvis's eye, and later nine stitches were needed to close the wound.

If I remember correctly, the scene had to be edited and Elvis's bandage over his eye was explained in the film as the result of a motorcycle accident.

Elvis and Rich had their problems. Elvis wanted to do a song with the Jordanaires called "Wheels on My Heels." But Rich argued that because Elvis was supposed to sing the tune when he was alone on his bike, the backup singers would be jarringly out of place.

Elvis won that one, but the moody Rich got back at him by making Elvis shoot take after take on a day when Elvis had a 104-degree temperature.

Costarring in the picture was Barbara Stanwyck, who played Maggie Morgan, the owner of the carnival. Hal Wallis originally offered the role to legendary sex symbol Mae West, then sixty-nine. In the original screenplay, Maggie was to be Elvis's mother. That was all West needed to hear. "I ain't never played mothers in my life, and I'm certainly not going to now," she reportedly said.

Elvis greatly admired Stanwyck and her work. Barbara had made her movie debut in 1927's *Broadway Nights* and quickly established herself as a dependable leading lady specializing in tough but vulnerable characters. She was a dedicated, no-nonsense actress who turned in exceptional performances over the years, most notably in Billy Wilder's classic *Double Indemnity*.

But Elvis's favorite movie of hers was an RKO Western B feature called *Cattle Queen of Montana*, and he told her so.

Barbara returned an even bigger compliment—she told Elvis that he reminded her of her one true love—former husband and Hollywood heartthrob Robert Taylor.

But it wasn't a love-fest between Elvis and Stanwyck right off the bat. Early in the shoot, Elvis arrived late on the set and assistant director Mickey Moore pointedly looked at his watch and commented on it. Now, the assistant director has the hardest job on the set, keeping everyone in line. He has to ensure everything and everybody is ready to go before the director can do his job. But for some reason Elvis thought it was Stanwyck who had complained about his tardiness, and he didn't like it.

"I don't give a damn if the big star Barbara Stanwyck is waiting for me, I'll get here when I'm good and ready," he announced loud enough for everyone on the set to hear. The ultimate pro, Stanwyck merely bowed her head and kept silent, though she had every right to chop Elvis off at the knees.

She was considerate of everyone on the set and insisted that we all call her by her nickname, "Missy." At the end of the picture, she presented to me a signed photo. Missy was a class act whom I liked and respected immensely.

I wish I could explain how Raquel Welch slipped under my radar screen. The future sex goddess made her movie debut in *Roustabout* as a member of a group of people who drive to a roadhouse called The Teahouse where Elvis is singing. But somehow I don't recollect noticing her at all, and I am sure the same goes for her about me.

One memorable moment during the filming was when we all met one of our football heroes—the great Jim Brown of the Cleveland Browns. Brown was making his film debut in *Rio Conchos* at 20th Century Fox. The meeting was set up through Gene Hickerson, a friend of Elvis's who was an All-Pro guard for the Cleveland Browns. Gene played football with us in the off-season but, of course, never went at full speed with us.

During football season, Elvis sat tubeside every Sunday with trays of soda, chips, and popcorn. He loved the Browns, and when they played on TV he was their biggest cheerleader.

We were all excited about meeting the game's greatest running back. When Jim Brown visited the lot, we told him how much we admired his skills and that we repeatedly watched a sixteen-millimeter film Elvis had of great football highlights from the season before. Most of them were of Brown's spectacular runs. Our favorite was one in which Brown got hit at the line of scrimmage by two defensive players, spun away from them, and, in midturn, was hit by another opposing lineman and bent over backward but still got away and ran for a touchdown.

We described the run in great detail, and Brown remarked, "You guys really do watch those films a lot, don't you?" Then he offered to demonstrate one of his favorite techniques to avoid being tackled if we promised not to give it away. Of course, we readily assented, and Brown instructed me to come at him. I did as ordered, and as I started to wrap an arm around him, Jim brought his forearm up and knocked my arm away. Nobody brought Jim Brown down with one

161

arm. The other technique he called the "limp leg," in which he would relax a leg when someone had a hold of it and they would sometimes loosen their grip a split second. That was all Jim needed, as he would snatch his leg free and continue his run.

The worst thing that happened during the filming of *Roustabout* didn't occur on the set. One day Elvis dispatched Richard Davis to the Perugia Way home to retrieve a piece of Elvis's wardrobe. Richard was rounding a curve in Elvis's station wagon when a gardener stepped back off the curb into his path. Richard didn't even have time to apply the brakes, and the gardener was struck and killed.

It was an unavoidable accident, but because the car was registered under Elvis's name, he got legal representation in case of a lawsuit. Thus began Elvis's long-term association with attorney Ed Hookstratten, who skillfully negotiated an out-of-court settlement with the gardener's family.

But the accident left lasting scars on Richard, who soon developed a drinking problem. It got to the point where Elvis finally told him, "Richard, man, I don't want to see a damn beer bottle or a can in your hand anymore."

Richard couldn't help replaying the accident over and over in his head. "I can't believe I actually killed someone, Sonny," he'd tearfully tell me. I'd tell him it was not his fault and weep with him, while telling him not to let it ruin his life, but that was easy for me to say.

Elvis himself went into an emotional nosedive thanks to Hal Wallis. Not long after *Roustabout* wrapped, Wallis told a reporter for the *Las Vegas Desert News and Telegram* that Elvis's pictures helped finance classier movies like *Becket*, starring Richard Burton and Peter O'Toole.

"In order to do the artistic pictures," Wallis said, "it is necessary to make the commercially successful Presley pictures. But that doesn't mean a Presley picture can't have quality, too."

The perceived confirmation from on high that his movies were lightweight schlock sent Elvis into morose seclusion for days. Nothing seemed to help—not the constant parties, the trips to Vegas, or dating starlets. Elvis's unhappiness with his singing and movie careers eventually sent him on a spiritual journey that took him to some pretty strange places.

Someone who tapped into Elvis's spiritual psyche was a twenty-four-year-old hairdresser named Larry Geller.

Larry came into the inner circle in April 1964 by way of Sal

Orifice. Sal worked for famous Hollywood hairdresser Jay Sebring, whose salon on Fairfax in West Hollywood catered to a clientele that was a who's who of the entertainment industry, including Steve McQueen, Paul Newman, Frank Sinatra, Glen Campbell, James Garner, and Andy Williams. Jay was the top men's hairstylist in the United States and was a major force in the development of a market for hair products and toiletries. Unfortunately, he was killed in 1969 by members of the Charles Manson "family."

Sal was originally my stylist. I was introduced to him by a singer friend of mine named Jerry Naylor. I was always amazed that Jerry's hair looked the same every day, and he recommended Jay's salon. The haircuts were $25 a pop back when most barbers charged around $1.50. After I started getting my hair cut by Sal, Elvis looked at me one day and asked, "Sonny, how do you keep your hair looking the same all the time?"

I told him about Sebring's hair salon, and soon thereafter Jay himself came to the Perugia Way home to cut Elvis's hair. Elvis was pleased with the results—until the next morning when his hair looked like a bird's nest and he couldn't straighten it out.

He ordered me to get Jay right back there, but Sal came instead, and Elvis liked him and his work so much that Sal ended up on the payroll.

Everybody liked Sal, who was sharp with a keen sense of humor. He eventually ended up opening up his own high-end salon called the Brass Rail on Melrose in Hollywood. That's when Sal's fellow employee, Larry Geller, became Elvis's hairdresser.

As Larry went to work on Elvis's hair, Elvis innocently asked him, "So, Larry, what are you into?"

Larry was into a lot of things.

Among other things, Geller—who was Jewish—claimed to have experienced a spiritual rebirth at the age of twenty-one in the Hopi Mountains near the Grand Canyon. That awakening, he told Elvis, opened him up to unorthodox ideas and philosophies, and he had tirelessly studied every world religion, philosophy, and metaphysical work he could get his hands on.

He had investigated the mysteries of yoga, tai chi, Scientology, reincarnation, transcendental meditation, and vegetarianism and had thoroughly studied the Bible, Kabbalah, Taoism, Buddhism, Judaism, and Christianity. All of which led him to the "universal

Christ" conclusion that Jesus, Muhammad, Buddha, Allah, and Krishna were all one and the same who astral-traveled around the world.

The haircut lasted three hours, and when they emerged from the bathroom, Larry had sunk his hooks good and deep into Elvis.

The rest of us were suspicious of Larry, but not for the reasons he has stated over the years. Larry says we didn't understand and like him, but that's only half true. We didn't like him, but only because he was so full of himself. Larry left the impression that he felt he was intellectually superior to us and pretty much rubbed our noses in it. "Oh, I'd tell you, but you just wouldn't understand," he'd say. Or, "You'd have to read that in order to fully comprehend what I'm saying." It was pure horseshit, but Elvis ate it up.

Let me emphatically state that, contrary to what Larry likes to say, he was never Elvis's spiritual adviser. Elvis had his own faith and never considered changing it. It was the same when Elvis got me to read *Masters of the Far East*. I found it to be interesting but not something I was going to embrace as my new religion.

We weren't the only ones who didn't care for Larry. Colonel Parker, who was intuitive about people, was distrustful and disapproving of Larry.

A voracious reader anyway, Elvis began poring over the books Larry brought over on a daily basis. The combination of them turned Elvis's head around pretty good. Where before he had enjoyed history, American literature, and joke books, Elvis was now immersed himself in *The Impersonal Life*, *Cheiro's Book of Numbers*, *Through the Eyes of the Masters: Meditations and Portraits*, *Autobiography of a Yogi*, and *The Tibetan Book of the Dead*.

As Larry's influence over Elvis deepened, we began calling him "the Swami," "Rasputin," and "the Brain Scrambler." His presence drove a wedge between us and Elvis, who was rarely interested anymore in tossing around a football or participating in the usual horseplay.

It got plenty stranger. Elvis announced that he possessed psychic healing powers and could cure the common cold or other ailments through his simple touch. He also thought he could make leaves move and turn the sprinkler system of the Bel-Air Country Club on and off through telekinesis. Once he even confided to Marty that he heard a bird's chirping turn into the voice of Christ.

On one of our road trips, Elvis and Larry talked well into the night. Elvis had asked Larry what was wrong with him and was told that if he "wanted tea, he must first empty his cup." Heavy, man.

The next afternoon, Elvis stopped the motor home in the middle of the desert near the Grand Canyon to survey a mysterious cloud formation. Then he announced that he saw the face of Joseph Stalin in the clouds.

"What's it mean, Larry?" he said. "What is he doing up there?"

Zen master Larry pronounced it was a "diffused" cloud and instructed Grasshopper Elvis to form his own conclusion. Elvis surmised that Stalin represented the evil part of his nature and that God was sending him a special vision to warn him about his over-inflated ego.

But then the cloud miraculously transformed itself into the face of Jesus, and, satisfied that he was right with God again, Elvis got back on board and was in high spirits for the rest of the trip.

Elvis's fascination with death turned into an obsession, and he started visiting morgues. Back in Tennessee, he made late-night visits to the Memphis Funeral Home where his mother had been prepared for burial, and he often popped in around 3:00 AM to take a look at the corpses on the slabs. Elvis talked in great detail about the embalming process, and he would lift the sheets off the bodies to describe various tricks of the mortician trade. He would nonchalantly show us how a jugular vein was cut to bleed the corpse out, and he seemed quite comfortable in that macabre setting.

His curiosity was unquenchable. Elvis read a new book on metaphysics, numerology, cosmology, or religion almost every other day. He carried a Webster's dictionary around to look up words he didn't know.

Larry also introduced Elvis to the Self-Realization Fellowship, a worldwide yoga organization headquartered on Mount Washington in Pacific Palisades. The association was founded in 1920 by Indian guru Swami Paramahansa Yogananda, who died in 1952. The fellowship then fell to the leadership of Sri Daya Mata (née Faye Wright).

Daya Mata reminded Elvis a lot of his mother, and she had a soothing effect on him. They talked for hours at a stretch, and he always came back to the house feeling better than when he left.

For a while Elvis flirted with the Church of Scientology, but in the end he dismissed it as "All head and no heart." In the early '70s, he gave it another shot and even went through an "auditing process" where they made up some charts for him at their center on Sunset Boulevard. Five minutes later he came bolting out of the place, cursing up a blue streak.

"F—— those people!" he screamed, shaking his head. "There's no way I'll get involved with those damn people. All they want is my money." Ironically, Priscilla and Lisa Marie involved themselves with Scientology after Elvis's death. And he is probably spinning in his grave over the fact they have aligned themselves with this strange religion.

As for Elvis, his path to enlightenment took a darker turn when he decided it was time to go even deeper into himself.

# Chapter 17

# Trippin'

**E**LVIS'S SEARCH FOR A HIGHER STATE OF CONSCIOUSNESS LED HIM TO TRY A LOT of things. But nothing got him there faster than the favorite hallucinogenic drug of the 1960s—lysergic acid diethylamide, or LSD.

He was not an experimenter by nature. But Elvis was intrigued by LSD's reputation for fueling creativity and bringing its users closer to God. While never a participant in the counterculture movement of the 1960s, Elvis didn't turn a blind eye to the social radicalism going on around him. He kept up with all the latest trends, listened to the latest music, and read the latest books. Two books in particular— Aldous Huxley's *The Doors of Perception* and Timothy Leary's *Psychedelic Experience*—piqued Elvis's interest. Leary, a Harvard professor turned counterculture guru, encouraged young people to "tune in, turn on, and drop out." Elvis never bought into that message, but he was willing to drop acid for the experience.

Elvis was something of an anachronism as an entertainer in the '60s. He stood staunchly in defense of his country and publicly was very much against any illegal activity, including drug taking. He felt members of the flower power generation were wasting their lives getting high, protesting the government, and fighting the system. He spent countless hours talking with many of them in Palm Springs in the late '60s and was truly interested in what they had to say. His movie star image turned off a lot of them, and they had trouble relating to him and his concerns. It was as if the walls of Graceland had served as a barrier between Elvis and the new counterculture.

The private Elvis was a whole different animal, of course. He knew that actors, writers, musicians, and filmmakers, including James Coburn,

André Previn, and Anaïs Nin, had used LSD and publicly endorsed it. Its best-known exponent was probably Cary Grant, who took LSD more than sixty times under the auspices of Drs. Mortimer Hartmann and Oscar Janiger.

Grant claimed he used the drug to straighten out his life. The debonair movie star was actually very insecure offstage, and he said in his memoirs that LSD helped him achieve the "peace of mind" that yoga, hypnotism, and mysticism had all failed to deliver. Thanks to LSD, Grant said, "I have been born again."

What was good enough for Cary Grant was good enough for Elvis—so long as he had us around to serve as his guinea pigs. He got Red to agree to take it by suggesting that it would help him write a great song. I was reeled in by the prospect of getting closer to God. I figured I needed all the proximity I could get.

Elvis promised to have Charlie Hodge and Larry Geller watch over us in case we had a bad trip. Knowing them as well as I did, that didn't bring down my anxiety level much.

Getting some LSD for our little experiment wasn't hard. Elvis's supplier was a UCLA student named Bonnie, a young woman in her early twenties who hung out in front of the Perugia Way digs. She got us several tablets of the stuff.

We popped the pills, and Elvis began reading from Timothy Leary's handbook to guide us through the experience. Red had a guitar, pen, and notepad with him for when his creative juices started flowing. I just held on for dear life.

After a few minutes, Red said he felt nothing. I didn't either. "You did take it, didn't you?" he asked suspiciously. I assured him I had taken mine. Meanwhile, Elvis paced around reading aloud from Dr. Leary's primer.

A half hour went by, and we were still sober as judges. Then all of a sudden it hit both of us. I saw flashes in the corners of my eyes, and my world went from black and white to a wild kaleidoscope of colors.

"Okay," Elvis said, "it says here that after a half hour you might start to feel creative and maybe even write a song." I personally believe that edict came from Elvis and not the book, but Red picked up his guitar to be ready.

The only urge I felt was to use the bathroom. En route there, Elvis advised me I should "start feeling a little more God conscious" anytime. As I stood there relieving myself, I tilted my head up and kept my eyes shut. All of a sudden, I saw this beacon of light that became more and more intense. I'm seeing the light of God, I thought, just like Moses did in the fire on the mount. Then a loud voice spoke to me.

"Sonny, are you finished yet?"

Opening my eyes, I saw not God's face but that of…Larry Geller. He had come in to check on me. Then, I looked up and realized that the divine light I had seen was actually the bulb hanging over the commode.

That's when my trip took a bad turn. As I washed my hands I looked into the mirror and saw looking back at me the ugliest wolf man I'd ever seen. I was clean-shaven at the time, so it was unnerving. I fled back to the bedroom and felt the walls closing in on me. Larry took me outside for some fresh air, and in the backyard I started playing with Elvis's collie, Baba. We romped in an ivy patch, and as I rolled around on the ground I ripped some ivy out and held it up to the sun for close inspection. The veins in the leaf began pulsating, and I told Larry, "Man, it's alive!"

Then it occurred to me that I was killing the ivy by taking it out of the soil, and I tried to replant it. My own skin suddenly became transparent, and I could see my veins, muscles, and tendons. They were all green, like the ivy's. It was overwhelming and enlightening at the same time. "We are all from God," I quietly intoned. "We are all the same inside. We just appear in different physical forms."

Larry was properly impressed, and he took me back inside to share my insight with the group. Everyone agreed that it was heavy, indeed.

Red was working with Elvis on his great psychedelic song. But they weren't getting too far because Red was all herky-jerky. He reminded me of one of those baseball coaches signaling to the batter with secret twitches and gestures.

Our LSD trip lasted about eight hours. It was an exhausting, emotional roller coaster and something I never cared to try again. More than four decades later, I still have flashbacks that last for a few seconds, which is why my memory of the whole event remains pretty much intact.

Several months later, Elvis decided to take the plunge himself at Graceland with Priscilla, Lamar Fike, and Jerry Schilling, while I kept an eye on them.

Not much happened. Elvis watched the movie *The Time Machine* and even ordered a pizza. He was mostly quiet and seemed more interested in watching everybody else.

Priscilla's trip was another story. She really got into Elvis's multicolored shirt. The yellow in it sent her off on a tangent about bananas. Then she suddenly became insecure and started pouring out her heart about a lot of different issues. It was a rare view into her psyche; normally Priscilla kept a safe emotional distance from everyone and always had to be in control.

Jerry was quiet and into himself, but at one point he described an Alice in Wonderland–type vision of Elvis as a fat little boy whose feet couldn't reach the floor.

Lamar was a hoot. He decided he was in love with this big tree in the front of the house. We went outside, and he walked over to the tree, gave it a hug, and planted a big kiss on its bark.

"I love you," Lamar said to the tree right before he gave it a big ol' smooch.

It was the last LSD experience for all concerned. No one in Elvis's inner circle that I know of ever did it again.

After we returned to Los Angeles, Elvis began seeing visions without the use of any hallucinogenic drugs. He, Priscilla, and I were standing in the backyard of the house overlooking the Bel-Air Country Club golf course, which was adjacent to the property, when out of the blue Elvis announced that he was seeing angels. Because he was staring at the sprinkler system as it sprayed the golf course, we were more than a little taken aback.

Our concern grew when Elvis ordered us to stay put while he went over to see what the angels wanted. He went off, and I followed at a distance. When he stopped by the sprinklers, I could hear him talking but couldn't make out what he said. Then he turned and walked back to his house, passing me without a word. He never mentioned the incident again.

Not long after the angels departed, the aliens dropped by. "Sonny, do you see that?" Elvis asked while we were in the backyard one night. I saw a light poking through the trees but had no reason to think it was anything other than a plane or maybe a helicopter.

"It's a flying saucer," Elvis proclaimed.

I didn't hear any engine noise, and the light kept coming toward us. Then it traveled through the trees and over the house and to the front of the house. Elvis told me to get Jerry so he could witness this bizarre phenomenon. I did as instructed, and when Jerry and I came out Elvis was gone. God almighty, had Martians kidnapped the King of Rock and Roll?

But he wasn't in outer space. At least not physically. We found Elvis three houses down, staring toward Westwood. "Man, Elvis," I said with a laugh, "I thought they had taken you." He smiled knowingly and replied, "They will come, but they won't hurt us. If they make contact we can't be afraid, because they won't hurt us."

Around this time, Elvis also started talking about biblical prophecies. One time while at his home in Palm Springs, he took to giving special Bible readings in the living room, and he sounded just like a hellfire preacher. Once he gathered us all around for a sermon. He started out reading passages in a quiet, sincere voice, and we listened enthralled. Then he got boisterous and profane.

"Whoa, all ye motherf———ers in high places," he yelled. "Be it known that it is easier for a camel's ass to go through the eye of a needle than for a rich man to enter the kingdom of heaven."

Then, possibly remembering that he himself was a rich man, Elvis quickly added, "Now, that doesn't mean it is impossible for a rich man to get into heaven. It just means he has to work harder for the Lord."

Continued Reverend Presley: "Moses, that white-haired sonofabitch, comes running down from this big mountain. Now his damn hair had turned white because he had seen the Lord, and those things can happen when you see the Lord."

Charlie started laughing out loud right about then, and Elvis asked what was so funny. When Charlie said that sure was a different version of the Bible than any he ever heard, Elvis had no idea what he was talking about. We quoted some of his chapter and verse back to him, and Elvis couldn't believe he had said those things. That was the last Bible session he presided over. Later he expressed that he was upset that he had twisted the words of the Bible, especially when quoting God and Jesus.

Elvis could have used some divine intervention to get his career jump-started. Instead, his next movie was *Girl Happy*, for MGM. It costarred Shelley Fabares and Gary Crosby.

Elvis was quite taken by Shelley's natural beauty and vivacious personality, and it was obvious he was interested in more than just a celluloid relationship with his new leading lady. But Shelley was seeing record producer Lou Adler at the time, and she politely but firmly declined to become more than friends with Elvis. He accepted that with good grace, but when they did another movie together he asked Shelley if she was still going with "that guy." No, she answered—now she was engaged to him. They did a third movie, and Elvis wondered if she was still engaged to that guy. Shelley smiled and said no—she was married to him.

Without missing a beat, Elvis grinned and said, "You were weakening, weren't you? Didn't think you could resist me anymore, right?" Shelley laughed and said, "Exactly!"

Shelley was faithful to Lou, and it was a tribute to the kind of lady she is. In spite of his failed attempts to lure her into a romance, Elvis truly adored Shelley, and they had a natural on-screen chemistry. But that's as far as it ever went.

Elvis moved on to another costar, former Miss America Mary Ann Mobley. Mary Ann was a true Southern belle. Beautiful and sweet, she also had a great sense of humor. When the movie was done, they went their separate ways but remained good friends.

During the shoot, plenty of celebrities dropped by to say hello to Elvis. One of them was Ann-Margret. A year had passed since their romance had cooled off, but they kept in touch sporadically. Ann always lifted Elvis's spirits, and now they seemed to pick things right up where they left off. He was less self-centered and easier to be around when Ann was near. It was heartwarming to watch them become totally alive around each other.

Another visitor to the set was Lynda Bird Johnson, daughter of President Lyndon B. Johnson. At the time, Lynda was dating actor George Hamilton and befriended both Colonel Parker and Elvis. George had recently finished filming *Your Cheatin' Heart*, based on the life story of country singer Hank Williams.

Of course, wherever the daughter of the president of the United States goes, the Secret Service isn't far behind. Never able to resist a good practical joke, Elvis decided to have some fun with these guys who really took their jobs seriously.

Elvis gathered us in his mobile dressing room beforehand and said he wanted us to go out and act as though we were his own personal security team. We were to wear sunglasses and copy everything the Secret Service agents did. If questioned, we were to say we were with "Elvis Presley Security."

The meeting with Lynda Bird and Hamilton was arranged in a big green field on the back lot of MGM behind the studio swimming pool. They showed up flanked by several stone-faced Secret Service agents. As we headed toward the group, we began to fan out in formation behind Elvis, just like the Secret Service agents had done behind Ms. Johnson. While Elvis chatted with Lynda and George, we stood stock-still about two feet behind, staring at the agents who were staring at us. They didn't laugh, but we did. Back in the trailer, of course. Despite the fact that we had a little fun at their expense, we knew the seriousness of the agents' duties and respected them very much for their dedicated service.

*Girl Happy* was another less-than-stellar movie. Elvis was far from ecstatic about the script and some of the songs he had to sing, but that was par for the course. There was always a song—or two—in his films that was lame and embarrassing for him to sing. In this case it was a ditty called "The Fort Lauderdale Chamber of Commerce," and filming the scene in which he crooned the song put Elvis in a foul mood. But Elvis did enjoy making the movie because of Shelley, costar Gary Crosby, and some other cast members in the film. Also, Elvis and us guys really liked the director, Boris Sagal, who was tragically killed in a helicopter incident years later while filming another movie.

In just a few months Elvis would turn thirty. His film and recording careers were stagnant, if not dead in the water. The future wasn't looking pretty, and it wasn't easy to jolly Elvis out of the funk this put him in.

# Chapter 18

# El's Angels

**B**Y THE MID-1960S, COLONEL PARKER HAD THE ELVIS PRESLEY MOVIE MACHINE in full production, churning out approximately three pictures and accompanying soundtrack albums a year. Elvis was paid close to $2 million annually and worked approximately twenty weeks a year. The rest of the time was his to do as he pleased, and what he did was a lot of brooding. His mood swings worried Colonel Parker, who decided to have Joe Esposito keep close tabs on Elvis for him. That basically meant Joe reported back to the Colonel on Elvis's daily routine. In other words, he was snitching on his boss. Joe told the Colonel that Larry Geller was filling Elvis's head with a lot of theories on religions and bringing him a lot of books that Joe felt were causing his mood swings.

That occasioned an emergency meeting with Elvis on the MGM lot right before Elvis and the rest of the guys were about to head back to Memphis in the motor home. I wasn't going because I was doing *Dr. Kildare* and some other TV and movie work.

The Colonel rarely got involved in Elvis's personal life, but now he sternly warned Elvis to get off his "religious kick" and back to reality. Elvis was silent throughout the tongue-lashing, but he was livid when he climbed into the Dodge motor home.

"My life is not a kick," Elvis sulked. "It's real."

Elvis drove in silence all the way to Amarillo, Texas, where they stopped for the night at a Holiday Inn.

Because Elvis usually traveled with a large group of people, he had a special arrangement with Kemmons Wilson, the founder and board chairman of Holiday Inns, Inc., which was headquartered in

175

Memphis. Wilson issued Elvis a letter of credit good at any Holiday Inn in the country.

Joe was in charge of the arrangements whenever we checked into a motel or hotel. When the group arrived at the Holiday Inn in Amarillo, there were photographers, television crews, and thousands of screaming fans staking the place out. Because the stop there was supposed to be shrouded in secrecy, Elvis went berserk, as I later learned from Marty.

While it smacked of Colonel Parker's handiwork, Elvis used it as an excuse to let Joe go. To this day, Joe claims he got fed up with Elvis and quit, which may be the case, but it was instigated by Elvis. Joe wanted to work it out, but Elvis was having none of it. Now what was Joe going to do? He had no other prospects going for him and a family to support in Los Angeles. Besides, he liked being Elvis Presley's foreman way too much to give it up on a whim.

I'm sure Joe hoped Elvis would change his mind once they got settled in back at Graceland, but Elvis was not in a forgiving mood. In fact, he refused to come out of his room for a whole week, hoping Joe would get the message and take a hike. It was just Elvis's way of dealing with the situation.

Joe, who kept the checkbooks for Elvis, finally turned them over to Marty and said he was leaving town. No sooner had he reached the front gate when Elvis came downstairs and asked if Joe was gone. Learning that was the case, Elvis turned chipper and asked for a big breakfast. Then he turned to Marty and said, "Looks like I've got me a new bookkeeper and foreman."

Marty didn't want the job at Joe's expense and said he wasn't interested. "I said, it looks like I've got me a new bookkeeper and foreman, and a raise goes with the job," Elvis said. Marty thought about it for a second, decided he wasn't *that* close to Joe, and took the job.

Over the next six months, Joe Esposito found out that being on the outs with Elvis also meant being on the outs with Elvis's entourage. He was hurt that most of the guys didn't stay in touch with him, but that's just the way it was. It's also the way it had been with Joe when he was riding high and somebody else got the boot.

Elvis also got fed up with Jimmy Kingsley and fired him. Jimmy was a snide fellow whose cutting remarks made it plain he was jealous of Elvis. He seemed to always be bitching and complaining about something. After Elvis canned him, Jimmy headed back to

Hollywood and worked as an extra in movies and television, and then he became a stuntman.

Joe's and Jimmy's slots in the entourage were filled by new guys Jerry Schilling and Mike Keaton. Jerry and Mike were buddies, but Mike was the more serious and reserved of the two. He was also very religious and a staunch member of the Assembly of God Church, which appealed to Elvis and gave him somebody else to talk to about the Bible. But what really sealed the deal was that Mike's mother was named Gladys, which Elvis took as a sign from above.

But life with Elvis wasn't so heavenly for Mike. He lasted only a few months because he really didn't like to do the same things we did. Most everyone in the inner circle had some sort of distinguishing characteristic that set him apart. I really can't remember anything distinguishing about Mike. He was a nice enough guy, but he held himself back from our games and pranks and seemed to prefer his own company. When he departed, the general feeling was that it was for the best.

In October 1964, Elvis reported to Paramount Studios for pre-production work on *Tickle Me*, an Allied Artists Pictures movie. The company was teetering on the brink of bankruptcy but scraped together Elvis's $750,000 salary and promised him 50 percent of the film's profits.

That didn't leave enough to pay for a movie soundtrack, but the wily Colonel Parker found a way around that. He handed over to the studio about a dozen previously recorded songs. It was the only nonoriginal movie soundtrack Elvis ever released.

In *Tickle Me*, Elvis played a rodeo rider who finds off-season work as a horse wrangler at a health ranch. The ranch is run by a mostly female staff whose advances he spurns while he searches for gold and finds love with leading lady Jocelyn Lane.

Jocelyn was British, and her beauty, brains, and dynamite body were offset by her snooty attitude. The other actresses mocked her behind her back. She warmed up to Elvis, though, but I'm not sure if they had anything going. I heard a few years later that she became a princess when she married into British royalty.

A prince of a guy was director Norman Taurog, who tapped Red and me for stunt and extra work on the picture. Red ended up playing a guy who picks a fight with Elvis in a restaurant, and he also doubled for the sheriff in a fight scene with Elvis.

I doubled for the chef in a fight scene that Elvis and I painstakingly choreographed. It was supposed to go for thirty seconds, but the sequence ended up taking up only thirteen seconds on film. I told Taurog that we could do it over and take up more time, but he liked the scene just the way it was and said he would make up the time elsewhere. He gave me a bonus.

While *Tickle Me* didn't tickle the critics, the viewing public ate it up to the tune of a $5 million gross, making it the third-highest-grossing film in the history of the studio. It kept Allied Artists out of bankruptcy for another year.

On the strength of *Tickle Me*, the Colonel struck a two-picture deal with United Artists for $650,000 apiece and a three-picture deal with MGM that would pay Elvis $1 million per movie. But Elvis was still personally unfulfilled.

For Christmas, some of the guys pitched in and got Elvis a special Bible with a "tree of life" motif on the front page. On each of the branches was the name of a person in the inner circle. Larry Geller's name was not included because to us he wasn't part of things, and he sure as hell hadn't kicked in for the gift. But Elvis wanted Geller included and insisted that his name be added to the cover of the Bible.

I don't know for sure, but it could have been that tree of life motif that spurred Elvis to look into his own family tree. Somehow he had recently gotten it into his head that he was Jewish. Geller probably had a hand in that, but Elvis later claimed he had been told as a child by his mother that his great-great-grandfather, White Mansell, had several wives at the same time, one of whom, Martha Tackett, was Jewish. (But until I see proof of that, I'll go with his cousin Billy Smith's version that the Presleys were of Scottish descent.)

Now that he was one of the "Chosen People," Elvis had a Jewish star put on his mother's gravestone and donated $12,500 to help build a $1 million Jewish community center in Memphis. In addition, he had Marty chase down kosher food for him from a local delicatessen.

He also began wearing a Jewish "chai" pendent around his neck. When a newspaper reporter once observed that he was wearing both a cross and a Jewish star, Elvis winked and said, "I like to cover all my bases. I don't want to be kept out of heaven based on a technicality." Elvis even ordered watches for himself and us guys with a Jewish star and a cross on the face that appeared and disappeared in a unique way.

Around the holidays, Elvis got wind that Joe Esposito wasn't doing so well and sent him a check to cover the bills. In the same envelope, Elvis included a $100 Christmas check for me. Joe called me, and I went over to get it. He asked if I thought Elvis would take him back. I suggested that he call Graceland and find out for himself.

If Joe came back, it meant that Marty Lacker, who did a great job as foreman in his stead, was probably going to have to share some of his responsibilities with Joe. When Joe called the house, Elvis asked Marty if they needed him. It was a crucial moment for Joe because if Marty turned thumbs-down, he could well have been out of Elvis's life for good.

"Yeah, we need him," Marty said after taking a deep pause.

Joe was back. He whisked his family back to Memphis and found an apartment near Graceland, with Elvis picking up the tab for the moving costs.

On January 8, 1965, newspapers around the country reported Elvis's thirtieth birthday as the end of an era. The once-dangerous icon was now considered part of the establishment. In fact, he had changed direction in his career, but he was still stuck artistically because he had no say in the scripts he was given.

Then came *Harum Scarum*, which called for Elvis to play a movie star in the mold of Rudolph Valentino unwittingly caught up in international intrigue. That appealed to him, and he reported to the set excited and eager to go to work.

When outfitted in the sheik costumes designed for him, Elvis's resemblance to Valentino himself was stunning. He looked every part the classic matinée idol.

But it was all downhill from there. The movie was produced by skinflint Sam Katzman, who could squeeze a penny until Abe Lincoln begged for mercy. The sets were ancient and rickety. The temple used in the film had been in mothballs since 1927, when Cecil B. DeMille used it for *King of Kings*. Some of the wardrobe was recycled from *Kismet*.

The script was equally threadbare. It cast Elvis as singing/action movie star Johnny Tyronne, who is kidnapped while on tour in the Middle East and enlisted by the Lord of Assassins in a plot to kill a foreign monarch. Elvis escapes from a dungeon to thwart the assassination scheme, woos a princess pretending to be a slave, and somehow ends up in Las Vegas surrounded by a harem of beautiful women.

Elvis gritted his teeth throughout the fifteen-day shoot. When the movie wrapped, he presented the entire cast and crew with Star of David watches designed by Memphis jeweler Harry Levitch. He also gave actor-dancer turned director Gene Nelson, who had earlier directed him in *Kissin' Cousins*, an autographed picture inscribed, "Someday, we'll do it right."

I worked as a stuntman on this movie, participating in a fight scene between the assassins and the subjects of the town. It was fairly dangerous because we were rolling around on the ground with the horses stomping around us.

As the movie was being edited, it was evident the production stunk to high heaven. Even Colonel Parker saw it and proclaimed that he had a solution to sell the movie, a novel one for sure. He suggested that a camel be the narrator of the movie. It was one of the few times Elvis overruled Parker and got away with it.

Amazingly, the film earned a cool $2 million profit for the studio, with Elvis receiving 50 percent off the top.

Elvis followed *Harum Scarum* with a period piece called *Frankie and Johnny*, based on the old folk song. This time the results were much better.

The movie was shot at Samuel Goldwyn Studios. The setting was a turn-of-the-century Mississippi riverboat, and United Artists built elaborate sets depicting nineteenth-century New Orleans. Elvis even got a chance to stretch his acting legs a bit. He was cast as Johnny, a compulsive gambler who has found a good-luck charm in Nellie Bly (Nancy Kovack), a spunky redhead who gives his girlfriend Frankie (Donna Douglas) a run for her money.

Buxom, blue-eyed Donna was best known for her role as tomboy Elly May Clampett in the popular television series *The Beverly Hillbillies*. (Later I landed a role as a veterinarian who courted her.) She was a sweet lady who got along well with Elvis. Not anything at all like her dim-witted Elly May character, Donna was intelligent and well versed on many subjects, especially religion. She was also professional about her acting craft.

The former Miss New Orleans was one of the few costars Elvis didn't try to seduce. She was a devout Christian and spent hours between takes talking with Elvis about philosophy, religion, and books.

While the movie was one of Elvis's better films, it didn't do so well overseas because the subject matter was pure Americana. But Elvis still got paid, and that along with his record royalties, BMI performance royalties, and income from merchandise, he wasn't hurting.

But Elvis couldn't spend money fast enough, and around then he embarked on the first of his famous buying sprees, kick-started when Jerry Schilling showed up at the house with a new Triumph 650 motorcycle.

Elvis owned a Harley-Davidson that he took for long rides with Priscilla, but on this day when he spotted that Triumph, he decided that he wanted not just one but an entire fleet for the whole gang. He had Alan Fortas order twelve bikes from Bill Robertson of Triumph Honda on Santa Monica Boulevard in West Los Angeles. Bill wasn't used to such large orders, and he said that while he had the bikes in stock, they were in crates and required assembly.

"Well, if I was you, I'd have them up here and assembled if you want to make the sale," Alan told him. Bill promptly loaded the crated bikes in a truck and had two of his mechanics assemble them on the drive to the Perugia Way house, about an hour away.

Almost everyone in the group got bikes but Marty, who declined because he didn't want to bust his head open. He really was scared of them and wouldn't even ride on the back of one as a passenger. Elvis bought him a Cadillac instead.

I had to teach Red how to ride his bike while Alan Fortas taught Joe Esposito. During a lesson they almost ran into each other and ended up in some bushes. But in time they became fairly good riders.

Every Saturday we'd hop on the bikes and ride around Los Angeles and the surrounding area. We often rode up the Pacific Coast Highway close to the edge of the Ventura County line north of Los Angeles County. Those were great times, and when the press caught wind of our rides we were dubbed "El's Angels."

But our snooty Bel-Air neighbors went crying again to the Beverly Hills Association about the racket the bikes made. To appease them, Elvis hired a driver to take the bikes by trailer to and from the entrance of the world's most famous gated community whenever we wanted to go out on the road.

What was the world coming to when the King of Rock and Roll couldn't make a little noise? Lord knows, enough noise was being made by the four mop-topped lads from Liverpool, England, who unceremoniously dumped him from the top of the musical charts.

# Chapter 19

# Meet the Beatles

IN THE EIGHTEEN MONTHS THEY INVADED THE UNITED STATES STARTING IN January 1964, the Beatles registered an amazing sixteen Top 10 hits, nine of which zoomed straight to Number 1. Album sales weren't too shabby, either: the Fab Four dinged the Top 10 nine times, six of them in the Number 1 slot. Acts today can build a whole career on just a single Number 1 hit or album. The Beatles scored one almost every time they issued a new record, making it appear as if they could do it in their sleep.

They also managed to conquer Hollywood their first time out of the gate, with the inimitable *A Hard Day's Night*. The viewing public loved it—including us. Elvis and all of us watched it at the Memphian Theatre and really enjoyed it, even getting a lot of the zany British humor.

The critics were gaga: "It's the *Citizen Kane* of jukebox musicals," proclaimed Andrew Sarris of the *Village Voice*. The *New York Times'* Bosley Crowther called it a "whale of a comedy," and since then famous film critic Roger Ebert has hailed the film as "exhilarating" and has shown it in the film class he taught.

Hollywood even rewarded the film with two Academy Award nominations—for best original screenplay and best original score. Talk about a good first impression!

Hollywood was never that receptive to Elvis. Sure, none of his films were *Gone with the Wind*, but *King Creole* deserved some sort of recognition at Oscar time. Actor Jack Lord once told Elvis he was appreciated by such heavyweight actors as Steve McQueen, Paul Newman, and Anthony Franciosa. After some of his early films they felt he had a great acting future. But by the mid-1960s, that window of opportunity was just about bricked up.

Say this for the Beatles: they always credited Elvis Presley as the man who inspired them to pick up their instruments and begin their rock-and-roll odyssey.

"Before Elvis, there was nothing," John Lennon once said.

Over the years Paul McCartney has done a pretty mean impersonation of Elvis. Listen to his version of "That's All Right" on his album *Choba B CCCP* or "All Shook Up" on *Run Devil, Run*, and it'll give you goose bumps. Elvis thought Lennon and McCartney were excellent songwriters, and he especially liked "Hey Jude," "Get Back," "Lady Madonna," "Yesterday," and "Something" (written by George Harrison)—performing the latter two songs when he went back to touring. He owned well-worn copies of their groundbreaking albums *Rubber Soul* and *Revolver*.

As the Beatles prepared for their U.S. invasion, they hinted in the press that Elvis Presley was the one person they really wanted to meet. Their first American appearance was in front of about seventy million people on *The Ed Sullivan Show*, and before the stodgy host brought them out, he read a telegram sent by Elvis and the Colonel congratulating the boys on their success.

The Beatles' manager, Brian Epstein, contacted Colonel Parker in hopes of getting everybody together, but the Beatles' recording and touring schedule and Elvis's movie obligations got in the way. Once, when the Beatles had an off-day in Atlantic City, McCartney did manage to have a friendly chat with Elvis on the telephone. Elvis told him he liked the cover on *Meet the Beatles* because it reminded him of the faces in the sci-fi thriller *Children of the Damned*. I don't know if you could count that as a compliment or not, but it certainly wasn't an insult.

Paramount Studios executives wanted to have the Fab Four appear in Elvis's upcoming movie, *Paradise Hawaiian Style*, but situations like that usually end up becoming a contractual nightmare, and nothing came of it.

While on location in Honolulu at the Ilikai Hotel, Elvis got a telegram from Alan Livingston, president of Capitol Records, which was the Beatles' label. It invited him to an August 24 reception for the group in L.A. at the Capitol Records Tower on Hollywood and Vine. Even though we were going to be back in Los Angeles in plenty of time for the event, Elvis balked on the grounds that the wrong party was being asked to make the pilgrimage.

"Hell, if they want to meet me, they're going to have to come see me," he said.

Was he touchy because the Beatles had eclipsed his popularity with younger fans? Sure. The Beatles had just done a concert at New York's Shea Stadium before a record-breaking fifty-five thousand screaming fans. United Artists had just released *Help!*, their first full-length motion picture in color, and the song and the album of the same title were racing up the charts. As Elvis had said so many times, there was plenty of room at the top for everyone. But this changing-of-the-guard business was tough on him.

So the negotiations continued, as delicately and intensely as if it was a nuclear arms pact being hammered out instead of a rock-and-roll summit. Finally, Colonel Parker and Brian Epstein agreed on a date for the grand event—Friday, August 27, 1965.

At around 10:00 that night, three Cadillac limousines pulled up to the house in Bel-Air in front of a phalanx of local police vehicles. They'd had to work their way through hundreds of screaming fans at the gates, for in spite of the secrecy both Parker and Epstein had insisted on, the cat somehow got out of the bag.

Later, I read an account by George Harrison in the Beatles' *Anthology* in which he said that the Beatles were so nervous about meeting Elvis that they got stoned on the way over. I know Elvis was a little apprehensive, too, but he was determined to play it cool. When the doorbell rang, he remained in the den while one of the guys went to let the visitors in. Several accounts of the meeting have said that Elvis answered the door himself to welcome the Beatles, but that didn't happen. Let the pilgrims approach the throne!

Elvis's red shirt with high Napoleonic collar contrasted nicely with his Hawaiian tan. He also wore black slacks and a black windbreaker. When the boys arrived, he was sitting in the middle of the horseshoe couch with his feet up, smoking a cigar, and channel surfing with the TV remote control. Also in the room were Priscilla, me, Red, Jerry Schilling, Joe Esposito, Richard Davis, Larry Geller, Pat Parry, Billy and Jo Smith, Alan and Jo Fortas, Marty and Patsy Lacker, and Colonel Parker.

Accompanying the Beatles were Epstein, road managers Malcolm Evans and Neil Aspinall, driver Alf Bicknell, press chief Tony Barrow, and British journalists Ivor Davis and Chris Hutchins.

As they approached the den, John Lennon launched into an Inspector Clouseau routine. "Oh, zere you are, Elvis!" he said as they entered. Elvis, who thought Peter Sellers was the greatest comedic actor around, smiled and said, "It's nice to meet you boys." He shook hands with everyone, and John and Paul took seats on his right and George and Ringo to his left. Epstein and Parker stood off in a corner.

Once everyone was settled, there was...nothing. The obviously starstruck Beatles sat there staring at Elvis, possibly because they were stoned or were just in awe. While Elvis waited for someone to get the conversational ball rolling, he again started clicking the remote control. Later, Paul McCartney remarked that it was the first time he'd ever seen a remote control.

About thirty seconds passed that way, and finally Elvis tossed the remote on the coffee table and announced, "Hell, if you guys are just gonna sit there and stare at me, I might as well go to bed. I didn't mean for this to be like the subjects calling on the king. I thought we might sit and talk and maybe jam a little."

One of them—I think it was John—said, "Yes, you are the King!"

"I didn't mean that kind of king," said Elvis. "I meant the King of England!"

That broke the ice, and Alveena the maid brought in Pepsi for Elvis (his favorite soft drink), and the Beatles had Scotch and Coke or bourbon and 7-Up. They also lit up cigarettes and chain-smoked for the rest of the night.

Some of the guys left the room and returned with electric guitars. Elvis began fiddling around with a bass plugged into an amplifier near the television. Looking at Ringo, Elvis said, "Sorry, there's no drum kit. We left that in Memphis." So Ringo played with his hands against the back of his chair. Later he got a pair of bongos.

When Elvis asked for a guitar pick, Paul turned to Mal Evans and said, "Yeah, sure, Mal always carries them around." Mal was a loyal member of the British Elvis Fan Club. He reached into his shirt pocket for a pick and discovered that the pocket had been sewn shut by the dry cleaner who had laundered it the day before. Mal went into the kitchen and broke apart some plastic spoons to use as makeshift guitar picks.

Elvis had the jukebox turned on, and they proceeded to jam to Cilla Black's "You're My World," Charlie Rich's "Mohair Sam," Chuck Berry's "Johnny B. Goode," and the Beatles' own "I Feel Fine." The last song had a tricky bass part, but Elvis had no problem with it, and Paul made the mock announcement, "And coming along quite promisingly on the bass...Elvis!"

Some of the songs Elvis stopped after only three or four lines, saying "Let's do something else." The Beatles deferred to him on the playlist.

Meanwhile, Colonel Parker and Brian Epstein got busy when Parker opened up a coffee table that converted into a roulette wheel and declared, "The casino is open!" They spent the night gambling, with Joe as their personal pit boss. Colonel bragged to me afterward that he won a nice sum of money from his Beatles counterpart.

After several songs, Ringo said, "I'm not going to beat up my hands anymore," and he excused himself to play pool with Red and me. We found Ringo quite funny and a great guy. He also was quite a ham and did a dead-on impression of Elvis, cradling his pool cue like a microphone. When Alveena brought him a drink, she accidentally stepped on his foot, and Ringo gave an exaggerated music-hall wince and said, "I think she's broke my bloody toe!" Ringo was definitely the most humorous and down-to-earth Beatle.

George also decided to break ranks and walked outside near the pool to smoke a joint. Larry Geller went to join him. Not surprisingly, they chatted about Far Eastern religions. Later, of course, George became a devout member of the Hare Krishna sect.

George rejoined Elvis, John, and Paul after a half hour, and their conversation was easy and freewheeling. Subjects included stardom, crazy fans, their mutual dislike of flying, and, of course, music. John, who was known for speaking his mind, bluntly asked why Elvis no longer made rock-and-roll records like the ones he did in the 1950s. I'm sure John didn't mean for the question to sound as harsh and judgmental as it did, but we all held our collective breaths waiting for the answer.

"It's my movie schedule," Elvis said evenhandedly. "It's so tight. But maybe I'll do one just for kicks."

"Then we'll buy it," John said with a smile, defusing the situation. John then asked Elvis what his next movie was about, and Elvis, tongue firmly in cheek, said, "I play a country boy with a guitar who meets a few gals along the way and sings a few songs."

Then Elvis sprang up from the couch and invited the group on a tour of the property. The first thing he wanted to show them was his brand-new black Rolls-Royce Phantom Five in the garage. The car was longer than the standard four-door Rolls-Royce, and it had extended leg room in the back. I believe it cost him around $50,000, which was a mint then. A car and racing fanatic, George Harrison especially admired the vehicle.

It was 2:00 AM when the Beatles headed for the door. John went back into Inspector Clouseau mode. "Sanks for ze muzik," he said, pumping a fist in the air, "and long live ze King!"

Before they left, Colonel Parker stepped up and handed each Beatle a gift bag containing a box of Elvis records and souvenir table lamps shaped like covered wagons. What the latter were intended to signify, I have no idea. But we got lamps from the Colonel, too.

Brian Epstein invited everyone to return the visit the very next night at the Beatles' rented home in Benedict Canyon, just a few miles away. "Well, we'll see," said Elvis, shifting uncomfortably. "I don't know if I'll be able to make it or not." He walked them out to the driveway and said, "If you ever get to Memphis, make sure you come and see us." And the Rock-and-Roll Summit was over.

It has been written by others that the Beatles left Elvis's house feeling disappointed, but that wasn't my recollection at all. I know Elvis enjoyed himself. "That was a lot different than I thought it would be," he said after the Beatles departed. "A lot better than I thought it would be. That's some good times there."

But not good enough for him to go to Benedict Canyon. The next night, me, Jerry, Richard, Billy, and Marty drove over to the Beatles' ranch-style place at 2850 Benedict Canyon, situated on a hilltop in an exclusive neighborhood. It was a madhouse. Police surrounded the house like a fortress to keep the screaming young girls and would-be groupies from storming it.

We got the okay to go inside, and what struck me right off was that each of the Beatles was holding court in a separate room.

Mal Evans showed us around the place, which offered a panoramic view of the Los Angeles valley. Ringo saw us and came right over with a friendly greeting. I asked if there was a pool table, and he said no. "We'll have to go back to Elvis's house to do that," he said with a smile.

As we saw the other Beatles in their separate enclaves, they politely nodded to us but mostly went on with whatever they were doing. John did come over and tell us, "Last night was the greatest night of my life!"

It's too bad Elvis and the Beatles didn't develop a closer relationship over the years, but that's how it usually goes with superstars. Most fans think that movie stars and entertainers see each other all the time, but you would be surprised how many of them never meet except when they work together or attend some awards show. Some are just very busy, and many celebrities spend time in various homes around the world. As much as he liked California, Elvis himself didn't care for the movie industry or Hollywood environment as a whole and pretty much kept to himself.

While Elvis liked John, Paul, George, and Ringo personally, over the years he came to disapprove of their public image, as some of them openly used and advocated drugs. He also bristled at the anti-Americanism that attended their increasingly strident criticisms of the war in Vietnam. He had put his own red-hot career on hold for two years to serve his country, and he didn't like it when foreigners—even ones as talented as the Beatles—went around bad-mouthing Uncle Sam. And, like many others, Elvis was appalled when John Lennon offhandedly said in 1966 that the Beatles were "more popular than Jesus."

Elvis would never have even thought such a thing about himself. It was enough to be "the King" and to have the Beatles, at least for one night, as his courtiers.

# Chapter 20

# Change of Habit

FOR NEARLY THREE YEARS, ELVIS KEPT PRISCILLA AT MORE THAN ARM'S LENGTH. About two thousand miles, specifically. She stayed at Graceland while he did whatever he liked in California and on location making his movies. But things started changing as the once meek and compliant Priscilla realized the considerable cachet available to her as Elvis Presley's girlfriend.

The changes in her were subtle at first, but more and more she began taking on Elvis's personality traits. She became cocky, confident, and imbued with a sense of entitlement. I began hearing stories from friends in Memphis about Priscilla's growing attitude and her free-spending shopping sprees.

She also spent a lot of time reading the gossip rags and perusing the scandal sheets' salacious coverage of Elvis. The constant photos of him with other women, and reports of his torrid affairs, bothered Priscilla. And she was no longer too timid to confront him about it.

"Don't you trust me, baby?" Elvis would always say, even in the face of pictorial evidence that maybe he wasn't so trustworthy. He blithely dismissed the photos as phonies or as stills taken during love scenes on a movie set. She bought it at first, but as the years passed she grew less malleable and gullible. She was insanely jealous of Elvis and suspected he was engaging in all sorts of wild, carefree behavior with other women while she was pining away at Graceland, waiting for him to pop the question.

She started trying to trip Elvis up, catch him off guard. Elvis suspected she rifled through his little black makeup kit, checked the bathroom trash containers for evidence of other women, and staked out the mailbox for love notes. For someone just out of her teens, Priscilla got pretty savvy in a hurry, and Elvis warned all of us guys to keep our guard up at all times.

One night, I answered the phone at the Perugia Way house, and a sultry female voice asked, "Hey, any big parties there tonight?" Nice try, Priscilla. I thought it was funny, so I replied, "Yeah, big party tonight. Elvis is getting a haircut right now, but come over after nine." I almost got a concussion hearing Priscilla slam the receiver down. Priscilla even staged a suicide attempt one night to get Elvis's attention when he was at Graceland. She decked herself out in a white satin gown, downed a couple Placidyls, and lay down on the bed. The amount she took wasn't enough to kill her, and she didn't even succeed at getting Elvis to feel sorry for her. He just chewed her out for acting stupid.

But he did finally agree to let Priscilla move back to California with him. In February 1966, they settled into a ranch-style home at 10550 Rocca Place, in Bel-Air. The secluded four-bedroom place in the hills offered them plenty of privacy from the outside world, but with Marty, Richard, Billy and his wife Jo, Jerry and his wife Sandy, and me living there, too, the place was plenty crowded. Richard and I shared a large den that had been converted into a fifth bedroom.

The house came with an intercom system connected to the front gate, which saved Priscilla from a jealous Elvis fan not long after we moved in. While Elvis and a few of the other guys were in the living room watching television, I was in my bedroom near the kitchen. All of a sudden I heard Priscilla's voice yelling over the intercom, "Sonny...Jerry...help!" I bolted for the door, yelling to Elvis that Priscilla was in trouble at the gate.

When I got there I saw a girl who appeared to be in her late teens and about 250 pounds grappling with Priscilla. When she saw me, the girl let go of Priscilla's hair, ran over to a car, got in, and locked the doors. Another girl and a guy were already inside the car.

I recognized Priscilla's antagonist. She was a regular at the gate who, because of her size, we called "Tiny." Later, in the house, Priscilla told us that Tiny had followed her as she drove home and had almost caused her to get into an accident. When Priscilla stopped at the gate, she confronted Tiny and demanded to know what she was doing.

"You whore!" explained Tiny.

Even though she was small, no one was going to talk to Priscilla that way. She promptly clocked Tiny with an uppercut.

After making sure that Priscilla was fine, I ran to Tiny's car and told her, through the rolled-up window, "You'd better get your ass out of here now, because if Elvis sees you, he won't like it!" Tiny's response was to stick her tongue out and start making faces at me.

I really wanted her to scram, because there was no telling how Elvis would react upon his imminent arrival.

His reaction was hot. He came pounding down the driveway, went right to Priscilla, and asked if she was all right.

"Yes," she replied, "but that girl is a big fat pig!"

Elvis advanced on her car with a full head of steam, screaming, "You big, fat, no-good bitch!" Then he began kicking the car and pounding on the windshield with both fists. "Open the door!" he yelled. "Open the door!"

Tiny stayed put and screamed back, "I'm underage! If you touch me, I'll sue!" Elvis was far past considering the legalities of the situation. He started looking around the roadway, and I knew he wanted a rock to break the car window. Before he could get a hold of one, I screamed, "Get the hell out of here now, or he's going to break that window and then that head of yours!"

Luckily for her and Elvis, Tiny started the car, hopped the curb, and peeled away. We didn't see her for a long time, but then she started showing up at the house on Monovale Drive. By then a regular, welcome visitor to the house was a woman named Pat Balasko, who was seriously into karate. Elvis called her "Karate Pat," and I still call her that, as she and I have remained close friends.

When Tiny reappeared, Elvis asked Pat to have a talk with her. Tiny hadn't changed. She started shooting off her large, filthy mouth, and then she made an even bigger mistake and tried to get physical with Karate Pat. Tiny ended up on the ground, and Pat warned her that if she ever blotted out our skyline again she would get it much worse. We never saw Tiny anymore, and Elvis presented Pat with a TLC necklace in gratitude.

A few weeks after they moved into the Rocca Place house, Elvis began filming *Spinout*, which paired him up again with Shelley Fabares. Priscilla sensed Elvis's attraction to Shelley, which caused one of their biggest blowups. From what I've been able to gather, Priscilla asked to visit the set for lunch and to meet the lovely Ms. Fabares, about whom Elvis always spoke so glowingly. Elvis wasn't thrilled with the idea and said so.

"Is there something going on you don't want me to know?" Priscilla wondered.

Tired of her attitude and nagging, Elvis said he had nothing to hide and then suggested it would be a good time for Priscilla to go visit her parents for a while.

"Well, I'm not going!" Priscilla yelled.

"Oh, yes, you are!" Elvis yelled back. "In fact, I'll help you."

He charged over to her closet and began tossing clothes on the bed. I was in my room at the time and heard their yelling. A moment later, Elvis emerged with the news that he had told Priscilla to "pack your shit and get out." He instructed Joe to get her on the first plane out of L.A.

He was using his brand of "reverse psychology" on her. Elvis had done it with us many times, letting us know that nobody but him was indispensable. After a while, he went back and told Priscilla to "unpack your things, dammit. You're not going anywhere."

When Elvis started filming *Spinout*, Cliff Gleaves came back on the scene. A bit of a drifter and con man, Cliff pestered Elvis for a part in the movie. Elvis gave in, and Cliff got a two-line part, courtesy of our favorite director and good friend, Norman Taurog. Cliff immediately started rehearsing his Oscar acceptance speech.

"Yeah, baby, this is going to be the start of an illustrious movie career," he crowed, snapping his fingers like a real hepcat. "Get ready, boys, this is the first step to getting my star on Hollywood Boulevard. This new gig is going to get me paid and laid."

He kept it up all the way up to the moment Taurog called "Action!" Then poor Cliff just froze, unable to move or recite his dialogue.

Elvis was livid, yanking Cliff aside and telling him, "Don't you ever—ever!—ask me to do something like this for you again. Got it?" Of course, as is often the case, Elvis laughed his ass off later when retelling that story.

Joe and I were in several scenes in the film, but nothing of Cliff's magnitude. We got to push Elvis's race car in one scene.

Actress Deborah Walley played a tomboyish drummer in Elvis's band. Notwithstanding her acting degree from the prestigious New York Academy of Dramatic Arts, Deborah mainly acted in bikini movies. Although a big Beatles fan, she switched teams the moment Elvis shook her hand at the first rehearsal and said, "It's such a pleasure to meet you and work with you. I am such a fan of yours."

They spent many hours hanging out, talking about acting and religion. Deborah was raised Catholic but had drifted away from church. Elvis apprised her of new philosophies and ideas, including meditation, even taking her to the Self-Realization Center in Palisades.

During a race scene shot in the L.A. hills, Elvis and Deborah were chatting between takes when a bedraggled German shepherd dog wandered up out of nowhere. Elvis sent someone out for dog food, and after the dog ate, he had it taken to a veterinary groomer to be cleaned up and checked out. Deborah ended up taking the dog, which she called "Missy." It was her pet for many years.

She was hoping to become Elvis's pet, and because we clicked as friends she confided her yearning to me. "I'm in love with him, Sonny, but I don't feel anything in return," she said one day. I let her down gently, explaining that Elvis felt more brotherly toward her than anything. The fact is that whenever Elvis met an obviously "good girl," he would usually put her up on a pedestal and never entertained romantic notions about her. It was just one of the many interesting dichotomies about Elvis.

*Spinout* marked the end of the Elvis's reign as a Top 10 box-office draw in the annual movie exhibitors' poll. Movie audiences were becoming more sophisticated in their tastes, and Elvis's core audience was growing up.

By then, Elvis's interest in moviemaking took a decidedly personal turn. He purchased an expensive reel-to-reel Sony video camera and recorder. It had just been introduced to the U.S. home market. The camera didn't include sound, and the film was in black and white. Elvis would often make his tapes and then close the door and view them privately in his room for hours on end. They weren't exactly intended for family audiences.

On one of the road trips we made back to Memphis, Elvis had one of his "regulars" rendezvous with him at the Western Skies Motel in Albuquerque, New Mexico. They engaged in a four-day private taping session while the rest of us just sat around. Some of the married guys got sore at Elvis because they were eager to see their families, but we stayed until the boss was done.

Elvis even turned his camera on Priscilla and another woman, filming them as they wrestled around in bras and white panties. He wasn't into black lace or rainbow lingerie, just white. I heard through the grapevine that Priscilla destroyed a large cache of tapes after Elvis's death.

Another expensive toy Elvis bought around this time was a retired Greyhound bus. Elvis took the bus to George Barris, who started the revolution in custom car building and designed one-of-a-kind hot rods for *The Munsters, Dukes of Hazzard, Route 66,* and *Batman.* George's Batmobile still draws crowds at car shows today.

The bus was George's most ambitious project yet. While he worked on it at his North Hollywood shop, Elvis would periodically drop in and check on his progress. George lined the rear engine with heavy-duty lead to contain the noise, installed and form fitted a hydraulic chair in the driver's seat, and set up a state-of-the-art stereo system, full kitchen, and sleeping quarters.

One night Elvis asked me, Marty, and Billy to take a drive with him in his black Rolls-Royce limousine to George's shop. I drove, and when we were done inspecting the bus, we headed back to Rocca Place. It was a beautiful California evening, and all of a sudden Elvis announced, "This is one of those baby blue Cadillac convertible nights" and instructed me to head for the Hillcrest Motor Company, a Cadillac dealership on Wilshire Boulevard and Beverly Hills Drive.

In the showroom, there was a beautiful brand-new black-on-black convertible with mahogany wood accent on display. Elvis introduced himself to the only salesman on duty and asked if he had any baby blue convertibles for sale. The guy said none were available, but he offered to try to locate one right away.

Elvis told Marty to stay with the salesman and then led me and Billy across the street to Hillcrest's used car lot. I thought he was looking for a used baby blue convertible in case the salesman couldn't find one for him. Nothing there appealed to him, and he asked if I knew of another Caddy dealership. I mentioned Lou Ehler's, down Wilshire near Fairfax. We drove right there, and I dropped Elvis and Billy off in front at the showroom door while I parked the Rolls in the back parking lot. As I walked up to the door to join them inside, Elvis, Billy, and the salesman were coming out. Elvis pointed to a fantastic black-on-black Caddy convertible and said, "Sonny, what do you think of that one?"

"God almighty, Elvis," I said. "That is beautiful. You sure you still want a blue one?"

Then he held out the keys and said with a smile, "It's yours."

Stunned, I told him, "No it's not, Elvis. I can't do it. No way."

Elvis just laughed and said he wanted me to have it. I choked up, and tears welled up in my eyes. I turned away and walked back to the Rolls and sat down in the driver's seat. Elvis had followed me and got in the front passenger seat. He looked at me and asked, "What's wrong with you, Sonny?"

What was wrong was that he had just given me a $1,600 motorcycle a few months earlier, and now this. But I couldn't say anything at the moment. Elvis and I had always had a playful relationship, and I never really told him what he meant to me. I loved that man like a brother. He was so good to me.

Finally, when I could speak again, I said, "Elvis, you're always giving, and we're always taking."

He smiled, "Naw, that's not true, Sonny," he said. "You're giving when you don't even know it. I hear how you always stick up for me when I'm not around. I know how loyal you are to me, and that means a lot to me, man. I put you guys through a lot, and you handle it well. This is just my way of saying thanks. So I want you to have this car right now."

Then he smiled and raised an eyebrow. "And you can't tell me that you didn't sit around seeing these cars go by and thinking one day you wanted to have one."

"Well, sure," I said, "every kid does that."

"I did, too," he said softly, handing the keys to me. "Now, you've got yours, so let's go get mine." Elvis and Billy got in the Rolls, and, with Elvis driving it, I followed them in my new Cadillac back to Hillcrest Cadillac. There, Marty told us that the salesman had found a baby blue Caddy in Long Beach. It would be delivered to Hillcrest as soon as it was serviced. But Elvis decided to cancel the order and take the black one on the showroom floor.

The next day Elvis started buying Caddy convertibles for every one of the guys, which took him several days to locate and complete. That was typical of the spontaneous generosity I witnessed many times during my sixteen years with Elvis. And it wasn't just his friends who benefited from it. Elvis made annual large contributions to Memphis charities, and he often reached out to individuals in need.

Elvis bought a specially equipped 1966 Chevrolet Impala for Memphian Gary Pepper, who was afflicted with cerebral palsy. From

1959 through 1963, Gary ran the International Tankers Fan Club, which was named after Elvis's army battalion. Elvis appreciated the work Gary did running the three-thousand-member fan club. Gary was present for several key events in Elvis's life, including his wedding reception. He often joined us for movie theater parties at the Memphian.

Elvis appreciated Gary so much that he arranged through Vernon to pay $400 a month for a personal nurse for him. He also gave Gary's dad, Sterling, a job as a gate guard at Graceland. Unfortunately, upon Elvis's death, Vernon promptly cut off Gary's benefits. He died at forty-eight in a Long Beach hospital in 1980.

Nothing touched me more than when Elvis bought a wheelchair for a poor elderly black woman who lived near Humes High School. Marty Lacker read a story about her in the newspaper. She had no legs from the hips down and got around on boards with roller skates affixed to the bottom. Marty showed the article to Elvis, and a nod of his head set things in motion. Marty and Richard Davis went to the medical supply store and bought an electric wheelchair. It was loaded into the station wagon. Richard and Alan drove that to the woman's home, followed by Elvis, Priscilla, Marty, Billy, and me in the limo. When we got there, the woman's husband answered the door, and we wheeled the chair into the tiny living room.

When the husband called the woman in, she saw the chair and asked, "What is this here for?"

"Ma'am, it's just a little something to let you go just about anywhere you want to go," said Elvis. "It's electric, so you don't need anyone to push you. It's just something we wanted to do for you to help you get around better." Her eyes teared up, and she asked in a soft tone, "Can I sit in it, please?"

Elvis and I reached down, picked her up, and set her in the chair. She ran her arms up and down the shiny wheels as the tears flowed. And I don't mean just hers. We said our good-byes, and outside Alan wondered if the woman even knew who Elvis was.

"It doesn't matter, man," Elvis said. "At least she knows someone cares."

Of course, Elvis was generous with himself, too. A gift to himself was a meditation garden built in the back of Graceland, inspired by the Self-Realization Park. Designed by Ann and Bernie Grenadier (Marty Lacker's sister and brother-in-law), the $21,000 garden featured Italian marble statues, stained glass panels, a fountain with fourteen different water features, and underwater light formations.

Elvis couldn't go to regular Sunday services, and the meditation garden provided him a sanctuary for private meditation. We chipped in to buy a statue of Jesus sculpted by a local artist that still sits in the garden today.

In May 1966, Elvis recorded his second gospel album, *How Great Thou Art*. It went double platinum (two million records sold) and garnered Elvis a Grammy Award for best gospel album of the year.

The recording session marked the beginning of Elvis's long association with RCA producer Felton Jarvis, a fine and talented man. He and Elvis connected deeply on a musical and personal level. Felton had a special gift for coming up with musical arrangements that impressed Elvis and everyone else in the studio. He always found a way to add a new dimension to a song. I remember when Elvis recorded one of my all-time favorite holiday songs, "If Every Day Was Like Christmas," written by my cousin Red. Felton came up with the idea of adding a steel guitar note in a couple of places in the song that was just the perfect touch.

A few years later, Felton was forced to undergo regular dialysis when his kidneys began to fail. When Elvis found out, he shelled out almost $100,000 for successful kidney transplant surgery.

Elvis's latest movie for MGM, *Double Trouble*, was an attempted takeoff on the Beatles' *A Hard Day's Night*, but it went nowhere. Elvis plays Guy Lambert, a London-based crooner who is pursued to Brussels by two women. Annette Day plays a love-struck adolescent heiress, and Yvonne Romain is an enigmatic temptress.

Annette was a seventeen-year-old actress discovered by one of the film's producers while she was working in an antique shop on London's Portobello Road. *Double Trouble* was her first and last picture. She was totally out of her element, and Elvis went out of his way to put her at ease. He even bought her a blue and white Mustang car.

The movie was shot on the back lot at MGM. I doubled for Elvis in a driving scene as well as for actor Michael Murphy in a fight scene against Elvis. Murphy played an assassin, and the script originally called for him to die when Elvis knocked him down a well. But Murphy's character almost got a reprieve when it was decided that Elvis shouldn't kill him and be responsible for his death. The fight scene was revised so that instead of Elvis knocking the guy into the abandoned well, the guy misses Elvis with a kick and falls into the well.

The stunt required split-second accuracy from me, because the circumference of the well was only about ten feet, and it had a metal rim. Elvis took me aside and asked me if I thought I could do it without hurting myself.

He knew that I hadn't ever performed a stunt like this before. I assured him that I would be fine. I practiced my fall diligently before the cameras rolled and hit my mark perfectly each time. There were large cardboard boxes at the bottom of the well with a mattress covering them. But during the money shot, I bounced off the mattress, which folded over on my head. I quietly lay there waiting for the Taurog to say "cut," but I never heard a word. The next thing I knew, Elvis was in the well with me, yelling my name and pulling the mattress off me. When I calmly asked what the problem was, he said, "Damn you, sonofabitch! Why didn't you answer us? Mr. Taurog yelled cut!"

I explained that with the mattress over me I couldn't hear a thing. "Man, you scared the hell out of us," Elvis said. "We thought you hurt yourself really bad."

When we got out of the well, Taurog came up and said he had bad news. The scene needed to be reshot due to a technical problem with the camera. That jolted me worse than the fall, but then Taurog said he was only kidding.

When George Klein visited the set, Elvis got a big kick out of his bebop attitude and inimitable voice. He dubbed George the "Eternal DJ." Whenever George entered the room, Elvis would announce in a deep bass voice, "Here comes GK the DJ!" and George would entertain us with some deejay patter.

It was around this time that Marty and Richard arranged a meeting with one of Elvis's favorite entertainers of all-time—the great Jackie Wilson. Elvis had admired the soul singer ever since he saw Wilson perform "Don't Be Cruel" and "Paralyzed" at the Frontier Hotel in Las Vegas in 1956. At the time, Wilson was the lead singer in the group Billy Ward and the Dominoes. With his black pompadour and electrifying dance moves, he was often called "the black Elvis Presley."

Jackie was playing a two-week engagement at The Trip, an intimate nightclub on Sunset Boulevard that featured mostly psychedelic acts popular at the time, such as the Byrds, the Lovin' Spoonful, the Velvet Underground, and Andy Warhol's Exploding Plastic Inevitable.

Also appearing after Jackie's engagement was over was James Brown, "the Godfather of Soul," who'd never met Elvis. Brown had wanted to meet Elvis for years, but every time he called, Elvis was sleeping. So when they finally met at The Trip, one of the first things Brown said was, "Man, you sure do sleep a lot!"

Brown really wanted Elvis to come catch his act the following night, but Elvis was noncommittal. He ended up not going, but he sent James a watch and a personal note that stated that he had to get up early the next morning to go to the movie set. Brown was upset and made no bones about it.

Jackie Wilson was a great gentleman and talented performer. Since going solo in 1957, he had registered fifty-five Top 100 hits and two dozen Top 40 singles. But his live act was really something to behold. After the show that night, Elvis told Jackie, "There's no reason you shouldn't be the number one singer in the world." Elvis invited him to the set of *Double Trouble* a few days later, and Jackie had a great time.

"Man, this is something!" he said. "I ought to get into making movies. You guys look like you're having fun."

Jackie asked for an autographed picture, and ever after, Jackie always told people Elvis was his favorite singer. But things ended badly for Jackie. The IRS slapped him with a large bill for back taxes after it was discovered that his manager had been ripping him off for years. In 1974, Jackie suffered a stroke and collapsed onstage in Cherry Hill, New Jersey. He spent his last years in a vegetative state in nursing homes, finally dying in 1984 at the age of forty-nine. On his bedside when he went was that autographed photo of Elvis.

I heard that Elvis paid up to $40,000 for Jackie's nursing home care. That's the kind of friend Elvis Presley was.

# Chapter 21

# Palm Springs and the Circle G

A S GREAT AND GLAMOROUS AS HIS LIFE WAS, ELVIS PRESLEY REQUIRED constant stimulation and diversion. While he should have been satisfied with his status as the world's greatest singer and box-office champion, there was an emptiness inside that he never could fill, although he tried in several ways—with cars, women, buying sprees, and a dazzling array of drugs. It was around this time that Elvis switched from uppers to downers. He started on Percodan and other pain pills, as well as such sleeping aids as Seconal and Tuinal.

Colonel Parker thought it might be therapeutic for Elvis to spend time at a desert hideaway between movies. Parker himself had a home in Palm Springs, and he arranged through the William Morris Agency for Elvis to stay at Jack L. Warner's Palm Springs house. The Spanish adobe-style home at 285 Via Lola was a royal residence, complete with solid bronze pharaoh-head doorknobs on the gates of the four-thousand-square-foot property.

Built in 1958, the C-shaped estate was lined with giant palm and olive trees and surrounded by a high security wall. Elvis rented Warner's guest cottage in the back, which came with its own swimming pool.

Celebrities flocked to Palm Springs for its blue skies, green golf courses, and enchanting mountain views. Today, Palm Springs and its surrounding cities boast a population of about 150,000 people, but in the late '60s only about 20,000 residents called "the village" home. They included Frank Sinatra, Bob Hope, Bing Crosby, Lucille Ball,

Desi Arnaz, Groucho Marx, Danny Kaye, Dean Martin, Liberace, Rock Hudson, Gene Autry, and Darryl Zanuck. Plus a Mafia chieftain or two.

The Coachella Valley was where U.S. presidents compared golf scores, movie stars played tennis, and studio moguls "auditioned" starlets.

And it's where Colonel Parker and Hal Wallis huddled many times in the latter's Rancho Mirage compound to chart Elvis's movie career, which, by late 1966, was almost off the charts. In fact, Wallis decided that his next film with Presley and Parker, *Easy Come, Easy Go*, would be his last.

Elvis enjoyed the laid-back desert lifestyle. "You can feel the tension leaving when you get out of Los Angeles," he said once as our caravan headed down Interstate 10 for the desert.

During the day, we mostly hung out by the pool. At night we'd either make a food run for hamburgers or pizza or take a cruise down Palm Canyon Boulevard to check out the ladies. We called it "trolling." As it was everywhere else, there were always plenty of females eager to come home with Elvis.

One night several of us joined Elvis for a guys' weekend. On these occasions, Elvis, Red, and I did our usual routine of settling down to watch the Friday night fights from Los Angeles. Channel 11 aired a full lineup of boxing matches from the Olympic Auditorium. This time we were surprised when, as soon as we sat down, Elvis broke out some pot that he had gotten from a gal in Los Angeles.

We lit up joints and sat back to watch the action. We'd all smoked a little grass before, but this stuff was really potent. After a while, Red exclaimed, "Damn, this is the longest round I've ever seen in my life!"

"What round is it?" I asked, having somehow lost track.

"Eleven," he said as if dealing with a hopeless child. When I asked how he knew that, he indicated the number eleven lit up on the side of the TV. "There it is right on the television: round eleven!"

Elvis was just about rolling on the floor. When he got his laughter under control, he informed us that eleven was the number of the channel we were watching.

A few minutes later, Red got up and walked right up to the TV set. He lit a match and held it in one hand, while with the other he covered up the channel number 11. When we asked what the hell he was doing, Red said he was "looking for the channel."

"You're covering it up with your hand, man," Elvis said, starting to laugh again. "It's right there in front of you."

"God almighty!" yelped Red, stepping back so fast he slipped on the throw rug and fell flat on his back. When Elvis decided he looked just like a frog that way, we all lost it. That particular fight seemed to last forever. When it ended, Elvis bid goodnight to Red and I and headed for his bedroom.

Then the munchies attacked. Red decided he couldn't live without a ham and cheese sandwich, and I had a huge hankering for a BLT. In the kitchen, I got out all the ingredients for my sandwich and went to work. The bacon took forever to cook; Red had eaten two sandwiches before I was done constructing one. After repeating for the umpteenth time how good those sandwiches were, he said goodnight as my bread popped out of the toaster. But I wasn't alone for long.

"Man, I could smell that bacon all the way back in my room," said Elvis, who was peering around the corner of the doorway. "You think you could make one for me?"

Elvis usually took a sleeping capsule called Placidyl at bedtime. I asked him if he had taken it yet, as it usually took only a little less than thirty minutes to work. He said he had taken it about ten minutes prior to his kitchen visit, so I knew he would never make it to the time it would take to make another sandwich. I'd seen him take one and then fall asleep in the middle of a meal. Figuring I had better not start from scratch on his sandwich, I handed him the one I'd made for myself, and he took it back to his room. I made myself another one and gobbled it quickly because I was afraid that Elvis was going to come back and want another. I would have made him another one, but I was going to eat mine first. No need to worry; Elvis didn't want seconds. I walked back to his room to check on him to make sure he was okay. He was sound asleep, and there wasn't a crumb left on his plate.

Wanting a place to call his own in Palm Springs, Elvis signed a one-year lease (at $21,000) on a home at 1350 Ladera Circle. The modern-style structure was called "the Alexander House," because it was built by famed Palm Springs contractor Bob Alexander. His construction firm popularized Palm Springs' signature midcentury modern architectural style. Alexander had originally created the circular-shaped spec home that Elvis leased for publicity purposes.

But his wife became so smitten with the design they decided to make it their permanent dwelling.

I couldn't blame her. Built in 1952 on a slope at the base of the San Jacinto Mountains in the Las Palmas district, the design incorporated glass and peanut brittle stonework to inscribe four perfect circles on three different levels. The centerpiece of the home was a three-octagon-shaped living room with a sixty-four-foot built-in couch, a freestanding fireplace, and thick shag carpeting. Other special touches included an open-air kitchen, gold-plated bathroom fixtures, and four bedrooms covered by an inclined shed roof. The raised circular master bedroom at the front of the home offered a spectacular view of the Santa Rosa Mountains and Coachella Valley.

The secluded grounds included a large swimming pool, a private garden, a fruit orchard, and a tennis court.

But the coolest feature of the place was a centralized vacuuming system. Each room had a plate mounted on the baseboard to which a vacuuming attachment was affixed. Then a single machine sucked the dust out of all the rooms simultaneously, making it unnecessary to drag a vacuum cleaner to every room.

*Look* magazine called it the "House of the Future."

Unfortunately, the Alexanders didn't enjoy their dream home for long. Tragedy struck on November 14, 1965, when the family's small Lear jet crashed outside of nearby Indio, killing everyone on board with the exception of a daughter.

After Elvis moved into the Ladera Circle home, he started work on *Easy Come, Easy Go*, his final picture for Paramount Studios. In it he played Ted Jackson, a former navy frogman enlisted to help a free-spirited woman, played by Dodie Marshall, to find a treasure in the hull of a sunken ship.

Actress Pat Priest usually played wholesome characters (she was the second Marilyn Munster in the TV series *The Munsters*), but in the film she was the villainous Dina Bishop. Pat was warm and friendly, with a great sense of humor, and I developed a good friendship with her. Interestingly enough, Pat's mother, Ivy Baker Priest, was a former treasurer of the United States, and at one time her signature was on every dollar bill printed by the U.S. Treasury Department.

Elvis ended up selling Pat a used black El Dorado Cadillac for $3,000. She drove the car for a few years and then traded it in for a

Pontiac, without telling the dealer that it had once belonged to Elvis. Later she joked that she had thrown away her retirement fund.

Pat Harrington, who played a nightclub owner in the movie, provided a lot of comic relief on the set. Elvis got a huge kick out of the actor who later became best known as Dwayne Schneider on the popular TV series *One Day at a Time*.

Pat was a gifted storyteller, and one day while we were on a boat on the soundstage, he started telling funny stories. Director John Rich, whose ego was blimp-sized, decided to match Pat story for story. But Rich's efforts were forced and not very funny, and his growing discomfiture made us break up more than his stories. One day Elvis and Pat had a running joke going, which all of us guys were in on, and it broke the two of them up. The two kept blowing their lines in the scene, and after a couple of takes, Rich exploded. "Okay, that's *it!* All you guys get off the set!" he yelled. "Let's go!"

Elvis stopped laughing and then took Rich aside. "I make these movies because I have fun while making them," Elvis said, suddenly turning serious. "When the fun stops, then I stop. And my guys go when I tell them to go."

We didn't have any more trouble with Rich, and the movie wrapped without further incident in November.

Back at Graceland that holiday season, Elvis got a call from Priscilla's father. He wanted to know when Elvis was going to follow through with his promise to marry his daughter. Both Priscilla and her dad have always vehemently denied this happened, even in the DVD version of *Elvis by the Presleys*, which came out in 2005. But Marty Lacker was there the day the call came in.

According to Marty, Elvis had been in a great mood because Marty's brother-in-law, Bernie Grenadier, had just finished redecorating his bedroom. But the phone call from the captain changed that. Elvis never told me or any of the guys he was actually engaged to Priscilla. As close as we were to Elvis, it's unlikely he would have kept such a huge secret from us. The fact is, he wasn't good at keeping any kind of secret. The joke among us was, "If you want everyone to know your secret, just tell Elvis."

Over the years, Priscilla has gone to great lengths spinning the fiction that theirs was a fairy-tale romance. If that was so, it ended very quickly, and fairy tales are supposed to be forever. Their marriage lasted but six years. Priscilla was quick to take back her maiden name as there was a condition in the divorce decree, according to Elvis, that she was forbidden to use the name Presley for a career name in the entertainment business. But after Elvis's death, she immediately took the name back and became Priscilla Presley.

In 1997, I even heard Bob Goen, a cohost of the TV show *Entertainment Tonight*, refer to her as "Elvis's widow, Priscilla Presley" in a story of her frantic efforts to get Elvis's Memphis Restaurant off the ground in time for Elvis Week in August. They had been divorced almost four years when he died, so she was hardly a widow. But it's a label that has benefited Priscilla greatly.

I know Elvis loved Priscilla, and he was saddened by the divorce. But he wasn't despondent about it. He was depressed, however, as their wedding date approached.

I personally think Elvis never should have married at all, as he just couldn't commit himself to one woman for long. He loved them and enjoyed being with them, but not forever. In my years with Elvis, there were just four women in his life who I think he *truly* loved: Anita Wood, Priscilla, Ann-Margret, and Linda Thompson, listed in the order in which they first appeared in his life.

Right before Christmas of 1966, Elvis bought Priscilla a four-year-old black quarter horse called Domino. Because Graceland had an old stable, tack room, and hayloft out back, the horse was quartered right on the grounds. Priscilla spent several afternoons riding Domino and started in on Elvis to join her. First he demurred and bought horses for his cousin, Patsy Presley, and Jerry Schilling's fiancée, Sandy Kawelo, in hopes that their company would be enough for Priscilla. Then one day Elvis took a ride on Domino, and he was hooked.

Jerry Schilling found him a golden palomino for $3,500. The striking horse was named Rising Sun. Within two months, Elvis bought twenty more horses—bays, quarter horses, sorrels, palominos, geldings, and buckskins. When I returned to Graceland in February 1967, after filming a movie called *The Hellcats*, the place looked like Gene Autry's Melody Ranch.

"You should have stuck around after the holidays," Elvis said. "I bought everyone a horse." I told him I didn't need one, but he insisted, and in short order I had my own golden palomino called Willie.

To accommodate all the horses on the thirteen-acre property, Elvis bought a bulldozer and razed the small home in back where

Billy Smith and his wife once lived, and he paid a tidy sum to have the barn renovated.

But even that wasn't enough, so Elvis began the search for a ranch. Priscilla found a 160-acre place near Horn Lake, Mississippi, called Twinkletown Farms. It was located off Highway 301 and Goodman Road, about ten miles from Graceland across the state line. Elvis paid a reported $437,000 for the spread, which included a small white-arched bridge across a lake, a barn with horse stalls, and a herd of Santa Gertrudis cattle. But what really clinched the deal for Elvis was the huge concrete cross that sat out in the pasture by itself. Elvis saw it as a message from God that the land was blessed. It was actually a landmark for a nearby airport, but no one wanted to tell Elvis.

One time at the ranch, Lamar mounted Charlie Hodge's horse. The animal immediately began to back up, and Lamar began sawing on the reins and calling out "Whoa...whoa!" Instead of stopping, the confused and frightened horse ended up flipping over backward with Lamar on him. Then the horse stepped on Lamar's leg while he was struggling to get up. Elvis almost fell off of his horse from laughing so hard, once he knew that Lamar wasn't hurt badly. He wasn't, but he did have a large bruise where the horse stepped on his thigh. All of us laughed with Elvis, except Priscilla, who jumped off of her horse and knelt to tend to Lamar, who was moaning and cussing the horse out.

Lamar fully healed after a few days, but that horse was never the same again. When Charlie tried to ride it a few days later, all the horse would do was go backward. Charlie got off, walked into the den where Elvis and some of us were watching TV, and started fuming about how Lamar ruined his horse. He said it would only back up. But Elvis had the perfect solution: "Just turn the saddle around and ride him backward," he told Charlie.

Elvis renamed Twinkletown Farms "The Circle G" and made Alan Fortas the ranch foreman. One day Alan went out on the front porch of the main house, and there was a line of new trucks parked in the driveway. "Take your pick, man," Elvis told him.

"But E," Alan protested. "I already have one." So Elvis pointed out one of the truck salesmen and told Alan to pick out a truck for him. He was told he already had a truck, too. Elvis threw up his hands and said to Alan, "Hell, find some sonofabitch to give one to!"

He ended up buying about twenty-five trucks in a week's time, mostly Ford Rancheros and Chevy El Caminos. Vernon just about choked when he got the bill for about $100,000. But that was mere chicken feed compared to the invoice that came in for the trailers he bought for all of the guys after that.

Elvis had gotten it into his head to give each member of his inner circle one-half acre of land and a down payment to build our own homes. He even was going to insert a provision in the ranch deed that if anybody stopped working for him or was fired, he would still have the option of buying back the land at current market value. He was also going to replace the small ranch house with a replica of Graceland. But those notions didn't come cheap, and Elvis needed some temporary cash flow to finance the $1 million deal. Colonel Parker arranged with United Artists for Elvis to star in *Clambake*, another beach-and-bikini romp.

Elvis had put on about twenty-five pounds since his last film. While he got plenty of exercise on the ranch doing chores and riding horses, he ate as he pleased, mostly his favorite foods: hot dogs, cheeseburgers, bacon sandwiches, pork chops, chicken-fried steak, cured smoked ham, deep-fried peanut butter and banana sandwiches, cakes, pies, ice cream, and brownies. Not your typical chuckwagon fare.

Elvis reported to the set a week before the cameras rolled in a foul mood because the script was the same old song and dance—sing a few songs, kiss a few girls, and punch out a couple of guys. Director Arthur Nadel was upset to find his star in less than stellar shape, and he had the wardrobe department work overtime to fit Elvis with clothes that concealed his new spare tire.

Colonel Parker enlisted the services of Joe Esposito and Charlie Hodge to keep an eye on Elvis's escalating drug use and report back to him, and when some of the guys found out about it, there was major infighting in the ranks.

Elvis's way of combating his weight problem was popping diet pills given to him by Dr. Max Shapiro, the notorious Beverly Hills dentist known around town as "Dr. Feelgood," whose clients read like a who's who of Hollywood stars.

Max was a scumbag of the highest order. In his autobiography *Been There, Done That*, singer Eddie Fisher fingered him as the man who got him hooked on speedball injections. A speedball is a mixture of speed and heroin and was the cause of actor River Phoenix's untimely death in 1993, as well as the deaths of John Belushi and Chris Farley.

But Max was more hooked on fame as far as I could tell. He plastered his office wall with pictures of himself and celebrities to show his regular patients what a big man he was.

Elvis got industrial-sized jars of pills from Max in every color, shape, and size. You name it, and Elvis most likely had it in his medicine cabinet—Dexedrine, Dexemyl, Demerol, Desbutal, Seconal, Tuinal, and Placidyl.

In Tennessee, Elvis's personal physician was Dr. George Nichopoulos, a Memphis-based son of Greek immigrants. He was introduced to Elvis through George Klein's then-girlfriend, Barbara Little, who worked as his secretary. "Dr. Nick," as we referred to him, came out to the ranch one Sunday in February 1967 to treat Elvis for, of all things, saddle sores. Elvis called him back out two more times that same day and the day after that.

It's too bad that the people who voted for Oscar nominees never saw Elvis perform when he wanted a doctor to write him a prescription. Marty Lacker told me about the time Elvis actually tracked down a Walgreen's pharmacist at his home. Marty and Richard Davis were there when the druggist opened his front door to find Elvis Presley standing there. Elvis recited a litany of ailments for which he needed immediate medication and said that he couldn't get a hold of his doctor.

"I know your store is closed today, and I sincerely apologize for bothering you at home, but I figured you might have some medication here to tide me over," Elvis said.

The kindly man led Elvis into his bathroom and opened up the medicine cabinet, which contained no end of drug samples. Elvis proceeded to load up with some of everything, "just in case." When the druggist fretted that he was doing something wrong, Elvis put an arm around his shoulder and, with that famous southern charm of his, said, "I'll get a prescription for everything I got from you." Then he and Marty left with enough drugs to medicate a wounded combat unit.

The night before *Clambake* was to commence shooting in the second week of March, Elvis tripped over a television cord in the bathroom of the Rocca Place house, fell, and hit the back of his head. Priscilla found him unconscious. She called Joe, who summoned Dr.

M.E. Gorson, who in turn called in a favor from radiologist George Elerding. Elerding came over with a portable X-ray machine, but except for a golf-ball-sized lump on Elvis's head, he was fine.

Colonel Parker was most definitely not fine. After calling the studio to report that his star was going to be two weeks late in reporting to the set, Parker gathered the troops and laid down the law. "You wouldn't be in this condition if your head was on straight," Parker told Elvis. The Colonel mostly blamed Larry Geller, whom he pegged as a master manipulator, responsible for filling Elvis's head with all kinds of mystical, highfalutin nonsense. Geller had even suggested that Elvis had divine powers and was meant for a much higher calling than the entertainment business.

"There are going to be major changes taking place around here," the Colonel said. "United Artists could tear up the contract they have with Elvis for this delay, and this could cost us millions!"

It was time, he said, to "scale it back some." Elvis was "spending way too much money and has gone beyond what he can afford." One of the Colonel's solutions was for everybody to take a pay cut. Then he said we were to stop bringing our personal problems to Elvis, and he reinstated Joe Esposito as chief foreman/informant. Marty was put in charge of "special projects," whatever that meant.

Then the Colonel looked directly at Geller, and his voice took on a razor-sharp edge as he continued: "And some of you think maybe he's Jesus Christ who should wear robes and walk down the street helping people. But that's not who he is. Elvis is an entertainer, and he shouldn't be distracted from what he is supposed to do. You're all lucky to be here. If you don't like it, there's the door."

As Parker spoke, Elvis sat in a chair looking down and not saying anything.

As for Larry Geller, he took his *Twilight Zone* library and departed for greener pastures. Elvis told me later that he and Priscilla gathered everything Geller left behind and turned it into a bonfire behind Graceland.

Now if only Elvis's career would catch fire again.

# Chapter 22

# Domestic Bliss

THE YEAR 1967 WAS A PIVOTAL ONE FOR SOCIETY BOTH POLITICALLY AND culturally. San Francisco's Haight-Ashbury district was the capital of the counterculture movement. The hippie lifestyle promoted an agenda of free love and social activism.

*Rolling Stone* magazine debuted, FM radio started changing the listening habits of millions, and the Beatles' *Sergeant Pepper's Lonely Hearts Club Band* musically and artistically broke new ground.

Cinema was also moving in a different direction, and audiences were getting hipper, feasting on rich offerings such as *Bonnie and Clyde, The Graduate, Valley of the Dolls,* and *In the Heat of the Night.*

The times, they were a-changing, but not for Elvis Presley. Sure, he was still loved by millions, but the entertainment business was and always will be a young person's game. Elvis had been on the scene for more than a decade, and his original fans had grown up, gone to college, entered the workforce, and started their own families. Elvis was fortunate to have had a second act when he came back from the army and transitioned safely into movies. Many of his 1950s peers weren't so lucky. By the mid-1960s, Bill Haley, Little Richard, Chuck Berry, Jerry Lee Lewis, Pat Boone, the Everly Brothers, Frankie Avalon, Dion, Fabian, Ricky Nelson, and Bobby Darin all gave way to the Beatles, the Rolling Stones, the Byrds, Simon and Garfunkel, the Doors, and the Beach Boys.

Colonel Tom Parker's philosophy was, "If it ain't broke, don't fix it." And as long as there was a studio willing to shell out big bucks for Elvis to star in movies, the system wasn't broke. Artistically speaking, it was a whole different matter, of course.

But that wasn't entirely the Colonel's fault. Elvis had always said that if things ever got bad, he'd just go back to the studio and cut a great album. From my vantage point, Elvis could have done both. Hell, Dean Martin and Glen Campbell were triple threats in the late '60s. They managed to balance hugely successful singing, movie, and television careers and performed concerts on the weekends. Elvis could have easily spread his wings had he chosen to do so. And it was getting increasingly difficult for the Colonel to get him to report to work and take it seriously. A pattern started to emerge: the less Elvis enjoyed making a movie, the more fooling around he did to get through it. That was the case when he started filming *Clambake*, which was based loosely on *The Prince and the Pauper*, in March 1967.

Director Arthur Nadel surrounded Elvis with a cast he knew Elvis would be comfortable with, most notably Will Hutchins, Bill Bixby, and Shelley Fabares, making her third picture with Elvis. Nadel wisely let Elvis and his guys cut loose on the set with water and pie fights and cherry bombs.

Red set the tone early in the shoot when he stationed himself up on the catwalk over Elvis's trailer and then, when Elvis came out after being in makeup for an hour, nailed him with a water balloon. Elvis didn't even flinch or react at all. He just stoically walked back into his trailer to get his hair and makeup redone.

Speaking of Elvis's dressing room, for the entire shoot he played an album by French actor Charles Boyer in there. It was called *Where Does Love Go?* and the French actor didn't sing "What Now My Love?" and "Softly as I Leave You" as much as he recited them. Elvis said that Boyer's resonant voice and French accent were so rich that there wasn't a woman in the world who could refuse him. Elvis liked the album so much he gave copies to the whole cast and crew.

Elvis joined in the fun on the set when he persuaded a well-endowed extra to undo her bikini top in a scene with Bill Bixby. Bixby's reaction was priceless, and the whole set exploded with laughter. The Incredible Hulk himself would have had a hard time getting mad.

Nadel was so nice about letting us screw around on the set that we waited till the final day of filming to nail his ass. Perhaps anticipating it, he showed up for work wearing a raincoat and hat. But we left him alone all day, and at the wrap party he let down his defenses. There he wore a nice suit because he had to go to a PTA meeting for one of his kids afterward. Elvis stood up and made a speech about how much he enjoyed working with everyone, and he particularly sang Nadel's praises as a director. Nadel got all choked up and rose to thank Elvis when someone came up from behind and smashed a pie in his face.

Four days after the film wrapped, wedding bells tolled for Elvis and Priscilla—but I never heard them.

It was May 1, 1967. I was in the San Fernando Valley acting in a motorcycle movie called *The Hellcats*. I was fourth billed in the picture, which translated to a costarring role. I also had a lot of fun making it. Motorcycle movies did big box office on the drive-in circuit, and after years of extra work and bit parts, I felt I was finally making some headway in the business.

At the end of the first day of filming, I flipped on the news and was floored to hear that Elvis and Priscilla had exchanged vows earlier that day at the Aladdin Hotel in Las Vegas.

I was surprised not to have heard anything about the wedding. Colonel Parker arranged everything and controlled the guest list, which included Mr. and Mrs. Beaulieu, Priscilla's sister Michelle (who served as the maid of honor), Vernon and Dee Presley, Joe and Joanie Esposito, Patsy and Marvin "Gee Gee" Gambill, Billy and Jo Smith, Marty Lacker, George Klein, and jeweler Harry Levitch. Plus a lot of Parker's own professional friends. Marty and Joe were co–best men for Elvis.

My cousin Red and his wife, Pat; Jerry and Sandy Schilling; Charlie Hodge; and Richard Davis all flew to Vegas thinking they were on the list, but they learned that they could only attend the reception. That wasn't right. They were all a big part of Elvis's life, especially Red. He had been friends with Elvis since high school and loved him like a brother.

Red was understandably hurt about being barred from the wedding. Pat wept. They didn't stick around for the reception but returned to L.A. This caused a serious rift between Red and Elvis that lasted a couple years.

It was Joe who had the unenviable task of informing Red and the others they would not be attending the actual wedding ceremony, to be held in Milton Prell's private quarters at the Aladdin. They would be attending only the reception afterward. Acting on Parker's orders, Marty said that there wasn't enough room to accommodate everyone.

"You tell the Colonel I'm going to take his cane, break it in half, and stick it up his ass," Red told Marty. Then Red borrowed $50 from jeweler Harry Levitch so he and Pat could return to Los Angeles. They ended up on the same flight as several members of the wedding party, including Vernon and Dee. But Red talked to no one.

Meanwhile, the newlyweds boarded Frank Sinatra's jet, the *Christina*, piloted by comedian Danny Thomas, and were jetted to Palm Springs. After a few days there, they headed to the Bahamas, where it rained constantly and Elvis was uncomfortable because of racial tensions he perceived. So they finished out their honeymoon in Hawaii.

Red and Elvis got into it later when Red was complaining on the phone to Charlie Hodge about his shabby treatment in Vegas. Elvis was sitting alongside Charlie, overheard the conversation, and grabbed the phone. "What the hell's going on, boy?" he spat.

"What the f—— you mean, 'boy'?" answered Red. Their conversation lasted just a couple of minutes as they went at each other. It wasn't a pleasant experience to hear two close friends fight. When Red hung up the phone, he was no longer affiliated with Elvis Presley. Red went to work as a stuntman on the TV series *The Wild Wild West* starring his good friend Robert Conrad.

Upon returning from the Bahamas, Elvis and Priscilla spent a month alone at the Circle G, taking walks, riding horses, and enjoying romantic sunsets. But I couldn't help but feel that Ann-Margret was still deep in Elvis's thoughts. Ann and actor Roger Smith married in Las Vegas exactly a week after Elvis and Priscilla tied the knot. About a month later, Elvis sent a guitar-shaped flower arrangement for one of her Vegas openings, which he did every time she started an engagement in Sin City. That July he went with a few of the guys to see her show, and he told Ann that his feelings for her had never changed.

Then it was back to the studio to begin filming *Speedway*, with Nancy Sinatra. Nancy had adored Elvis for years and was recently divorced from singer Tommy Sands. While I wasn't there, I heard through some of the guys that she and Elvis were flirting like mad, having pajama parties in his trailer, and grinding up against each other whenever the opportunity arose. Nancy has claimed over the years that they never became intimate because she didn't want to get involved with a married man.

And an expectant father, to boot. Just two weeks into filming, Priscilla phoned Elvis with the news that she was pregnant. Elvis told reporters it was the greatest thing that ever happened to him, but I believe the news took him aback. His entire career was based on his sexy image, and fatherhood didn't go with that. In fact, he was so upset about Priscilla's pregnancy that when she was in her seventh month, he proposed a trial separation so he could think things through. He ended up buying Priscilla a shiny ring and never brought up the idea of separating again.

But that didn't mean he was interested in becoming a full-time family man.

Elvis was a man whose interest in something could fade without warning. That was the case with the Circle G ranch. In September of 1967, he decided to get rid of the place. I think it had something to do with the fact that since his marriage a lot of the guys weren't around anymore. Priscilla has said over the years that his entourage placed demands on him and added to his pressures. That's bunk. If anything, we kept him loose and free of worry because we demanded nothing of him. We did our jobs, and when the time was available, we hung out with him. If Elvis didn't want us around, he had no problem telling us to hit the road.

Two years after it was put on the market, the Circle G was purchased for $440,000 by a man named D.L. "Lou" McClellan. He added a swimming pool and a second building and planned to put a recreation center on the land, but he ended up defaulting on his loan after making three payments of $50,000. Ownership of the ranch reverted to Elvis, who held onto it for four years and then sold it to the Boyle Investment Company for a tidy profit.

After Elvis died, the ranch fell into the hands of W.F. McLemore, who owned a chain of McLemore's convenience stores. In 2002, a developer paid the McLemore family a fee to turn the land into a $600 million destination resort called the Presley Ranch. The site plans included two hotels, two championship golf courses, a go-kart racing complex, 650 luxury condominiums, three wedding chapels, and several honeymoon cottages. The site would also house shops, restaurants, a concert auditorium, horse trails, an Elvis museum, and a replica of the dream house Elvis wanted to build on the property when he was alive.

The developer also announced plans to hire me, Marty, Billy, Lamar, and Red as official greeters, telling visitors the history of the place and stories about Elvis. For that we would receive an annual salary and a place to live on the property. But the developer could never get the project off the ground. As of this writing, Presley Ranch still hasn't gotten off the ground, and I'm not so sure it ever will.

Elvis's next picture was a modern Western called *Stay Away, Joe* for MGM. In it he played Joe Lightcloud, a Navajo Indian rodeo rider turned cattle rancher.

Elvis reported to the set looking as fit as I'd ever seen him. He weighed about 165 pounds, was tan, and looked relaxed and happy.

I had a good role in the picture, but it wasn't from Elvis this time. Michael Hoey, who had worked on several pictures with Norman Taurog, was the dialogue director. He had hired me to do a small role in a film he wrote and directed called *The Navy vs. the Night Monsters*. Michael called and asked if I'd be interested in reading for a part in Elvis's picture. I read for director Peter Tewksbury, who had directed television shows such as *Father Knows Best* and *My Three Sons* and was a nice man. I initially read for the role of Hike Bowers. Only later did I find out that Red also tried out for the same part. Neither of us got it. It went to Warren Vanders. But Tewksbury thought I was perfect for the role of Jackson He-Crow, Joe Lightcloud's childhood friend who roughhoused and chased women with him.

Elvis was pleased to hear we would be working together. Our friendship survived his surprise wedding and my exclusion from it. Once I mentioned how fast it had all happened, and he said it was over almost before he knew it. Otherwise, we avoided the topic.

I was no longer a person working for Elvis but someone who worked with him. It was the acme of our personal and professional relationship. As far as I was concerned, that respect went both ways.

While I always had an appreciation for Elvis's acting ability, I really examined his technique on this picture. I'm convinced that had he been offered the right roles, Elvis would have equaled Frank Sinatra and other singers who also made a real mark in Hollywood. His musical timing was fantastic, and it was the same thing with his acting. He had such great timing with his double takes in a scene. Elvis usually nailed most of his takes on the first or second attempt.

Elvis had a natural flair for comedy, which any actor will tell you is the hardest category to tackle. Unfortunately, Elvis wasn't being offered great dramatic roles until years later when Barbra Streisand approached him for the lead role in *A Star Is Born*. By then Elvis didn't seem to care about leaving his mark as an actor.

The movie was filmed in gorgeous Sedona, Arizona. Located about one hundred miles north of Phoenix, Sedona has long been admired for its natural beauty. In 1923, Zane Grey's book *The Call of the Canyon* first introduced Sedona to the masses. It was rediscovered in the 1980s by devotees of the New Age movement.

Today Sedona is littered with million-dollar homes and more than four hundred New Age–related businesses. But back in 1967, the city consisted of a small motel, gas station, bank, post office, drugstore, and grocery store.

My home was the cozy Kings Ransom Motel. I stayed there with a handful of other actors, including Burgess Meredith, Katy Jurado, Quentin Dean, Joan Blondell, L.Q. Jones, Henry Jones, Michael Lane, Warren Vanders, Douglas Henderson, and Thomas Gomez. The latter introduced me to escargot for the first time when he invited me to eat with him at the motel dining room. He was a nice man, and I enjoyed many conversations with him on the set, especially about his impressive résumé and the people he worked with over the years. Some of us mostly passed the time hanging out at the pool and playing cards when we weren't working.

Elvis stayed at a private home and passed his time getting to know Quentin Dean. Quentin, a ringer for a young Linda Evans, played the character Mamie Callahan, a naive young girl who was coming of age and exploring her sexuality. She did a lot of the latter with Elvis offscreen, too, although when Priscilla visited the set things cooled down for a while. Quentin was first noticed in the business as the sexy young woman who changed clothes in front of a window in her home in the hit movie *In the Heat of the Night*. Elvis still found her sexy a few months later.

*Stay Away, Joe* was an offbeat comedy in which Elvis sang a love song to a bull called Dominic, which I know was a front-runner when it came to the most-hated songs in his catalog. The movie was one of my favorites because of how much fun I had working on it, not only with Elvis, but with the director and the cast. However, it didn't lasso many box-office dollars and was not considered a hit.

When the movie wrapped in November, Elvis and Priscilla moved into a $400,000 home at 1174 Hillcrest Drive in the exclusive Trousdale Estates. She'd found the split-level, six-year-old French Regency–style home in an ad in *Variety* magazine.

The house was definitely an upgrade from the Rocca Place home. It had three bedrooms, a security gate around the property, a swimming pool, and a guest cottage. My gut feeling was that Priscilla hoped to put even more distance between Elvis and the rest of us. Hell, I couldn't really blame her, with a baby on the way. Charlie Hodge stayed in the guest cottage while Patsy; her husband, Gee Gee; and their daughter, Dana, occupied one of the bedrooms. The other was reserved for Elvis and Priscilla's baby due in February. I dropped by to visit from time to time, but it sure wasn't like it used to be.

Things livened up with the birth of Lisa Marie Presley on February 1, 1968, exactly nine months to the day after her parents were married. Elvis was as happy as I'd ever seen him, and he viewed his daughter as the eighth wonder of the world. He was absolutely amazed that he and Priscilla had created this precious child.

"She's so perfect," he said to me, grinning from ear to ear. "I can't believe she's mine."

There was no doubt in my mind what a wonderful and attentive father Elvis would be. Not only would Lisa Marie's every material desire be provided for, but Elvis would shower her with unconditional love.

Priscilla was a different story. It didn't come easy for Elvis to be a committed husband. Elvis viewed her as a mother first and a wife second, and he had hang-ups about making love with her.

I think it went back to his extremely close relationship with his mother, Gladys. She gave him so much love and attention while he was growing up that he came to put all mothers on a special pedestal. The idea of sex with a mother was, to Elvis, out of the question.

So he continued to seek it elsewhere. And pretty soon Priscilla did likewise.

# Chapter 23

# The Comeback King

**W**HILE ELVIS WAS AT AN ALL-TIME HIGH IN HIS PERSONAL LIFE WITH THE birth of his daughter, professionally he was just treading water. He was recording mostly tunes that accompanied his movies, and the movies themselves were no great works of art.

MGM and Elvis's multipicture deal ended when Elvis finished the movie *Live a Little, Love a Little*. His last film, *Stay Away, Joe*, got bad reviews and did not do well at the box office, grossing only $1.5 million. The film ranked sixty-fifth on *Variety's* list of top-grossing films that year.

*Live a Little, Love a Little* was director Norman Taurog's ninth and final collaboration with Elvis. The movie was a comedy similar to some others he had made, but it contained some adult themes not seen in previous Elvis pictures. There was a sprinkling of expletives, a scene in which Elvis and his costar share a bed, and even a psychedelic sequence. But that was as far as the envelope was pushed.

The movie was shot in and around Los Angeles over a six-week period. The idea on everybody's mind was to take the money and run. Red and I were used in a key fight scene filmed at the *Hollywood Citizen-News* on Wilcox Drive. I believe this was perhaps the first time Red and Elvis had seen one another since the wedding debacle. As was always the case, things worked out between them, and when Taurog called "Action!" we all collaborated on what, I think, was our best stunt work together on celluloid.

The scene, filmed inside the newspaper office where Elvis's character worked as a photographer, called for us to toss him out on his ass. All told, the fight was supposed to last about a minute and a half.

The only direction we got from Taurog was to start at point A and end up at point B in the obstacle-filled room. He left the rest to us. We worked it out and got the sequence shot in one take, and when it was done Taurog exclaimed, "My God, I just love watching you guys work! It's so real! I thought you guys were knocking the hell out of each other." Then he gave Red and me $600 each for our work.

Elvis clicked with costar Michele Carey. The sultry brunette was a former child prodigy on the piano, and her beauty matched her talent. Elvis took instantly to the twenty-two-year-old former Powers model from Denver, and, taking their cue from the film's title, they loved a little.

On the home front, there was no romance at all between Elvis and Priscilla. She claimed that after Lisa Marie was born, Elvis didn't even touch her for two months. Once she dolled herself up in a black negligee, snuggled up to Elvis, who was in bed with a book, and began nibbling at him in hopes of lighting his fire. Nothing. Then she found out she could have set him on fire and Elvis wouldn't have felt anything, because his sleeping pills had already kicked in.

Increasingly frustrated, Priscilla enrolled in a modern jazz dance class under the pseudonym "C.P. Persimmons." The class was taught by Steven Peck, a former New York stage dancer with a small studio in Beverly Hills on Robertson. Distinctive and refined, the then-forty-five-year-old instructor still had the lean and taut body of an athlete.

He also had the ability to spot vulnerability a mile away. For the most part a very closed-off person, Priscilla did open up and express herself through dance. She also opened herself up to her handsome, dark, Sicilian instructor, and the two did a little more than the tango. It was the first time, to my knowledge, Priscilla ever stepped out on Elvis.

Soon she was taking so many classes that it was obvious to everyone in Elvis's inner circle what was going on. But it wasn't clear to Elvis himself, who was too ensconced in his own private world to take notice. The fairy-tale marriage Priscilla likes to rhapsodize about today was, in reality, a complicated mess from the get-go. The truth of the matter is that they both led double lives, and the only thing they had in common was their love for Lisa Marie.

In mid-May, Elvis, Priscilla, and Lisa Marie flew to Hawaii, but it was no second honeymoon. For one thing, Elvis invited his housemates and several others along. Joe and Joanie Esposito, Patsy and

Gee Gee Gambill, and Charlie Hodge all stayed with them at the Ilikai Hotel Nikko in Waikiki.

The Espositos had a bungalow right next to Elvis and Priscilla, and one night they heard Priscilla screaming, "You don't love me anymore since the baby was born! We never make love anymore! You never take your pajamas off anymore with me! We're always in the dark!"

In Hawaii, Elvis and Priscilla attended the 1968 Karate Tournament of Champions. It was hosted by Elvis's friend and associate, Ed Parker. Mike Stone, one of Bruce Lee's pupils and Parker's best black belt, shone like a diamond in the tournament and caught the attention of both Presleys. Elvis admired Stone's fighting prowess, while Priscilla admired him physically.

Back on the mainland, Priscilla pursued her affair with Steve Peck with a vengeance. The two were spotted together all over Los Angeles. Word got back to Elvis's attorney, Ed Hookstratten, who talked about hiring private detective John O'Grady to tail Priscilla. Whether Hookstratten actually followed through, I don't know. But he did mention something to Joe Esposito, and Joe spilled the beans to Elvis on the set of *Charro* in Apache Junction, Arizona. His reaction surprised everyone.

"You tell everybody to stay out of Priscilla's business and leave her the hell alone," Elvis said. Apparently, as long as Priscilla didn't embarrass him publicly, Elvis seemed to have no problem with her behavior.

Before Elvis began shooting *Live a Little, Love a Little*, Colonel Parker inked a deal with NBC and executives from the Singer Sewing Machine Company for a Christmas special. Today it's nothing for an actor to go back and forth between movies and television, but back then it was a risky move. But it saved Elvis's career.

While Elvis was taping the special at NBC studios in Burbank, California, I was in Tucson, Arizona, filming *Five Angry Men*, starring Keenan Wynn, Henry Silva, and Michele Carey, the latter having just finished the most recent movie with Elvis. I was gone for a few weeks, and when I got back Elvis took me to the studio to show me the tape of the Christmas special. He was excited, and when the film started rolling I saw why. It blew me away.

The songs, the sets, and Elvis's raw energy jumped off the screen. Elvis the rebel was back, clad in skintight black leather and prowling the stage like a panther. I was speechless and in awe. At the end, when Elvis stood in front of his own name in large red neon, wearing a pristine white suit and tearing out his soul in "If I Can Dream" (which would be his first million-selling record in three years), I was beside myself. "This thing is going to be a smash!" I told him.

Was it ever! When "Singer Presents Elvis" aired on December 3, 1968, 42 percent of the U.S. viewing audience was tuned in. The program boasted a higher audience share of women between the ages of eighteen and forty-nine than any other program that year and was NBC's highest-rated show of the week. The album soundtrack cracked the Top 10. More than three decades after the show aired, *TV Guide* named it as one of the one hundred greatest moments in television history.

Today it's commonly known as "The Comeback Special," because it put Elvis's career firmly back on track. The critics rediscovered him and loved him again. Representatives of the International, a new Las Vegas hotel opening the following summer, wanted Elvis to be its charter act.

Juiced by the overwhelming response to the special, Elvis canceled an RCA Nashville recording session with producer Felton Jarvis scheduled for January 1969. It was time to step outside his comfort zone and try something different.

They say that success has many fathers, and over the years lots of people have taken credit for putting the bug in Elvis's ear to record his next album at American Sound Studio in South Memphis. But I think the credit goes to Marty Lacker. He had quit working for Elvis in '67 to start Pepper Records, a jingle factory that did approximately 75 percent of the radio spots in the Southeast. Marty also did a lot of production work with Lincoln "Chips" Moman, the producer at American.

Moman was already a legend by the time Elvis met him. The Georgia native was a founding partner of Memphis-based Stax Records in the 1950s, working with artists such as Otis Redding, Aretha Franklin, Sam and Dave, and Booker T. and the MGs. Chips left Stax in a dispute over money and successfully sued his former company for $3,000. He used it in 1965 to convert a run-down dairy across town into a hit factory. Chips assembled the American Sound Band, a house band that scored 120 R & B, pop, and country hit records over a three-year span.

Of those, fifty-four became million sellers. Artists such as Neil Diamond, Dionne Warwick, Wilson Pickett, Dusty Springfield, the Box Tops, Joe Tex, Roy Hamilton, and Herbie Mann recorded at American Sound.

Making up the house band was Reggie Young on lead guitar, Tommy Cogbill and Mike Leech on bass, Bobby Emmons and Bobby Wood on organ and piano, and Gene Chrisman on drums. They created what was known as "the Memphis sound," a tight rhythm section with a punchy horn section that gave a lift and commercial gloss to every song they touched.

The band was unique in that its members were not cold and clinical in their approach to music. Like Elvis, they waited for the mood to hit them before they got started. Once they got in a groove, they started recording.

Even though the studio was practically in Elvis's backyard, he was mostly oblivious to the incredible streak of hits coming out of the former dairy. That ended when he was in the Jungle Room one day with Marty and, of all people, Felton Jarvis. Marty said, "Dammit, Elvis, I just wish for once you'd record here in Memphis. Chips Moman is the hottest thing going right now. That Memphis sound is tailor-made for you."

Elvis thought about it and told Marty he had just a couple days to make all the arrangements. Marty promptly phoned Chips to set things up, but the problem was that Neil Diamond was scheduled to start a recording session at American Sound. Diamond was big, but Chips made a gutsy spur-of-the-moment call. "F—— Neil Diamond," he said. "Neil Diamond will just have to be postponed. Tell Elvis he's on." (Diamond agreed to the postponement in exchange for getting Elvis to record one of his songs, "And the Grass Won't Pay No Mind.")

Chips and the American Sound Band could make the Chipmunks sound good. The question about Elvis was, could they make him relevant again? For years, Elvis picked songs to record from the Hill and Range catalog. It was pretty standard pop fare. When the Beatles and Bob Dylan came on the scene, everything changed. They ushered in the era of the singer-songwriter. Not only did the music have to have a hook, but the lyrics had to have some meaning. The record-buying public demanded more from artists, and now Elvis was in the position of having to prove that he hadn't lost his touch. Colonel Parker sent over his right-hand man, Tom Diskin, along with Freddy Bienstock of Hill and Range and RCA vice president Harry Jenkins, to give Elvis several songs from which to choose for the session. Only Eddie Rabbitt's "Kentucky Rain" made the cut.

When Elvis openly wondered why he couldn't get better songs, Marty spoke right up. "They don't need you anymore, Elvis," he said.

"What do you mean, they don't need me?" Elvis said in the shocked silence that followed Marty's statement. So Marty laid it out for him, explaining that when he ruled the charts in the late '50s and early '60s, Elvis was the only artist with the sort of power to demand a piece of the publishing profits and get away with it. It was a shrewd business deal the Colonel and Hill and Range developed with the songwriters, but artists were starting to get hip to the fact that the big money was in publishing, not performing. Selling the publishing profits was almost tantamount to selling their souls.

Dolly Parton likes to tell the story about the time she was approached by Colonel Parker when Elvis wanted to record her song "I Will Always Love You." Lovely—but he and the moguls at Hill and Range wouldn't budge unless Dolly gave up 50 percent of her publishing rights. Now, Dolly Parton is no country bumpkin. She wasn't going to give anything away, not even to Elvis Presley. She said no thanks, and everybody said she was nuts. But when Whitney Houston recorded "I Will Always Love You" on Dolly's terms in the early 1990s, it made Dolly more money than all of her own recordings put together.

Many people have asked me over the years why Elvis didn't write his own songs. The answer is that he just didn't have the patience. He had too much nervous energy to sit down and concentrate on composing. He appreciated the work of good songwriters, and he had a great ear for lyrics. He liked haunting lyrics, and when he heard something that blew him away, he announced it by proclaiming "My boy! My boy!"

Chips Moman spent more time chasing down good songs than anything else, and he was willing to open up his vault for Elvis. The Hill and Range brass wasn't happy, but they kept their powder dry until the end of the ten-day recording session that started on January 13, 1969.

Because the studio was in a less-than-ideal part of town, Chips assigned an armed security guard and a not-so-friendly dog to watch over the parking lot. Elvis entered through the back door, looked around the place, and said, "What a funky, funky place. Good Lord, what have I gotten myself into?"

The first order of business was to listen to the songs Elvis and the Colonel's men had picked for the session, and Chips and his troops quickly made it clear that they wouldn't settle for anything ordinary. The first song Elvis played got the thumbs-down from guitarist Reggie Young and pianist Bobby Wood. That made Felton Jarvis and Harry Jenkins blanch, but Elvis was impressed by their honesty and listened to what they had to say.

Elvis was coming off a bad cold, but he soldiered on through that first session and put down three vocals—"Long Black Limousine," "This Is the Story," and "Wearin' That Loved On Look." When they wrapped it up around 5:00 AM he was dead tired, but I'd never seen him more exhilarated.

"Man, that felt really great," Elvis said on the way to Graceland. "I really just want to see if I can have some great songs out there again." Toward that end, he opened himself up to new ideas and let himself be pushed like never before. The payoff was tremendous.

The best example I can think of is when he recorded "In the Ghetto," written by Mac Davis. At Chips's request, Mac came to play the song in person for Elvis. Chips and Elvis were at the control board as Mac played his guitar and sang, and when he was done Elvis said he liked the tune but that its message about poverty seemed a little too political and controversial for him.

Chips decided on some reverse psychology, at which he was as good as Colonel Parker himself.

"Elvis, I've got to tell you, this is a hit song," he said as Elvis stood with his hands on his hips, staring at the floor. When Elvis said nothing, Chips said, "If you don't want to do it, can I have the song?" Then he said it would be perfect for Joe Tex and Joe Simon, two black recording artists he was working with.

That did it. "No, I'll do it," Elvis quickly said.

He recorded the song, and I remember watching Elvis listening to the playback. When it was done, he took a deep breath and said, "Whoa!"

"In the Ghetto"—actually recorded in the ghetto—became his first Top 10 single since 1964, selling more than a million copies.

Another high point came when Elvis met R & B singer Roy Hamilton, who was working on an album for Chips's label, American

Group Production. Elvis admired Hamilton's vocal style, and upon meeting him Elvis presented Hamilton with a song he had planned to record himself. The song was "Angelica," and the two worked on it together so that Roy could record it that same day. Roy returned the favor by giving Elvis "You'll Never Walk Alone," which he later recorded. As it turned out, "Angelica" was Hamilton's last single. A year later, the thirty-nine-year-old singer had a stroke and died.

But the biggest song to come out of those sessions almost didn't get made because of a publishing dispute. "Suspicious Minds," written by Mark James, had actually been released by James in 1968 for Scepter Records, but it didn't go anywhere. Chips owned the publishing rights and felt the song was perfect for Elvis. Using the same arrangement as in James's version, it took Elvis only four tries to nail it. Elvis loved it and played it over and over. Everyone knew it was a hit.

That's when Tom Diskin and Freddy Bienstock tried to strong-arm Chips into giving up half the publishing. That brought everything to a screeching halt.

"Gentlemen, I thought we were here to cut some hit records," Chips said. "Now, if that's not the case, let me tell you what you and your group can do. You can take your f——ing tapes, and you and your whole group can get the hell out of here. Don't ask me for something that belongs to me. I'm not going to give it to you."

Diskin tried to get Elvis to back him, but Elvis knew he had gold and wasn't about to let them screw it up. He took Diskin, Bienstock, and Jenkins into another room and told them that he appreciated them looking out for his business interests. Regardless, though, he was recording the song.

In November 1969, "Suspicious Minds" became his first Number 1 song in seven years and the centerpiece of his Las Vegas shows. Three decades later, it was unanimously voted by fans around the world as their favorite Elvis Presley song of all time.

All told, Elvis cut thirty-six songs at American Sound Studio, most of which were released on *From Elvis in Memphis* and *From Vegas to Memphis*. It was his best work to date. From those sessions came four singles that charted on Billboard's Top 40—"Kentucky Rain" (Number 16), "Don't Cry Daddy" (Number 6), "In the Ghetto" (Number 3), and "Suspicious Minds" (Number 1), the last two certified as million sellers. "Rubberneckin'" was also recorded then and later remixed as a single in 2004.

Many fans have wondered why, given his great success at American Sound Studios, Elvis never recorded there again. The answer is complex. It took a lot of effort for Elvis to buck the Colonel, RCA, and Hill and Range that one time, and had his career not been between a rock and a hard place, he might not have done it at all. I wish Elvis had taken the reins of his career for good, but I don't really think he had the will.

But the other reason was that in 1972, Chips Moman left town in a huff. He was unhappy about all the attention his former studio, Stax, got when Memphis promoted itself as "Soul City"—a not-so-subtle reference to his rival. Chips moved to Atlanta for six months, and then he headed for Nashville, where he enjoyed more success. In 1975, Chips cowrote and produced B.J. Thomas's "(Hey Won't You Play) Another Somebody Done Somebody Wrong Song," a Number 1 smash that was named the Country Music Association's Song of the Year. Two years later, Chips cowrote the Waylon Jennings country hit, "Luckenbach, Texas." During his Nashville period, he also produced and played with Johnny Cash, Willie Nelson, Jerry Lee Lewis, Roy Orbison, and Carl Perkins.

After Chips departed, the Memphis recording industry started to flounder. In 1975, Stax Records went belly-up. In 1985, the city lured Chips back by offering him a twenty-year studio lease for just one dollar a year. He called his new place 3 Alarm Studios, but it never caught fire, and before long Chips was mired in lawsuits and foreclosures.

In the early 1990s, the native Georgian opened a studio in West Point, Georgia. In 2001, Chips started an Internet label offering a combination of unreleased material recorded during his glory years and some new artists. The label seems to fill a nice niche in the marketplace. As always, Chips remains the eternal rebel in the music industry.

And, thanks to him, in the late 1960s the King of Rock and Roll reclaimed his throne.

# Chapter 24

# Viva Las Vegas

**E**LVIS'S CAREER WAS BOOMING AGAIN WITH HIS HUGELY SUCCESSFUL TV SPECIAL, a new batch of recordings, and an upcoming engagement in Las Vegas, while my own was coming to a crossroads.

For almost a decade I had been pounding the Hollywood pavement in search of my big break. Like most struggling actors, I needed a regular job while I pursued an acting career. When I wasn't with Elvis, I worked as a car valet at a club on Sunset Boulevard and as a bouncer/doorman at a couple of nightclubs.

In the mid-1960s, Clint Eastwood's successful trilogy of "spaghetti Westerns" created overseas opportunities for actors whose careers were struggling in the States. A bunch of American leading men and character actors packed their bags for Europe in search of stardom and handsome film offers. Actors such as Lee Van Cleef, Gilbert Roland, James Coburn, Edd Byrnes, Joseph Cotton, Broderick Crawford, Jack Elam, Woody Strode, John Ireland, Ty Hardin, Guy Madison, and Lex Barker found film work there.

From 1960 to 1975, European production companies churned out nearly six hundred titles, created several international movie stars, and earned lots of fast cash. I was considering heading across the pond in early 1969 with an actor buddy of mine named Bruce Fischer. But then I got called to act in a horror film/biker flick called *Bigfoot*, starring John Carradine and John Mitchum. Mine was a small role, but it paid big dividends because, thanks to being in this movie, I landed the leading lady of my dreams—the beautiful and talented Judy Jordan.

She looked like Kim Novak with a flowing mane of dark hair. But she had other things going for her as well—piercing green eyes that lit up any room, a voluptuous hourglass figure, and something else—that X-factor that isn't so definable. I was instantly so incredibly attracted I walked right up to her on the set and told her exactly what was on my mind.

"I'm going to marry you," I said. "You're crazy," she shot back. "I'm engaged!" It turned out that Judy was engaged to a man named Jimmy James in Florida. He happened to be a multimillionaire, but that didn't really bother me so much. I was a man on a mission.

I asked where her fiancé was, and Judy said he was in Miami. "Well, then, he's lost you already," I said like a poor man's Cary Grant. "He just doesn't know it yet."

Such bravado was uncharacteristic of me. But Judy inspired me to reach beyond myself. All of our conversations and time spent together were on the set, but after a few days, I managed to finagle a date out of her. Then I courted her the old-fashioned way with flowers, cards, and phone calls. We developed a great relationship without sex entering into things.

I found out quickly that Judy was just as beautiful on the inside as on the outside. I loved her sweetness, sincerity, honesty, unselfishness, and all the other wonderful qualities one could want in a woman.

I also liked the fact that Judy was an accomplished actress and an emerging starlet. From 1966 through 1968, she was the original "And Away We Go!" girl on *The Jackie Gleason Show*. She appeared in theatrical films such as *The Gatlin Gun*, *Coma*, and *Airport*, along with several TV movies. Judy landed parts on *Dragnet*; *The Mod Squad*; *Marcus Welby, M.D.*; and *It Takes A Thief*, and she had two recurring roles on *The Beverly Hillbillies*, appearing in thirteen episodes.

I was especially impressed with Judy's moral fiber. In our picture, director Robert F. Slatzer asked Judy to go topless in a scene even though it wasn't in the script. Judy refused, but rather than fire her, Slatzer wrote in a new part for actress Joi Lansing to spice things up. Judy found herself in a similar situation a few months later when she was offered the "Lieutenant Dish" role in Robert Altman's *M*A*S*H*.

Unlike in *Bigfoot*, the seminudity was in the *M*A*S*H* screenplay from the beginning. Judy, who was raised in a very religious home, still refused to do it. She had been offered the part by director Robert Altman and producer Ingo Preminger. At the time, she was being represented by International Creative Management, a powerful, high-profile agency. ICM was so enraged when Judy refused the role and opted for a smaller part in a Western playing the love interest of Guy Stockwell, that she was dropped as a client. The part in *M*A*S*H* went to actress Jo Ann Pflug instead, and she went on to have a successful career. But Judy has no regrets. She can look at herself in the mirror every day and be proud that she didn't forsake her values.

One thing I didn't do in courting Judy was play the Elvis card. I needed to be certain that she liked me for me. She passed that test with flying colors. Then it was time for me to pass a test—meeting Judy's mother, Opal Jordan. Judy and I had been dating for several months, but we both maintained our own apartments—hers in the San Fernando Valley and mine in West Hollywood. Her mom had flown out from Florida in April, and I asked Judy if her mother was an Elvis Presley fan.

"I don't know," Judy said. "Why do you ask?"

"Would you and your mom like to meet him?" I asked. Judy looked at me skeptically, and I spilled the beans.

As it turned out, Opal was indeed an Elvis fan. At Universal Studios, Elvis was filming *Change of Habit*, which costarred Mary Tyler Moore. Elvis had a particular affinity for Mary and was a big fan of hers from *The Dick Van Dyke Show*. He thought Mary was the total package: sexy, funny, talented, and extremely professional in her approach to her craft.

In the movie, Elvis plays John Carpenter, a do-good doctor with a ghetto practice. (According to set gossips, he reserved his best bedside manner for costar Jane Elliot.) When we stopped by the set, Elvis was a great host and made everyone feel welcome. I teased him about his new hairstyle, which was longer and parted differently. His mutton-chop sideburns were also long and shaggy, in the style of the day. He looked good and in excellent shape. We visited for a while in his trailer, and he graciously posed for pictures with Judy and her mom.

Later that night I went by Elvis's house to get his reaction to Judy. He gave her a big thumbs-up but laughed and gave me a big thumbs-down. "Sonny, you're not ever going to get married," Elvis said.

"I thought so too, until I met her," I said seriously. "I'll believe it when I see it," he replied. A little less than two years later he not only "saw it" but was my best man.

Elvis then invited me and Judy to be his special guests at his first live stage show in almost nine years at the Las Vegas International

Hotel a few weeks hence. "It's going to be fun being back on the stage again," Elvis said.

Alex Shoofey, the hotel's general manager, had wanted Elvis to be the first star to grace its stage when the hotel opened for business, but Elvis demurred because he didn't want his show marred by the technical problems with the sound and lights that were sure to occur in a new showroom. Barbra Streisand did the honors instead, and as it turned out she had her fair share of sound and lighting glitches during her monthlong engagement. She didn't appear again on a Las Vegas stage for several years.

Meanwhile, Elvis built a stage act from the ground up. After interviewing more than two hundred musicians, he assembled a world-class band. They included James Burton on guitar, Jerry Scheff on bass, Ronnie Tutt on drums, Larry Muhoberac on piano and organ (later replaced by Glen D. Hardin), John Wilkinson on rhythm guitar and backup vocals, and Charlie Hodge on acoustic guitar and backup vocals. James Burton was the only one who didn't have to audition, as Elvis knew his work from Ricky Nelson and as a member of the Shindogs, the house band on the popular TV show *Shindig*.

Also on the bill was forty-one-year-old Borscht Belt comic Sammy Shore. Sammy (father of comedian Pauly Shore) used lots of blue humor, and while he kept older audience members in stitches, the younger and hipper crowd found him annoying.

Opening for and backing up Elvis were the Sweet Inspirations, who sang backup for Wilson Pickett, Aretha Franklin, and Chuck Jackson, to name a few. The Imperials, a gospel quartet, also backed up Elvis. They were replaced by J.D. Sumner and the Stamps Quartet the next year due to a contract obligation with country star Jimmy Dean. Also there was the hotel's thirty-piece orchestra, conducted by Bobby Morris. There were more than fifty people onstage with Elvis, and they made a lot of beautiful noise.

Judy and I arrived in Las Vegas on July 31, and everywhere we looked we saw Elvis. Billboards, posters, taxi marquees, and radio and TV ads shouted his name. The marquee in front of the International featured his name in letters taller than I am. In the lobby was an Elvis souvenir booth that sold posters and 8-x-10s of the man of the hour. The excitement was something even for Las Vegas.

234

The Colonel pulled out all the stops and even arranged with hotel owner Kirk Kerkorian to have music critics from New York flown in on a private DC-9 jet for the premiere.

When Judy and I stepped into the Showroom Internationale, we marveled at the spacious and ornate two-thousand-seat venue and at the glitterati who'd turned out for the invitation-only extravaganza. In the crowd were Sammy Davis Jr., Cary Grant, Xavier Cugat, Carol Channing, Juliet Prowse, George Hamilton, Paul Anka, Dick Clark, Charo, Shirley Bassey, Fats Domino, Phil Ochs, and Sun Records founder Sam Phillips.

As the Sweet Inspirations warmed up the audience, I felt a tap on the shoulder. A showroom captain said that Elvis wanted to see me backstage. I was escorted through a side door and along a hallway to a staircase leading down to Elvis's dressing room. Inside were Elvis, Joe Esposito, Lamar Fike, Richard Davis, and Charlie Hodge.

Elvis looked spectacular. His wavy jet black hair and gold jewelry meshed well with the dark blue karate-style Cossack suit and macramé belt designed by Bill Belew. We hugged, and after visiting for a short time, we headed upstairs to the backstage area. Elvis was nervous as we started the stretching routine we had always done before our karate workouts. We placed our right feet side by side, barely touching. Then Elvis leaned way back, pulling me forward, and I leaned back pulling him forward. Then we switched hands and feet and duplicated the process. Elvis said repeatedly, "It is here, it is here," almost as if he were in a trance. When we finished, he shook his arms as if to release all that nervous energy.

It's no secret that Elvis's first Las Vegas engagement, in 1956 at the New Frontier Hotel, was not a great success. Sandwiched between the Freddy Martin Orchestra and comedian Shecky Greene, Elvis played to a mostly geriatric crowd that sipped cocktails and clapped tepidly after each song. That first outing in Sin City was a huge blow to his ego, and the memory of it still haunted him. Elvis's fans were too young for Vegas at that time, but that would certainly change in the future.

As he paced back and forth, beads of sweat forming on his forehead, I told him, "Elvis, you're going to kick ass. I just know it." "Man, I hope so," he replied nervously.

When the lights in the showroom dimmed and Elvis's opening music filled the room, the crowd was on its feet. The gold lamé curtain began its ascent, and Elvis looked up as if to say, "Help me, God, do the best I can." Then he took one last deep breath and exhaled. He nodded to me and then walked out onstage. The crowd roared its approval, and the sound seemed to move through him like an electrical current. All of a sudden, he was home.

There's an old saying in show business that was made for Elvis that night: "A singer needs songs, but an entertainer just needs a stage." He grabbed the microphone, paused, and launched into a raucous version of "Blue Suede Shoes." It was as if a surge of electricity traveled through his body. The audience was screaming, swooning, and dancing. Sammy Davis Jr. was right up front, pounding the stage in excitement and yelling, "Yeah, yeah, kick it, babe!" Sammy kept it up all night. Elvis did the same thing himself when he attended other entertainers' shows.

There came a time in the show when Elvis introduced celebrities in the audience, and he gave Sammy a special introduction that night. When Elvis did the Frank Sinatra TV special in 1960, Sammy was there and noticed how nervous Elvis was. He went up to Elvis and spoke with him and succeeded in calming him down, telling him, "You're the man! Don't worry about anything. Just do your thing!"

Elvis graciously told the audience in Vegas that night about it, and then to thunderous applause he knelt down and took a huge black star sapphire ring off his finger and presented it to Sammy, moving "Mr. Bojangles" to tears.

For ninety minutes, Elvis's manic energy never waned. It was just him and a microphone. No pyrotechnics or backdrops, just pure raw talent. He electrified the crowd with rolls, kicks, and gyrations. It was crazy, spontaneous, frenzied, and over the top. That one show changed the face of Las Vegas–style entertainment forever and added a gilt-edge page to the Elvis legend. He was a superstar again.

And he knew it. "Damn, Elvis, that was great!" I said excitedly when he came offstage.

"Thanks, Sonny," he said, wiping his face with a towel. Then he said, "Yeah, I did it. I knocked them on their butts!"

The celebrities in the crowd paraded backstage to congratulate him. Sammy Davis Jr. and Cary Grant were especially effusive in their praise. Singer Shirley Bassey showed her enthusiasm by stroking Elvis's hair, which made him slightly uneasy.

Meanwhile, Colonel Parker was getting stroked by Alex Shoofey. Always the shrewd one, Parker had refused to talk long-term deal until the show was over, knowing he'd be in the catbird seat then. He and Shoofey agreed on a five-year contract (written on a tablecloth!) that paid Elvis $1 million annually for two thirty-day engagements. At the time, it was the highest fee ever paid in Las Vegas.

After the Colonel was done with business, he went backstage. The crowd parted as he and Elvis fell into a tearful clinch. Parker's body was literally shaking with pure emotion. "We did it! We did it!" the Colonel said. "Yes, we did, Colonel," said Elvis. "We sure did." Then Parker reverted to his normal self and ordered Joe and me to get Elvis to the press conference on time.

Later we all adjourned to Elvis's suite on the twenty-ninth floor. Judy and I had a wonderful time, and when it was time to go, Elvis asked me to come back to work for him as his chief of security.

I had to think it over. It was a great honor that Elvis wanted me to head up his security detail, of course. But I had my heart set on acting. In fact, I had just finished filming my first lead role in a movie called *Outlaw Riders*, plus I had a guest-starring role as a veterinarian on *The Beverly Hillbillies* that could become a recurring role with me as Elly May's love interest.

There was also the matter of my relationship with Judy, still in its infancy. I told Elvis I needed to talk to her before deciding for sure. Judy said she didn't see any reason I couldn't run Elvis's security operation for his two thirty-day hotel stints and still audition for parts in between. I didn't either, so I signed on at $250 a week, all expenses paid. I flew back home that day with Judy, gathered more clothes for the month-long engagement, and caught a plane back to Vegas that same day. The job started that night and would last for the next seven years.

It didn't take me long to get into the groove, and I took to my position quickly. To and from each show, I assigned two guards on each side of Elvis and one in the back. I took point. I wanted to be the person in front of Elvis because of my good eyesight and instinct for potential trouble. I didn't miss much, which is why Elvis nicknamed me "Mr. Eagle."

Because Elvis was naturally wired after his shows, it wasn't unusual for us to hit the sack around 4:00 or 5:00 AM. Often we needed help falling asleep. Elvis started taking Placidyls, which were nonaddictive. They took about twenty to thirty minutes to kick in and didn't leave you groggy when you woke up. We'd take them and then bet on who would fall off to sleep first.

I usually got up around 2:00 or 3:00 PM the next day. My normal routine was to shower, eat breakfast, read the paper, and arrive in Elvis's suite around 5:00 PM. That's when he got up. Elvis's breakfast rarely varied—a pound of crisp bacon, toast, Spanish omelet, beefsteak tomatoes, coffee, and orange juice.

Around 7:00 PM we escorted him to the backstage area for the first show, and he'd start getting dressed about thirty minutes before he went on. We'd perform our stretching exercises backstage, and then Elvis would say to himself, "My boy, my boy," as he was being introduced. Then the curtain went up and he'd say, "Here we go."

Elvis was an iron horse in those early Vegas engagements as he performed two shows a night, at 8:15 and midnight. He didn't care particularly for the earlier show because people were finishing up their dinner, and he could hear the dishes clattering while he performed. At the midnight show the crowd was loose and ready to party.

He liked to crack the audience up with silly jokes ("Good evening, my name is Pat Boone") or rambling monologues about the necessity of keeping his throat moist.

"A lot of singers have a problem with what they call a 'Vegas throat,'" he said. "It's either too dry, or you swallowed too many chips."

After his last show, his suite filled up with old and new friends paying homage. Cliff Gleaves, Marty Lacker, and George Klein caught a few of his earlier shows. Singer Tom Jones was a regular visitor, and he and Elvis often stayed up to the wee hours of the morning. Elvis was Tom's biggest booster and praised him as one of the greatest talents around.

Not such a favorite was fellow Memphian Jerry Lee Lewis. Jerry Lee's career had been in perpetual decline ever since he married his thirteen-year-old cousin, but he acted as though he and Elvis occupied the same stratosphere.

"Shit, Elvis, put the two of us out on the road and we'd outdraw everybody, including the Beatles and the Rolling Stones," Jerry Lee ranted. "The King and the Killer." At least he gave Elvis top billing.

When Joe finally rescued Elvis by telling him that Colonel Parker wanted to see him, Lewis exploded. "Elvis, why the hell do you listen to that old bald-headed sonofabitch manager of yours? He should come to you! That's what ole Jerry Lee would make him do."

Without missing a beat, Elvis stood and said, "Jerry Lee, I guess that's why I am where I am and why you are where you are. I gotta go, see ya. Let's go, guys." With that we headed out of the room, and I told one of the security guards to escort Lewis's group out and lock the dressing room door. Later Elvis said that Jerry Lee had lots of talent but probably should be locked up in a cage when not performing.

The most memorable visitor I can recall was actor Charlton Heston, who attended the show one weekend with his wife and another couple. Elvis was a huge Heston fan and screened *The Ten Commandments* and *Ben-Hur* numerous times at the Memphian Theatre.

Entertainers always kick it up a notch when another entertainer they admire is in the crowd. Elvis really threw it into high gear that night. Afterward, I brought Heston and his party back to the dressing room, and when he saw Elvis he intoned in that commanding voice, "The aura, the presence, the charisma, the magnetism, the electricity were nothing short of magnificent."

Elvis was thrilled, naturally, but he didn't want to talk about himself. Instead, he said to the actor, "Say, me and the guys have heard so many stories about all the stuntmen who were injured or killed in that chariot race in *Ben-Hur*. How about you give us the straight scoop on what happened?" Heston obliged, bringing all his actor's skills to bear. After a few more stories, it was time for them to leave, and I had a guard escort Heston and his group to their car out front.

Elvis stood there for a moment with an odd look on his face, and then he spoke: "You know what guys? I started getting a little nervous when Moses started talking about me like that." We all broke up.

It's a Las Vegas tradition that on the closing night of a performer's engagement he announces the artist replacing him on that stage. In Elvis's case it was Nancy Sinatra who would follow him at the International Hotel.

Everyone in Elvis's entourage attended Nancy's opening night, and afterward we attended a party hosted by her father, Frank, in the hotel's convention hall. When Elvis and Priscilla entered the room, all conversation stopped as everyone's attention shifted to Elvis. Frank ordered all of the reporters to the other side of the room as he turned to us. He obviously mistook me as a reporter and said, "Did you hear what I said? Beat it!" I stared back at him and said politely, but with stoic conviction, "I work for Mr. Presley. I move when he tells me to move." The Chairman of the Board blinked first. "Oh...okay," he said. "Sorry about that." Elvis got a big kick out of that. He always referred to Frank after that as "one of Sonny's favorite people," although I never held any bad thoughts toward Sinatra for the incident. He was actually running interference for Elvis.

Frank had been holding court at his table, and he escorted the Presleys over. Elvis told me beforehand that when he turned and looked at me, that was the signal for me to escort him out of the place. He was uncomfortable being the center of attention at a table with Frank Sinatra.

As they continued talking, I glanced around and saw Burt Lancaster and Kirk Douglas with their wives at a table close to Sinatra's. They seemed to be sizing up Elvis, and Burt and Kirk were nodding in approval. Telly Savalas and Don Rickles were also present. Rickles was one of Elvis's favorite comics, as well as mine.

After a few minutes I got the signal from Elvis and moved in to escort them out. "Well, it's been very nice visiting with all of you, but it's been a long thirty days, and I'm very tired," Elvis said to the Sinatras. Then he looked at Nancy and added, "You'll know the feeling, Nancy. Thank you for inviting me tonight."

Every one of Elvis's shows on each of the thirty days sold out, drawing a total attendance of 101,500 customers and gross receipts of approximately $2 million. It was the first time an entertainer actually made money back for a hotel/casino. In 1999, the *Las Vegas Review-Journal* listed Elvis along with Howard Hughes, Kirk Kerkorian, Steve Wynn, Liberace, and Don Laughlin among "The First 100 Persons Who Shaped Southern Nevada."

No one could argue with that.

# Chapter 25

# Taking Care of Business

**E**LVIS PRESLEY'S LAS VEGAS TRIUMPH OPENED THE DOORS FOR MANY OTHER new opportunities and put Colonel Parker firmly in the driver's seat when it came to leveraging deals for his client. The Colonel's phone began ringing off the hook with all sorts of offers. Soon after the Vegas engagement, MGM came calling and signed a two-deal picture to film a couple of documentaries, which eventually became *Elvis, That's the Way It Is* and *Elvis on Tour*.

But a more intriguing offer came from Management III Productions and Concerts West, a concert promotion company that put arena-style rock shows on the map. They would eventually take credit for bringing Elvis to the masses in the '70s.

Founded in 1964, the company was run by Tom Hulett and Jerry Weintraub, a pair of successful businessmen who had courted the Colonel for two years. They had put on close to seven hundred shows a year, featuring Jimi Hendrix, Bob Dylan, Cream, Neil Diamond, Frank Sinatra, Three Dog Night, the Beach Boys, Creedence Clearwater Revival, Eric Clapton, and Led Zeppelin.

Jerry was the more flamboyant of the two. He started his career in the mail room at the William Morris Agency in the 1950s. He later managed Jack Paar, Norm Crosby, John Denver, and singer Jane Morgan, whom he married. Jerry eventually conquered Hollywood as a big-time producer, bringing to the silver screen hits such as *Nashville*; *Oh, God!*; *The Karate Kid*; *Oceans Eleven*; and *Oceans Twelve*.

But back in 1969, Tom and Jerry practically got on bended knee to do business with the Colonel. In fact, Weintraub called Colonel Parker every day for a year.

"You want to do business with the Colonel?" said Parker. "Fine. Bring me a million dollars in cash by noon tomorrow, and then we'll talk."

Weintraub showed up the next day with a cashier's check for a million. The Colonel put it in a desk drawer and said, "Now let's talk business." It was the start of a great relationship that lasted until Elvis's death in 1977.

Elvis's first foray outside of Las Vegas was a six-show engagement at the Houston Astrodome's Livestock and Rodeo Show from February 27 to March 1, 1970.

Colonel Parker personally tapped me to do the advance work with him. The Colonel always treated me with great respect. Over the years, Parker has gotten a bad rap for making bad decisions regarding Elvis's career. The fact is, a lot of the bad decisions were made by Elvis himself. But the Colonel took the heat and kept doing what he did best, which was promoting and managing Elvis's career. No one is right all the time, but if I could be right half as many times as the Colonel was, I would feel I had done a lot of great things in my life and be satisfied.

Once, Elvis asked Parker if he could send one of the other guys out with him to do the advance security and let me stay back and travel with him for a while. The Colonel told him that he had trained me well and I knew what was expected of me. He didn't want anybody else out there with him because he'd have to start over again. Both Elvis and Parker told me that, and it made me proud.

In Houston, the Colonel and I established the blueprint for how we conducted most of Elvis's tours. He arranged for limousines and a large police escort to be on the tarmac when Elvis landed at the airport. Then a customized Greyhound bus with black-and-white cowhide seats took Elvis to the Astroworld Hotel, compliments of a wealthy family who made their fortune in the trucking industry. The bus driver was the son and heir apparent of the company's founder. He gave us a hearty Texas welcome, and then he scared the hell out of everybody by driving like a maniac, tailgating cars, honking his horn, and swerving all over the road as he made his way through traffic.

"Sonny, I'm not going to ride on that bus again unless that sonofabitch stops driving like that," Elvis told me. The Colonel tactfully arranged for a new driver.

Arriving at the hotel, we went in the back and walked through the kitchen to the service elevators that took us to Elvis's suite. We occupied the entire eighth floor. Of course, the Colonel and I mapped out all of that way before Elvis ever got there.

I liked to add little touches here and there to make it as comfortable for Elvis as possible. When he got to his room, the TV was on and the beds were already turned down. Depending on the view, I'd open up the drapes in the living room. If the hotel didn't have blackout drapes in the bedroom, I'd put tinfoil over the windows. He liked the bedroom dark and cold enough to hang meat. I turned the ringer off on all the phones in Elvis's suite because inevitably some resourceful fans would find out what floor we were on and start dialing the rooms on it one at a time to see if Elvis would answer.

The accommodations in Houston were outstanding, but it was a different story at the Astrodome. It was a great place for a football game but not a rock concert. The acoustics were terrible. The delay from the sound bouncing back off the ceiling was about seven seconds, which made it difficult for the people onstage. Elvis had monitors brought up onstage so they didn't have to rely on the soundboard. It was a far-from-perfect arrangement, but there was nothing else to do but try to relax and have some fun.

There was a funny incident that happened when we came back to town a couple of years later. Elvis made his dramatic entrance in a Jeep, waving to the crowd. The place was roaring with people, and flashbulbs were going off like strikes of lightning. When the driver pulled up to the stage, Elvis got out of the Jeep and walked a few feet to a stairway. All of a sudden the roaring stopped and there was raucous laughter. Elvis looked up to see what had happened, and Charlie pointed at Red and me dusting ourselves off the dirt floor where we'd fallen. The Jeep driver had let the clutch out too quickly and lurched forward, promptly dumping Red and me. Elvis thought it was hilarious, too.

It was a great performance. I remember one fan who jumped from the stands and outran the security, who chased him to the stage, where he had to be wrestled to the ground by police officers. Elvis told them to take it easy on the guy, who was screaming, "He's my idol!" At a press conference later, someone dropped a rope from a balcony to get in. It got scary sometimes, and the security people earned their money.

Elvis set an indoor record when approximately forty-three thousand people attended his Saturday night performance. That stood until the late '80s, when George Strait finally outdrew the King. But the music industry was vastly different then.

Professionally, things were getting better and better. But that wasn't the case on the home front for Elvis. His marriage was crumbling. When he started performing in Vegas, Priscilla was there every weekend. By the second thirty-day stint, though, she was allowed in only on the opening and closing nights and once in the middle. Finally, Elvis banned everybody's spouses from coming on the road with us.

It was tough living in Elvis's world because everything had to revolve around him. Elvis stifled individuality in his women because he did not want them having a career. As far as he was concerned, his wife had one career—pleasing him.

That may have suited the impressionable fourteen-year-old Priscilla Beaulieu, but it wasn't good enough for the adult version. Priscilla felt suppressed, and she began searching for diversions outside the home. She took calligraphy, cooking, and Spanish classes at UCLA, and she took ice-skating lessons for fun. In time, she also took up karate, which led her into another realm.

Elvis's interests were simpler—and they usually wore makeup and lipstick and smelled pretty.

When Elvis didn't arrange his own date, some of us guys kept our eyes out for girls we thought were his type. Upon finding one, we'd ask if she wanted to meet Elvis. Nobody ever said no.

Of the parade of women Elvis romanced in Las Vegas, two stand out in my memory.

Joyce Bova was a beautiful twenty-five-year-old brunette from Washington, DC, who worked for the House Armed Services Committee. She was one of my favorites and had an identical twin named Janice. They were both sweet and fun to be around. Joyce and a friend had flown in to see Elvis in August 1969 and were picked out to meet him by a greeter at the International Hotel. Elvis liked Joyce's exotic features, long black hair, and sweet personality. Elvis dated her over a two-year period and always made it a point to see her when in the nation's capital.

Another of my favorites was twenty-three-year-old actress and model Barbara Leigh, one of the most beautiful women Elvis ever dated. Tall, with long brown hair, big eyes, and high cheekbones,

Barbara was totally exquisite. Barbara was a starlet on the rise in Hollywood and was dating MGM studio head Jim Aubrey, known as "the Smiling Cobra."

Jim brought her to a show in August 1970 and made the mistake of introducing her to Elvis backstage. A notorious womanizer himself, Aubrey was the exec who green-lighted the documentary *Elvis: That's the Way It Is*. But he might as well have been the janitor once Elvis got a look at Barbara. "Man, that's Venus sitting down over there," he said. Elvis, sometimes as wily as the famous cartoon coyote, got Barbara to write her phone number on a piece of paper. They began getting together whenever the opportunity arose. But she was smart—she continued seeing Jim Aubrey and movie star Steve McQueen when her calendar permitted.

Elvis dated Joyce and Barbara intermittently and often flew in one as the other was leaving. Of course, there were other women sandwiched in between, including Kathy Westmoreland, who replaced Millie Kirkham as the beautiful soprano voice in the show.

In August 1970, a woman named Patricia Ann Parker filed a paternity suit against Elvis in Los Angeles Superior Court. The twenty-one-year-old waitress claimed she'd slept with Elvis during his early 1970 engagement in Vegas, and she wanted $1,000 a month in child support for the child she named Jason Peter Presley.

Parker's only proof that she and Elvis were ever together was a snapshot of the two of them taken in the corridor near his dressing room. Elvis gladly posed with anyone who wanted a picture, and when he saw this one he was frankly appalled. "Guys, does this look like anyone I would ever sleep with?" he asked.

That wasn't the first time Elvis had been accused of fathering a child. Actress Joanna Moore, his costar in *Follow That Dream*, one night showed up at the Perugia Way house around 11:00 demanding to see Elvis. They'd had a little off-set romance, but Joanna was quite possessive, and Elvis broke it off. Now she was sobbing and saying that she was pregnant—and that she had taken a bunch of sleeping pills. We carted her off to the UCLA emergency room, where Joanna's stomach was pumped. The doctors told us she wasn't pregnant.

We never saw Joanna again except for on television or in a movie magazine. She later married actor Ryan O'Neal. They had two children, actress Tatum and a son, Griffin.

With the Patricia Parker case, Elvis wasn't going to get off as easy. Parker enlisted the help of high-profile attorney Paul Caruso, whose clients included Audie Murphy, James Mason, Jane Russell, and Kirk Douglas. He also once represented Charles Manson follower Susan Atkins.

The judge decided the quickest way to arrive at the truth was to order blood tests to establish the baby's paternity. The baby obviously needed to be tested, too, and in those days the blood was drawn from a small cut made in the child's heel. Elvis and Parker were present for the procedure, and as the doctor made his incision, the child shrieked. Elvis clenched his jaw, turned to me, and said, "That damned bitch! Putting her baby through all this pain for nothing."

The blood tests proved that the child was not Elvis's.

But our relief was short-lived, because about two weeks later Elvis got his first serious death threat. There had been other threats over the years. About six weeks after John F. Kennedy's assassination, a postcard arrived at Graceland from Huntsville, Alabama, addressed to "President Elvis Presley." The message from the anonymous sender said, "You will be next on my list," which included Johnny Cash, President Lyndon B. Johnson, and Alabama governor George Wallace. It was obviously from a nutcase.

This threat, though, was different. It started with a phone call to a security guard at the International Hotel from someone identifying himself as "Jim Reeds," who reported a plot to kidnap Elvis by two men who'd met him at a party. The same man also called Joe Esposito's house in L.A. the next day and said that Elvis was going to be shot at his August 30 show. "Reeds" said that in exchange for $50,000 in small bills he would provide the identity of the assassin.

Meanwhile, in Las Vegas, Joe picked up an envelope left for him at the front desk of the International. In it was a showroom menu with Elvis's photo on the front and a drawing of a gun pointed at his head.

The FBI met with us in Colonel Parker's office and suggested that Elvis cancel his Saturday night show. Hotel officials seconded the motion, but Elvis wouldn't hear of it. "I'm not going to cancel anything for some no-good coward sonofabitch," he said. "I wouldn't give him the satisfaction."

Elvis had Joe summon Ed Parker from Hawaii and Jerry Schilling from Los Angeles, and he told me to contact Red in Memphis and bring him out to beef up security. When he and Red saw one another, they hugged. Red's and Elvis's estrangement was officially over. No one was more pleased to see them back together again than I was.

In the dressing room before the show, FBI agents said it was likely someone planning to shoot Elvis would do it from close range. Agents would be in the crowd, and we were to shout out the word "floor" if any of us sensed any danger during the show. That would be the signal for Elvis to dive to the floor and the rest of us to spring into action.

I stationed myself onstage behind the organ and put Jerry by Glen D. Hardin near the piano to give both of us a plain view of the front of the stage. Red walked the perimeter of the room with a contingent of FBI agents and local policemen. We were all armed.

The International's house doctor, Thomas "Flash" Newman, stashed oxygen tanks and other medical supplies backstage and arranged for an ambulance to be standing by outside.

Before he went on, Elvis called Red, Jerry, and me together. His voice choked with emotion, and tears streamed down from his eyes. He said, "I have never done anything to anyone for them to try and kill me. But if it happens, I want you guys to get to him first, before the police. I want his face f——ed up and his eyeballs ripped out of his head. I don't want him sitting around afterward like Charles Manson with a grin on his face saying, 'I killed Elvis Presley.'"

Then, he went around to everyone and said good-bye. That was quite emotional for me. Just before the curtain went up, Elvis slipped a small derringer gun into each of his boots.

The tension was unbelievable. When the show started, Red saw someone who looked suspicious and got into a stare-down with him. It turned out to be an FBI agent. I had locked in on a guy down front with dark glasses who looked suspicious because he never applauded during the entire show. He turned out to be a "high roller" who was there because his wife wanted him to be.

Elvis stood sideways for most of his performance, offering the smallest target possible. Once, when he momentarily turned his back to the audience, our eyes met, and I saw real fear.

In the middle of the show, someone in the balcony yelled out "Elvis!" and we all flinched. Elvis dropped to one knee to fish out one of his derringers, but the guy just wanted to hear his favorite tune.

"Would you sing 'Don't Be Cruel'?"

Elvis heaved a sigh of relief and said, "Sure." It was a cruel night, but nothing happened.

When we embarked on the fall 1970 tour, Elvis and Priscilla and a jeweler designed the logo that became our calling card. It was the letters "TCB" over a lightning bolt. The letters stood for "Taking Care of Business," a saying Elvis started using in the '60s. It became a code in the inner circle that meant we were to instantly drop whatever subject was being discussed.

Elvis commissioned Beverly Hills jeweler Schwartz & Ableser to make a dozen fourteen-karat gold charm necklaces with the new logo for his entourage and his close male friends and family. I went down with him to pick them up when they were ready in October 1970. He put the first one, which I still have, on my neck, and then he put one on his neck, and then we took the rest up to the house for him to hand out to the others. Not long after, Elvis had "TLC" ("Tender Loving Care") necklaces made for all the women in his life. Then he had bracelets made for all of us with a round bar with a rope chain that had our first name on the front and our nickname on the back. Mine was "Hunk."

He eventually put the TCB logo on almost everything—T-shirts, rings, guns, badges, backstage passes, a wall at Graceland, and the tail of his jet plane, the *Lisa Marie*. It's also on his tombstone at Graceland.

By the way, one of those original necklaces that cost $90 apiece in 1970 was offered three decades later on an Internet auction site for more than $1 million. I still have mine, which was the first one Elvis gave out. I guess technically that makes me a millionaire.

With all the craziness, insanity, and heartache I endured in the last couple of years of Elvis's life, I can honestly say I earned every penny.

# Chapter 26

# Elvis Meets Nixon

OVER THE YEARS, NUMEROUS BIOGRAPHERS, JOURNALISTS, FANS, AND ARM-CHAIR psychologists have tried to delve deep into Elvis Presley's psyche to understand his passion for guns and fascination with law enforcement.

I can tell you this: Charlie Manson had plenty to do with the gun fetish. A week into Elvis's Vegas comeback, Manson and his cult murdered Abigail Folger, Voytek Frykowski, Sharon Tate and her unborn baby, Jay Sebring, and Steven Parent in the Hollywood Hills. Sebring's death—he was stabbed seven times and shot once—was particularly disturbing to Elvis because Jay had been an acquaintance, having come to Elvis's home to cut his hair.

After that death threat in Vegas, Elvis's interest in guns picked up even more. Not only did he want to be armed himself, he wanted all of us packing heat, too. And really, what's so difficult to understand about that? When a celebrity becomes a target of a death threat, he understandably switches from a passive to a proactive stance regarding his own personal safety. If John Lennon had an armed, professional bodyguard with him on that fateful December night in 1980, the bodyguard would have been instantly alert when Mark David Chapman stepped out of the shadows with a gun in the hallway outside the Dakota. The end result would probably have been much different with the injury or death of either or both, but Lennon would most likely have been safe and alive. (And I can honestly state that if a group of men like the Memphis Mafia had been protecting Lennon that night, he probably wouldn't have been shot and killed by the sick sonofabitch.)

Elvis was also a collector by nature. Look at Graceland; it's filled with stuff Elvis acquired over the years—records, guitars, jewelry, civic awards, trophies, karate outfits, gold-plated belts, and stage clothes. So why not guns and law-enforcement badges, too?

In September 1970, Elvis embarked on a short tour as a test run for future tours. He played Phoenix (where there was a bomb threat), St. Louis, Detroit, Miami, Tampa, and Mobile, Alabama. The tour had its kinks to work out. It was the first and only time Elvis used pickup horns and strings players in each city, which caused a few headaches.

Colonel Parker was not much help this time, either. In Mobile, he booked everyone into the Admiral Semmes Hotel, once the crown jewel of local hotels. However, that was a long time ago, and now the place was pretty grungy. But the Colonel was friends with the manager and apparently was doing him a favor.

The Colonel and I got there the day before the concert with other members of the advance team, including George Parkhill, an executive with RCA records; Pat Kelleher, also with RCA; and Loanne Miller, a secretary for RCA assigned to the Colonel (who later married him).

It was my first taste of Alabama humidity, and it turned out that the Admiral Semmes had no air-conditioning. This was going to be a problem when Elvis arrived. He liked his room refrigerated.

Sure enough, he wasn't very happy. "Shit, I'm not staying here," he said before we even got upstairs. He told Joe to book us another hotel pronto. Joe tried the Howard Johnson's first, and when he said he needed ten rooms, the manager laughed and said, "Hell, there ain't even one room available within fifty miles of here. Don't you know that Elvis Presley is in town?"

An angry Elvis ordered Joe to get the crew back out to the plane so he could stay in his air-conditioned jet. He also told me to tell the Colonel that he wanted to leave after the show that night and fly to the next city. He then got dressed there for the show, took a limo to the concert, and, when he finished, hopped back on the plane and jetted to Memphis, as Mobile was the last city on the tour.

It was on that tour that Elvis's interest in law enforcement really took hold. He met a lot of cops and appreciated their willingness to put their lives on the line for him. Four he befriended around this time were Dick Grob, a training specialist with the Palm Springs Police Department, and Bob Cantwell, Ron Pietrafeso, and Jerry Kennedy of the Denver Police Department.

About a week after the tour concluded, Shelby County Sheriff Roy Nixon, who was one of Elvis's longtime friends, made him a chief deputy. Some books have stated that Nixon made him an "honorary agent," but that is flat-out wrong, and the badge he gave Elvis is on display in his collection at Graceland.

Elvis was thrilled and asked Nixon to deputize all of us. Nixon agreed but said he would have to run mandatory background checks on everybody first. He did so, and when he handed me my badge Nixon remarked, "Damn, Sonny, there's nothing on your arrest record that's criminal, but you sure did get into a lot of fights when you were younger."

When I replied that I hadn't started them, Nixon said, "No, but it looks like you pretty much finished them." He must've approved, because he made me a lieutenant.

The emblem Elvis really coveted was a federal narcotics badge. Through John O'Grady, a former L.A. narcotics cop who did investigations for Elvis's lawyer, Elvis learned that a Federal Bureau of Narcotics and Dangerous Drugs (BNDD) shield would permit him to travel anywhere in the country with a gun without being stopped. Now he really had to have one.

Vice President Spiro T. Agnew was a friend of Frank Sinatra's and often stayed in one of Frank's guest houses at his Rancho Mirage estate. When Elvis found out that Agnew was there, he wrangled a special audience with the second-most-powerful man in the free world. (Or third, counting Frank.)

Elvis brought along a beautiful, gold-inlaid .357 Magnum revolver with hand-carved ivory handles in a commemorative box. It cost him $5,000 and was intended as a gift for Agnew. It raised a few Secret Service eyebrows, but Elvis was allowed to present the gun to the vice president. But Agnew told him that as an elected official he wasn't allowed by law to accept gifts. However, he added, he would be glad to have it once he left public service. Elvis happily agreed to hang on to the gun until then.

(Not long afterward, Agnew was forced to resign the vice presidency when it was learned that he had taken about $30,000 in bribes while governor of Maryland. When I told Elvis it was probably all right for him to send the gun to Agnew now, he said, "Hell, man, he got caught as a crook. He don't get shit.")

In their meeting at Sinatra's place, Elvis explained to Agnew that he was concerned about rampant drug use by young people, and he said he was sure he could help if he had a federal narcotics badge to back him up. Agnew replied that Elvis needed to get in touch with that department to pursue the subject of a narcotics badge. The meeting broke up shortly with Elvis no closer to getting the badge he desperately wanted.

Elvis consoled himself by going on one of the wildest spending sprees I'd ever seen. Not long after he donated $7,000 to the Los Angeles Police Department (and got a permit from Beverly Hills Police Chief Joe Kimball to carry a weapon within the city limits), Elvis spent almost $20,000 in a three-day gun-buying frenzy at Kerr's Sporting Goods.

Elvis also shelled out $339,000 for a new home for himself and Priscilla located in the exclusive Holmby Hills section of Beverly Hills, put a $10,000 down payment on a home in West Los Angeles for Joe and Joanie Esposito, and ordered Mercedes Benzes for Charlie Hodge, girlfriend Barbara Leigh, and himself. He also paid for George Klein's and Dick Grob's weddings, and he gave Grob a Cadillac as a wedding present.

Because Grob's name has entered the fray, I would like to address some disparaging remarks he has made about me over the years since Elvis's death. I'll start with the ridiculous statement he made that when Elvis fired me, Red, and Dave Hebler, it was because he wanted a better grade of security, thus making Grob his new chief of security. That never happened. Sam Thompson, Linda's brother, was brought in and given that job after our departures. Grob was given the position of chief of security of Graceland by Vernon Presley *after* Elvis's death. One of Memphis's newspapers ran a story the day after the Ten Outstanding Young Men awards ceremony in January 1971 that stated, "The Secret Service could take lessons from Elvis Presley's security." I must point that out because Dick Grob had nothing to do with the security detail I ran, other than to follow instructions. Grob was a bodyguard who worked in the detail and took instructions from me as to the procedures, just as I took mine from the Colonel.

I haven't read his book *The Elvis Conspiracy?* and don't intend to as I know it is full of untruths and exaggerations, such as his claim of being an ace fighter pilot. I was shown a passage in his book that refers to my being "hypnotized" by the Colonel and doing some things that he felt were "embarrassing" and "degrading." Grob concluded with, "I guess there is no determining for what price someone will sell their soul." If that was supposed to be a profound statement, it should be saved for something a lot more profound than the Colonel and some of us guys having a little fun.

I'm sure that Grob didn't know that we were doing the hypnosis gag of pretending all the way back to the movie years, while he was pretending to being an "ace pilot." The Colonel did it with several of us, and we had a lot of fun with it. Guess what, Grob? Elvis enjoyed it also.

Grob also states that it was either Sam Thompson or himself that took Lisa Marie back and forth on the plane between Elvis and Priscilla, but he failed to say that it was after I was gone in July of 1976. Also, Grob did not start working closer with the Colonel after I departed as he has stated, according to Lamar. It was Lamar that replaced me working with the Colonel on the advance team, not Grob.

I mention these things only because Dick, as in the "ace fighter pilot" fiasco, was always trying to make himself more important than he was. According to Billy Smith, Grob was going to get fired near the end by Elvis, until Billy interceded and told Elvis his security was getting too depleted.

I know that Christians are supposed to forgive someone who has spoken against or harmed them. I do try, but I am not always as strong as I'd like to be.

Getting back to the weddings of Klein and Grob. Their weddings reminded Elvis to ask how come Judy and I weren't married yet. I told him we were saving up for a wedding. He promptly offered to pay for everything and wanted us to move into his big new house. Judy and I were already engaged, so I asked her if she wanted to get married soon, and she said yes. We picked the date, December 28, 1970. I asked Elvis if he would be my best man, to which he readily agreed. Elvis then asked Marty to take care of the details, and everything was set in motion.

When all the bills for the cars and homes arrived on Vernon's desk back in Memphis, Vernon nearly keeled over. He went to Priscilla, and they confronted Elvis about it when he returned to Graceland for the holidays, just before our wedding. "Son, if you keep spending like this," Vernon said, "we're gonna end up on the poor farm."

Elvis didn't want to hear it. "Daddy, I earned the money, so I can damn well spend it as I see fit," he yelled. "I don't need anybody sticking their nose in my business where it don't belong. Just pay the bills and I'll go out and earn my keep!"

With that, he stormed out of Graceland and drove off alone. I didn't even know he was gone until the next day, when I got a call from Jerry Schilling. "Sonny, get to Washington, DC, right away," he said. "Elvis wants you. Take a taxi at the airport and meet us at the Hotel Washington on Pennsylvania Avenue."

When I asked what they were doing there, Jerry would only say, "It's a long story, Sonny." Then he told me to let Vernon and Priscilla know that Elvis was okay, but not to tell them where he was.

Later I found out that Elvis had left Graceland, gone to the Memphis airport, and boarded a flight to the nation's capital. There he checked into the Hotel Washington on Fifteenth and Pennsylvania Avenue and called a girlfriend, Joyce Bova, who lived in Baltimore. After they talked, Elvis checked out and headed for L.A. On a layover in Dallas, he called Jerry to have him and his new limo driver, Gerald Peters (who once was Winston Churchill's chauffeur), pick him up at the Los Angeles airport and bring him $500 in cash.

When Elvis got off the plane in L.A., he had his arms around two stewardesses to whom he had promised a ride home. He'd also made friends on the plane with a serviceman who'd just done a tour of duty in Vietnam. Elvis told Jerry to give the soldier all their cash, including the $500, and insisted on it when Jerry hesitated and informed him that was all the cash they had.

They drove to the Hillcrest home, and a doctor was summoned to treat Elvis for an allergic reaction he had to some medicine had had taken for an eye infection that was exacerbated by chocolate he'd eaten on the plane.

Then it was back to the airport for a flight back to Washington, DC. En route, Elvis learned from a stewardess that U.S. senator George Murphy of California was on the plane. Elvis introduced himself to Murphy and inquired about how to go about meeting with Bureau of Narcotics and Dangerous Drugs director John Ingersoll and FBI director J. Edgar Hoover to get the badge he wanted so badly.

Murphy suggested that Elvis eliminate the middlemen altogether and write a personal letter to President Richard Nixon. Elvis went back to his seat, got some American Airlines stationery, and wrote out a five-page missive to the commander in chief:

Dear Mr. President:

First, I would like to introduce myself. I am Elvis Presley and admire you and have great respect for your office. I talked to Vice President Agnew in Palm Springs three weeks ago and expressed my concern for our country. The drug culture, the hippie elements, the SDS, Black Panthers, etc. do not consider me as their enemy or as they call it The Establishment. I call it America and I love it. Sir, I can and will be of any service that I can to help The Country out. I have no concern or Motives other than helping the country out. So I wish not to be given a title or appointed position. I can and will do more good if I were made a Federal Agent at Large and will help out by doing it my way through my communications with people of all ages. First and foremost, I am an entertainer, but all I need is the Federal credentials. I am on this plane with Senator George Murphy and we have been discussing the problems that our country is faced with.

Sir, I am staying at the Washington Hotel, Room 505-506-507. I have two men with me by the name of Jerry Schilling and Sonny West. I am registered under the name of Jon Burrows. I will be here as long as it takes to get the credentials of a Federal Agent. I have done an in-depth study of drug abuse and Communist brainwashing techniques and I am right in the middle of the whole thing where I can and will do the most good.

I am Glad to help just so long as it is kept very Private. You can have your staff or whomever call me anytime today, tonight, or tomorrow. I was nominated this coming year one of America's Ten Most Outstanding Young Men. That will be in January 18 in my hometown of Memphis, Tennessee. I am sending you the short autobiography about myself so you can better understand this approach. I would love to meet you just to say hello if you're not to busy.

Respectfully,
Elvis Presley


P.S. I believe that you, Sir, were one of the Top Ten Outstanding Men of America also.

> I have a personal gift for you which I would like to present to you and you can accept it or I will keep it for you until you can take it.

The gift to which he referred was a commemorative World War II chrome-plated Colt .45 pistol encased in a handsome wooden chest. It was not the gun he tried to give Agnew.

When Elvis's plane touched down at National Airport around 6:00 AM on Monday, December 21, he and Jerry were picked up by a driver by the name of Ben with the Liberty Limousine Service. Elvis instructed Ben to take him to the northwest gate of the White House to drop off his letter. The guard who accepted the letter assured Elvis that he would give it to his superiors as soon as they arrived that morning.

Then Elvis and Jerry checked in at the Hotel Washington, where I joined them later. Elvis had eaten more chocolate on the plane, and his face was very swollen. The hotel doctor came for a look and told Elvis to stay off chocolate when he was on meds.

Later that morning, Elvis presented himself alone at the office of John Ingersoll at the Bureau of Narcotics. Ingersoll wasn't in, and Elvis was shown to the office of Deputy Director John Finlator. All the secretaries were beside themselves, of course. None had been fooled when Elvis checked in at the front registry as "Jon Burrows."

Elvis offered Finlator a $5,000 donation for the Narcotics Bureau, but the assistant politely declined it on the ground that the bureau couldn't accept donations. Then Elvis pulled out some of his police badges and asked Finlator for one from the bureau. Finlator said he couldn't do it, and, if he thought his morning wasn't strange enough already, Elvis asked him, "Would you mind if I asked President Nixon for a narcotics badge?" Not sure if he was kidding, Finlater told him, "That's the only way you'll ever get it."

Then came a call from Jerry Schilling at the hotel. "Come back right away, Elvis," he said. "The president wants to meet with you in a half hour."

Elvis's letter had ended up with White House aide Dwight Chapin, who read it and called Nixon's deputy counsel, Egil "Bud" Krogh, at about 8:45 and asked if he was sitting down. "You won't believe this," Chapin said, "but the King is here right now and he wants to meet with the president."

Krogh got upset. He controlled Nixon's schedule, and there were no kings on the president's schedule that day. "King who?" he asked. "No one told me there was a king coming today!"

"Not a king," said Chapin. "*The* King!"

"Elvis?" said Krogh. "Bingo!" answered Chapin. "I'm reading a letter he wrote to the president asking for a meeting."

Krogh, an avid Elvis fan himself, rushed over to see the letter. He was touched by its sincerity and decided on the spot that it wouldn't do any harm to have Richard Nixon, who most young voters were convinced had come out of the womb wearing a suit and a five o'clock shadow, meet with the King of Rock and Roll. Nixon's schedule was usually open from 11:30 to 12:30, and Elvis was penciled in.

I had no idea about any of this when I reached the hotel. Jerry filled me in a little. When I asked where Elvis was, he said he was coming around in the limo to pick us up. Minutes later, we were sitting in the backseat with Elvis, and he announced grandly, "Boys, we're about to meet the president of the United States!"

Elvis was sporting new, oversized jeweled aviator glasses and wearing a white, high-collared shirt open at the neck, a deep purple Edwardian jacket and cape, matching pants, a gold lion's-head pendant courtesy of Sol Schwartz, his prized tree of life necklace, and the monolithic gold belt the International Hotel gave him for his record-setting run in Las Vegas. Not exactly Sunday go-to-meetin' clothes for us, but for him it was just fine. On his lap was the box containing an expensive firearm and silver bullets.

A few minutes later, our driver dropped us at the northwest gate of the White House. We were taken through a doorway into the West Wing lobby, where several Secret Service agents were waiting. The first thing they wanted to know was what was in the box Elvis carried. He said it was a gift, and they wondered what kind of gift it was.

"It's a gun," Elvis said nonchalantly. Bill Duncan, head of the president's Secret Service detail, immediately called Bud Krogh and asked what he should do. Krogh told him to accept the gift on behalf of the president but under no circumstances to let that gun into the Oval Office.

About a minute later, Krogh himself joined us in the lobby; and, while Jerry and I were escorted by White House aide Jeff Donfeld to the Federal Building next door, Krogh led Elvis through the Roosevelt Room and across the hall to the northwest door of the Oval Office.

Elvis later told us that when he met Nixon, the president was quite taken by his threads. "You dress kind of wild, don't you, son?" said Nixon. "Mr. President," Elvis coolly replied, "you've got your show to run, and I've got mine."

"You're right," Nixon said, breaking into laughter. "Very good."

I thought that after Elvis and the president were alone for a few minutes discussing the war on drugs, Jerry and I would be invited to join them in the Oval Office. But Donfeld told us not to count on that happening because the president was a busy man. I begged to differ. "You don't know Elvis," I told Donfeld. "We will meet the president."

A few minutes later, Donfeld's phone rang. He picked it up, listened for a moment, and then said, "We'll be right over" and hung up the phone. Then a slight grin crossed his face. "I'll be damned! You're going to meet the president," he said. He took Jerry and me over to meet President Nixon in the Oval Office.

Bud Krogh later wrote a book called *The Day Elvis Met Nixon*, and reading it, I was touched to find out how hard Elvis pushed to get us in the Oval Office that day, telling Nixon it would mean a lot to us and him if we could come in and say hello.

The president was sitting behind his desk when we walked in. Strewn over the desk of the leader of the free world were Elvis's aviator glasses, police badges, and two photos autographed to Nixon. Elvis was standing nearby, acting as if he owned the place.

"Come on in, guys," Elvis said. "Mr. President, these were the guys I was telling you about."

Nixon got up, extended his hand as he walked around the desk, and said, "How are you gentlemen?"

"Fine, Mr. President," I said, shaking his hand. "Thank you."

Nixon sized us up and smiled. Then he playfully jabbed me on the shoulder and said, "You're a couple of pretty big fellows. You guys take good care of him, do you?"

Elvis answered for us, saying, "Oh, yes sir, they sure do."

"Well, that's good," said the president.

Meanwhile, White House photographer Ollie Atkins slipped into the room to take pictures. I never even noticed him and found out about the photos only when they were mailed to us at Graceland a few weeks later. Atkins had already taken shots of Elvis and Nixon while Jerry and I were in the Federal Building.

"I've got something for you fellows," Nixon suddenly announced. He walked to his desk, opened a drawer, withdrew two fourteen-karat gold key chains with the presidential seal, and handed them to us. We thanked him, and then Elvis totally amazed me by saying, "Mr. President, they have wives, too."

Nixon returned to the drawer and pulled out a couple bow-shaped pins with the presidential seal. He gave them to us, and we thanked him again. Then we all looked over at Elvis, who was busily rummaging through the president's drawer in search of more mementos.

"Elvis, see anything you like?" asked Nixon, smiling.

"You've got some pretty good stuff here, Mr. President," Elvis said, pulling out a few more items for himself.

But the most important memento was still to come. President Nixon had instructed that an official Bureau of Narcotics and Dangerous Drugs badge be issued to Elvis.

After bidding Nixon good-bye, we were taken to lunch in the White House cafeteria by Bud Krogh. When we finished, John Finlator was in Krogh's office with Elvis's badge. Elvis was almost overcome with emotion as he accepted it. The King was, at long last, a federal agent.

# Chapter 27

# High Times and Low Places

IT WAS EXCITING TO MEET PRESIDENT NIXON AT THE WHITE HOUSE, BUT that was nothing compared to making Judy Jordan my bride.

I had the love of my life ready to walk down the aisle with me in a beautiful church setting, Elvis Presley as my best man, and his wife, Priscilla, as Judy's matron of honor (which is quite a story in and of itself). Even Vernon Presley lent me his black 1967 Lincoln sedan to drive to and from the wedding. I don't know if he did that at the suggestion of Elvis or on his own volition, but it was the nicest thing Vernon ever did for me.

Having Elvis Presley as my best man was a pretty big risk, because he was the main focus of attention wherever he went. Judy was worried that Elvis would do something wild or crazy on our special day, and it probably didn't calm her fears when he showed up at the Trinity Baptist Church in Whitehaven wearing a fur cloth black bell-bottom suit, white tie, belt with gold eagles and chains, two guns in a white shoulder holster, and two pearl-handled pistols tucked inside his waistband. Elvis also had a derringer stashed in his boot and carried a fifteen-inch metal Kel-Lite police flashlight.

Many fans have asked over the years what the deal was with that flashlight. What happened is that Elvis began wearing sunglasses everywhere he went, even indoors. When he couldn't see something, he'd start shining that flashlight around. Plus, he could use it as a weapon.

Like any groom, I was nervous. There's a funny picture of me in my wedding album in which Elvis is wiping the sweat off my brow with a handkerchief as we waited in the pastor's office. It wasn't an act for the camera.

Judy's fears were for naught. When I approached Elvis about Judy's concerns (actually I had some too), he looked at me warmly and said softly, "Sonny, this is your night," pinning on my boutonniere. "Tonight, I will strictly be in the background." It was one of the most touching things he ever said to me, and when I told Judy about it later, she was moved to tears.

When the pastor said it was time to enter the sanctuary, Elvis followed behind me. Marty came up and tried to take the flashlight out of his hand. Elvis resisted at first, but he relented when Marty told him, "Elvis, you don't need to carry the flashlight up there."

"Damn, I hate to give this up," Elvis said, handing the flashlight over.

The twenty-minute ceremony in front of approximately 150 of our closest friends and family went without a hitch. Afterward there was a reception in the church hall downstairs. Elvis and Priscilla stood in the reception line and greeted everyone who attended. Then Elvis hugged Judy and me and told us to enjoy the reception and that we should come over to Graceland for another reception when we finished.

When we got to Graceland there were presents to open from the guys and our other friends there, and also from Elvis and Priscilla. When Judy and I went back to California a few weeks later, Elvis gave us a Mercedes 280 SE four-door sedan.

It was at the Graceland reception where a famous picture of the Memphis Mafia was taken. Sheriff Roy Nixon had given us our deputy badges several weeks earlier—not on my wedding night, as has been written in so many books and articles. We were proud of those badges, and we carried them everywhere. Sheriff Nixon and former sheriff Bill Morris were at the Graceland reception, and somebody offhandedly mentioned that there were enough professional law-enforcement people there to start a war. The notion tickled Elvis, and he had our wedding photographer, Frank Carroll, take our picture with the badges. George Klein was the only guy in the room without a badge, but Elvis gave him one from his collection of police emblems so he wouldn't be left out. The photo was taken in the living room, and it showed Billy Smith, Bill Morris, Lamar Fike, Jerry Schilling, Roy Nixon, Vernon Presley, Charlie Hodge, George Klein, Marty Lacker, Dr. George Nichopoulos, Red West, and me gathered around Elvis, who was sitting there like the don, surrounded by the Memphis Mafia and friends, flashing badges instead of guns.

The photo was taken as a pure lark, but over the years unscrupulous people used it as Exhibit A to prove that the Memphis Mafia was a dangerous bunch of badasses. I hate to blow our cover, but we were just a bunch of guys having fun at a wedding reception.

As the party wound down, Elvis suggested that we all go to the Memphian to see a movie or two. "Elvis, I don't think I'm going to the movies on my wedding night," I said. "Judy would never forgive me." Elvis laughed and agreed that it probably wasn't a good idea. Judy and I checked in at the Howard Johnson's down the road from Graceland.

It was a short honeymoon. Two days later, Elvis rounded up the troops for a return trip to Washington, DC, where he hoped to compare law-enforcement strategies with the head G-man himself, J. Edgar Hoover.

Judy understood that working for Elvis was a 24/7 job. As I kissed her good-bye in the driveway at Graceland, Elvis walked by and snickered, "I thought that stuff stopped when you got married."

"Are you kidding?" I said with a smile. "It's just starting."

Our group included Bill Morris, who arranged for us to visit FBI headquarters and the office of the National Sheriffs' Association.

When we arrived at the FBI building, two agents met us outside as we exited the limos and said that any weapons we had on us would have to be left in the vehicles. I took out the gun in my shoulder holster and put it on the jump seat as others in the group did likewise. Elvis removed the guns from his twin shoulder holsters and then one from his front waistband and still another from the back of his waistband. The agents' jaws dropped as the artillery piled up in front of Elvis like a scene from a cartoon.

We got the grand tour, seeing the files and exhibitions on the biggest crimes in history, including weapons captured from Machine Gun Kelly and John Dillinger. At one point, Elvis said he had to use the restroom, and a couple agents accompanied us. As Elvis bent over the sink to wash his hands, a .25 automatic pistol hidden in his waistband fell out and clattered to the floor. I looked at the agents for their reaction. They looked at the gun on the floor, then at each other, and never said anything or indicated they even saw it. "Sorry about that, fellas. I guess I missed that one," Elvis mumbled as the agents blanched and then quickly looked away. They didn't know about the derringer in his boot, but that obviously wouldn't have mattered, either.

He never did get to meet J. Edgar Hoover. They said there was a "schedule conflict," but I've always wondered. Later it was revealed that the FBI had a 633-page dossier on Elvis dating back to the 1950s. Among the items in it were a photo of Elvis taken at my wedding, attached to which was a memo written the day before we arrived there that said, "Presley's sincerity and good intentions notwithstanding, he is certainly not the type of individual whom the Director would wish to meet. It is noted at the present time he is wearing his hair down to his shoulders, and indulges in the wearing of exotic dress."

That was rich, given the later revelation that J. Edgar was pretty fond of "exotic dress" himself, especially in the company of his right-hand man, Clyde Tolson, for whom, it is rumored, Hoover liked to put on women's clothes.

Elvis's growing obsession with stamping out illegal drug use moved him to recruit his stepbrothers, David, Ricky, and Billy Stanley, as his own personal narcs at Hillcrest High School in Memphis.

"We're gonna stop drug trafficking in this country," Elvis told them. "I'm tired of f——in' John Lennon talking about drugs. I'm tired of this free-spirited crap. I'm tired of all these drugs. They're destroying our youth. They're demoralizing our country. Young people are going straight to hell because these damn drugs are being made out to be so great by people in a position to influence them."

Elvis asked the Stanley boys to be his "eyes and ears" at school and report back to him about any drug use they saw. When David protested that they could be killed for ratting out drug users at school, Elvis said, "Then you'll be put under the Federal Witness Protection Program."

After school, he gathered the boys around and asked if they'd seen "anything suspicious today?" When the boys said no, he admonished them to "keep at it."

But the most memorable time he pulled that badge, he did it on another member of the entourage, one James Caughley.

Known as "Hamburger James" because his main responsibility was to fetch hamburgers for us while we watched movies at the Memphian Theatre, James was short, stocky, bald-headed, and cursed with a uni-brow (his other nickname was "the Brow"). He was also desperate to be considered a tough guy. He jawed nonstop about his expertise with guns, gave everybody the skunk eye, and acted as if everything was a government secret. He came off as a combination of Inspector Clouseau and Agent 86, the character Don Adams played in the TV series *Get Smart*.

Sometime in 1973, Elvis made the mistake of taking Caughley along to Las Vegas. Elvis gave him $500 as a bonus, and James promptly went into the casino and blew the whole wad. Rather than tell Elvis this, James said his money had been stolen. Elvis held a meeting with all the guys and decided to give James another $500. Then, shortly after that, it was discovered that he had been forging Elvis's signature on some checks. He had also gotten into some personal Polaroid photos that Elvis had of Priscilla and another woman.

The thought of someone in his own entourage stealing from him enraged Elvis, and after stewing about it all night, he decided to have a chat with our hamburger helper. When I informed him that James was already at the airport on a flight bound for Memphis, Elvis screamed, "We're going to get that sonofabitch right now!" He, Red, and a security guard took one of the hotel's security cars and headed for the airport. After hurriedly getting dressed, I got into our courtesy car provided by the hotel, and the chase was on, just like in the movies.

Elvis and Red got to the airport first and pulled up to the gate just as the plane was preparing to pull away. Elvis ran onto the tarmac and waved his federal narcotics badge at the pilot, who obediently stopped the plane and let him and Red aboard, thinking Elvis had missed the flight. Elvis informed the pilot he was looking for a fugitive and would like to take him into custody. The pilot remarked, "Aren't you Elvis Presley?" To which he replied he was, but more important, he was also a federal agent. The pilot sent his first officer with Red. Elvis asked the pilot what time the plane was getting into Memphis, to which he replied, "Elvis, this plane isn't going to Memphis. It's going to San Francisco!" Elvis called out, "C'mon Red...we got the wrong damn plane," and they exited the plane as fast as they had entered it, leaving the pilot and his crew in total amazement.

Shortly thereafter, I arrived at the airport and spotted James inside one of the terminals and hauled him out to the car. I opened up his briefcase and found a .357 Magnum and a ring worth $20,000 that Elvis had received from the Sahara Tahoe for setting an attendance record. When I confronted him about the ring, he said that he was holding onto it for safekeeping. I said it was safe enough in Elvis's jewelry case where it was supposed to be. It was hard for me not to slap the hell out of him right then and there for stealing from Elvis.

I was in the process of confiscating the items when Elvis arrived, flashing his badge. He proceeded to give James his own special version of the Miranda rights: "You have the right to remain silent, you have the right to an attorney. ..." Then, not being able to remember the rest of the Miranda rights, he continued, "And all the rest of that shit. Now get the f—— in the car! Sonny, Red, I'll see y'all back at the hotel."

Elvis and the security guard left in the station wagon. After we made James load his suitcase into the trunk of the car, he and Red got into the backseat, and I drove. James's suspicious nature kicked in, and he said, "Y'all are taking me to the desert, aren't you?" He was obviously referring to the many bodies that are supposed to have been buried out in the desert by the mob during the fight for control of the city in the early days of Las Vegas. It didn't sit well with him, and we remained silent. Then he continued, "My dad knows that I'm supposed to be on that plane, and he's going to wonder why I'm not on it." I spoke up and said, "We are not taking you to the desert." He started to say something else, and Red barked, "Shut the f—— up, before I slap the shit out of you, you damn thief!"

We went back to the Hilton, where Elvis yelled at him for a while and actually popped him on his head, with a ring on Elvis's finger bringing forth a little drop of blood, resulting in Elvis's taking pity on James. He began speaking to James in a tone of voice that indicated he was even considering letting him stay, an idea that Red and I both quickly talked him out of, foreseeing major trouble down the road.

Finally, Elvis said, "Go on, James. Go on back to Memphis. Nobody's going to bother you anymore. Just keep your mouth shut, or these two guys will find you."

For once, James did just that. We never saw him again, but I understand he still lives in Memphis.

Meanwhile, Elvis's personal arsenal continued to grow, and it included a Thompson machine gun, an M-16, .357s, .45s, shotguns, rifles, and derringers. He especially liked the craftsmanship of German guns, and he paid $5,000 for an over and under 410/.22 shotgun custom made for Hermann Göring, Adolph Hitler's air force field marshal. Elvis also enjoyed target practice with a German Luger I bought him for Christmas in 1971.

For a while, one of his favorite weapons was a prototype .45 rifle that converted into a fully automatic weapon with the placing of a ball bearing into a slot. A manufacturer in Utah that he met through Ed Parker made it for him. One day the gun literally exploded in his hands while he was taking target practice at Graceland, which could have caused serious injury, especially to his eyes. After that, Elvis stuck with Smith & Wesson, Colt, and other well-known firearms manufacturers.

Elvis used a shed door that was adjacent to the office behind Graceland for target practice. Some days it sounded like the Hatfields and the McCoys were potshotting each other back there. Once Vernon came out of his office and told Elvis he was going to kill someone in there if Elvis didn't stop shooting in that direction. "Daddy, I'm a damn good shot," Elvis told him. "I'm shooting at the door on the shed. So tell the girls that they don't need to worry, or you either, okay?"

As if the badges and guns weren't enough, Elvis also began buying law-enforcement equipment like a police radio, handcuffs, and a blackjack that fit into a special holster on the inside of Elvis's forearm.

He also got a revolving blue light that he put in his Lincoln Mark IV, and he started patrolling the streets of Memphis in search of evil-doers. When he didn't find any of them, Elvis contented himself by pulling over speeders.

"Man, do you know how fast you're going?" Elvis asked one motorist he'd stopped.

"No, sir, I don't," came the reply.

"Well, I don't either," said Elvis said, "but you were haulin' ass, my friend."

Then the guy realized who he was talking to. "Hey, aren't you Elvis Presley?"

"Yes I am, but I'm also a licensed sheriff's deputy here in town. I watch these streets because it's speeders like you that can cause serious accidents."

The guy promised not to drive too fast again, and instead of a ticket he drove away with Elvis's autograph.

Shortly before Elvis's thirty-fifth birthday, the Junior Chamber of Commerce of America—also known as the Jaycees—named him one of the nation's Ten Outstanding Young Men for 1970. It was a prestigious award given out to outstanding professional men thirty-five and under. Past honorees included John and Robert Kennedy, Richard Nixon, Howard Hughes, Orson Welles, Leonard Bernstein, Pat Boone, Jesse Jackson, Joe Louis, and Henry Kissinger.

Elvis was rehearsing at the time for an upcoming Las Vegas engagement, and he interrupted his preparation to fly to Memphis for the award ceremony at the Holiday Inn Rivermont. George H.W. Bush, then the U.S. ambassador to the United Nations and later the first President Bush, was the main speaker at the luncheon. He and Elvis chatted amiably. Later, an impressed Elvis remarked that Bush was a true gentleman.

Elvis was proud of his award, and he carried the medallion with him for years. Today it hangs in a display case in the Big Room at Graceland.

Elvis resumed rehearsals for his Las Vegas appearance. He seemed to be irreverent for that particular engagement; during one of his shows, he donned a gorilla mask and sang "You've Lost That Lovin' Feeling." Another time, he grabbed one of those battery-operated laugh boxes, turned it on, held it up to the microphone, and said, "I'd like you to meet Colonel Parker!"

He delivered rambling speeches and started giving karate demonstrations, one of them even lasting twenty minutes. And he'd sing "Happy Birthday" to band members even when it wasn't their birthday. On the final night of that engagement, he even had a water fight onstage.

In the spring of 1971, at Elvis's insistence, Judy and I moved into his new Holmby Hills residence in Los Angeles with him, Priscilla, and Lisa Marie. For the next two years, we occupied the large room above the den. Even though the house had a security system, Elvis gave me a Ted Williams–model .20-gauge pump shotgun and had me keep it in my room.

As a fail-safe, Elvis hired a private security firm, which sent a security guard named Al Strada to stand watch while we slept. Al was a young college student at UCLA and was juggling school and work. One night while we were away on a tour, Judy caught him sleeping on the job. She mentioned it to me, and I took him aside when we returned and laid down the law as bluntly as possible.

"Elvis would shoot you himself if he knew you fell asleep while his wife and daughter were inside the house," I said. "I understand you're burning the candle at both ends, but get your sleep somewhere else. Sleep in class if you have to, but don't ever sleep here again."

It never happened again, and Al ended up joining Elvis on the road, working in wardrobe. He became a trusted confidant and good friend.

Although he loved and doted on Lisa Marie, Elvis left most of the parenting duties to Priscilla. I doubt he ever changed a diaper in his life. He also wasn't big on discipline, and Lisa Marie got away with plenty. She was a bright child who was quick to tell staff members who stood in the way of her getting whatever she wanted, "I'm gonna tell my daddy, and then you'll be fired!" It worked on some of them, including Elvis's aunt Delta, who asked how high when Lisa Marie told her to jump.

Judy and I saw firsthand the growing tension between Elvis and Priscilla. He grew increasingly edgy and temperamental, thanks in part to his growing dependency on Dexedrine to control his weight. When he needed to come down, he took pain pills and chased them with sleeping pills.

The real heart of the matter was that Elvis wanted Priscilla to exist only for him. He was proud of her taking dance lessons and karate, but he basically wanted her to be at his beck and call the rest of the time. As it turned out, she had an affair with both her dance teacher and her karate instructor.

Elvis loved to cruise around on his Harley, and he did a lot of car buying. The car dealers were even coming to him. One night we got a visit from Jules Meyers, who owned a Pontiac dealership on Santa Monica Boulevard. Jules drove up in a gorgeous 1971 Stutz Blackhawk. He was the only dealer in California licensed to sell the car, and he was making the rounds of his celebrity clients to see if they might be interested in purchasing the $30,000 vehicle. He had already taken an order from Frank Sinatra.

Made in Italy, the Blackhawk used a Pontiac Grand Prix chassis to hold a big-block V-8 engine. A GM TH400 automatic transmission allowed the car to accelerate to sixty miles per hour in 8.4 seconds. Fuel economy wasn't part of the deal: the Blackhawk got just eight miles per gallon.

Naturally, Elvis fell instantly in love with the car and told Jules he'd take it. Jules got out his order pad and started scribbling. He figured he could have one delivered in a few weeks.

"No," said Elvis. "I'll take this one."

Jules started to explain that he couldn't turn over that one to Elvis because it was his demo car to show potential buyers. "I can't sell this car if no one sees it," he said.

"Mr. Meyers, let me ask you something," Elvis said. "Who do you think is gonna sell more of these cars driving it? You or me?"

Ka-ching! Elvis cut him a check for thirty grand and had someone drive Jules back to his dealership. He and I got into the Stutz and cruised Sunset Boulevard, with Elvis blowing the car's musical horn, always an attention getter.

Cars weren't Elvis's only distraction, of course. There were still new women in his life. While he was performing in Lake Tahoe in the spring, he spotted a beautiful young woman sitting in the second row with her mother. Elvis winked at the woman throughout the performance, and afterward he sent me to bring her and her mother backstage.

Here's how charming Elvis Presley could be when the mood hit him: he talked the mother into going home alone. The daughter, named Paige, ended up staying with him for the duration of his engagement.

One weekend they traveled to his place on Chino Canyon Road in Palm Springs. Elvis had a bottle of prescription Hycodan, a powerful cough medicine loaded with codeine. Taken in large quantities, it's a dangerous narcotic.

Elvis and Paige kept swigging from the bottle all evening and finally retired for the night to Elvis's bedroom. The next day, when Elvis wasn't awake at his usual time, I went to check on him in the master bedroom. Nobody responded to my knock or when I began calling out Elvis's name in increasing volume, so I went in. The room was freezing, and Elvis was lying in bed on his back with the covers pulled up to his chin. His breathing was erratic.

"Boss! Boss, snap out of it!" I yelled, taking him by the shoulders and shaking him. "Wake up, Elvis!" He moaned a bit, so I left him and went to Paige. She made a rasping noise when she breathed and didn't even respond when I shook her hard and slapped her hard across the face twice. I noticed the bottle on her nightstand, and it was almost empty.

I yelled for Charlie to call for a doctor, and within minutes, Dr. George Kaplan arrived. By then, Elvis had regained consciousness, though he was still plenty woozy. As the doctor checked Paige, Elvis said, "She'll be okay, Dr. Kaplan, just give her a shot of Ritalin." That pissed me off. Clearly, Elvis just wanted everybody to go away. He even argued when Dr. Kaplan said an ambulance was needed immediately, but he relented when the doctor explained that Paige was in critical condition.

Charlie and I followed the ambulance to the hospital. I wasn't much of a praying man at the time, but I asked God to spare her life. She had her stomach pumped and was put in the intensive care unit. "This girl is in bad shape," said Dr. Kaplan. "I'll be honest: I can't promise anything."

He said there was no reason to stay there as he wasn't sure how long it would be before there was a new development. Dr. Kaplan told us to return home, promising to call us with any news. We returned to the house, where, thanks to a dose of Ritalin, Elvis was up and about. "I told her not to drink that much," he said guiltily.

A few hours later, the doctor called to say that Paige was coming around. I went to the hospital. She had tubes down her throat and seemed to be sleeping, but when I touched her arm her eyes jerked open, and she started making awful noises. I asked the doctor if she was all right, and he said that depended on how long her brain had been deprived of oxygen. In the meantime, Elvis had called the Colonel and apprised him of the situation, and the Colonel swiftly went into action.

He told Elvis that all of us should leave for Los Angeles immediately and he would take care of everything. After a few days, the Colonel had Paige flown to her home on a private jet, with Elvis picking up the tab for the plane and her medical bills. Thank God, Paige eventually recovered.

But Elvis didn't visit her or even call for a long time. Later that year, Paige and her mother came to the Hilton to one of his shows. He didn't want to see her, but I got them into the showroom after asking Paige not to come down front to the stage or attempt to go backstage, to which she readily agreed. I found out they were going to sleep in their car for the night before driving back to the Bay Area, which I wasn't going to let happen. I got them a room for the night, but I'm sorry to say that Paige wasn't the same person. Her personality wasn't as radiant as before.

Another time, Elvis invited several female fans into the house in Palm Springs. This time it wasn't a sexual thing. He just enjoyed their company, and we all had a good time hanging out for a couple of days. We were goofing around once, and one of the girls struck her tongue out at Elvis. "Good God almighty, would you look at that tongue!" Elvis said. "You've got a tongue like a lizard!" From then on, the girl was known as "Lizard Tongue."

When the girls left, "Lizard Tongue" sent a letter to Elvis at the Palm Springs address, signing it with her nickname. When Priscilla and Joanie went down to the house to hang out, Priscilla found the letter and went ballistic. Elvis was back in Vegas, and Priscilla called Joe demanding to speak to him. Joe said he was sleeping.

When Elvis called back later, he chewed Priscilla out, and she apologized. But then she did something I still don't understand. She told Judy about the letter from "Lizard Tongue," said it was addressed to me, and insinuated that I was fooling around.

Why Priscilla would go out of her way like that to try to cause trouble in my marriage, I don't know. Maybe she wanted Judy to be as unhappy as she was. Years later, after her divorce from Elvis, Priscilla apologized to me, which was fine, but she needed to apologize to Judy because Judy was the one Priscilla had hurt so badly. She never did. What she did to Judy changed things between Priscilla and me for good, especially because I had been there for her on several occasions to prevent problems between her and Elvis.

Over time, Priscilla withdrew from everyone. We all spent Christmas at Graceland, but Priscilla was distant and cold. Elvis had promised her a new car for Christmas, but she told him not to waste his money. He instead presented her with ten $1,000 bills. She stuck them in her purse and the next day lammed out for Los Angeles with Lisa Marie.

It was evident to me that the New Year would present plenty of changes.

# Chapter 28

# Separate Ways

O N JANUARY 8, 1972, ELVIS'S WIFE AND DAUGHTER WERE TWO THOUSAND miles away. So he flew Joyce Bova to Memphis to help him celebrate his thirty-seventh birthday.

Meanwhile, in Los Angeles, Priscilla was getting deeper into her affair with karate instructor Mike Stone. When that started has been a matter of much speculation. According to Priscilla, they didn't even meet until early that year when Stone, acting as a bodyguard for record producer Phil Spector, visited Elvis backstage in Vegas. Her version is that Elvis encouraged her to train with Stone, almost as if Elvis pushed her into involvement with him.

But others insist that Priscilla and Stone began their affair in the summer of 1971. That's when Ed Parker, her karate instructor at the time, told her that if she wanted to improve, she should study the great fighters. So Priscilla, Joanie Esposito, and instructor Bob Wall attended a tournament in Orange County in which Stone fought. Three years earlier, Priscilla and Elvis had seen Stone at a tournament in Hawaii, and Priscilla was infatuated with him. Now her interest was rekindled.

A few weeks later, Priscilla dragged Lamar's wife, Nora Fike, with her to Stone's karate studio in Huntington Beach. After attending a few of his classes, Stone invited Priscilla to his home to meet his wife, Fran, and their four-year-old daughter. Fran was pregnant at the time, but that didn't daunt Priscilla in the least. In her book *Elvis and Me,* Priscilla never even mentioned that Stone was married, which is a telling omission.

I learned about their affair way before Elvis even had a clue. I was with him in Vegas in January 1972 when Judy called to tell me she might be expecting. I flew home to go with her for a pregnancy test. I was at the Monovale house when Priscilla drove into the driveway. She and Mike got out of her white Mercedes 380SL and walked up to the door. When I opened it, Priscilla was stunned and said, "Sonny, what are you doing here? Where's Elvis?"

"He's not here," I said. Then I explained that I had come home to be with Judy for the day, and Priscilla said, "Oh, okay. You remember Mike, don't you?" We acknowledged each other coolly, and then he walked back to the car and got in. Priscilla went into the house for a moment, and then she went out and drove away with Stone.

Judy had her own suspicions. She saw Mike pick up Priscilla at the house late one night. "There's something going on," she told me.

We weren't the only ones who thought so. Red heard through Elvis's maid Henrietta that Stone was spending a lot of time at the house. Red bet Joe Esposito $100 that Stone and Priscilla were having an affair. "That's impossible," Joe said. "Priscilla would never cheat on Elvis."

It was the easiest $100 Red ever made.

Priscilla and Mike even rented a small Huntington Beach apartment in Belmont Shores to use as a love nest.

One day while Priscilla was taking a "karate lesson" at Chuck Norris's studio, Elvis asked me to contact her. I called Norris's studio in Sherman Oaks and was told Priscilla was at a karate tournament. I then called the tournament site, but she was nowhere to be found.

To buy some time, I told Elvis that Norris's line at his studio was busy. A couple hours later, the red light went on in the box behind Elvis's desk, signaling that the front gate was opening. He didn't notice it, but I did, and I went outside to meet her. When Priscilla got out of her car I told her that Elvis had been looking for her for several hours and that I had covered for her as best I could. Now, it was up to her.

"Where ya been, 'Cilla?" Elvis asked as she entered the house.

"Oh, I just went to another studio to watch a karate tournament with some students there," she blithely answered. Elvis didn't pursue the matter, but if he had, I am sure Priscilla would have had all the right answers.

In late February, Elvis finished his engagement at the Hilton Hotel in Las Vegas (formerly the International). Between shows one night, he summoned Priscilla to his suite, and what happened next leads me to think that he knew all about what was going on between her and Mike Stone.

As Priscilla herself has told it, Elvis was in bed when she got there. Then he, as they say in paperback romances, "forced himself on her." "This is how a real man makes love to his woman," he said, according to Priscilla.

That was interesting given that Elvis's aversion to sex with women who'd given birth was well known. But I suppose it could have happened if he was upset about Mike Stone. Either way, it was a case of too little, too late. After his midnight show, Priscilla told Elvis she was leaving him.

"What do you mean you're leaving me?" he screamed. "I have given you everything you want! You can't mean that, Satnin'. I don't believe what I'm hearing!"

Priscilla told him they had both lived separate lives for some time, and it was finally time for her to start over. After a lengthy discussion, Elvis finally resigned himself that he had lost Priscilla. They hugged and said good-bye.

Elvis immediately called in Red, Lamar, Charlie, Joe, and me and announced, "Well, another man has taken my wife." We were stunned, not because we didn't know about it but because Elvis was always very guarded about his personal life.

The first thing that came to Red's mind was what happened when Priscilla begged Elvis to let her come to Vegas more often. He told her no, and then he told Red: "I wish she would find someone else to mess around with and quit bugging me."

So Red said to him, "Hell, man, ain't that what you wanted?"

"No, not that way, man," Elvis replied forlornly. "Not that way."

But then he started ranting. "Hell, man, I tried giving her all the freedom I could. Sometimes a man and a woman have to have separate lives. I gave her all the time she wanted. I encouraged her to take those lessons from Mike Stone and everything."

Red looked at Elvis in disbelief and said, "Elvis, don't you know that Mike Stone is the guy she's seeing?"

"Damn," Elvis said, shaking his head.

There was nothing more to say right then, so we left.

Looking back, I wonder if Elvis would have been that upset if Priscilla just left him to strike out on her own. Clearly, what upset him the most was the involvement of another man. I'm certain he wondered how that would look to the public.

Over the next few days, his emotions were all over the map. He'd go from hurt to despair to sorrow to absolute fury. "How could that bitch leave me?" he asked as we sat at breakfast. "I gave her everything a man could offer, and she ends up leaving me for another man? What the f—— does she want?"

That he'd been screwing around on Priscilla from day one somehow didn't enter into it as far as Elvis was concerned. He just couldn't get over that Priscilla had left him, and it galled him no end.

To get his mind off things, he began delving anew into metaphysical books—and even more into drugs.

He also threw himself into his work. In 1972, Elvis played one hundred–plus shows, touring virtually nonstop. He squeezed in some recording sessions, too, and "Burning Love" hit Number 2 on *Billboard*'s Top 40. Red wrote a song called "Separate Ways," which was about Elvis and Priscilla. It became a Top 20 hit for Elvis later that year.

He also performed at Madison Square Garden in New York for the first time, though it took some arm-twisting to get him there. "I'm not really a New York kind of artist," Elvis told Jerry Weintraub after the promoter proposed the date. "They're not going to like me there. They like me in Alabama, Georgia, and Tennessee, but you're gonna have trouble selling shows in New York City."

Elvis couldn't have been more wrong. Weintraub ended up selling approximately eighty thousand tickets, and to get them, fans slept outside the box office on cots and in sleeping bags for two weeks. Nobody had ever seen anything like it. Elvis became the first entertainer to sell out the Garden four nights in a row.

Those were among the best shows Elvis ever did. Colonel Parker capitalized on the triumph by releasing *Elvis as Recorded Live at Madison Square Garden* just eight days later after the last Garden performance. It sold more than three million copies.

About that time, MGM released the documentary called *Elvis on Tour*. It contained live and unrehearsed scenes of Elvis on the road, including one filmed the morning after a concert in Jacksonville, Florida. The same day he performed there, a rocket had been launched from Cape Canaveral. The camera caught me asking Elvis as we were crossing the Jacksonville Bridge if he'd seen the rocket launch. And his bawdy reply: "No, Sonny, I didn't, man. I was having a launch on a beaver about that time," breaking everyone up.

One scene that didn't make it into the movie was when we traveled to Indianapolis. As we approached the back entrance of the Fairgrounds Coliseum, about five policemen were there with German shepherd dogs, who were barking at the crowd. It almost looked like a scene from the civil rights era, and Elvis flashed.

"What the hell are those dogs doing out there?" Elvis asked in a harsh tone.

"I don't know, boss, but I'll find out," I said. He was angry that dogs were being used to hold back his fans, and he looked to me to take care of the situation quickly.

After I escorted him to the dressing room, I took the officer in charge of the security detail and pulled him aside.

"Why are you using those dogs for crowd control?" I asked. "This is very upsetting to Elvis." He informed me that the dogs weren't being used for that purpose at all but to patrol the lot to prevent people from breaking into cars. He said the officers with the dogs were just gathered there to get a look at Elvis before they went back out to the parking lot. Once I found out the scoop, I went back to Elvis and told him. He was pleased with the answer and calmed down. I always admired his respect and concern for his fans.

There were, however, exceptions. In Lubbock, Texas, Elvis got smacked by a jealous boyfriend in the 1950s. The guy called him over to his car to ask him for an autograph for his girlfriend, and when Elvis leaned down to the window to sign it, the guy sucker punched Elvis in the face. Elvis said he, Red, and Scotty Moore drove around all night looking for the guy, but they never found him. Elvis said in 1972 before he played the Lubbock Municipal Coliseum, "I wonder if that sonofabitch is still out there. He's probably an old pot-bellied dude by now. I'd still like to kick his ass."

But Elvis could go from a fighter to a lover in no time flat. In July, Elvis met Linda Thompson, a twenty-two-year-old former Miss Tennessee attending Memphis State University. His friend Bill Browder, who later became a country music singer under the name of T.G. Sheppard, arranged the meeting. Linda came to the Memphian Theatre, where Elvis was screening some movies, and he was instantly smitten. "Hello, honey, where have you been all my life?" he said to her.

"Growing up," Linda shot back with a smile. Her tongue was as quick as she was beautiful. When Elvis sat down next to her, she took in his high-collared black cape with its red satin lining and teased, "Dressed a little like Dracula, aren't we?"

"Well I'll be damned," laughed Elvis. "Don't get upset if I try and bite your neck tonight."

Unaware of his impending divorce from Priscilla, Linda resisted his advances at first, and finally Elvis told her, "Honey, you know I'm not married anymore." He never forgot her reply.

"No I didn't," Linda said. "But you know, I'm sorry that it didn't work out for you, but you should have married a Southern girl."

Linda was fifteen years younger than he was, but for the next four and a half years, she and Elvis were together.

Like Ann-Margret, Linda wasn't intimidated by the guys and never felt threatened by our presence. In fact, she embraced us, and we loved her in return. She was classy and erudite yet down-to-earth and kind to everyone. I still think of her as a good friend today.

Though Linda was his love, Elvis was still Elvis when it came to women. It seemed his breakup with Priscilla freed him to resume a lifestyle he enjoyed when he first started out as a young rock and roller in the mid-1950s. All women were fair game, and he went about trying to prove it. Around the same time he met Linda, he also dated another former Memphis beauty queen and model. This one had considerably more notoriety.

Elvis first met actress Cybill Shepherd in Memphis. Cybill was going through one of her many breakups with Peter Bogdanovich, who had brilliantly directed her in *The Last Picture Show*. Elvis saw the film many times and felt a strong attraction to the sexy actress. He arranged to meet her through George Klein, who had met Cybill when he emceed the Miss Teenage Memphis pageant a few years before.

Like the character she played in *The Last Picture Show*, Cybill definitely didn't lack self-confidence. But there was nothing wrong with that; Lord knows, there's enough insecurity in the movie business. Cybill was forward and didn't pull any punches. If she didn't like you, you knew it. She liked Elvis, but her schedule was as crowded as his, and eventually she returned to Bogdanovich.

Elvis also began seeing another beauty queen that year, only her crown was given to her by Hugh Hefner. Sheila Ryan was a *Playboy* playmate whom met Elvis in 1972 when she came backstage in Vegas with singer James Darren. Sheila was a beautiful, statuesque young woman with light brown hair, which she wore in a shag-style cut. She was quiet by nature and had a shy, demure manner. Elvis always seemed relaxed and in good spirits when Sheila was around. The two cared deeply about each other, and their relationship lasted about eighteen months. She later married actor James Caan, with whom she had a son, Scott Caan, who has followed in his father's footsteps.

There were many other women in between over the years. Back then if *People* magazine ran its "sexiest man alive" issue, there is no doubt in my mind that the first recipient would have been Elvis Presley.

For years, overseas producers had tried unsuccessfully to get Elvis to tour England, Germany, Japan, Italy, and Spain. It has been speculated that he didn't because Colonel Parker was in the United States illegally (Parker was born in Holland, and his real name was Andreas Cornelis van Kujik), which would've come out when he tried to get a passport. But the real reason we never toured abroad is that Elvis would not give up his guns and pills, the combination of which Parker feared would have caused an international incident or two.

By then, Elvis was into guns for more than just self-protection. He was regularly shooting up hotel rooms, television sets, chandeliers, and anything on which he chanced to draw a bead. Once he blew away a TV set when singer Robert Goulet appeared on a show Elvis and Lisa Marie were watching as they ate dinner. Goulet had screwed up the lyrics to "The Star-Spangled Banner," and Elvis never forgave him for it. So when Goulet materialized on the screen in front of him, Elvis grabbed a gun and blasted away. "That'll be enough of that shit!" he said, returning to his meal.

When Lisa Marie wondered why he'd killed their television, Elvis told her, "Aw, daddy didn't like what was on, so I just turned it off from here."

But I have since learned there's an interesting backstory to this tale: supposedly when Elvis was stationed in Germany, Anita Wood constantly stayed in touch through letters. In one of the letters, Goulet added a postscript in a very sly manner indicating that he was "personally taking good care of Anita," which Elvis didn't take to kindly. He had harbored ill feelings ever since, and it finally manifested when he saw Goulet on television.

As for Elvis, millions of fans from all over the world would be able to catch their idol on *Elvis: Aloha from Hawaii, via Satellite*, thanks to the efforts of Colonel Parker. The January 1973 concert from Honolulu was expected to reach in excess of one billion people in more than forty countries. An album soundtrack was scheduled for release afterward.

The historic event would be the pinnacle of Elvis's amazing career.

All the downers Elvis was using in Vegas—mostly Dilaudid and Demerol—had given him a powerful sugar jones. He ate Popsicles, Dreamsicles, and Fudgsicles by the box, and when the Honolulu concert was announced, he was tipping the scales at a hefty 195 pounds. When Marty Pasetta, the producer-director of the *Aloha* special, got his first gander at Elvis, he came right out and said Elvis had to drop some weight before the concert.

Joe, Lamar, and I had just dropped about forty pounds apiece on a stringent diet, and Elvis came to me and said he wanted to do the same thing. The catch was that he wanted me to go on the diet with him. He was the boss, so we started on the thirty-day regimen in December. In addition to minuscule portions of bland foods frozen in plastic bags and then boiled in hot water, the diet included a daily injection of protein taken from the urine of a pregnant woman, to burn up fat in the system. We weren't allowed to use anything with fat in it, even including lotions, shaving creams, and shampoos.

We stuck to it and lost about twenty pounds each. The first time I went on the diet it had been rough, but it was nothing like the second time. Elvis looked great, and he arrived in Honolulu on January 9, 1973, raring to go.

When we landed at the airport, so many leis were placed around Elvis's neck that you could hardly see his face. We went by helicopter to the Hilton Hawaiian Village Hotel, where hundreds of fans welcomed Elvis. It was a thrill just to be a part of it. He loved it, of course, but he was also a little tense. He would be performing live before an estimated billion and a half people around the world, and he wanted everything just right.

Elvis worked hard in rehearsals and had his performance down to a science. He had his hair restyled and cut by longtime close friend Pat Parry and had designer Bill Belew go to work on an outfit that would scream "America!" to the world. Bill and Gene Doucette, who did the embroidery and designs, came up with a white jumpsuit and cape emblazoned in gold studs, with red and blue stones on the front and back in the design of an American eagle.

Even though Elvis had a lot on his plate, he spent a good deal of time trying to lure actor Jack Lord to his show. We were all big fans of *Hawaii Five-O*, and more than once I heard Elvis say the famous Steve McGarrett line, "Book 'em, Dano."

While Jack wasn't filming, he usually hibernated with his wife, Marie, in their Honolulu condominium because of the long hours he kept on the show. They were an early-to-bed couple, but because Elvis was so gracious, they made an exception. I learned years later when Elvis took the time to introduce Jack to the worldwide audience, he was floored by his introduction.

"My favorite actor in the whole world is sitting in the audience, and I want to introduce him," Elvis said. When Jack later visited with Elvis backstage, he returned the compliment.

"You know, Elvis, many of the actors I worked with in New York really admired your work," Jack said.

"Really? Who?" Elvis asked.

"Steve McQueen, Paul Newman, Tony Franciosa, and Robert Mitchum," Jack replied. "They all thought you were dynamite." You could have knocked Elvis over with a feather. He admired all of those actors and yet never felt he earned their respect. Elvis was deeply touched by the comment.

Jack later told a reporter, "The moment we met and shook hands it was as if we had known each other all of our lives." By the way, have you ever noticed that Jack had a lock of his hair that fell over his forehead, much like Elvis did in the 1960s?

There were subsequent meetings in Las Vegas and lots of correspondence over the years. The two men had a deep and profound respect for one another. Like all of us, Jack was crushed when he heard the news of Elvis's death.

The special was filmed at the Honolulu Convention Center at 12:30 AM, so as to be beamed live to other countries around the world in prime time. (The special wasn't broadcast in the United States and Canada until a few months later, after additional songs and island footage were added to make it a ninety-minute special.) It was a blockbuster show that proved Elvis Presley was still the King. He came out and for the next hour rocked the universe with a powerhouse performance that was beamed to an estimated 1.5 billion people.

To put it into proper perspective, for a moment in time a quarter of the world's population stopped whatever they were doing to watch an Elvis Presley concert. It's a Herculean achievement that hasn't been duplicated in more than three decades.

The next day we were supposed to visit the USS *Arizona* memorial, a project that Elvis kick-started in 1961 at a charity show. Red, Marty, Joe, I, and a few of the other boys went to Elvis's suite to pick him up. We knocked and knocked, getting no response. Finally, Linda Thompson came to the door shaking her head in dismay. "He can't go anywhere," she said. We went inside, and there was Elvis on the couch, his head lolling back. There was a towel around his neck, and he was sweating profusely. I suspected he had taken some Demerol, because when he greeted us his words were slurred and he could hardly keep his eyes open. He looked like a zombie, and our hearts sank.

"Well, I guess we won't be doing anything with him," someone piped up.

"No, it doesn't look like it," Linda said, looking absolutely crestfallen.

Nobody knew it then, but the day after one of the greatest performances in entertainment history, Elvis Presley started on a toboggan slide at whose end was a crash landing none of us could have ever imagined.

# Chapter 29

# T-R-O-U-B-L-E

IN EARLY 1973, ELVIS WAS RIDING HIGH ON THE CREST OF THE *ALOHA* SPECIAL concert and soundtrack. The latter shot straight to Number 1, selling four million copies. It would be Elvis's last time on top of the charts.

Since his comeback in August of '69, Elvis had worked practically nonstop, and his output of product was unmatched by any other artist of his era. But, instead of winding down, Elvis cranked it up a notch, performing 168 shows in 1973—the most of his career. Looking back, it was apparent he needed a break.

In late January, he opened his eighth Las Vegas engagement at the Hilton. It was around then that some reviewers noted that his energy level was low and that his shows lacked zip.

But there was a personal high for Elvis not long after that, when he met boxing great Muhammad Ali. Ali came to town to fight British champion Joe Bugner on February 14. He was staying and training at Caesars Palace, but he came to see Elvis perform at the Hilton.

When Elvis really liked and admired someone, a backstage greeting wasn't enough. At Elvis's direction, Ali was brought to his suite.

Like Elvis, Ali was in a class by himself. They both had incredible charisma and magnetism. They admired each other immensely, and I can't even begin to describe what it was like to be there with the "King of Rock and Roll" and "the Greatest" in the same room.

"Elvis, now I know why the women like you so much!" said Ali in that inimitable rapid-fire manner of speech he had. "You're almost as pretty as I am!" Ali went on to say how much he'd enjoyed Elvis's show, and then he began admiring the jumpsuit Elvis was wearing. That's when Gene Kilroy, a member of Ali's staff, took me aside. Ali liked Elvis's jumpsuit so much, Kilroy said, that he wondered if who-ever designed Elvis's jumpsuits would make a robe for him. Specifically, Ali wanted a robe that proclaimed him to be "The People's Champion" on the back.

Ali lost his heavyweight title bid to Joe Frazier in their 1971 fight at Madison Square Garden. Then Frazier lost the title to George Foreman. Foreman wasn't interested in fighting Ali then, so Ali gave himself the title he wanted emblazoned on the robe.

When I told Elvis about Kilroy's request, he excitedly said that he would pay for the robe himself and give it to Ali as a present.

When I gave Ali's measurements, I emphasized that the hem should drop somewhere between ankle and midcalf, and the sleeves should be wide enough for Ali to easily get in and out of the robe wearing boxing gloves. A few days later, the robe was done. I called Kilroy, and we made arrangements to get it to Ali on the night of the Bugner fight.

I went with a security guard from the Hilton in one of their vehi-cles to personally pick up Ali and his entourage at Caesars at the appointed time. As we began making our way through the casino, Ali had the look and intensity of a panther, which was, coinciden-tally, a species close to one of our nicknames for Elvis, "Tiger." People began chanting "Ali! Ali! Ali!" The energy coming off him was going through me as if I had an electric wire attached to me.

Outside, as we walked to the car, Ali asked where I was going to sit. I said in the front, and he said he would, too. He squeezed in between the driver and me. In the back were Ali's people—Gene Kilroy, Angelo Dundee, Dr. Ferdie Pacheco, and Ali's brother, Rahaman.

I was still pretty jacked up from the thunderous reaction of the casino crowd and the energy Ali gave off. He noticed I couldn't stay still and asked me what was the matter.

"Ali, you have me so wired I'm ready to whip his ass for you!" I blurted out. He responded with, "All right, Sonny!" breaking up him and everybody else in the car.

At the Hilton, we went to the back entrance and straight to Elvis's suite. Ali and Elvis greeted one another warmly, and Ali produced a pair of gold Everlast gloves, on one of which he had inscribed, "Elvis, you are the greatest!"

Then Elvis handed over the large wrapped box containing the robe. Ali opened it, took out the robe, and expressed great delight.

He put the robe on, and as he started to turn around to see himself in the large foyer mirror, Gene Kilroy whispered to me that the inscription on back of the robe was wrong. Sure enough, instead of "The People's Champion," the robe said "The People's Choice."

When Ali noticed, he seemed perplexed. "That's my fault," I quickly offered. "I told Bill the wrong words. I'll get it changed for you." Ali stood there for a moment looking at the back of the robe in the mirror. Then he flashed that incandescent smile and repeated "The People's Choice" a couple times with growing enthusiasm.

"Naw, Sonny, I like it!" he proclaimed. "'The People's Choice' is nice! Anybody can call himself 'The People's Champion.' But 'The People's Choice'—that sounds good!"

No matter how he really felt about the robe, Ali didn't want to get me in trouble with Elvis. As if I wasn't already grateful enough for that, then Ali turned to Elvis and said, "I know Sonny is one of your main guys and that you need him for your shows, but I was wondering if you could let him come to the fight tonight?"

The greatest of all time? I would say so! "Yeah, Sonny can go," Elvis said. "And he can represent all of us in your corner, Ali." That was one hell of a proud night for me.

Ali didn't wear the Elvis robe for the Bugner fight, but he did when he fought Ken Norton on March 31, 1973. Kind of. I've seen the video of that fight. Ali stepped into the ring wearing a blue robe on the back of which it said, "The People's Champion." The robe Elvis presented to him at the Hilton was white, with jeweled studs.

Ali never wore the robe again after the Norton fight—but not, as has been said by many, because he considered it unlucky, because Norton broke his jaw and won a twelve-round decision from him. The fact is that the Elvis robe was heavy and cumbersome. It stayed in Ali's closet for more than three decades until it was recently unveiled at the grand opening of the Muhammad Ali Center in Louisville, Kentucky, in November 2005.

Ali called me a couple of times at the Monovale house over the next few months. The first time, the housekeeper buzzed me on the intercom in my room to say I had a call. When I picked up the phone, Ali said, "Sonny, how you doing?" We chatted for a few minutes, and then I asked if he wanted to speak with Elvis. His answer endeared Ali to me even more, if that was possible. "Sonny, if I want to talk to Elvis, I'll call Elvis. If I want to talk to Sonny, I call Sonny."

Elvis loved Ali, and the feeling was mutual. "I don't admire nobody, but Elvis Presley was the sweetest, most humble, and nicest man you'd want to know," Ali once told a reporter.

A few days after Ali won a decision over Bugner in Vegas, we could have used his help in an incident that occurred during Elvis's midnight show. Four well-dressed men were seated right up against the stage, and one of them suddenly jumped up during Elvis's performance and made a beeline for him. His coat was draped over his right arm, and for all we knew he was hiding a weapon. Red ran up behind the guy, got him in a headlock, and delivered him to a hotel security guard backstage.

Meanwhile, another member of the foursome stood up, and there was tape covering his right knuckles. J.D. Sumner pushed him back, and as the other two tried to mount the stage, Jerry and I knocked them off the stage. The ringleader brandished a cane, which later turned out to be a sword cane.

The whole time Red, Jerry, J.D., and I were grappling with the intruders, Elvis was onstage spinning around, throwing karate chops, and kicking the air without ever touching a soul. I ended up having to grab him in a bear hug to calm him down as he screamed, "Let me at him!" Vernon came out and helped settle Elvis down. As he prepared to resume the show, Elvis told the crowd, "I'm sorry about that, ladies and gentlemen.... I'm sorry I didn't break his god-damned neck, is what I'm sorry about." That got the biggest cheer of the night.

After the men were arrested, our good friend Gene Dissel, chief of security for the hotel and a former member of the Las Vegas Police Department, got copies of their rap sheets and mug shots. They were strip club owners and pornographers who had been arrested before on concealed weapons charges.

Elvis got it in his head that they were assassins sent by Mike Stone. He was so upset about it that he needed sedation after the show. The next day, while he was in his bedroom with Linda, he summoned me and Red. When we entered, Linda looked nervous, and Elvis, sitting cross-legged on the bed in white silk pajamas, was sweating profusely and looking frantic. He started raving about Mike Stone and how Stone had sent those guys to kill him the night before.

Then, he turned to me with pleading eyes and held out his hands. "Come here, Sonny," he said, slurring his words. "Come here, man."

When I knelt down in front of him, he commanded me to look him in the eye. Then he said, "The man has to die. You know the man has to die; the sonofabitch must go. You know it, Sonny, you know it. There is too much pain in me, and he did it. Do you hear me? I am right. You know I'm right. Mike Stone has to die. You will do it for me—kill the sonofabitch. Sonny, I know I can count on you. I know I can."

Linda was crying, and I started to tear up myself, fearing Elvis was on the brink of a nervous breakdown. I tried to reason with him. "No, boss, let's forget that talk," I said gently. "I know he has caused you pain, but you can't talk like that. It ain't right; it just ain't right."

But there was no calming him down. "Mike Stone must die," Elvis said repeatedly. "He must die. You will do it for me. You must. He has no reason to live."

Suddenly he pushed back the covers and rolled out of bed. As he did so, Elvis's traveling library of religious books, including the Bible, went flying.

"What is wrong with him?" Linda screamed. "Can't somebody do something? Will somebody tell me what's happened? Calm him down for God's sake."

Elvis went to the closet and began rummaging around. When he found what he was looking for, I heard Red whisper, "Oh, Lordy! Oh, Lordy!"

It was a gray-green M-16 rifle.

Elvis advanced toward me, holding the rifle out for me to take. I took the rifle and backed away, saying, "No, boss, please! No, please don't!"

"Doesn't anyone understand? Oh, God, why can't anyone understand?" Elvis ranted. "Why can't you all understand why this man must die?"

Then he leaped back into bed and started scaling the headboard as his tirade continued. "He has hurt me so much; you all know that. He has broken up my family. He has taken my wife away from me. He has destroyed everything and hurt me so much and nobody cares. He is the one who has done it all!"

Linda tried to calm him. "Baby, don't honey," she said. "Don't, please don't."

It was a sight I will never forget. I couldn't watch anymore, so I left the room with the M-16 and tossed it into a wastebasket in the hall. Then I collapsed on the couch across from Lamar, who took one look at me and realized something terrible was happening.

"Lamar, it's bad," I told him. "You know what he wants me to do? He wants me to kill Mike Stone. He was in there trying to inflict his will into me to kill him. He put that M-16 in my hands and told me to go out and waste Mike Stone, just blow him away."

Lamar leaned back, putting his feet up on the table, and said, "Son, it's going to be a long night."

I knew better. "Naw, it's going to last longer than a night," I said. "This is going to last a long time, and I don't know what to do."

Back in the bedroom, while Linda called Dr. Elias Ghanem, Elvis's personal physician in Vegas who was on call for him twenty-four hours a day, Elvis turned to Red and started in on him.

"Dammit, Red, you know he has to die. Find somebody to wipe him out. I want the sonofabitch dead. Make some calls; find someone. I could find someone in ten seconds. You can do it. Just do it. This man Mike Stone has just caused me too much suffering."

Red just listened and nodded until Dr. Ghanem arrived and gave Elvis a shot of Valium to put him to sleep.

But the nightmare wasn't over. The next day, Elvis went to Red and asked if he'd put out the call for a hit man to kill Mike Stone.

"I'm working on it, boss," Red told him. "I've made some calls. It's going to take a little time. I'm working on it." Of course, Red hadn't called anyone. He was buying time until he could figure a way out of this mess.

Finally, Red did call his friend and mentor, actor Robert Conrad, and laid it all out for him.

"Look, don't get into it man," Conrad said. "Don't go near it. Stay well away. I've seen guys act like this from a reaction to pills or shots. Just go along with what they say, and just keep putting the thing off until they calm down and realize what they are asking. He will come to his senses and forget all about it. We hope."

But it didn't go away, and Elvis kept after Red until finally Red did it to placate the boss. It didn't take too many calls to find someone willing to help out Elvis Presley. When the guy said it would cost $10,000, Red said he would get back to him.

Red went to Elvis and told him that he had made preliminary arrangements for the hit and how much it would cost. All that was necessary was for Elvis to give the final word. Red was crossing his fingers that Elvis would have a change of heart.

Elvis stared at the ground for several long moments, and then he looked up and said, "Aw, hell, let's just leave it for now. Maybe it's a bit heavy. Let's just leave it alone for now."

Red was so relieved that after the show he went out and got rip-roaring drunk. Mike Stone was almost a phone call away from being taken out.

Not long after that, Priscilla's lawyer called to tell Elvis that the divorce would cost more than anticipated.

Ed Hookstratten, Elvis's lawyer, had originally arranged a settlement of $100,000 plus several thousand dollars a month in spousal and child support. Also, Priscilla would keep her new 1971 Mercedes, a 1969 Eldorado, and a 1971 Harley-Davidson motorcycle. That was fine with her at first, but when Priscilla mentioned the deal to her friend and interior decorator, Phyllis Mann, who had worked on the Monovale house, Mann said it was a ridiculous amount.

Priscilla promptly contacted Hookstratten to demand a bigger windfall. He said no, and she hired attorney Arthur Toll, whose name was given to her by Mann. He got her a new settlement calling for an outright cash payment of $725,000 and $4,200 a month in spousal support for a year, plus $6,000 a month for ten years. Priscilla would also receive $4,000 a month in child support and half the price of the sale of the Hillcrest home. And the real kicker—5 percent of Elvis's publishing company. The divorce would cost him about $1.5 million.

Elvis didn't fight the deal because he didn't want any public speculation that he didn't have the money and that he was trying to stiff his ex-wife and daughter. But the fact was that he really didn't have the money then, and he was forced by the settlement to make a shortsighted business decision.

For some time, RCA, Elvis's recording label, had been after Colonel Parker to sell all the rights to Elvis's back musical catalog and its control. His royalties generated around $500,000 annually through repackaging and other artists' covers of his songs. Back then, nobody envisioned CDs or any technology supplanting vinyl, but RCA knew how valuable backlists were and offered $5.4 million for the whole shooting match. Elvis grabbed it—a decision that would end up costing the Presley estate untold millions.

Ironically, the loser was Lisa Marie, who eventually inherited the estate. Even though his estate generated approximately $50 million in 2006, the estate owns Elvis's recordings from only 1973 to 1977.

The real shame of the RCA deal was that after Colonel Parker and Uncle Sam got their cuts, Elvis received only about $1.5 million. And almost all of that went to pay off Priscilla in the divorce settlement.

The strain of it all really began to show. In May 1973, when Elvis opened a seventeen-day engagement at Lake Tahoe, he was about thirty pounds overweight.

Around that time, we added Dave Hebler to the security detail. Dave was a seventh-degree black belt and a buddy of Ed Parker's. His personality was a good fit. Dave was quiet, confident, respectful, playful, and always deferential to Elvis. And, like Red and me, Dave feared no man and was brutally honest when asked his opinion.

Too bad Dave didn't get to see Elvis at his best. When he started another engagement at the Las Vegas Hilton, Elvis was having breathing problems. He had several respiratory treatments and even hired a masseur to pound on his back and break up mucus filling up his lungs.

Joe Esposito and Jerry Schilling left for a European vacation that had been booked for some time. Elvis wasn't happy about that. "I'm stuck in this damn room getting these treatments, and you guys are going to Europe to have fun," he complained. But the tickets had been paid for, so Joe and Jerry left. To help fill the void, Ed Parker flew in from Los Angeles to join me, Charlie, Ricky, David, and a new guy we'd just hired, Kenny Hicks.

Elvis was getting only a few hours of sleep a night, and it was a big strain on me. I had to pick up most of the slack.

The shots given by Dr. Ghanem to help Elvis sleep weren't helping much. Once I was up with him for twenty-six hours straight. Finally Dr. Ghanem came over and gave Elvis a double dose of Valium that did the trick. It was around 5:30 AM, and I got the doc to give me a shot of Valium to put me out, too. About two hours later, I was awakened by a loud banging on my door.

I staggered across the hall into his room, and Elvis was standing at the bathroom counter. "Sonny, we need to call that old sono-fabitch. He's not going to call here," he said in a deeply slurred voice.

He meant Colonel Parker. I called Parker's office at MGM Studios in Culver City, California, and got his assistant, Tom Diskin. When the Colonel came on the line he heard my own slurry voice and asked me what was wrong. I told him about the Valium shot, and he said to call him later. I turned the phone over to Elvis and quickly returned to my room for five more hours of sleep.

On our return trip to Los Angeles, Elvis gave me a new Cadillac Eldorado for hanging in there. He also bought Ed a new Cadillac Sedan DeVille for coming over and helping out, and he got a Corvette for Kenny as a "welcome to the group" gift.

Colonel Parker had to cancel some of Elvis's shows and, along with Vernon Presley and attorney Ed Hookstratten, decided to act on the matter of Elvis's growing problem with drugs. Hookstratten hired John O'Grady to find out who was supplying Elvis with his drugs, and he reported back that it was mainly Drs. Nichopoulos and Ghanem and the dentist, Max Shapiro.

By then, others were noticing Elvis's deteriorating condition. After a Vegas show in August 1973, actress Lucille Ball joined Liza Minnelli, Petula Clark, and Joan Rivers in his suite. As Ball talked to Elvis, it was apparent he wasn't right. "What are you on, son?" she finally asked, looking him dead in the eye. "You don't need whatever it is you're taking."

Embarrassed, Elvis quickly turned his attention elsewhere and shot me a look that let me know they were no longer welcome in the suite. I walked Ms. Ball and her husband, Gary Morton (who Elvis had introduced during his show as "Mr. Ball"), out, and she wouldn't let it drop. "Why is he taking that stuff?" she said. "Why is he doing this to himself?"

I told her that Elvis had been sick. But I'm pretty sure Ms. Ball wasn't fooled, and the question occurred to me: how long would I be able to cover for Elvis?

As the monthlong engagement progressed, his behavior got increasingly erratic. One night, while giving a karate demonstration in his suite, Elvis accidentally broke the ankle of a fan named Beverly Albrecq, who'd gotten cute and said, "Well, what if I did this?" and made an unexpected move toward Elvis. We called Dr. Ghanem, and she was taken to the hospital. Elvis paid her medical costs and gave her a $5,000 settlement.

Another night, he slapped a guest when actor Lee Majors visited the suite. Everyone liked Lee, especially Elvis, because Lee was a pretty down-to-earth guy with a playful sense of humor. So when a woman slapped Lee in the face, it caught Elvis's attention. I got up to run interference, but Elvis told me to sit down because he was going to handle the matter personally. Elvis pulled the woman aside and asked, "Did he [Majors] say something to offend you?" The woman responded no, she just didn't like his attitude. Elvis took exception to the fact that this woman had insulted one of his guests, so he slapped her in the face. "There, now you know how it feels," Elvis said. "Sonny, get her ass out of here!"

In October 1973, Vernon and I accompanied Elvis to the Los Angeles Superior Courthouse in Santa Monica. The occasion was the finalization of his divorce decree. Elvis's melancholy mood didn't match his stylish jogging suit. "Damn, I don't look forward to this, but it's finally over," he said. "It weighs heavy on my heart, but once I sign those papers, it's over and done and we can go about our lives."

I waited outside while Elvis and Priscilla entered Judge Laurence J. Rittenband's chambers. After twenty minutes, they strolled out hand in hand and smiled for the waiting press. They hugged and exchanged good-byes. As she walked away, she turned back to wave. He winked back. The fairy tale was officially over.

Elvis was about to embark on a new chapter in his life. It was one I wish I could have skipped.

# Chapter 30

# Freefallin'

**F**OR ELVIS PRESLEY ENTERPRISES (EPE), THE ORGANIZATION THAT OWNS Elvis's image and likeness, the years 1974 through 1977 are a black hole. That's because in March 1996, EPE decided in a super-secret summit with licensees that Elvis's image would be forever frozen in time from 1973 backward. The last three and a half years of Elvis's life marked his mental and physical meltdown, and it's an image EPE cannot market. Unfortunately for me, it's an image I can't get out of my head.

Many have pointed to Elvis's divorce from Priscilla as the catalyst for his unraveling, but there were so many other factors as well. Yes, the divorce and the breakup of his family did play a part. So did Elvis's declining health and his growing disinterest in his career. But the common denominator linking all of those things was his escalating abuse of prescription medication.

Once at the Monovale house, I accepted a delivery from Schwab's drugstore. In the bag were several prescription bottles for Elvis, one with my son Bryan's name on it. The latter was a four-ounce bottle of liquid Demerol. I checked the bag for a receipt or a copy of the prescription, but I found nothing. When I realized that everything was for Elvis, I was livid.

It wasn't the first time I intercepted Elvis's drugs. It also happened in Memphis with the help of Elvis's aunt Delta when she gave me a package from Dr. Ghanem in Las Vegas. It contained two plastic bottles with pain pills. There must have been five hundred pills in each of the bottles, which were still sealed from the manufacturer. Elvis often came home with industrial-sized bottles—Placidyl, Quaalude,

Valium, Percodan, and Phenaphen with codeine. At least those bottles had his name or someone else's on them, but not my son's.

I jumped into my car and went to Schwab's, on Sunset Boulevard at the Laurel Canyon intersection.

"I work for Elvis Presley, and this was just delivered by a driver from your store," I told the pharmacist. "See this? This is liquid Demerol. And that is my son's name on there."

"What's the problem?" he asked.

"My son is less than a year old," I replied.

"No, that can't be," he said. "It's got to be a mistake."

"Let me tell you something," I said. "It's intended for Elvis Presley and was prescribed by Dr. Max Shapiro. Just so that I'm very clear and there's no misunderstanding—I don't ever want anything sent up to that house again in my name, my son's name, or my wife Judy's name by Shapiro or I promise you I will go to the authorities."

"Mr. West, we won't do that again," the unnerved pharmacist said.

My next move was to call Max Shapiro. The first time I tried, he was with a patient. When I finally got hold of him, I said, "Dr. Shapiro, this is Sonny West. I'm glad I didn't connect with you the first time because I've had a chance to cool off. I would have confronted you in a very bad way."

"What is it, Sonny?"

"I've got a bottle of liquid Demerol in my possession prescribed by you in my son's name and delivered by Schwab's drugstore."

"Oh?" he replied, clearly taken off guard. "There must have been some mistake."

"I'm telling you, Dr. Shapiro," I said. "The next time you do that, I will be paying you a house call. Don't ever write another prescription in my family's name again or I will report you."

Shapiro didn't confirm or deny that he had written the prescription. As far as I know, he never did that again, because he knew I would make good on my promise. I'm sure he told Elvis, although Elvis never brought it up with me.

I was thoroughly pissed at Elvis for giving my son's name to Shapiro, but I couldn't take it out on him because Elvis was good to Bryan. When Bryan was an infant, Elvis and Linda "kidnapped" him one morning when we were at Graceland for the holidays. Judy was in the kitchen warming up Bryan's formula when the intercom buzzed. "Judy, are you missing something?" teased Elvis. He and Linda loved spending time with Bryan.

When Bryan was a few months old, Elvis heard he was sick with a high fever and called instantly with a request that tugged at our heartstrings. "Would you mind if I came over and prayed over him?" Elvis asked. Fifteen minutes later, he showed up with Linda. Around Elvis's neck was a large green scarf, and on his head was a white turban with a big, bright gem on the front of it.

Elvis asked me if he could "lay hands" on Bryan or try to heal him through the power of prayer. We set Bryan down on Elvis's green scarf (green is the color of healing, he explained), and he knelt down alongside Bryan and moved his hands in circles over him, praying softly with his eyes closed.

Transfixed by that bright stone on Elvis's turban, Bryan reached up, grabbed it, and gave it a pull, causing the turban to fall forward onto Elvis's face. "No, no little guy," Elvis said calmly. "Let go. Let go." I looked over at Judy and Linda, who were working hard to suppress their laughter. I bit my lips to do the same. We didn't want to spoil this for Elvis, who was totally serious about helping Bryan. I tried to pry Bryan's hand off the turban, but he had a tight grip on it. "Strong little fella, isn't he?" Elvis said. I finally freed the turban, and Elvis pushed it back on his head and resumed his circular hand movements and silent prayers over Bryan.

Then he announced, "I think the fever's starting to pass." I put my hand on Bryan's forehead and really couldn't tell if it was or not. But I didn't want to ruin the moment for Elvis, so I said, "Yeah, I think you're right. I think he's cooling down."

When Elvis and Linda left, he told me to call when Bryan's fever went down. About a half hour later, it was a little below 100 degrees, which amazed Judy and me. I called Elvis, and he was pleased.

The next day, Elvis asked me how Bryan was doing. "Very good, Elvis," I said. "I think your prayers were very helpful and he's a lot better. His temperature was just a little over 99 about an hour ago when we last checked."

"Well, good," Elvis said. "That's good. Call me if there's a change."


Over the years I've been asked many times why we didn't confront Elvis earlier about his misuse of prescription medicines, and the answer is that we did, and his answer was always the same: "This is none of your damned business." Then Elvis would let us know that if we pursued the matter, it could cost us our jobs.

Somehow, he continually ignored the warning signs that he was headed for a giant fall. One of the signs came when he was on a charter flight to Memphis, and he began experiencing difficulty breathing. He was taking large quantities of Demerol at the time. When he arrived in Memphis, Linda called Dr. Nick, who checked Elvis into Baptist Memorial Hospital.

When he arrived, Elvis was bloated, semicomatose, and in shock. A team of doctors worked on him and thought at first he might be suffering from congestive heart failure because of the severe buildup of fluids in his body. They were astonished by the black-and-blue marks all over his body, and when Elvis finally came to he told them they came from "acupuncture needles." Joe told Dr. Nick they were needle marks all right, but not from acupuncture needles.

Dr. Nick called Max Shapiro in California and told him Elvis was very sick and even close to death. Shapiro finally confessed that he had been giving Elvis daily shots of Demerol. That's when Dr. Nick realized for himself that Elvis had a full-blown addiction.

Elvis was immediately put on phenobarbital and methadone. The latter is commonly used to treat heroin addicts. Elvis had never used heroin, but the fact that he was put on methadone meant serious business.

Linda stayed in Elvis's room on a bed rolled in for her.

Getting Elvis back on his feet wasn't easy. He popped sleeping pills from a secret stash when a nurse wouldn't give him any. He had Ricky Stanley fetch him Krystal burgers and meatloaf made by Lottie Tyson, one of the cooks at Graceland.

Before he was discharged, Drs. David Knott and Robert Fink, both drug addiction specialists, spoke to Elvis about the dangers of prescription abuse and recommended that he sign himself into a drug-treatment center. Elvis listened, but it was clear that he had no intention of taking their advice.

Performing in Vegas and Tahoe and going on the road was now fairly routine to Elvis. But he got excited when George Waite, a movie producer, came to him with a two-page summary and sketches of a proposed karate film. Waite had studied karate with Ed Parker in the early '70s.

Elvis flew Waite and his girlfriend to Vegas to meet with him about the movie. They attended his show at the Hilton, and nobody was more surprised than Waite when Elvis announced during his performance, "Ladies and gentlemen, I want you to meet George Waite. I'm going to produce his next film called *The New Gladiators.*"

In Elvis's suite after the show, Elvis gave Waite a check for $50,000 to get production of the film started. The idea at first was that it would be an action vehicle for Elvis himself. Jerry Schilling brought in his friend, writer Rick Husky, who worked on TV's *The Mod Squad, Cade's County*, and *The Rookies*, to hear what Elvis had in mind.

"I want to be the baddest motherf——er there is," Elvis said. His slurred speech and out-of-shape body kicked that notion right out of consideration, and it was decided to make a documentary instead of a feature film. Documentaries cost less to make, but good ones could make a huge profit. *Endless Summer* and *On Any Sunday*—well-made documentaries on surfing and motorcycle riding—made studios take notice and introduced cult sports to a mainstream audience. Elvis wanted to introduce karate to the masses.

Elvis would finance, appear in, and narrate the educational documentary depicting karate competitors and their training leading up to tournaments around the world. A segment of Elvis's doing some chi exercises was shot on September 16. About thirty-two minutes of film was shot. A snippet of it can be seen in the 1981 documentary *This Is Elvis*.

Elvis was one of the first actors to use karate in his films. He also promoted karate in his concerts, sometimes to the dismay of those who only wanted him to sing. Elvis was a great ambassador for karate, and *The New Gladiators* would be his greatest contribution to the martial arts.

The main focus of the documentary was five American fighters taking on some of the best fighters in the world. It took about a year and a half to film, and after Elvis's film company, TCB Productions, had sunk about $125,000 in the project, Colonel Parker, who normally stayed out of Elvis's personal business, heavily influenced him in this case to pull the plug. I believe the Colonel felt that Elvis was becoming too consumed with the project instead of his career. Waite was never able to finish the picture, and it sat dormant for two and a half decades until he finally released it as a ninety-three-minute documentary on the twenty-fifth anniversary of Elvis's death in 2002.

For such an ardent devotee of karate, Elvis abided less and less by its main tenet—to be of "sound body and mind." The rumor mill in Vegas was churning about his suspect health and behavior. At the end of his engagement in early September, Elvis launched into a diatribe about how he was not "strung out" but was in the hospital receiving medical treatment.

"In this day and time you can't even get sick. You are strung out!" Elvis said to the audience. "Well by God I'll tell you somethin' friend. I have never been strung out in my life—except on music."

But on Friday, September 27, 1974, he was in as bad of shape as I'd ever seen him in public when he arrived in College Park, Maryland, to start a fifteen-city tour. When he exited from the limo at the hotel, he looked as though he'd been on a huge bender. His hair was a mess, and his speech was pretty slurred.

There were policemen standing nearby to help me with the security detail. I tried to cover up Elvis's condition in front of them by saying, "Not awake yet, huh, boss?" and then whisked him up to his suite. After I got him settled in, I gathered Red, Dave, Jerry, and a couple of the other guys and asked what was going on with Elvis. He had never shown up for a tour in this condition. "Sonny, I didn't even know if he was going to make it here," said Red. "It's getting harder and harder to get him up and moving."

I didn't know what else to do but pray. I gathered all of the security detail, and we formed a prayer circle, asking God to please help cure Elvis of his prescription drug habit and whatever else was bothering him.

When we went into Elvis's room, he started handing out checks to everyone. The checks ranged from $10,000 for the "old-school" guys down to $2,500 for the younger and newer ones. I got a check for $5,000, and Elvis told me to forget about paying him back for an $11,000 loan he'd made me a couple of months earlier in July for a down payment on a home that Judy and I bought in Woodland Hills, California.

Tears came to my eyes, and I said, "Elvis, are you sure, man?" "Oh yeah, I'm sure," he said, smiling.

I thanked him, and we hugged. Then I turned to Elvis's dad, Vernon, and thanked him, too. "It was his idea," he said testily, nodding at Elvis. I knew that, of course. I just was trying to be respectful to Vernon.

Elvis could break my heart in so many ways.

After a nap, Elvis was still feeling the effects of whatever drugs he'd been doing. Dressed in a white peacock jumpsuit, he stepped onto the stage and told the crowd of fifteen thousand, "I just woke up."

He just about sleepwalked through the performance, hanging onto the microphone for dear life, mumbling unintelligibly, and screwing up the lyrics of "Love Me Tender."

The show was cut twenty minutes short. The next night, Elvis was only slightly better.

But it wasn't the quality, or lack thereof, of the show that caught the attention of the *The Washington Post* reviewer as much as Elvis's weight gain. In his story in the next day's paper, the reviewer riffed on Elvis's "paunch," and when Elvis saw the article, he was very upset. When he took the stage for his second show in College Park, he told the crowd, "Those of you who saw the morning paper, er, the evening paper, whatever it was, they gave...they gave me a fantastic write-up. No, they did. Except they said I had a paunch here, and I want to tell you something...I got their damn paunch!

"I wore a bulletproof vest onstage. True. You know, in case some fool decides to take a .22 and blow my...belly button off. That's the truth. I got his paunch...sonofabitch."

He also ranted about the tabloids, which had been hinting that Elvis was no longer the boy next door. He told the audience he was a federal narcotics agent and an eighth-degree black belt.

"I don't drink booze or take this or that," he announced. "Don't say boo to me when I tell you that because it's the God's honest truth."

The crowd cheered, but school officials made the decision that Elvis would never be invited back to the University of Maryland.

Things continued to get worse as the tour progressed. A few days after the College Park fiasco, Red and a couple of the other guys got wind that Tim Batey, a bass player in Voice, a backing group for Elvis, had a shipment of cocaine he was holding onto for Elvis. They marched to Tim's room. When he answered the door, Red pushed it open hard when entering, breaking one of Tim's toes when he leaned against the door to keep him out. "The next time I find out you've been giving Elvis drugs, I'm going start with your legs and work my way up," Red told him.

Then we put the word out that anybody getting drugs for Elvis was in for a serious ass-kicking. Elvis's stepbrother, Ricky Stanley, told Elvis what we'd said. It wasn't long thereafter that Elvis called Red and me into his room. He laid into us. "You guys need to stay out of my business," he said angrily. "I know what I'm doing. I can quit whenever I want to, but right now I need it."

"What about the good old days when you didn't need that shit?" Red asked.

"Red, there are no more good old days," Elvis said flatly.

I felt like a knife had been plunged into my heart.

"If you don't stop, you are going to be looking for other jobs," Elvis told us. We certainly didn't want that, but we hated even more the idea of him destroying himself.

When the tour ended in late October, Elvis went to Dr. Ghanem for help losing weight. Ghanem put him on a "sleep diet" he concocted, which consisted mostly of liquid nourishment and lots of sedated rest. Elvis stayed with part-time girlfriend Sheila Ryan in a special wing Dr. Ghanem had added to his cavernous Las Vegas home.

After two weeks, Elvis walked out ten pounds heavier than he had been when he walked in.

He was in such bad shape that Colonel Parker postponed his annual January engagement at the Las Vegas Hilton to February. Two weeks after his fortieth birthday, Elvis was admitted to Baptist Memorial Hospital when he couldn't catch his breath. Dr. Nick told the press that Elvis was having liver problems, but the truth was that his drug abuse was out of control.

A few months earlier, *The National Enquirer* had published a nasty story headlined: "Elvis at 40—Paunchy, Depressed and Living in Fear."

"I hate those sonofabitches," Elvis said. "I'd just like to destroy their whole place. All they do is write a bunch of lies." But what they'd written wasn't far from the truth.

While Elvis was in the hospital, Vernon suffered a heart attack at his home on February 5, 1975. He recuperated in the room next to Elvis's.

A ray of hope appeared in late March via singer/actress Barbra Streisand and her boyfriend, hairdresser turned movie producer Jon Peters. They turned up backstage after one of Elvis's midnight shows in Vegas and said they wanted to discuss an idea with him. For the next three hours they huddled in a room, and after Streisand and Peters left, Elvis came out with a big grin on his face.

"Well guys, I was just offered the lead role in the remake of *A Star Is Born*," he said. We were thrilled to see him so excited. He had always wanted to be taken seriously as an actor, and this was the role that could show everyone he had the goods. It was a role made for him, and I know he would have had to clean up his act and invest his whole heart and soul in it.

When Elvis said he was going to do the picture, Red got right in his face and said, "You swear? Shake hands on it!" Elvis shook on it. But a few days later, he was singing a different tune.

"You know, Streisand has been known to take control of a picture, and I don't know if I can deal with that," Elvis announced. "And that hairdresser boyfriend of hers might end up directing it, and I might have to slap the shit out of him." But I think what was really bothering him was the prospect of having to get off drugs, lose weight, and get in shape.

Colonel Parker has often been cast as the villain for allegedly demanding too much when contacted about what it would cost to get Elvis for the movie. He said $1 million in salary, $100,000 in expenses, 50 percent of the gross profits, and a separate deal for soundtrack rights. Then, to kill the deal for good, Parker insisted that Elvis get top billing in the movie.

Any time Elvis wanted the Colonel to get him out of something, the Colonel did it by making impossible demands. It was always that way with him and Parker. (I personally know of that happening once before in the '60s when Elvis was approached to make a children's record with Judy Garland. Elvis didn't want to do it but didn't have the heart to tell Garland no. So the Colonel put the price out of reach and got Elvis out of the deal.)

By then, Elvis hadn't had a Top 10 record since "Burning Love" in 1972, and he had been touring almost nonstop for five years. His behavior became more and more impulsive and outlandish. One day in mid-June, he called me into his bedroom at Graceland and introduced me to a Dr. Asghar Koleyni. Then Elvis asked, "Sonny, do you notice anything different about me?"

I didn't notice anything, but because Elvis obviously wanted me to see something, I said, "Yeah, but I'm not exactly sure what it is."

"Look into my eyes," Elvis said, smiling. Contact lenses? I couldn't put my finger on anything. Finally, Elvis pointed underneath his eyes and told me the doctor had excised some fatty tissue. Then he pulled his ears forward so I could see the incision marks where he'd had his double chin tightened. I really didn't notice much difference, but I complimented Elvis anyway.

About a month later, I got a letter from Blue Cross Blue Shield denying coverage of cosmetic surgery I had done at Mid-South Hospital. Trouble was, I hadn't had any cosmetic surgery. I went to Vernon Presley, and he said I shouldn't worry about it. What had happened, of course, was that Elvis had checked into the hospital under my name.

His behavior onstage was getting more bizarre all the time. On his third tour that year, Elvis introduced singer Kathy Westmoreland one night and then told the audience, "She will take affection from anybody, any place, any time. In fact, she gets it from the whole band." As a result, Kathy became the target of lots of indecent propositions. She complained to Joe Esposito, who gingerly asked Elvis to stop referring to Kathy like that.

Onstage the next night in Norfolk, Virginia, Elvis said, "Ladies and gentlemen, this is Kathy Westmoreland, our soprano singer, who doesn't like the way I introduce her...and if she doesn't like it, she can get the hell off the stage." Estelle Brown and Sylvia Shemwell of the Sweet Inspirations began to cry and walked off-stage, followed by Kathy.

A few days later at the Civic Center in Asheville, North Carolina, the crowd wasn't responding the way Elvis wanted, so he started saying things like, "Y'all can clap you know?" and, "This is the part where the audience usually applauds." In Elvis's hotel room later, Dr. Nick said he was cutting off Elvis's supply of medication, and Elvis pulled out a Beretta pistol and started waving it around. The gun accidentally went off, and the bullet ricocheted off the television and a chair and was spent by the time it thumped Dr. Nick's chest.

"Son, good God almighty!" exclaimed Vernon. "What in the world made you do a thing like that?"

"Aw hell, daddy, so I shot the doc," Elvis said blithely. "No big deal. He's not dead."

At the second show in Asheville, Elvis was again unhappy with the audience. He passed around a request box hoping to whip up interest and enthusiasm, but that didn't fly. So then he introduced J.D. Sumner of the Stamps and said, "J.D., hold up that right hand and show them your jewels." J.D. did as instructed, and then Elvis said, "Now hold up my hand," meaning J.D.'s left hand, which held about $100,000 worth of jewelry Elvis had given him over the years. The line always drew a laugh, but what happened next triggered a near riot.

Elvis twisted off a ring, bent down, and handed it to a man in the front row. A woman rushed the stage, and Elvis gave her a ring. Then he tossed one out into the crowd and started handing jewelry to members of the band. The crowd was going nuts, and so was Vernon, watching from the wings with his hands on the sides of his head. Elvis got his roar of approval, but it cost him $35,000 in jewelry.

One night as we were in the dining room of the Imperial Suite in Las Vegas, Elvis took out a gun, put his feet up on the table, and proceeded to shoot up the ornate chandelier. At Graceland, he blasted a black commode to pieces because he didn't like the color.

He spent $140,000 on fourteen Cadillacs and gave them away. One went to a complete stranger who just happened to be in the showroom at the time. She was checking out a very expensive model when Elvis sidled up and asked, "Do you like it?" She did, and Elvis promptly bought it for her.

When cars weren't enough, Elvis started buying planes. He bought himself a Jet Commander, which is a small corporate jet, and a G1 prop plane for Colonel Parker, who declined the gift because it would cost so much just to maintain the aircraft. Then Elvis decided to upgrade to an 880 Convair, a four-engine jet previously owned by Delta Airlines with a hundred-passenger capacity. That set him back about $250,000, and he spent another $800,000 having it customized by an outfit in Dallas.

The 129-foot plane he called the *Lisa Marie* had a bedroom (with a seat belt over the queen-sized bed), three closed-circuit TVs, a six-seat conference room, a lounge area with gold-plated seat belt buckles, a fake fireplace, two half baths, and gold wash basins with flecks of twenty-four-karat gold and brass fixtures imported from Spain. To give it his personal touch, he had the "TCB" logo painted on the tail. It set him back about $400,000 a year in operation costs.

While the *Lisa Marie* was getting its makeover, Elvis shelled out close to $900,000 for a business jet called *The JetStar* to use in the meantime.

Elvis gave Dr. Nick a $200,000 interest-free loan to build a home out of redwood. The staff payroll alone was about $100,000 a month, and Graceland's monthly upkeep came to around $40,000.

As Elvis was en route to Vegas on a Jet Commander for the start of another summer engagement, the plane had to make an emergency landing in Dallas after he suffered severe shortness of breath. Joe and I were already in Las Vegas waiting on them to arrive there, but Red was on the flight and told us Elvis had taken a bunch of pills before takeoff and was in trouble once up in the air.

"I can't breathe!" Elvis gasped, "I can't breathe!"

Red said he spotted an open vent on the floor of the plane, with air streaming out. He grabbed Elvis and placed his face in front of the vent. Elvis thought he was done.

"I'm not going to make it," Elvis screamed hysterically. "Land!"

The group landed safely in Dallas and checked into a motel for five hours, until Elvis had recuperated enough to continue the trip.

The date of that incident was August 16, 1975. Exactly two years later, Elvis wouldn't be as lucky.

# Chapter 31

# Moody Blue

WHEN I SIGNED ON TO WORK FOR ELVIS PRESLEY IN 1960, IT WAS A DREAM job. Fifteen years later, it was turning into a nightmare. Going through Elvis's mood swings, erratic behavior, and odd habits with him was tough sometimes, but watching him on a self-destruct course was when the nightmare began.

But because I loved him so much, I stuck around, hoping he'd change. When he didn't, there were some of us who tried to help him change. Once in a while there were flashes of the fun days we used to share on vacations in between movies and touring—like the ten-day vacation we took in Vail, Colorado, for his forty-first birthday.

In January 1976, Elvis flew seventeen people to Denver in the *Lisa Marie*. From there we took a charter bus to Vail. We sang "Happy Birthday" to Elvis on the two-hour ride through the majestic Colorado mountainside. He laughed and said, "Man, they're just coming way too fast."

Elvis rented a house for himself and Linda Thompson, and the rest of us had our own condos. The group included Denver police officers Jerry Kennedy, Gerald Starkey, Bob Cantwell, and Ron Pietrafeso. Elvis befriended them in the early 1970s, and they helped out with our security detail whenever we visited the Mile High City. Jerry was a captain, Gerald was a police doctor, and Bob and Ron were undercover narcotics officers. We called them the "Mini-Narcs."

Another member of our group was David Leach, an aptly named used-car salesman who wormed his way into Elvis's life when he delivered a new car to Patsy Lacker. Leach wore white patent leather shoes, but it never took long for his big mouth to draw your attention away from them.

305

On Elvis's birthday, January 8, Linda brought out a cake for him at their house. Nobody had said there was going to be a party, and most of us were off doing our own thing at the time. Later, Elvis called everyone together and said how disappointed he was. He seemed to be high at the time.

"Sorry, Elvis," somebody said. "We didn't know to come over."

Then Leach opened his yap. "Well, maybe if security was around more…" he started very sarcastically. Dave Hebler cut him right off.

"Hold on there, tough guy. You don't have a right to say anything about security being around here. That is none of your business. We're around. In fact, the security detail is the tightest part of this operation."

Dave was plenty worked up. When he finished speaking, Elvis told him, "There'll be no bullying tactics around here."

"I'm not bullying him, Elvis," Dave said. "I'm just saying that this guy has no idea what he's talking about. He just got here, and this used-car salesman is already judging your security detail? I'm not going to have it."

"And I'm not going to have it either, Dave," Elvis shot back. Then he asked the wives and girlfriends to wait there in the living room, and he led us into the bedroom. On the bed were several photographs and police rap sheets. We recognized the men in the pictures as the ones who'd caused the ruckus at the Las Vegas Hilton in February 1973.

Three years later, Elvis was still convinced that they were after him. "We need to find these guys and wipe them off the face of this earth," he said.

We were all too stunned to speak. Why in the world was he obsessing about that again? Then it occurred to me that what happened in Pontiac, Michigan, might be responsible.

Elvis had played a New Year's Eve show just a few days before the Vail trip at the Pontiac Silverdome. When I arrived the day before the show to set up security, the police told me about a mentally challenged male who threatened to kill Elvis. This guy went around threatening every celebrity who visited the area, so the cops said it wasn't a problem. But I still asked them to take the guy into custody before Elvis hit town and hold him until after we left—just as a precautionary measure.

They did so, releasing the man when we were on our way back to Memphis. Unless you count Elvis's ripping his pants onstage, the show had gone on without a hitch. Or so I thought until a few days later, when I got a call from Red at the Memphian Theatre.

I wasn't feeling well and so stayed home from the moviefest that night. When Red called, he asked if there had been a death threat against Elvis in Pontiac. I explained what had happened in Michigan, and Red told Elvis.

The next thing I knew, Elvis was on the phone. "Sonny, I want to know when there is a threat against me, whether you have it under control or not. I'm the one on that stage, and I want to know if some sonofabitch is going to shoot me. So don't hold anything from me ever again. Okay?"

The reason I hadn't told him about the threat in the first place was I feared just such a reaction from Elvis. If I'd told him, it would have been on his mind through the whole show, especially because he was performing on a twenty-foot-high stage and was feeling especially vulnerable.

I assured Elvis I would do as he said, and I later heard from Red that Elvis found out about the Pontiac incident through a Memphis cop who was buddies with a deputy in Pontiac. Red told me that Elvis was getting increasingly paranoid and even delusional.

That was painfully obvious in Aspen. Dave Hebler later told us that Elvis had told him the real reason he went to Denver was to participate in an undercover raid with the "Mini-Narcs." According to Elvis, they'd had a couple of drug runners surrounded when a guy with a sawed-off shotgun snuck up behind him. But Elvis dispatched the guy with karate chops, breaking his neck. It was a great story, but it was also pure fiction.

In Elvis's room in Aspen, Jerry, Gerald, Bob, and Ron noticed a container of Dilaudid on the bedside table. They knew it was a painkiller five times more powerful than morphine and that it was often prescribed for last-stage cancer patients. It was also sold on the street for big bucks.

When we left the room, one of them asked if Elvis had cancer. I averted my eyes and said no. When they asked what he was doing with Dilaudid, I bobbed and weaved like a prizefighter under fire. "Well, he has occasional pain now and then," I said.

The look they gave me made it clear I was fooling nobody. "No, he really doesn't need it," I admitted.

"This is crazy," one of them said. But that was the end of it for the time being, because before anyone could confront Elvis he went on another car-buying spree. The four police officers and Kennedy's wife got Lincoln Continentals, and everybody else got Cadillacs. My wife, Judy, got a brand-new white 1976 Cadillac Seville after Elvis asked her what her favorite color was. She told him baby blue. Not being able to find her one in that color, he purchased her a white Cadillac with baby blue interior instead. Elvis playfully asked her if that was okay. Needless to say, Judy was overwhelmed. With tears in her eyes, she answered, "Oh yes, Elvis!" then hugged him. Pat West got a new Eldorado, and Linda Thompson received a new Seville. All told, the cars cost about $70,000.

Denver television reporter Don Kinney heard about the spree and broke the story on the local news. He wound up his report by joking, "By the way, Elvis, if you're listening out there and you've got an extra one of those Cadillacs, I sure could use one." The next day, a Cadillac Seville was delivered to the station. Elvis did it just to blow the guy's mind.

Another huge black cloud appeared over the vacation when Elvis decided for some reason that he wanted to move into the condo where Jerry Schilling and Myrna were staying. It was 3:00 in the morning when Elvis called Jerry to let him know. Naturally, Jerry and Myrna were sleeping then. "Elvis, can't this wait until the morning?" Jerry asked. Elvis blew a gasket.

"Listen, Jerry, when I say 'Jump,' you jump," he said. Then Elvis went to Jerry's condo with Red and instructed Red to beat Jerry up. Red tried to calm him down, but then Elvis put a bullet into the gun he was carrying and cocked the weapon. That tore it for Jerry.

"Listen, Elvis, you can have the condo because I quit," he said. "There are some things more important than money, like friendship." Jerry left immediately. He went back to California and got a job in the film industry.

In late January, Elvis returned to Denver to attend the funeral of police officer Eugene Kennedy, Jerry's brother. At the service Elvis wore a tailor-made Denver police captain's uniform, which surely raised a few eyebrows. While he was in town he made frequent trips to the Colorado Gold Mine Company, a famous restaurant that served a killer peanut butter and jelly sandwich called the "Fool's Gold Loaf."

Elvis loved those sandwiches so much that one day in early February 1976, as he was preparing for a recording session in Memphis, he decided he had to have one for lunch. Elvis had two pilots on call at all times—Milo High and Elwood Davis. He told them to fire up the *Lisa Marie* and had Joe call the Colorado Gold Mine Company to set up shop on the tarmac of Stapleton Airport.

It was the mother of all take-out orders. One Fool's Gold Loaf consisted of a loaf of Italian white bread, two tablespoons of butter, one pound of lean bacon, one large jar of smooth Skippy peanut butter, and one large jar of Smucker's grape jelly. I can't even begin to estimate the caloric content of the sandwich, but its suggested serving size was eight to ten people.

Elvis ordered twenty-two of them.

When the plane arrived in Denver, it taxied to a private hangar where the Colorado Gold Mine Company folks delivered the sandwiches on a silver tray, along with champagne, Perrier water, and Pepsis over cracked ice.

Each sandwich cost $49.95, and the entire tab was $3,387 (today that would be around $12,000), but the round-trip airplane ride to Denver added about $40,000 to the total.

Back in Memphis, Elvis went to work on what would be one of his final recording sessions, for the album *From Elvis Presley Boulevard, Memphis, Tennessee*. Elvis was so passionless about making music that he didn't even want to leave home for the sessions, so RCA brought the recording studio to him. They parked a mobile unit outside Graceland; it contained a control room to mix the sound. To improve the acoustics, the technicians put expensive equipment in the den, such as baffles and partitions to separate Elvis and the musicians, just as they would be in the studio.

Producer Felton Jarvis assembled several members of Elvis's road band and a few Los Angeles and Nashville session musicians to play on the tracks. J.D. Sumner and the Stamps were there, as was soprano Kathy Westmoreland.

Elvis showed up for the first session wearing the Denver police uniform. He cut three tracks, but it was obvious that his mind was elsewhere. The next night he went back and forth from his bedroom to the den. In the latter he sang of lost love (Neil Sedaka's "Solitaire"), while in the bedroom he ranted about wiping out Memphis drug dealers, whom he blamed for getting his stepbrother Ricky hooked on heroin. Ricky even went to jail for forging a Demerol prescription for Elvis. Elvis bailed him out and pulled some strings to get the charges dropped.

Red and I were summoned to Elvis's room during a break from recording. We found all his weapons strewn about the floor—pistols, automatic weapons, rifles, and rockets. We knew some serious shit was about to go down.

Elvis handed us a list of names and police-file pictures. "These sons of bitches need to be wiped out," he said. His plan was for us to slip out the back of Graceland, knock off some drug pushers, and then come back and record some hits.

"You're getting into something very heavy here, Elvis," I said.

"Hell, the police want them," he countered. But the one Elvis himself especially wanted was a local hood who ran a pool hall. According to Elvis, the guy knocked Ricky down with a pool cue, and now Elvis was going to take him out himself.

We managed to convince him to put off the mission for a while.

Elvis's recording sessions were flat and uninspired. He just wasn't interested. Felton hoped to get at least twenty tracks, but he called it quits after just a dozen.

Not long afterward Elvis jetted off to Colorado to check out some real estate he was interested in for a vacation home. I didn't accompany him this time, but Dave Hebler went and filled me in on what happened. Elvis hooked up with his Denver police buddies and asked Gerald Starkey, the doctor, for Dilaudid to ease the pain of an ingrown toenail. Starkey stalled him and mentioned Elvis's request to Ron Pietrafeso and Bob Cantwell.

From what I was told, the two men approached Elvis at a Denver hotel and said they knew he was using. And they said it was personally and professionally embarrassing to them, as narcotics officers and as his friends. They recommended that Elvis check himself into a nearby detox center that was very discreet. Instead, Elvis immediately checked out of the hotel and flew back to Memphis.

Elvis was totally unreachable, even by the people who loved him. One night Red tried talking some sense into Elvis when he had not yet zonked himself out. He said that Elvis had changed and needed to do something about the situation. To Red's great surprise, this time Elvis didn't go ballistic. Instead, he just looked at Red and said, "Yeah, Red, I agree with you."

But Red's hopes for a breakthrough dissolved first thing the next morning when Elvis ripped into him. "So, I'm not myself anymore, huh? Dammit, I don't want to hear that shit! I wish people would

310

stay out of my personal life. I'm going to do whatever it is the f——
I want to do. I don't need anybody preaching to me."

It was around this time when Elvis's aunt Delta brought in a
package sent by Dr. Ghanem. It contained two large containers
whose seals were unbroken. They were Phenaphen with codeine. I
opened one up and took out several pills to get Dr. Nick to confirm
what I already knew due to the seals still being in place. I had
approached Ghanem before about what he was giving Elvis, and he
assured me they were placebos. Well, this package made him an
out-and-out liar and a deceitful, self-serving bastard. I never trusted
him again after this incident.

"Delta, this package never got here," I told her. She didn't argue.
"I can't believe that sonofabitchin' doctor is sending stuff like this to
Elvis," Delta said.

A lot of people have criticized Colonel Parker for pushing Elvis
out on the road so much, but there was a method to his madness.
Touring was the only thing that kept Elvis clean for any period of
time. That's why Elvis's tours were done in shorter bursts during the
last year and a half or so of his life.

When Elvis returned from the road, he'd go to his room for two
or three days of rest and recuperation. Those R & R sessions began
getting longer and longer, and sometimes they lapsed into weeks
before we had to drag him out of his room to go on tour again.

Where before he would mostly get high between engagements,
now he was doing it all the time, and it showed in his performances.
He slurred his words, forgot lyrics, and occasionally had to resort to cue
cards to get through songs, when and if he felt like completing them.

Every now and then, there was a rare and brief ray of sunshine.
On April 25, 1976, I made arrangements for Judy and our son,
Bryan, to visit before a show in Long Beach, California. Bryan was
about three and a half at the time, and he spent some time before
the show with Linda Thompson at the hotel. He didn't feel well that
day and was a little cranky.

"Hi precious little Bryan," Linda said, going for a hug. "No! No!"
Bryan said, shaking his head. That was unlike him, because he loved
Linda very much. But he was just not himself that day. Linda
laughed it off and said she'd see us at the show.

When we got to the dressing room at the arena, Bryan was still
in a funk and wouldn't have anything to do with anyone, including

311

his second cousin Red, J.D. Sumner and the Stamps, and the Sweet Inspirations, who all loved him.

It was different, though, when Bryan saw Elvis. Elvis was sitting in the middle of the dressing room, kind of quietly within himself, when Judy and I walked in with Bryan between us. Elvis and Judy exchanged greetings, and then he said, "Come here, little Bryan." Bryan walked right into Elvis's open arms, and when Elvis said "I love you," Bryan said, "I love you too, Elvis."

As Judy, Bryan, and I prepared to leave, Elvis stroked Bryan's hair and said, "He's such a sweet boy." I told Elvis we were proud of our son, and then I turned to Bryan and said it was time for Elvis to go to work. "Bye, Elvis," he said. "Bye, little Bryan," Elvis replied.

I fully understood then that Elvis had a truly tender heart that kids recognized and were drawn to. That particular exchange between he and Bryan will always remain a special memory for Judy and me. It was the last time Elvis and Bryan ever saw each other close up.

But Elvis's good days were no match for his addictions. A week later, Elvis opened an eleven-day stand in Lake Tahoe and was visited by John O'Grady. Elvis probably tipped the scales at 210 pounds then, and his bulk was beginning to cramp his stage style. He was very bloated, and he took hits from an oxygen tank backstage to catch his breath between songs. His appearance so alarmed John that he called Elvis's attorney, Ed Hookstratten.

Ed in turn contacted Priscilla, and they discussed enrolling Elvis at the Scripps Clinic in San Diego for a three-month stay, to be followed by a vacation in Hawaii. Priscilla later made a special trip to Memphis to broach the idea to Elvis, emphasizing that their daughter needed a healthy father. But Elvis said nothing doing to the detox center.

Not only was his addiction out of control, so were his finances. In addition to his usual freewheeling spending habits, Joe Esposito and Dr. Nick got Elvis to go in with them in a chain of fifty racquetball courts called Presley Centre Courts. Elvis thought at first that he had only to lend his name to the project in exchange for 25 percent of the profits. But after a while he was asked to put up $80,000 to hire a secretary for the enterprise. Elvis told them he wanted out of the deal, and he even told Lamar he was going to fire them, but then he backed off.

On July 3, Elvis was appearing in Dallas, Texas, at the Tarrant County Convention Center. I had made special arrangements with him when the tour began in late June to fly my wife and son into Memphis when we wrapped it up there on July 5 at the Mid-South Coliseum. That was my birthday, and Elvis gladly offered to pay for their airfare from California.

But when I called to check on Judy, she was crying. Her and Bryan's reservations, which had been made on Elvis's American Airlines account, had been canceled. When Judy called Wally Jones, a supervisor at American Airlines, he said that Vernon Presley had personally canceled the tickets.

I had calmed down by the time Elvis arrived at the hotel. After I had escorted him to his room, I asked him if I could speak to him about something. I then told him what his father had done. Elvis was changing from his traveling clothes into pajamas, and he said it probably was just a mistake.

"No, I don't think so," I told him. "Wally said that your dad said no a couple of weeks ago when I made the reservations, telling him, 'Judy and Bryan are not on Elvis's expense account.'"

"Well, there have been a couple of guys abusing it, so Daddy set it up where he or I would have to okay it," Elvis said. "I must have forgotten to tell him. I'll call Daddy and tell him it's all right. You call Judy and tell her to get ready."

"Okay, thanks boss," I said. "I appreciate it." "Okay," he said, then added, in his best Strother Martin imitation from *Cool Hand Luke*, "Just a failure to communicate."

I called Judy and told her to pack her bags. But about an hour later, Ricky Stanley came to my room and breathlessly asked, "Man, what did you say to Elvis?"

When I asked what he meant, Ricky said, "Oh man, he was ranting and raving and cussing you, saying you put down his daddy. Boy, he sure was mad." Not believing what I was hearing, I said I would go talk to Elvis right away. But Ricky said he'd gone to bed a half hour ago. So I figured I would talk to Elvis when we met up at our next stop in Tulsa, Oklahoma.

In Tulsa, Elvis greeted me as he always did, with no hint of anger toward me. I decided to let the matter drop. No sense stirring up the pot.

I drove him to his last show of that tour at the Mid-South Coliseum in his white Lincoln limo. Red, Joe, Vernon, and Linda were in the car also. Elvis was acting strange—cold and aloof to everyone. He hardly said a word and stayed by himself in his dressing room until it was time to hit the stage. He gave an especially powerful performance for the hometown crowd of approximately twelve thousand fans.

"Let me tell you," he started off. "I'll sing all the songs you want. It's the end of the tour, and I have as much time as you want tonight." And he gave them quite a show.

After the concert, I took him back to Graceland. He had on a white jumpsuit, aviator sunglasses, and a towel around his neck, because he was still sweating from the show. "Goodnight, boss, and great show," I said. "I'll see you in a few days." I knew he needed a couple of days to recuperate, and he knew I was going to spend time with my family. We would be in touch again in about a week.

"Okay, Sonny," Elvis said. And then: "By the way, happy birthday." I was touched that he remembered, and I told him that Judy had made me a cake with white icing and asked him if he wanted some. "Oh yeah, Linda's gonna bring me some," he said.

"Okay, boss, fine," I told him. "Goodnight."

"Goodnight," Elvis said. Then he walked on up the stairs and into his bedroom—and, as it turned out, out of my life.

I spent most of the next week lounging poolside at the hotel, enjoying the company of my wife and son, and resting up for the ten-city concert tour coming up in three weeks.

On the morning of July 13, I went to the office of Dr. Lester Hoffman, who was also Elvis's dentist. I had a bridge that needed some work, and Dr. Hoffman was preparing to fix it when he told me I had a call.

"Sonny, Vernon Presley is on the phone," Dr. Hoffman said. My heart skipped a beat because I thought something must have happened to Judy, Bryan, or Elvis—three of the most important people in my life.

"Yes, Mr. Presley?" I said into the receiver.

"Sonny, I was hoping that after your visit with Dr. Hoffman you might come out here to the office so I can speak with you," Vernon said.

"What's wrong?" I asked. "Is something wrong?"

"No, no, no. I just need to talk to you about a personal matter is all," Vernon said.

"Mr. Presley, please don't do this," I said, getting a little agitated. "I'm a grown man, and if there's a situation or something wrong, please tell me now. I'm in the middle of a dental appointment, and I'm going to be here for a while, and I'm not going to feel too good when I leave here."

After a moment of silence, Vernon let me have it.

"Well, I wanted to tell you in person, but since you're being persistent...We're going to have to make a few changes around here and cut back on expenses..."

I thought for a second it might be a salary cut, but that wasn't it.

"...And in order to do that we're going to have to let some people go."

Then it hit me. I was being fired.

"And I'm one of those people?" I said.

"Yeah, you are, Sonny, but there's others as well," Vernon said.

"Who else?" I asked.

"I'd rather tell them myself," Vernon said.

"Okay," I said. "Good-bye."

When I hung up the phone, I felt gut-shot. I was no longer employed by Elvis Presley, but as I sat in the dentist's chair, it hit me that Elvis was upset because I had gone to him after Vernon canceled my wife's and son's plane reservations.

When I got back to the hotel room, I looked out the window and saw Judy and Bryan splashing around in the pool. I watched them with tears spilling down my cheeks. Judy saw me and waved with a big smile on her face that turned to a frown when she noticed my expression. She got Bryan out of the pool and came to me.

"Honey, what is it?" she asked. "Is something wrong with Elvis? Vernon called here and said he needed to speak to you. I told him you were at the dentist's office."

It took a moment or two for me to find my voice. "No, Judy, Elvis is fine. I've been fired."

"Why?" she asked, her own eyes welling up.

"Vernon said it was to cut back on expenses. He said there were others, but he wouldn't tell me who."

Just then the phone rang. It was Dave Hebler, who asked if I had heard from Vernon yet.

"Yeah, I did, and I suspect you did, too," I answered.

"Yes, I did," Dave replied. "Quite a shock." After commiserating with one another for a few minutes, I told Dave I was calling Red.

315

When Red answered, I knew from the tone in his voice that he had walked the plank, too.

I asked if he'd talked to Vernon, and Red replied, "Yeah, I talked to that sonofabitch. I can't believe it." Red said that he told Vernon that he wanted to speak to Elvis directly but was told that Elvis had left for Palm Springs the day after the tour ended. Obviously, Elvis hadn't wanted to be around when we got the ax.

Red said he was going to move back to California and get back into the movie industry. That sounded appealing to me, too.

After we hung up, I called the Palm Springs house. I don't remember who answered, but when I asked if Elvis was up yet I was told no. I called back later and got a recorded message that the number had been changed.

Dave Hebler called me a couple of days later and reported that Elvis had flown from Palm Springs to Las Vegas and was staying at Dr. Ghanem's house. Dave immediately flew out and walked right past Ghanem's security gate and pounded on the front door. Several of the guys were there—David and Ricky Stanley, Dick Grob, and Al Strada—and their eyes got real wide when they saw Dave standing there.

"What's going on, guys?" Dave casually asked as he walked past them into the house. Nobody had the 'nads to try to get in the way of a pissed-off seventh-degree black belt. But Elvis was securely stashed away, and when it was clear that Dave would have to break down every door in the place to find him, he told the boys, "Well, see you around," and left.

"I could see their asses tightening up," Dave told me a few minutes later from a pay phone. We laughed, which was better than crying. But I wasn't ready to let things go until I heard from Elvis himself why we were fired. I called Ghanem's house, and he answered. When I asked if Elvis was awake, Ghanem replied, "Yes he is; he just finished eating." When I asked Ghanem to see if Elvis would speak to me about the situation, he said he would ask.

Ghanem came back on the line after a minute and said, almost apologetically, "Sonny, he doesn't want to talk about it." So I asked him to try again. "Tell him I am not asking for my job back; I just want to know the real reason why I was fired. He can even tell you and you tell me if he doesn't want to get on the phone with me." Ghanem did as I asked, but he came back with the same answer: "Sonny, I'm sorry, but Elvis doesn't want to talk about it."

"Okay, I see," I said. "I see. Well, tell him I won't be calling back."

"I will," Ghanem replied, and I said "Bye," and hung up the phone.

I could try now to describe the hurt I felt because Elvis wouldn't even get on the phone with me, but after all these years it's still impossible. Losing the job was one thing, but I felt that I had just lost my best friend. And that was really tough to bear.

After sixteen years of dedicated service, Vernon gave us three days' notice to clear our things out of Graceland and Elvis's other properties, and he gave us one week's severance pay.

# Chapter 32

# Elvis: What Happened?

I HAVE HAD ALMOST THIRTY YEARS TO PONDER WHY I WAS FIRED BY ELVIS Presley. In no way, shape, or form have I ever believed that it was decided by Vernon. While it's true there was never a two-way love affair over the years between the guys and Vernon, he was merely acting for Elvis when he cut us loose from the organization. Elvis steered clear of giving us the pink slip himself, not wanting a confrontation.

With the wisdom and clarity of hindsight, I believe I was fired for several reasons.

First and foremost, Red and I practically grew up with Elvis, and as we got older he didn't feel he had a hold over us anymore—especially when we would not look the other way as his drug habit spiraled out of control. More than once we went so far as to intercept shipments of drugs to him. And we told him to his face several times that he needed to get help.

Elvis couldn't stand that. He had a huge ego, and he didn't like anyone holding up a mirror for him to see what he had become in the last years of his life. When Lucille Ball confronted him about his drug use that night in Vegas, she was summarily shown the door. So were we.

Also, Elvis and his father were increasingly nettled and stressed by all the lawsuits piling up against him. Some of them Elvis blamed on me, as his security chief, but I was personally responsible for only one while doing my job.

It happened when Elvis was playing a ten-day engagement at the Del Webb Sahara in mid-1974. A Grass Valley, California, land developer named Edward Ashley attended the May 20 show with three women. One was his date; the others were friends of his date. After the show, a showroom waiter named Louie notified me that Ashley had slipped him $50 to have his female friends taken up to Elvis's suite, and he wanted to know if it was all right. He even offered me half the money.

The waiters and showroom staff had always been good to us, so I told Louie to keep the $50 and send the girls up to our floor and I'd meet them at the security desk by the elevator.

I did so, and then I escorted them into Elvis's suite. After making them drinks, I left them to wait for Elvis, went over to an arcade game the hotel had provided for us, and began playing.

All of a sudden the electricity in the suite went off. Then Ricky raced in and said, "There's a guy out here turning out all the lights!" I knew there was a breaker panel on the wall in the hallway. When I ran out, I found Ashley getting ready to punch David's lights out in the doorway of the stairwell and the hallway. His left hand was on David's chest, measuring him. His right fist was cocked, but before he could get the punch off I brought my left forearm down on his and then hit him with my right. He spun around off the wall and fell in a heap to the concrete floor of the stairwell. Red and Dick Grob appeared and helped me lift Ashley up and get cuffs on him. We took him to the security room, and when he came to he was loud, obnoxious, ill-tempered, and pretty drunk. What happened was, he'd come upstairs with his date hoping to get to Elvis's suite, too. But that didn't happen because Elvis had a strict rule about having any husbands or boyfriends he didn't know personally let in his room. Ashley didn't like this, and after his lady friends went in, he turned out the lights and then tried to bully his way inside.

As a couple of security guards took Ashley to the elevator, he turned and got a glimpse of Elvis as the door of the elevator was shutting. He yelled, "You sonofabitch" at Elvis, who lunged at the elevator, but the doors closed just in time, preventing Elvis from getting his hands on Ashley.

Ashley filed a $6.6 million lawsuit in the state of Nevada against Elvis, me and several John Does, the Sahara Tahoe Hotel, and its parent company, Del Webb International. The hotel and Del Webb International countersued because Ashley had turned off the electricity and put the guests on that floor in danger of potential injury. Ashley promptly dropped them as defendants.

Then I was dropped from the suit for legalistic reasons, chiefly that I was not a resident of Nevada or earning a paycheck in the state. For the record, my pay came from Tennessee. That left Elvis and the several John Does as the defendants. "Damn, Sonny, you hit the guy, and he's suing me and some John Does, whoever the f—— that is," Elvis said.

Right before Elvis and I were scheduled to give depositions in the case, we saw Ashley near a room where we were deposed at the Sahara Tahoe. Elvis spoke civilly to him, and when he didn't reply Elvis leaned toward me and said, "I wished you would have killed the sonofabitch."

Ashley had no case, of course, but because these things can be drawn out, Elvis decided to pay him a settlement so he would just go away. I don't know how much he got, but he didn't deserve a penny of it.

A year earlier, Red had mixed it up with another souse who'd gotten into Elvis's suite in Vegas and was bothering some female guests. After people complained about him, Red and I collared this guy, named Kaijo Peter Pajarinen, and headed for the elevator. He got abusive and made a threatening gesture toward Red. Red broke his nose.

In May 1975, Pajarinen filed suit against Elvis, and Elvis made a settlement to dispose of the case.

There were a couple other cases where we had to get physical to protect either ourselves or someone else, but overall we handled ourselves with remarkable restraint and performed our jobs admirably.

After we were fired, we learned from Linda Thompson that Elvis had told Vernon to give each of us $5,000 and he was going to hire us back, but he "had to show us he was still the boss." What we got instead was three days' notice and one week's pay. I still have the check stub.

Judy, Bryan, and I flew to California to begin a new life without Elvis. Red and I immediately found stunt work on the set of *The Six Million Dollar Man* at Universal Studios. We knew actor Lee Majors through Elvis, and he was helpful to us. Lee had spent some time in Vegas with Elvis, and one night, when Elvis introduced him, Lee stepped out onto the stage and went into that slow-motion run that was part of the opening sequence of his show. The audience went nuts, and it broke Elvis up.

Bryan really loved *The Six Million Dollar Man*, and when Lee autographed an 8-x-10 photo to him, it made Bryan quite the hit with his friends and classmates at preschool.

Red eventually got a permanent acting gig on NBC's *Black Sheep Squadron* thanks to the show's star, Robert Conrad, who pulled a few strings for his old buddy.

Dave also moved back to the Los Angeles area. As a seventh-degree black belt, he had no problem getting back into teaching the martial arts.

In addition to the stunt work, Judy and I raised and showed Arabian horses. We also made and sold custom-made Western costume jewelry on the side. It was different, but looking back on it, I now realize the change made me grow up. For years I had put Elvis's needs before those of anyone else, including my own wife and son. While I was with Elvis in Tennessee and on the road, Judy was virtually raising Bryan by herself in California.

The durability and strength of our marriage came from Judy's strength, patience, and understanding. She held us together through some trying times. She accepted my job responsibilities and the sacrifices they entailed.

Our favorite song was "The Wonder of You." At one performance when Judy was in the audience, Elvis said, "Judy, Sonny, this is for you." Then he sang that song. Judy and I both got a little misty-eyed.

For years, Red turned down offers to write a memoir about his friendship with Elvis. When you think about it, we did a decent job of keeping Elvis's personal life pretty much under wraps for more than two decades. In 1971, Jerry Hopkins came out with *Elvis: A Biography*, based mostly on old newspaper stories and interviews with fans, studio flacks, former associates, and bit-part actors. Elvis never even bothered to read it.

I stayed in touch with Al Strada, one of Elvis's wardrobe assistants. He kept me abreast of Elvis's escalating drug addiction and the associated physical and emotional problems. Elvis was not only addicted but grossly overweight. He also had an enlarged heart and colon and intestinal blockages. He gorged on cheeseburgers, cakes, Popsicles, Eskimo Pies, and banana splits, and then, a week before he was to go on the road, he would starve himself to lose a few pounds. Just like everything else in his life, it was feast or famine.

I heard about financial problems, too. From what I understand, at the end of his life Elvis had $1 million in his checking account and $1,000 in his savings account. That kind of says it all to me.

Al told me that eventually Elvis didn't even want the guys who were left on the payroll around him, except for Billy Smith, and Elvis barred them from the house except on the days when tours were starting. Elvis needed only one person there for running errands, which the younger guys did in shifts. Most of his time was spent in his extra-king-size bed with Linda and, after she left, Ginger Alden. When he ventured out of the room, anything was possible.

Billy Smith said that once when Patsy Presley's son, Jimmy Gambill, was outside having a mock gunfight with Billy's kids, Elvis heard them from his bedroom, looked out, and saw Jimmy sitting on the fence that surrounded Graceland firing an old-fashioned cap gun. Thinking that someone was coming to shoot him, Elvis grabbed a shotgun and ran outside yelling, "I'll kill the sonofabitch. I'll kill him!" Only Billy's intervention settled him down and saved him from doing something rash. Some of the medicine that Elvis was taking caused delusional behavior.

The only time Elvis ever appeared to sober up was when Lisa Marie came to visit, which wasn't for long stretches at a time due to his addiction. Her visits were just a brief interruption in a long, downhill slide.

Those closest to him knew he could no longer go down this road, which was a descent into madness with the pills fueling the ride. It is also why in August 1976, Red, Dave, and I sat down and began planning the book *Elvis: What Happened?*

"You know, a book could generate some money for us and scare the hell out of Elvis, to the point where he does something about his problem," Red said in proposing the idea to us at his house. "If we can scare him enough, maybe he'll clean up."

I called attorney John Irwin, who'd once been a member of Ed Hookstratten's firm, and he put us in touch with Jeff Cooper of the Frank Cooper Agency, a highly regarded literary agency in Beverly Hills. Jeff was pretty much running the show for his semiretired father, Frank, but both of them listened to our story and agreed to represent us.

They began shopping the book proposal around to publishers, and almost every one reacted with horror. They were afraid of lawsuits by Elvis, sure; but what I think mostly bothered them was the idea that Elvis Presley was hooked on prescription drugs. Who was more beloved in pop culture than Elvis? Nobody wanted a tarnished idol.

We did get an offer of $50,000 from *The National Enquirer*, but they just wanted to run articles over a period of several weeks, and we said no. A book would have more impact and shelf life.

When *The Star*, the *Enquirer's* rival tabloid owned by Rupert Murdoch's World News Corporation, offered us a total of $125,000 and the services of ace reporter Steve Dunleavy to help us write the book (which would be excerpted in *The Star*), we accepted. Dunleavy, an Australian, had a reputation as a dogged and fearless scribe with an eye for the sensational. I didn't have a problem with him until much later.

The three of us signed the contract with World News Corporation, which in turn inked a deal for an original paperback book to be published by Ballantine, the paperback division of Random House. We began taping interviews for the book in a suite at the Continental Hyatt House on the Sunset Strip in early October 1976.

It didn't take long for Elvis to find out what we were up to.

About a week into our interviews with Dunleavy, he got a call from John O'Grady, who asked to speak to me. I took the call in the suite's bedroom.

"Sonny, I'm calling as an emissary for someone whom I'm representing," O'Grady said. "We don't need to say whose name it is or refer to who it is. I would just like to tell you that there are interests out there that prefer you not publish this book that the three of you are planning on writing."

When I began to tell him that he knew Elvis had a problem, O'Grady cut me off. It hit me at that moment that either Elvis was listening in on an extension or that O'Grady was taping the conversation and didn't want Elvis to hear that he and I had previously discussed his prescription problem.

"Sonny, I'm not here to talk about anything else other than possibly coming up with a figure for you guys not to do the book. I'm authorized to see if I can get you three to come up with a figure that I can take back to the person I'm representing. If you come up with an agreeable amount, we can take care of this matter quickly," he said.

"So, he's trying to buy us off now, right?" I said.

"No, let's just call it overdue severance pay," answered O'Grady. John always did have a way with words.

I told him that we'd already signed a contract and received the first two payments on our advance, but O'Grady countered: "Sonny, you're not listening to me. If we can come up with an agreeable amount, you three can walk out of that room and not do that book. We will pay for any legal costs that might occur and refund any monies that have already been advanced."

I promised him I would talk with Red and Dave about what was discussed, and O'Grady said he would call back in fifteen minutes. I told him it would take only five. I had a pretty good idea what the others would say.

I have read in some books a claim by O'Grady that he offered us $50,000 apiece and an "education allowance" to use for training in new careers, but that is an outright lie. No sum was ever mentioned to me. And we certainly didn't require any new career training.

When I hung up the phone, I called Red and Dave into the room and reported my conversation with O'Grady. Then I said, "I know what my answer [to his offer] is, and I think I know yours. He's trying to buy us off. What do you say, guys?"

Red shook his head and declared, "No, not this time, man."

Dave made it unanimous: "Nope. That would just make us like everybody else. Give them a car, give them money, give them whatever they want. But we're not going to be that way."

We knew that unless we went ahead with our plan, Elvis would not change his life. If we wrote the book, maybe he would.

When O'Grady called back, I gave him a firm no. "Is that your final decision?" he asked.

"Yeah," I said tersely.

"Well, I'll convey your answer," O'Grady said, and we said good-bye.

After that call and the day's taping with Dunleavy, Red, Dave, and I huddled together and decided to *pretend* to write a long statement and put all our documentation with it and give it to our lawyer to put in his safe for safekeeping. It was a ploy against the possibility of something of suspicious origin happening to us to prevent the book from being finished. Then we let it be known, through our attorney, where those documents and statements were filed and that their release to the authorities and media would occur if something unfortunate happened to us.

We were well aware of Elvis's sometimes-uncontrollable temper and rage that could induce him to make rash decisions at times. And we weren't just paranoid. In his 1986 book entitled *Life with Elvis*, David Stanley wrote that he had to talk Elvis out of hunting us down and killing us.

According to his account, David was staying with Elvis in Linda Thompson's Santa Monica apartment when Elvis kicked in his bedroom door, rousing him from a deep sleep. Elvis was dressed in a black jumpsuit adorned with a Drug Enforcement Agency patch, and he was carrying two .45s and a Thompson submachine gun.

Elvis hustled David into his new Ferrari, and they took off down Santa Monica Boulevard with Elvis ranting about finding us and putting us out of his misery. He turned back only after David told him that Lisa Marie could forgive a father who abused medication but would never live down his cold-blooded murder of three former associates.

That November, Linda Thompson also decided that she could no longer stick around and watch Elvis self-destruct. She once said that she could keep Elvis alive for another five years or she could wake up one morning and find him dead. Both options were going to tire her out as well as age her internally. Linda had become romantically involved with his keyboard player, David Briggs, and left soon thereafter. The sad part was, she really loved Elvis, and she continued to check on him through Charlie Hodge and Rick Stanley. She was and is a very special lady.

A few weeks after Linda left, George Klein introduced Elvis to nineteen-year-old Ginger Alden. I never knew Ginger, so I don't know if it's true that she and Elvis became engaged. But I have a hard time believing that Elvis would ever have married again. He loved Linda, and I wish they had married. During my shows, people often ask me whether Elvis would be alive today if Linda had been with him that night at Graceland. I tell them that I can't say for certain that he would be alive today, but I do tell them, "If Linda Thompson had been with him, he wouldn't have died that night." Of course, there's no way to know for sure, but that statement is a reference to how well Linda looked after him.

Elvis played his last Las Vegas engagement in December 1976. From all reports, his performances had become weak and bizarre. He read lyrics right off the sheet and was likely to burst out with declarations such as, "I hate Las Vegas!"

The wheels had fallen off his incredible comeback ride since 1969. His career careened from legitimate to ludicrous, and Elvis had become a caricature of himself.

Bill Burk of the *Memphis Press-Scimitar* was there for his closing night and filed a story that shook the faithful back in Tennessee:

After sitting through Elvis Presley's closing night perform-ance at the Las Vegas Hilton, one walks away wondering how much longer it can be before the end comes, perhaps suddenly....

This may seem like one person's opinion. It isn't. Dur-ing Presley's last three nights here, these opinions, or various forms of them, were heard time and time again from former Presley groupies who openly expressed con-cern for him....

And yet they keep coming back and they will pack his next road tour. Once a king, always a king. Maybe that's it. And just maybe they're still coming around because they think it might be the last time around.

Years later, Bill confirmed to me that when he wrote that piece he had been aware of Elvis's drug habit since December of 1973 but was kept under strict orders to keep his lip buttoned.

"The people think of Elvis as baseball, apple pie, and Chevrolet," Burk was told by his editor. "And we will *never* ruin that image."

Singer Elton John recently mused that if Elvis had been covered by the no-holds-barred British press, his problem would probably have come to light much sooner, forcing him to deal with his addic-tion. But as Red, Dave, and I learned, not even the threat of public humiliation was enough to stop Elvis from abusing drugs.

You have to be willing to admit you have a problem in order to get the help you need, and Elvis was never willing to do so. I'm aware of several opportunities he had to clean himself up at treat-ment centers, but Elvis wasn't having any of that. He was so afraid his fans would desert him. Actually, they would have loved him even more for acknowledging his human frailties and dealing with them. But it didn't seem that was ever going to happen.

With all that is in me I feel that if Elvis had accepted the challenge our book presented to him and corrected his course in the year before it was published, he would have become a greater hero than ever. Then, when the book came out, he could have called us liars, and we would have left it at that just to have him healthy again.

Instead we learned, as the book progressed, that he wallowed in rage and disbelief. "Man, I loved those guys," he would say to any-one within earshot. "Why would they do this to me?"

About a week after O'Grady's call, Charlie Hodge phoned Red. Charlie was so determinedly nonchalant that Red suspected Elvis was listening on an extension. The conversation was short, and when it ended, Red had the feeling that it was the precursor of a call from Elvis himself. "Elvis is going to call me," he said. "I just know it."

Sure enough, the next morning around 7:00, Red was awakened by a call from Elvis, who was in Memphis. His voice was heavily slurred. Because of his premonition that Elvis would call, Red was able to tape the conversation. It is fully transcribed in *Elvis: What Happened?* but the words on paper don't give a full sense of Elvis's awful state. Often he made no sense at all. He actually told Red that he was in the best shape of his life. Elvis mentioned the book and said he wasn't worried about it at all.

That bizarre episode strengthened our resolve to go ahead with the project.

Ballantine ordered an initial print run of four hundred thousand copies of our book and slated it for release on August 1, 1977. But before that, the book was serialized in England and Australia, and word of mouth created a sensational buzz in the States.

The morning of August 16 was one of the first interviews I ever gave about the book, and it was with Bob Greene, a well-known columnist for the *Chicago Sun-Times*. When Greene and I talked over the telephone about the revelations in our book on August 16, he asked, "So it wouldn't shock you if one day you opened the newspaper and found out [Elvis] suddenly died?"

"No, it would not," I replied straightforwardly, but not without a pang of despair at that prospect. Neither of us knew it at the time, but Elvis was already dead, and his demise would make headlines around the world.

After that interview, Judy and I took our Arabian mare to see if she was ready for breeding with a beautiful Arabian stallion named Asdar, owned by a good friend of ours, Dr. Harvey Cohen. It was not a typical California day. The sky was drearily overcast, and a light rain was falling that had not been in the prior evening's weather forecast. There were 0.19 inches of rain that day, which still stands as the record amount for an August 16 since records have been kept. The next day, August 17, the whole world was mourning the loss of Elvis. The rainfall for that day was 2.06 inches, which also set a record for August 17.

Perhaps even God was weeping over the fact that he had to take one of his favorite sons home.

We were walking toward the barn with the mare when Harvey came out of his house. He looked concerned and walked over to us and said, "Have you heard?"

I blurted out the first thought that came into my head.

"Elvis died?"

"Yeah," Harvey confirmed. "Isn't that something?"

I let go of the mare's halter rope, dropped to my knees, and began sobbing.

"*No! No!*" I shouted. "Oh God, he doesn't deserve this! He can't be dead!"

Crying too, Judy put her arms around my shoulders and said, "Oh no! Oh honey, I am so sorry. I know how much you loved him."

When I could stand again, I walked over to a wooden fence and punched it, cracking the top board. Alarmed, Judy asked if I was all right. I looked at her and wailed, "Judy, baby, he didn't deserve this! Why? Why?"

The anguish I felt was unlike any pain I had ever experienced. Upset that he had broken the news to me, Harvey told Judy, "I'm sorry. I wouldn't have said anything if I'd known he'd get this upset."

I don't remember the ride home, but I do recall walking aimlessly from room to room, wondering what to do with myself. The phone rang incessantly. Judy told everyone I was unavailable. Red and Pat came over, and he and I stumbled into each other's arms and cried uncontrollably.

Since then, I have lost my brother, who was a gambling addict, to suicide. At the end, he sold or hocked all his personal belongings for money to feed his gambling addiction. That addiction took my brother away from me.

Another addiction, drugs, killed my friend and hero, and they did it in the most humiliating and gut-wrenching way. They robbed Elvis of everything—his family, friends, music, finances, and his future—and it seemed there wasn't a damn thing I or anyone else could do about it.

That night, I cried myself to sleep. In the years since then, I have wondered when the tears would stop. But they never have.

# Chapter 33

# Memories

**T**HE DAY ELVIS PRESLEY DIED WAS THE WORST ONE OF MY LIFE. ALL I COULD think of were the wonderful memories of my life with him. I so desperately wanted him back.

In a way, I was even glad I had been fired, because it would have been so difficult for me to watch him die. I loved him too much. He was so good to me and my family, and his kindness and warmth enveloped everyone who knew him.

When I got up the morning after Elvis died, my attorney, John Irwin, called to say that Steve Dunleavy, the writer of our book, was going to be on ABC's *Good Morning America* to talk about Elvis. Journalist Geraldo Rivera would also be appearing on the show to be interviewed by host David Hartman.

It didn't take long for the fur to fly. The two obviously didn't like or even respect each other, perhaps even harboring a past vendetta. Rivera puffed out his chest and claimed that Elvis may have had a minor flirtation with drugs, but to call him a "junkie" was a lie. He said he had met him on several occasions and he was "as straight as anyone in this room." We never called Elvis a "junkie" in our book or at any other time. (Years later, in his book *Exposing Myself*, Rivera admitted that he met Elvis only one time, for all of ten minutes backstage at Madison Square Garden in 1972. So much for his credentials as an Elvis expert.)

Rivera accused Dunleavy of manipulating the story to make it as sensational as possible, and Dunleavy demonstrated his professionalism by calling Rivera "Jerry" instead of Geraldo, for which he was reprimanded by Hartman. I did agree with Rivera about Dunleavy's "sensational" style of writing. He was a reporter for *The Star* magazine, which pretty much says it all.

Their childish, idiotic bickering made me angry, and I knew something had to be done to set the record straight. I called John Irwin and had him set up a press conference that afternoon. Red was working on *Black Sheep Squadron* and wasn't available, but Dave Hebler met the press with me at John's law office.

The media was hungry for answers about why forty-two-year-old Elvis Presley had suddenly dropped dead, and a large crowd of journalists, photographers, and television crews turned out. Wearing sunglasses because I had been crying for the previous twenty-four hours, I said that while I stood by every word in our book, I disavowed our coauthor Dunleavy and ripped into him and Rivera for their disgusting appearance on Good Morning America.

Then I went into detail about Elvis's drug problem, and from the tenor of the questions, it was apparent the reporters couldn't fathom why no one close to Elvis was able to get through to him about what he had been doing. Dave put the whole matter into perspective with a simple question: "How do you protect a man from himself?"

When executives from Ballantine Books caught our press conference on TV, they canceled a planned publicity tour for the book, fearing a backlash. It didn't make any difference. Elvis's death sent people to bookstores in droves in search of answers. *Elvis: What Happened?* sold about three million copies, making it the best-selling original paperback in history at the time.

But the book's success didn't bring us much happiness. To hell with the book. We wanted Elvis back.

The years immediately after Elvis Presley's death seem like a blur now. I remember bits and pieces, but there was a huge shadow over my life for quite some time. It didn't help when people like Geraldo Rivera and author Albert Goldman dredged up sensationalistic pieces of his past.

On September 13, 1979, Rivera did a piece called "The Elvis Cover-Up" on the primetime ABC news magazine *20/20*. This marked the first time a major network cast a spotlight on rumors of Elvis's drug-related death.

While the official cause of Elvis's death was given as cardiac arrhythmia, or heart failure, it was clear to all of us close to him that the fourteen prescription drugs discovered in his system (several of them in toxic amounts) contributed to his demise. This was subsequently confirmed by Dr. Eric Muirhead, head of the autopsy department at Memphis's Baptist Memorial Hospital, who issued a statement saying that Elvis died of "poly-pharmacy." It simply meant that too many drugs were in his system. Dr. Eric Muirhead was reportedly astonished that cardiac arrhythmia had been given as the cause of death.

Rivera had dumped all over Red, Dave, and me on *Good Morning America* the day after Elvis's death. Yet, he had the nerve to call Red and ask for an interview for the *20/20* segment. Red told him fine, as long as Rivera apologized to us on the air for having called us liars. That ended that. Instead, Rivera went with the man who had tried to bribe us to abandon our book project, John O'Grady, who now was claiming to have tried to help Elvis overcome his addiction.

Albert Goldman was a respected author whose book *Ladies and Gentlemen: Lenny Bruce* was considered a classic. Goldman approached Lamar Fike to help him write an in-depth biography of Elvis, in exchange for which Lamar would get a share of the royalties. Lamar asked me to help out, and I agreed. But I laid down strict ground rules. I warned Goldman that I didn't want to be misquoted or have anything I said taken out of context. He promised and came to my house twice for lengthy interviews.

After Goldman's book *Elvis* was published, he sent me an autographed copy, but I didn't read it until I started hearing unflattering things about it. I flipped through the index and read all of the parts mentioning and/or quoting me. Goldman had kept his promise. I hadn't been misquoted. But I was appalled by the many other distortions in the book and Goldman's interjection of his own voice. He painted a vile picture of Elvis, and anyone who read the book could only come away convinced that Goldman hated his subject and had utter contempt for him.

I got Goldman's phone number from Lamar and called him up.

"Albert, I want to tell you something," I said. "First of all, I have to say you kept your word to me by not misquoting me or taking what I said out of context. But you wrote about some personal things that didn't need to be written or divulged. Your disgust and contempt for Elvis was so obvious throughout the book, as you tried to tear down a wonderful person. Don't ever contact me again."

Shortly before Vernon Presley died in June 1979, Priscilla was named executor of the estate so she could look after the estate for Lisa Marie, Elvis's sole heir, who would inherit everything in 1993 when she turned twenty-five.

A Tennessee judge deemed Elvis's estate to be worth in the neighborhood of $7 million. The estate owed the Internal Revenue Service close to $10 million in inheritance taxes, and Graceland cost about $500,000 a year to maintain.

Elvis had no investments, no trusts, and no money socked away for a rainy day. Fearing that the IRS would take Graceland and Lisa Marie would be left with nothing, Priscilla rolled up her sleeves and went to work. She combed through all of Elvis's canceled checks going back to the start of his career and found many that had been made out to his friends and marked "personal loan." Elvis did that only so that the recipients wouldn't have to pay taxes on the money he gave them.

Priscilla saw this as a way of getting some quick cash and also getting back at some of the guys she had never much cared for. Just a week after Marty Lacker signed a release so Priscilla could strike a $250,000 deal on a home movie package, she expressed her gratitude by suing Marty for repayment of $10,000 in past loans from Elvis. The rest of us had no doubt we were on her list, too.

But Marty filed a countersuit for the $50,000 plus a percentage of the profits we had all been promised by Elvis when he made the film *The New Gladiators*. In no time, Priscilla's lawyer was on the phone. "If you drop your lawsuit, we'll drop ours," he said.

In 1982, Priscilla opened Graceland to the public. Now the Presley estate is a thriving enterprise to the tune of $40 to $50 million a year. Elvis has been the top dead celebrity earner for the past decade, his image and memory bringing in more than those of Marilyn Monroe, John Lennon, George Harrison, and James Dean.

A year after Graceland opened, I called Jack Soden, chief executive officer of Elvis Presley Enterprises, and asked to visit along with Jeff Cook, a member of the group Alabama. Jack has always been a gentleman to me despite the fact that Priscilla and I haven't maintained a friendship. He said to come on over and met us on our arrival.

When I entered the foyer at Graceland, my mind raced back to the first time I saw Elvis there in 1960, after he came home from the army. That was also where I last saw Elvis—on July 5, 1976, after we returned from the concert at the Mid-South Coliseum.

As we stepped into the dining room, the hostess began to tell our group how Elvis would share meals there with his family and friends. Jack Soden nudged me and suggested I add a personal reminiscence. I mentioned how Elvis loved the holiday season and how we used to decorate the white Christmas tree every year. Once, Priscilla told Elvis to hang the tinsel on the tree, and he asked some of the guys to help. Priscilla specifically ordered us to put the tinsel on one strand at a time, but after a few painstaking minutes of that, Elvis got tired of it and just started heaving gobs at a time on the branches. After Priscilla ordered us to put down the tinsel and leave the decorating to her, Elvis gave us a huge grin and said, "Guess I got us out of that, huh guys?"

Each room at Graceland held great memories for me of the years I spent there with Elvis. When it came time to go outside and visit the grave site, I told Jeff that I would skip that part of the tour and meet him at the racquetball court behind the house.

I didn't go back again until fifteen years later. My friends Russ Howe, Bud Glass, Tom Salva, Tom Beattie, and I were in one of the museums across from Graceland that displayed one of Elvis's old cars. It was the eve of the twentieth anniversary of his death, and there was a constant line to and from the grave site to pay tribute to Elvis.

"Come on, guys, I'm gonna try and go up there," I told them. When I got there the crowd was two and three people deep. When I stopped and turned to look, I saw Elvis's grave. It overwhelmed me, and I turned to my friends and said, "I've gotta get out of here," and I headed back to the street.

Just then, a woman stopped me and asked if I was Sonny West. I said I was, bracing myself because some of Elvis's fans were still upset about the book Red, Dave, and I had written two decades earlier.

"I just want to thank you so much," said the woman, "because I really feel that we had Elvis as long as we did because of you and Red." She was crying, and my eyes welled up with tears, as did the eyes of my friends. She then hugged me, and I broke down and cried.

A lot of the anger at us has dissipated over the years as people have come to accept the truth of what we wrote in *Elvis: What Happened?* Sure, some still view us as modern-day Judases, but the majority of fans have come around.

I'll never forget the time in the mid-1980s when singer Johnny Cash introduced me to country artist Waylon Jennings at a Fuddruckers restaurant in Nashville's Rivergate Mall. I told Waylon that I had been a big fan of his for a long time, and he replied, "Naw, I'm a big fan of you and your cousin for what you tried to do. I wish I had you two around me to try and straighten my ass out when I was into that shit. I admire the hell out of both of you guys for that."

Do I have any regrets about writing *Elvis: What Happened?* A couple. I mostly regret that we didn't accomplish what we set out to do, which was to help Elvis get his life straightened out. And I regret that we weren't able to have a writer with the sensitivity and compassion to convey the Elvis Presley we knew and loved.

People ask me everywhere, "If Elvis were still alive, would he and you be friends?" I have no doubt about it. If our book had succeeded in its purpose and Elvis had changed his behavior, I'm sure we would have resumed our friendship. We had our differences over the years, but they never lasted long. You don't spend that much time with someone and not retain a core friendship. I loved Elvis and was grateful to him for bringing me into his life and giving his friendship to me, which I will always cherish.

I was one of the few in the Memphis Mafia who would have died to protect Elvis from harm. But I couldn't protect him from his deep-rooted frailties. I believe Elvis really thought he could stop taking pills whenever he wanted to, but that was always sometime later because he just "needed them right now."

Though I've made my peace with Elvis, that sadly has not been the case where Priscilla and Lisa Marie Presley are concerned. I hold no animosity toward Priscilla, but she has never apologized to my wife, Judy, for trying to instigate trouble by lying about the infamous "Lizard Tongue" letter. She did apologize to me once over lunch at the Hamburger Hamlet on Sunset Boulevard, and I appreciated it. But Judy is the one who deserved to get an apology. In 1984, I bumped into Priscilla at the Nashville Airport; we exchanged pleasantries, and I congratulated her on the success of Graceland. We gave each other a hug, wished each other well, and went our separate ways. I haven't seen her since.

Lisa Marie is on record as hoping that Red, Marty, and I "rot in hell." This happened after she caught us, in her words, trying "to take away her father's dignity" in the *E! True Hollywood Story: The Last*

*Days of Elvis.* Her behavior in private and public has done more to "take away her father's dignity" than anything I have ever said or done in regards to her father's memory. Regardless of what Priscilla says about Elvis being proud of his daughter today, you must remember, Priscilla is her mother. Period.

The TV show was not, I concede, a sterling production. But that wasn't our fault. A couple years earlier, we had participated in another documentary for E! Entertainment called *The Hollywood Years* and were pleased with how it turned out. When it came time to do *The Last Days of Elvis*, the producers used clips from the first documentary and edited them to put Elvis in the trashiest possible light. For example, Lamar mentioned Elvis's heavy use of Brut cologne and said, "You could smell him coming a mile away." But in the second documentary, that was edited to make it seem as if Lamar was complaining about Elvis's body odor. We were all disgusted with the show and told the producer we would have nothing more to do with him or E! Entertainment.

In an interview with *Rolling Stone* magazine, Lisa Marie said that the Memphis Mafia was a bad influence on her father. "They scared the hell out of me when I was a kid, too," she said. "I remember seeing the *Playboys*, the drugs, the women—I watched it all, and I watched them. I know the real story behind all of them, and I know what they're out there doing." She is so full of herself, and if it wasn't so pitiful it would be funny. The memories of the Memphis Mafia are not the only subject that she has invented about her childhood days.

The only thing I ever influenced Elvis to do was get his hair cut by Jay Sebring. Maybe Lisa Marie saw somebody in the group with a date, but the impression she left was that there were wild orgies going on. It didn't happen. Elvis wouldn't have allowed it, especially in front of his little girl. My wife and son lived there at Graceland while she said things were going on. I can promise you, they weren't.

Lisa Marie's comments hurt because some of us were like a second father to her. I personally escorted her to and from California many times after Elvis and Priscilla were divorced, and I watched over her as if she were my own child. She knew more card games than anyone, and that's how we spent our time during the flights. There were plenty of times I could have used a nap, but Lisa Marie would have none of it, pleading more games out of me until we landed.

The fact is that Lisa Marie was just nine years old when her father died. He wasn't around much after his divorce from Priscilla. He was usually on his best behavior whenever Lisa Marie was around, and the rest of us certainly were. For her to claim with a pointedly raised eyebrow that she "watched it all" is a joke.

Her own track record since her father's death is nothing to brag about. She has admitted dalliances with open sex and drugs and had brief and embarrassing marriages to Michael Jackson and Nicolas Cage. She has been married a total of four times as of this writing. If Elvis were still alive, I think he'd come down on her like a ton of bricks. Her "tell-it-like-it-is" attitude, foul mouth, and blunt demeanor would be a constant source of embarrassment to him.

My pastor told me once that those in heaven are able to see the good things their loved ones here on earth do, and it makes them happy. But God doesn't let them see anything that would upset them or cause them unhappiness. If this is true, then Elvis hasn't seen much of Lisa Marie lately.

Lord knows, I have not been seen by my loved ones who are in heaven for long periods of time, either. However, I have tried to be someone they would be proud of every day since 1990, when I rededicated my life to the Lord. I had just moved to a new home with my wife and children and started going to a church led by a minister called "Pastor Mac." I developed a close relationship with him as my pastor, my friend, and my guidance counselor. Before God called him to the ministry, Pastor Mac had been a professional musician. He was truly my inspiration for rededicating myself to the Lord God and his son Jesus. Pastor Mac's philosophies and teachings during the sermons seemed to always be right on for me.

Judy, my wife of thirty-five years, always maintained that I was a "godly" man, but today she proudly boasts that I am a "spirit-filled man." Every day I give thanks to the Lord for the many blessings he bestows upon me. I try to avoid prayers for myself and instead pray for my family and friends, their health, their prosperity, and their acceptance of the Lord Jesus as their savior.

I am frequently asked, "Was Elvis a Christian when he died?" To fully answer that question, you have to look at the road map of his life, not just his last years. He was raised in utter poverty, and his mother relied on the Lord to help her family through the rough times. Gladys passed on her love and faith in Jesus Christ to Elvis,

338

and even at the peak of his fame he never forgot his place in the grand order of things. I remember during one performance in Las Vegas when a woman approached the stage carrying a pillow on which rested a crown. "It's for you," she told Elvis. "You're the King." Elvis took her hand in his, smiled, and said, "No, honey, there is only one King, and his name is Jesus Christ. I'm just a singer." This story is true, but I don't think people who refer to Elvis as the "King" mean it in a religious form, just as a shortened version of the "King of Rock and Roll."

Whenever female fans told Elvis they "worshipped" him, he would ask them to "love my music, but don't ever worship anyone but the Lord."

There's no doubt in my mind that Elvis is in heaven, singing with that angelic voice to his creator for all eternity.

The word *legend* is not big enough to describe Elvis. His contributions to popular music and culture are unparalleled. He is the stand-alone icon of the century and the greatest entertainer this world has ever seen. Paul McCartney recently said, "Elvis could sing the way Picasso could paint." He painted a song like no other.

According to a recent Harris Poll, 71 percent of all Americans say they are Elvis Presley fans. Almost one-third of the American population owns an Elvis record, CD, or video. And they're not just of his generation. Half of all the folks who tour Graceland are thirty-five or younger—pretty impressive in this hip-hop, boy-band era that we live in today.

Elvis is bigger than the Beatles, James Dean, Marilyn Monroe, Muhammad Ali, and Bob Dylan, and other than Ali running a close second, no one else has even come close to possessing his electric charisma. Almost thirty years after his death, the man they call "the King" still reigns from beyond the grave.

For the past five years, Elvis Presley Enterprises has raked in approximately $40 million to $50 million annually. In February 2005, Lisa Marie Presley sold 85 percent of the corporation's assets for $114 million to Robert F.X. Sillerman of SFX Entertainment. Lisa Marie retains possession of Graceland and most of Elvis's personal effects plus 15 percent of the business, but she has arranged a ninety-year lease with Sillerman.

Sillerman now owns Elvis Presley's name, image, likeness, and trademark. He plans to spend $20 million over the next few years to promote Elvis in this country and abroad. As of this writing, on the drawing boards are Elvis-themed restaurants, a large hotel and convention center, and a Graceland-themed casino in Las Vegas. I expect Elvis will become an even bigger icon in the years to come.

The problem with icons is that they are typically viewed as one-dimensional. Elvis was anything but. He was a dichotomous and paradoxical human being, and yet he treated everyone the same from the groundskeeper to the president. There wasn't a day that went by in which something interesting, funny, warm, touching, or bizarre didn't happen. Every day with Elvis was an adventure.

Over the past five years I have performed in shows called "Moments with Elvis" or "Memories of Elvis—An Evening with Sonny West." My objective is to portray Elvis Presley as a human being and to put audience members right there in the same room with him and me—to make them the proverbial fly on the wall, as it were.

At the end of my show I take questions, with nothing off-limits or taboo. I address any and all rumors, facts, myths, and famous stories the audience cares to bring up, and, of course, I offer lots of stories of my own.

A crowd favorite concerns the time in the late 1960s when Elvis found himself locked in the Jack L. Warner compound in Palm Springs. We were unwinding there late on a Friday after a hectic week of filmmaking. In the morning a couple of the guys went into town to do some shopping before Elvis got up, and I took the opportunity to go to the grocery store to get some items for Elvis's breakfast. We pretty much did everything for Elvis, even dialing the phone when he wanted to call someone.

Elvis woke up earlier than usual, and everybody was gone. Not wanting to sit there alone, he decided he wanted to go shopping and picked up the phone, dialed the operator, and asked her to send a cab to fetch him.

"I don't do that sir," she replied and then continued, "I can give you the number to call the information operator if you like." Elvis then dialed the number.

When the operator answered, he told her he needed to get a hold of a cab company.

340

"Which cab company would you like, sir?" she asked.

"Anyone will do, ma'am," he replied.

The operator rattled off a few names, and when she said "Yellow Cab," he recognized that one and said it would do fine. She gave him the number, and he called for a Yellow Cab. But when the dispatcher asked where the cab should pick him up, Elvis had no clue. He didn't even know what street the house was on.

Finally, in exasperation, he said, "Look ma'am, I'm Elvis Presley!"

"Oh, you are," the dispatcher said sarcastically.

"Yes, ma'am, and I don't own the house. I just rent it. Jack L. Warner of Warner Brothers Studios owns the house."

It was a well-known residence, and the cab was dispatched, but only after a stern warning. "I don't know if you're Elvis Presley or not, but you'd better be there when the cab shows up," the dispatcher said.

When it arrived, the cabbie pushed the button at the front gate to let Elvis know he was there. There was a speaker box in the kitchen, but Elvis didn't know how to use it. He also didn't know how to open the gate to let the cab in as he didn't have a key. So he ran outside and told the cabbie not to leave until he figured out a way to open the gate.

That's when I pulled up. When I asked the cabbie what was going on, he said, "There's a guy who says he's Elvis Presley over there, and he can't get the gate open."

"Elvis?" I yelled. "Sonny?" he yelled back. "Get this damn gate open!"

When I did, Elvis said, "Damn, Sonny, where y'all been? I've been sitting here waiting. I want to go shopping!"

He told me to give the cab driver $100 so he could leave, to which the guy said with a big grin, "Thanks, Elvis. If you ever need me again, just call," and handed me his business card. I quickly took the food in the house and placed the perishables in the refrigerator; then I drove Elvis to meet the others while he told me the whole story. We laughed until tears rolled down our faces.

In my show I don't try and convert people or get them to like me, but I do promise they'll have a different perspective on Elvis Presley and Sonny West when they leave.

Elvis might have left the building, but he has never left my heart. Not a day goes by without something said, heard, or seen that makes me think of him. I think he would be enthralled by the entertainment scene today—the action films and special effects. He would have liked *The Aviator*, as he was a big fan of Howard Hughes; *Independence Day* with Will Smith; and *Gladiator* with Russell Crowe, to name just a few.

The same goes for music. I think Céline Dion would probably be his favorite female singer. He would have admired Mariah Carey's vocal range and absolutely loved Shania Twain's sexiness and voice. He would have liked U2 and Collective Soul and some of the male groups (e.g., Boyz II Men) because he loved harmony and melody.

Almost thirty years after his death, Elvis Presley lives on through his music, his films, his timeless talent, his beautiful spirit, and his legendary countless acts of kindness. His story as the ultimate symbol of the American dream will live on forever. I hope that this book contributes to that symbol and his legacy. I guess you could say I'm still taking care of business.

I loved being a part of it all, and I love telling his story. And I will be honored to keep telling it for as long as Elvis Presley fans want to hear it.

God bless.

# Appendix **A**

# All the King's Men

**M**ANY PEOPLE HAVE WONDERED OVER THE YEARS WHAT HAPPENED TO ALL the King's men after Elvis's death on August 16, 1977. I have compiled a list with several categories, and the names are listed alphabetically. The first is the original members of the Memphis Mafia— the guys working for Elvis in the early 1960s when the name was bestowed. Members of the original Memphis Mafia are designated by (OMM) after their names. A second category is employees who joined us later. These members are marked (MM). I've also included some good friends who never actually worked for Elvis. They're (GF). And some that aren't marked, well, I'll just leave to your imagination where they fit in the grand scheme of things.

If I have overlooked anyone, it is strictly by error or on purpose.

**Richard Davis (MM)**—Elvis's valet manager, movie stand-in, and wardrobe assistant, he was employed in the early '60s and was with Elvis for about seven years until fired by Vernon Presley in a cost-cutting move. Richard eventually found employment in the security division of the Horseshoe Casino in Tunica, Mississippi, where he later became a supervisor. In August 2004, he died in his sleep of an apparent heart attack, leaving behind a thirty-three-year-old wife and young triplets. He was sixty-four.

**Joe Esposito (OMM)**—"Diamond" Joe first met Elvis in the army in the late '50s and eventually became road manager and foreman of the group when he and Elvis returned from Germany in 1960. After Elvis's death, he worked as a road manager for the Bee Gees and owned his own limousine service. Joe authored *Good Rockin' Tonight* in 1994 as well as a picture book and DVD, the humbly titled *Elvis: His*

*Best Friend Remembers.* Joe remained friendly with Priscilla Presley and has appeared as a spokesman for Elvis Presley Enterprises. Today he is a casino host at the Wynn Hotel in Las Vegas. Joe and I got along well during the time we were employed by Elvis, but in recent years he has exaggerated his relationship with Elvis to boost his own ego (and perhaps to market himself for his own interests). He also said some disparaging things about me and some of the other guys that I didn't appreciate. We saw each other again for the first time in years in 2003 at a convention in Palm Springs, California. He issued an apology of sorts, and I sort of accepted.

**Lamar Fike (OMM)**—The incomparable Lamar was always entertaining and possessed a razor-sharp wit, which is what Elvis liked about Lamar when he hired him in the late '50s. After Elvis died, Lamar went back to the music business, working with Jimmy Bowen and pretty much running his publishing company. In 2005, Lamar was diagnosed with lymphoma, a form of cancer that causes cells to mutate and multiply. Luckily the cancer was detected early, and Lamar is expected to make a full recovery. Today he is a consultant for a major memorabilia collector and resides in Dallas.

**Alan Fortas (OMM)**—Known affectionately as "Hog Ears," Alan was employed by Elvis from 1960 to 1969. But his friendship with Elvis dated back to the late 1950s. Alan spent many years with Elvis in Hollywood and later became foreman of the Circle G. Alan left after a financial dispute with Vernon over ski equipment. He stayed in California for a while and worked as a movie extra. Eventually, he went back to Memphis and worked as a bartender, and he later sold municipal bonds. In 1992, Alan authored *Elvis: From Memphis to Hollywood.* He died of kidney cancer that same year.

**Marvin Gambill (MM)**—Nicknamed "Gee Gee," Marvin worked for Elvis beginning sometime in 1967. Marvin was married to Elvis's first cousin, Patsy Presley, and they had a daughter named Dana. Marvin was a valet and chauffeur for Elvis before leaving the group after a couple of years. He was a customer service specialist for Mapco Express in Nashville when he was struck and killed by a motorist in February 2005 while walking to work. He was sixty-one.

**Larry Geller (GF)**—I would just as soon leave him out, but the record must be set straight. Contrary to his claims, Geller was not Elvis's "spiritual adviser," nor was he with Elvis for thirteen years. It was more like a total of three years. He got the job as Elvis's stylist in 1964 and was sent packing in '66 by Colonel Parker. Somehow Geller wormed his way back in after Red, Dave, and I left in 1976. Today he resides in Southern California and sells hair products.

**Cliff Gleaves (GF)**—The most original and flaky character in the inner circle, Cliff first met Elvis in 1957. After Elvis was drafted into the army a year later, Cliff accompanied him to West Germany. But because Elvis could take Cliff only in small doses, Cliff drifted in and out of Elvis's life until 1972. Cliff could have been a successful comedian or actor, but he never picked an occupation and stuck with it. He eventually found work as a disc jockey and died in 2002 of complications from diabetes.

**Dick Grob (MM)**—He was hired as a part-timer in 1970 and eventually became full time with the security detail. After Elvis's death, Dick said publicly that Elvis fired Red, Dave, and me because he wanted a better grade of security and that toward this end Grob had been made chief of security. Neither statement was true. As a matter of fact, Billy Smith told me that Elvis had wanted to fire Dick but didn't because the security force was so depleted at the time. In recent years at conventions, Grob has played up his military status and his role in Elvis's life, both of which are dubious. In 1996 he self-published a book called *The Elvis Conspiracy?* He lives in Las Vegas and, the last I heard, was still in the security business.

**Dave Hebler (MM)**—A tenth-degree black belt and kenpo grand master, Dave was hired by Elvis in the early '70s. Dave was fired along with Red West and me in July 1976, and he coauthored *Elvis: What Happened?* Now a resident of Gardnerville, Nevada, Dave is a card dealer at a casino.

**Charlie Hodge (OMM)**—Elvis credited Charlie with keeping his spirits up after his mother's death and was with Elvis until his death. A former member of the Foggy River Boys, Charlie lived at Graceland for many years, including when Elvis died. Charlie probably had the hardest adjustment to make, for he existed for Elvis. In 1988, he wrote a memoir called *Me 'n Elvis* and had a regular spot for years at the Memories Theater in Pigeon Forge, Tennessee. Charlie died in March 2006 from lung cancer. He was seventy-one.

**Mike Keaton (MM)**—Mike worked for Elvis for just a short time before moving on. He was a little different and didn't fit in well with the organization. I bumped into his wife in October 2005, and she said Mike is retired and living on the Texas Gulf Coast.

**Jimmy Kingsley (MM)**—Jimmy was hired with Richard Davis in 1962. Jimmy didn't really have a defined role within the group, and he always seemed jealous of Elvis and his success. He was around only a couple of years before he quit to get into the movie business. After a few years as a stuntman, Jimmy drifted back to Tennessee. His wife of just eleven days left him to go on tour with a singer with whom she was having an affair. In despair, Jimmy put a gun to his head and committed suicide in 1989.

**George Klein (GF)**—George was never considered a member of the Memphis Mafia, but he was a good friend of Elvis's. George would take a vacation from his work and come out to visit with Elvis on a movie set or go out on tour. George was a leading deejay in Memphis for years and today is an executive host at the Horseshoe Casino in Tunica, Mississippi, about thirty minutes south of Graceland. George still has a hand in entertainment and hosts a radio show for Sirius Satellite Radio on the Elvis Channel.

**Marty Lacker (OMM)**—Marty was employed by Elvis from 1961 until 1967. He became foreman when Joe Esposito left, and they shared the job after Joe came back. Marty left Elvis's employ for good in 1967 to start his own company, but he stayed close to Elvis and was a co–best man at Elvis's wedding. Since then Marty has remained involved in the music business, first in California and then in Memphis, to which he returned in 1977. In 1979, Marty wrote *Elvis: Portrait of a Friend* with his wife, Patsy, and in 1995, he coauthored *Elvis Aaron Presley: Revelations from the Memphis Mafia* with Lamar Fike and Billy Smith. He still lives in Memphis and does consulting work in the music industry. He also has an Internet enterprise launched with his daughter Sherry. Marty has three children, Sherry, Mark, and Angie, and several grandchildren. He never remarried after his divorce from Patsy, and they remain close friends to this day.

**Sal Orifice (MM)**—A real artist with a scissors and comb, Sal began cutting Elvis's hair in the early '60s. He met Elvis through me, and eventually Elvis convinced Sal to work for him. The only thing I hold against Sal is that when he left the group to open up his own salon, he brought Larry Geller in to replace him. I often needled Sal about this at his new salon called the Brass Rail. I haven't been in touch with Sal for years, but I assume he still lives in the Los Angeles area.

**Ed Parker (GF)**—Long considered the father of American kenpo karate, Parker first met Elvis in 1960. He became a member of the security team after Red, Dave, and I were fired. Ed was a good friend to Elvis and almost everyone within the group. He gave me private lessons in kenpo to help me improve my bodyguard skills as much as possible. In 1978, Parker wrote a book called *Inside Elvis*, in which he made the astounding claim that Elvis did not have a drug problem. I was sad to hear that Ed died of a massive heart attack at age fifty-nine in December 1990.

**Tom Parker**—Not an employee or Memphis Mafia member, "Colonel" Tom was Elvis Presley's legendary manager. Parker moved to Las Vegas in the 1980s and enjoyed the life of the high roller. He continued to work with the Hilton Hotel, bringing second-tier acts into the showroom that once housed the King. The Colonel was honored in 1994 when Nevada governor Bob Miller declared June 25 "Colonel Tom Parker Day" throughout the state. The final curtain came down on January 21, 1997, when Parker passed away at eighty-seven from complications of a stroke. At his funeral they played one of Elvis's songs, "How Great Thou Art," a fitting tribute.

**Pat Parry (GF)**—Pat was the only female around consistently from 1960 until Elvis's death. She was adopted by Elvis and the group, and over the years she has remained close to most of us. She cut Elvis's hair often, most notably for his *Elvis: Aloha from Hawaii, Via Satellite* show. Elvis had a special place in his heart for her, as do I. Pat jokingly refers to herself as the "only female member of the Memphis Mafia." There was never a female in the Memphis Mafia, but if there had been, it would have been Pat. Pat is semiretired and still cuts hair twice a week in a Beverly Hills salon.

**Jerry Schilling (MM)**—Jerry met Elvis in the 1950s when he was a young boy and was hired by Elvis in 1964. Over the years, Jerry would leave and do other work in the entertainment business and then come back into the fold. Jerry left the group for good after he and Elvis had a blowup in Vail, Colorado, in January 1976. Jerry then took a job in the film industry. Eventually he became the tour manager for singer Billy Joel and also briefly managed the Beach Boys and Jerry Lee Lewis. He even served as Lisa Marie Presley's manager for several years. Jerry still lives in the Los Angeles home Elvis bought him in the mid-1970s.

**Ray Sitton (MM)**—One of the numerous "Chiefs" in Elvis's life, Ray was expelled from the tribe by Elvis after he wrecked a couple of Elvis's cars and got into a fight with a Memphis police officer when he was pulled over for driving under the influence. Chief worked as an extra in Hollywood and died in the late 1980s.

**Billy Smith (OMM)**—Billy was Elvis's cousin and was raised by Elvis as a younger brother. Although he wasn't officially employed by Elvis in the early '60s—Billy was too young—he was part of the close-knit group of guys even before I joined up in March 1960. That's why I have him down as an OMM. In the last year of Elvis's life, Billy was the only one Elvis wanted to be around between tours. In 1995, Billy coauthored *Elvis Aaron Presley: Revelations from the Memphis Mafia* with Marty Lacker and Lamar Fike. Today, he works for a machine company and lives in northern Mississippi with his wife of more than forty years, Jo. He has two sons, Danny and Joey, and several grandchildren.

**Gene Smith (OMM)**—Perhaps Elvis's closest relative at one time, Gene accompanied him on the road and to Hollywood in the '50s. He officially went on the payroll when Elvis got back from the army in 1960. Gene moved back to Memphis in 1963 to spend more time with his wife and family. In 1994, Gene authored a book called *Elvis' Man Friday*. Five years later, in March 1999, Gene died of heart failure.

**Billy Stanley**—The oldest of the Stanley brothers and Elvis's stepbrother, Billy lacked personal drive, which disappointed Elvis. If memory serves, Billy went out on tour once, to help out with the wardrobe, and that lasted only about two weeks. He wrote a book in 1989 called *Elvis, My Brother*, but many of his stories were exaggerated or untrue. In 1998, Billy and a former *Boston Globe* editor enlisted the aid of Jack Gordon, former husband and manager of singer La Toya Jackson, to produce a screenplay called *My Memories of Elvis*. It went nowhere, which isn't surprising given its claim that Elvis was diagnosed with terminal cancer prior to his death.

**David Stanley (MM)**—The youngest Stanley brother and Elvis's stepbrother, David went to work for Elvis in 1972 as an assistant. David worked in wardrobe and ran errands. The last couple years that Elvis was on tour, David was a bodyguard. David has written and coauthored four books about his life with Elvis. Today, he owns and runs a film production company in Dallas, Texas.

**Ricky Stanley (MM)**—The middle Stanley brother and Elvis's stepbrother, Ricky started working for Elvis in 1970 as his personal assistant. He also helped with Elvis's wardrobe. After Elvis's death, Ricky kicked alcohol and narcotics and graduated from Criswell

College in Dallas on a full scholarship provided by Dr. W.A. Criswell, who was impressed by Rick's story. Rick went on to receive a graduate degree at Southwestern Baptist Theological Seminary in Fort Worth, and today he has a ministry. He speaks at schools, businesses, prisons, churches, and alcohol/drug rehab facilities, sharing a message of compassion and encouragement. Ricky is the author of three Elvis books. He lives in Niceville, Florida, with his wife and children.

**Al Strada (MM)**—Al was hired in 1972 by Elvis after a stint as a security guard with a private security firm assigned to Elvis's Monovale home in California. Later, he worked in wardrobe. Al was the first one to respond to Ginger Alden's call downstairs after she found Elvis dead on August 16, 1977. During Elvis's last year, I stayed in touch with Al to check on Elvis's condition. Like many, I'd heard that Al died of cancer, but I recently learned that he is alive and well and driving a truck in California.

**Sam Thompson (MM)**—Linda Thompson's brother, Sam was a deputy with the Shelby County Sheriff's office before he went to work for Elvis after the three of us were fired. Elvis made him, not Dick Grob, chief of security. I liked Sam a lot, and we became friends over the years. After Elvis's death, Sam became a judge in Memphis. Now he and his wife, Louise, live in Las Vegas, where he was recently appointed by Governor Kenny Guinn to the Transportation Services Authority.

**Red West (OMM)**—Elvis's protector and bodyguard since they attended Humes High School in Memphis, Red had a tight bond with Elvis. Red accompanied Elvis to Germany in 1958 and stayed there with him for about six months before going to Hollywood to get into the movie business. Red and Elvis fell out when Red was not invited to Elvis's wedding, and the two were estranged for a couple of years. Red came back for good in 1970 after Elvis received a death threat in Las Vegas. Fired with Dave Hebler and me on July 13, 1976, Red coauthored *Elvis: What Happened?* I'm proud to say that Red has enjoyed the most success of all the Memphis Mafia members. He's a veteran screen actor with more than one hundred film and television appearances, is a successful songwriter (Elvis recorded a handful of his tunes), and runs a thriving acting school in Memphis. He has been married to his wife, Pat, for almost forty-five years. They have two sons, Brent and John Boyd, and several grandchildren.

**Sonny West (OMM)**—Employed by Elvis in 1960, I performed a wide variety of jobs for him until I became his chief of security in 1969.

After my dismissal in 1976, I earned a living raising Arabian horses and making Western costume jewelry. In 1982, I was chief of security for a tour sponsored by the Salem Division of R.J. Reynolds Tobacco Company called "Salem Country Gold 82," featuring Alabama, Mickey Gilley, Johnny Lee, Juice Newton, the Thrasher Brothers, and comedian Eddie Jay. This lasted two years, and then I went to work for Sonny Simmons, who taught me the ins and outs of the talent-booking business. A few years later, I went to work with country singer Eddy Raven, running the concession side of his business in conjunction with his manager at the time, Charles Stone, a longtime dear friend of mine back on the tours with Elvis when he worked for Concerts West III. After I left Eddy in early 1988, I joined my wife, Judy, in a construction cleaning service she had started with another woman who quit because of the hard work involved. The pay was good, and I got to spend much more time with my wife, which hadn't happened a lot in our earlier years together. At the same time, I hosted a radio show on WMRO in Gallatin, Tennessee, on Saturdays from noon to 4:00 PM called *The Doo Wop Show*. I spun oldies from the '50s, '60s, and '70s and conducted trivia contests for prizes about my years with Elvis.

For the past few years I have produced a show called "Memories of Elvis: An Evening with Sonny West," recalling my life with the King and sharing stories with audiences around the world.

My wife, Judy, and I have been married since December 1970 and live near our two children, Bryan and Alana, just outside of Nashville.

# Appendix **B**

# Myths, Facts, and Frequently Asked Questions

PEOPLE WHO COME TO MY SHOW OFTEN ASK ME TO ADDRESS A NUMBER OF facts, so-called facts, and outright myths regarding Elvis Presley's life. I'm always happy to do so, because over the years, there has been such an explosion of myths and untruths about Elvis. I'll list some of them here and set the record straight. Then I'll answer some of the questions I get over and over about Elvis.

**Myth:** Elvis Presley faked his death on August 16, 1977, and is still with us today under a different identity.
**Fact:** Absolutely, 100 percent *not true*. I think this myth got started because so many fans weren't ready to let Elvis go. Then others set out to profit from their grief and wrote books that became best sellers because people wanted so badly to believe that Elvis was still alive. I wish he were, but he isn't. If he was, you can be certain that Elvis would never have let his daughter, Lisa Marie, marry Michael Jackson. If that didn't bring Elvis Presley out of hiding, nothing would. Had Elvis not died, he would never have permitted his daughter to even date Jackson.

**Myth:** X-rays taken after Elvis's death showed that he had degenerative arthritis and cancer, which is why he needed strong painkillers.
**Fact:** Not true. Elvis did not have cancer. There was a spot on a leg bone, about the size of a pinhead, but the autopsy report specifically

ruled out cancer as a disease in Elvis. Such spots are not unusual in most people, according to doctors. I never heard that Elvis had degenerative arthritis, and I'm not aware of any immediate Presley family history of that condition.

**Myth:** Elvis Presley was a racist.
**Fact:** Absolutely untrue. Elvis was a caring person who recognized the suffering of different races and ethnic groups throughout history. He had several close friends of different races whom he respected and greatly admired.

**Myth:** Elvis Presley did not like to bathe in his later years.
**Fact:** The sad truth is that as Elvis got more into the drugs he was not as concerned about his personal hygiene as before. He washed himself in ways without taking showers or baths, but he was not unclean.

**Myth:** Elvis Presley did not like to go out in public, which is why he had so many bodyguards.
**Fact:** Not true. Elvis enjoyed getting out, especially in the 1950s and '60s, the movie years. After he started doing live shows again in 1969, it became more difficult, but he still ventured out. The last year of his life, as his drug addiction took firm hold of him, Elvis did become more of a recluse.

**Myth:** The Memphis Mafia was a bad influence on Elvis, shielding him from family and friends.
**Fact:** Not true. We were definitely not a bad influence on him and shielded him only from those Elvis specifically instructed us to keep away from him.

**Myth:** The Memphis Mafia's out-of-control behavior, including careless use of firearms, resulted in many embarrassing lawsuits.
**Fact:** Not true. We were not out of control, and we took pains to conduct ourselves as professionals. Yes, we did carry guns and were licensed to do so, but nobody ever pulled a weapon on anyone. (Elvis himself pulled a gun on someone more than once, when he lost his temper.) And, yes, there were lawsuits over the years. But they were filed by people strictly out for a buck. Elvis was an inviting target for

such people, as they knew he was reluctant to be mired down in lengthy litigation and would offer a financial settlement to avoid all the negative trappings of a trial.

## Frequently Asked Questions

**Q:** It's been said that Elvis had an obsession about his twin brother, Jesse Garon. Did he ever speak of Jesse?

**A:** Elvis sometimes wondered what life would have been like had Jesse Garon lived. In public, he was drawn to twins and would go out of his way to talk with them about shared sensations and experiences. But it wasn't an obsession, and Elvis never "talked" to Jesse Garon as if he was in the same room with him.

**Q:** How often did Elvis talk about his mother, Gladys, after her death, and what did he say about her?

**A:** He spoke often of his mother, always in the most warm and endearing terms. Elvis had warm memories of her gentle and giving side, but he also reminisced—usually with a laugh—about her hair-trigger temper. I think Elvis inherited her sweetness and giving nature as well as her temper.

**Q:** How did Elvis honestly feel about his father, Vernon?

**A:** Elvis clearly loved his father, but at the same time, he was disappointed in Vernon. I know Elvis didn't like it when Vernon got involved with Dee Presley, whom he felt was responsible for breaking up her marriage to Bill Stanley. That it happened mere months after Gladys died also hurt Elvis. Vernon often bragged and acted cocky about some of the women he knew in Las Vegas, which was rough on Elvis. Vernon was not exactly a role model, but Elvis loved him regardless.

**Q:** Did Elvis hate any of the songs he recorded?

**A:** I can really think of just one—"Dominic." The reason he hated it so much was that he had to croon it to a bull in *Stay Away, Joe*.

**Q:** What female artists did Elvis enjoy listening to? Male artists?

**A:** Timi Yuro, Connie Francis, Olivia Newton-John, Tom Jones, Jackie Wilson, Roy Orbison, to name but a few.

**Q:** Was there anyone with whom Elvis would have liked singing and recording a duet?

**A:** Elvis admired many female singers, but I never heard him express any interest in a duet with anyone. I'm sure that if Elvis had really wanted to perform a duet with anyone, it would have happened.

**Q:** What was Elvis's absolute favorite meal?

**A:** For breakfast he usually ate a Spanish omelet with a pound of very crisp bacon, beefsteak tomatoes, and several pieces of toast. For dinner, nothing beat a hamburger steak with gravy and potatoes and a vegetable (e.g., green beans). Occasionally he liked the famous fried peanut butter and banana sandwiches or a cheeseburger. Simple and Southern.

**Q:** Did Elvis have any rituals he performed before he went onstage?

**A:** Elvis often did a stretching exercise known as "Indian Wrestling." He and a partner—usually me—placed the sides of their feet together and then leaned back pulling one another with their hands. He also would shake his arms vigorously as they hung at his side. Both routines eased tension.

**Q:** How did Elvis really feel about his fans?

**A:** Elvis Presley had a unique relationship with his fans. He loved and respected them in a way I haven't seen anyone else do, and they rewarded him with the kind of adulation and support most performers have only dreamed about. Elvis was well aware that without his fans he was nothing, and he was eternally grateful for their support and love.

**Q:** Did Elvis ever read his fan mail? What did he do with it?

**A:** Elvis often went to the office behind Graceland to visit with his father and the secretaries, and they would show him some of the more touching letters—and also the most bizarre ones. He was genuinely touched by the sincere expressions of love, and he was moved to laughter by the others and their outrageous proposals. Some of the letters from ardent female fans included a photo or two that they would not have wanted their parents and pastors to see.

**Q:** How much plastic surgery did Elvis have?

**A:** Elvis had his nose cartilage reduced in the '50s by a plastic surgeon named Dr. Maury Parks. Elvis said in my presence at a later time that the same doctor had tucked Priscilla's ears closer to her head. And Elvis had his eyelids, chin, neck, and face done in 1975, using my name.

**Q:** What is your favorite Elvis song?

**A:** In the '50s it was "I Was the One." In the '60s, "Fame and Fortune." After I met my wife, Judy, my favorite song became "The Wonder of You," which Elvis sang especially for us one night.

**Q:** How did Elvis decide which jumpsuit he was going to wear before a concert?

**A:** Sometimes he would pick a specific jumpsuit for a certain occasion, but most of the time his outfit was chosen by the people in the wardrobe department.

**Q:** What was the happiest you ever saw Elvis?

**A:** I wasn't there when his daughter, Lisa Marie, was born, which I am sure was his happiest time. Another was when he received his badge from President Nixon in 1970 and when he earned his first-degree black belt in karate in 1960. The successes of the '68 comeback special and the opening night in Las Vegas in July 1969 as well as the *Aloha from Hawaii* special were great personal triumphs. I'm sure there were many others, but these stick out in my mind.

**Q:** What was the saddest you saw Elvis?

**A:** At the funeral of my Uncle Tom, Red's dad, Elvis stumbled into the room at the funeral home crying. He hugged Red and told him he understood his loss, because Elvis had just lost his mother that same day and was still extremely upset about her death.

**Q:** What is the angriest you saw Elvis?

**A:** I saw Elvis lose his temper many times. The one that sticks out in my mind was when he hit me in 1961 because he believed I had said something derogatory about him to his cousin Gene after Tuesday Weld and a friend visited his house. Another time he went ballistic was after he heard that a bellhop at the Hilton in Vegas had told people Elvis was "strung out on drugs."

**Q:** Had he lived, would Elvis had done more movies?

**A:** I would like to think that, had Elvis turned his life around and kicked his prescription drug habit, he would have returned to acting and done better movies.

**Q:** What were some movie roles Elvis passed up?

**A:** *A Star Is Born; Dirty Harry; Thunder Road; The Rainmaker; West Side Story; Splendor in the Grass; A Walk on the Wild Side; Too Late Blues; Baby, the Rain Must Fall; Midnight Cowboy;* and *Butch Cassidy and the Sundance Kid.* Most of these roles were either turned down or automatically defaulted because Elvis already had multipicture deals and was not available.

**Q:** Did Elvis ever wish aloud that he could go back to the days before he was famous and do things like a normal human being?

**A:** I never heard Elvis make this statement in all the years I was with him, and I don't think anyone else did either. Elvis loved being Elvis. I think Elvis enjoyed his celebrity and never looked back.

**Q:** What did you think of the movie *Elvis Meets Nixon*, which was loosely based on his meeting with the president? And what did you think of the actor who depicted you?

**A:** I never saw it because I was told by people who did that it was totally ridiculous and tasteless. I have yet to meet anyone that liked it, so I won't waste my time on watching it.

**Q:** Jerry Schilling wrote in his 2006 book *Me and a Guy Named Elvis* that you had personally tried to recruit him to be a coauthor for *Elvis: What Happened?* Is this true?

**A:** Absolutely 100 percent false. We never considered him or anyone else for the book. It was just us three, period. That conversation never took place. The conversation we did have took place after we finished the manuscript but several months before the book was published. Jerry wanted to know if I told the story of the time he, Lamar, Priscilla, and Elvis took LSD at Graceland in Memphis. I told him no, that we didn't want to hurt anyone and that we were trying to get Elvis to see that what he was doing with the prescription drugs was wrong. He was headed down a bad road. Jerry was obviously worried about his image with the people he was working for at the time. Yet I wasn't surprised when he wrote about it in his book. Things change over the years. There were quite a few statements in Jerry's book that were not true. For example, he mentions that he and Elvis worked out a stretching routine when it actually was a continuation of what Elvis and I started the first night he performed in Las Vegas in 1969. A small thing, I know, but it was irritating to me. It seems Jerry took credit for some things individually that he was actually just a part of. The people who were there know the truth.

**Q:** In your opinion, who has given the best Elvis portrayal in either a television or movie production?

**A:** I think Kurt Russell stands out as the best Elvis in the 1979 TV movie *Elvis*.

**Q:** Did Elvis ever express a desire for more children after the birth of Lisa Marie? Specifically, did he ever want a son?

**A:** I can't say he mentioned wanting another child, but if he did I suspect he would have hoped for a son. After the birth of Lisa Marie, Elvis had a different outlook about children. When my son was born in 1972 while we were living with him, Elvis loved Bryan to a fault, and he and Linda Thompson enjoyed their time with Bryan. They nicknamed him "little Santa," after they gave Bryan a little Santa Claus outfit when he was three months old.

**Q:** Had Priscilla not left Elvis, would he have divorced her or continued the marriage as long as he could?

**A:** This is an interesting question. I believe he would have let things go on as they were. But I don't think Elvis and Linda would have had a relationship if Priscilla had not divorced him, as dating a married man was not in Linda's nature.

**Q:** Did Elvis express a desire to remarry Priscilla?

**A:** Never to me. I know Priscilla has suggested this, and maybe Elvis did say or indicate to her that they could get back together. But he told us guys that she was the one hinting at reconciliation and that he wasn't interested. After she broke up with Mike Stone, both were available but chose not to go down that road again.

**Q:** How important was Elvis's faith to him?

**A:** Elvis's belief in God was strong and something he cherished. His reading about and investigations of other religions were done out of curiosity. Elvis never considered converting to Scientology or some other out-of-the-mainstream faith. He was against Scientology and stated so after visiting a center in Los Angeles once.

**Q:** Is it true that Elvis had a sleeping disorder dating back to his childhood, which is why he could not get more than a couple of hours of sleep at night?

**A:** Yes. Elvis had a tendency to walk in his sleep, and a few bad childhood experiences made him apprehensive at bedtime. One happened when Elvis was an infant and his father, Vernon, thought the house was on fire and threw Elvis into a wall instead of out a window to safety.

**Q:** If you'd had the chance, would you have gone back to work for Elvis as his chief of security?

**A:** I would have gone back in a flash, but I would not have compromised my convictions about his drug problem.

**Q:** Elvis knew karate, but could he have handled himself in a street fight?

**A:** Most definitely. He was very capable of taking care of himself.

**Q:** How did Elvis's fashion sense evolve or develop?

**A:** I am not sure, but I do know he always liked clothes that were different and eye-catching and that added to his aura.

**Q:** Elvis met many celebrities over the years. Who impressed him the most?

**A:** Probably actor Jack Lord, star of the TV series *Hawaii Five-O*. Both men treated each with other with class and sensitivity, and they respected each other's talents immensely.

**Q:** What do you think of the way Elvis Presley Enterprises has run the estate?

**A:** I don't feel it right to judge, as I haven't been on the inside. But I will say that I don't think EPE has been fair to the fans over the years. Many of the fans I meet are unhappy with EPE because they are viewed as walking dollar signs.

**Q:** Did Elvis have any pets other than Scatter?

**A:** Elvis usually had a dog in his life, and his favorite one was a chow he named Get-Lo on account of the expression on the dog's face.

**Q:** What do you think of the recent remixes of Elvis's music, specifically 2002's "A Little Less Conversation" and 2004's "Rubberneckin'"?

**A:** I really like the new versions, especially "A Little Less Conversation," and I'm sure Elvis would be pleased, too, as it has introduced him to a new generation of listeners.

**Q:** What do you think of Elvis Presley tribute artists?

**A:** As long as they realize they are performing a tribute to Elvis and don't try acting like him when not on the stage, I have no problem with them. Some I have seen and worked with are very good. Seeing a well-done Elvis tribute show gives people who never saw Elvis perform in person an idea of what he was like, especially the younger generations. Let me tell you, they missed out!

**Q:** Do you think there will ever be another entertainer like Elvis Presley again?

**A:** Not in this lifetime or the next. Most likely never.

# Index

Meeting President Nixon was a thrill and was also indicative of Elvis's tenacity when it came to getting what he wanted—a federal badge. That's me to the right of the president and Jerry Schilling to the right of me. *Photo courtesy of the Richard Nixon Library.*

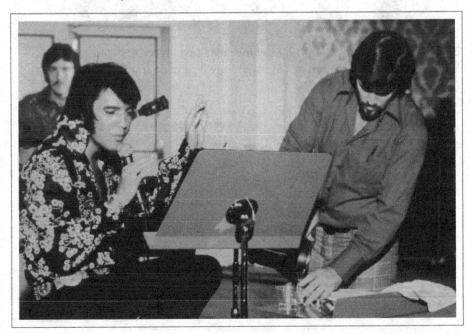

I'm keeping Elvis hydrated as he rehearses for a show in the convention room area at the International Hotel, which later became the Las Vegas Hilton Hotel. This photo was taken in 1970 during the filming of *Elvis: That's the Way It Is.*

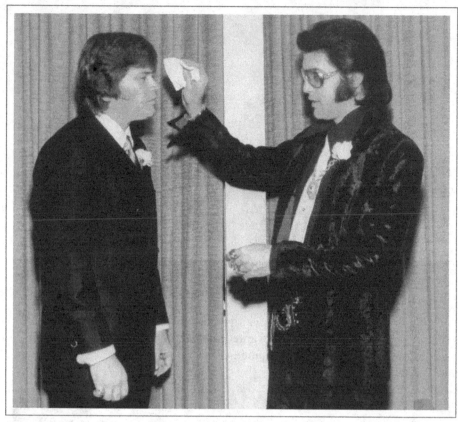

Elvis wipes some perspiration off my forehead just before my December 28, 1970, marriage to Judy Jordan. Elvis was my best man and Priscilla served as Judy's matron in waiting.

The reception at the church following Judy's and my wedding. From left are Sheriff Roy Nixon, Priscilla, Elvis, Judy, myself, Red, and Richard Davis. A second reception was later held at Graceland.

A scene from the film *Wild in the Country*. From left are Bitsy Mott (Colonel Parker's brother-in-law), Tuesday Weld, Elvis, and me, playing the state trooper who appears to be sleeping on the job. Actually, I happened to blink as the photo was taken.

Here I'm leading the group while on tour in Terra Haute, Indiana, on July 9, 1975. *Photo courtesy of the Derek Phillips Collection.*

Elvis is honored in Memphis at one of the functions for the 33rd Annual Congress of America's Junior Chamber of Commerce's Ten Outstanding Young Men of the Year Awards for 1970. The actual award ceremony was held on January 15–16, 1971. Elvis was especially proud of this honor.

From left, Red, an unidentified plainclothes Metro policeman working with hotel security, Elvis, and I pose for a photo outside the Las Vegas Hilton Hotel dressing room corridor, circa 1972–1973.

Elvis makes his grand entrance for a show inside the cavernous Houston Astrodome on March 3, 1974.

Elvis, Linda Thompson, and I leave Graceland to take in an all-night movie session at the Memphian Theatre in the mid-1970s.

Backstage at Garrett Coliseum in Montgomery, Alabama, Elvis was received by then-Governor George Wallace and his second wife, Cornelia, on March 6, 1974.

Elvis sponsored a flag football team named Elvis Presley Enterprises, which included a few members of the Memphis Mafia, such as Red West (middle row, second from right), Alan Fortas (middle row, far right), and me (middle row, far left). We were pretty good, too. We were cochampions of Memphis one year.

Here I'm about to escort Elvis in his Mercedes-Benz limousine to a medical clinic in California for a blood test in a paternity suit. The other gentleman in the picture is Gerald Peters, who was our driver. Gerald also drove for Sir Winston Churchill at one time.

Joe, Gee Gee, and myself, along with an unidentified security officer, escort Elvis to the dressing room prior to a show while on tour in 1970.

Elvis performs a number during the filming of *Viva Las Vegas*. That's me with the huge bottle and cowboy hat, with Red to my far left.

Here I'm signing photos at a convention with Judy, my beautiful bride of 36 years.

Elvis and Lee Majors on the set of *Clambake*. Lee was a great guy and one of the few celebrities whose company Elvis thoroughly enjoyed.

Elvis and me rehearsing a fight scene in the movie *Double Trouble*, in which I doubled actor Michael Murphy. As usual, Elvis won.

"The King and the Greatest." Elvis and boxer Muhammad Ali in Elvis's suite at the Hilton Hotel in Las Vegas, February 1973. The two greatly admired and respected each other but also really liked each other, and when in the same room, they generated an enormous amount of energy.

Moving Elvis through the crowd at Waikiki Beach near the Hilton Hawaiian Village Rainbow Towers. We were there for the live telecast of *Elvis: Aloha from Hawaii via Satellite,* January 1973.

Playing football during a break on the set of *Flaming Star*, 1960. That's my cousin Red trying to block me while Elvis tries to run the sweep. I was able to tackle the boss and still keep my job.

Sitting on the curb in Idyllwild, California, during a break on *Kid Gallahad*, 1961. From left to right: Red West, me, and Elvis. Marty Lacker is behind us, leaning on me and Red.

Juliet Prowse and Pat Boone pay a visit to Elvis on the set of *Wild in the Country*, 1960. That's me sitting in a cast chair listening to the conversation. *Photo courtesy of the Derek Phillips Collection.*

The beautiful cast of *Blue Hawaii* on the set.

Elvis shown at Graceland in the late 1950s. There was never a shortage of fans at Graceland wanting an autograph, and Elvis was always appreciative of their love and support.

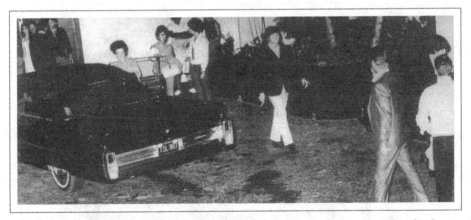

This photo of the night the Beatles met Elvis Presley remains one of only three known pictures (taken by a fan) of that historical summit, which took place on August 27, 1965. Elvis and the Beatles enjoyed their brief time together despite what other books have written. At the front door at the far left are Priscilla, Billy Smith, and Elvis, who is talking to an unidentified man with his back to the camera. John Lennon is in the center of the photo walking to the Beatles' limo, and at right are Red (in suit), George Harrison, and myself (white shirt).

This is an action shot from the 1967 film *Stay Away Joe*, which we shot on location in Sedona, Arizona. Elvis, playing the lead role of Joe Lightcloud, is joined in the water by other cast members while I'm standing in the water at the right, playing my character, Jackson Hee-Crow. On the river bank are extras played by members of the Navaho Indian Tribe.

Also taken during the filming of *Stay Away Joe*, this photo features actors Thomas Gomez (to my right, in hat) and the great Burgess Meredith (in headband with back to the camera).

Here we are boarding a train from Memphis to Hollywood in 1960 to begin filming the movie *GI Blues*. On board the train directly behind Elvis are, left to right, myself, Joe, and Charlie.

Elvis taking the stage, circa 1974–75, with myself, JD Sumner, Ed Hill, and Bill Baize of the Stamps Quartet. I am not sure which city we were in, but the Show Member badge I am wearing means we were on tour, not in Vegas or Lake Tahoe.

This picture was taken of me and Colonel Parker in December 1983 at the MGM Grand Hotel in Las Vegas. I had not seen the Colonel for some time before then, and it is the only photo of the two of us that I currently have. *Photo courtesy of Sonny West.*

Red is bringing up the rear with me on point as we escort Elvis to a show. This was in Macon, Georgia, when Elvis performed there on April 24, 1974. *Photo courtesy of Paul Lichter's archives/ elvisunique.com.*